Cleanth Brooks

Robert Penn Warren

MODERN
RHETORIC

Shorter Third Edition

Harcourt Brace Jovanovich, Inc.

New York / Chicago / San Francisco / Atlanta

to **David M. Clay**

© 1972 by Harcourt Brace Jovanovich, Inc.

ISBN: 0–15–562813–5

Library of Congress Catalog Card Number: 79–177381

Printed in the United States of America

Preface

This Shorter Third Edition of *Modern Rhetoric* takes account of the many major revisions which appeared in the Third Edition of the larger book. Thus the first four chapters have been thoroughly revised to give greater emphasis to the stage of "prewriting"; Chapter 5, Exposition, has been reorganized; a new Chapter 7, Persuasion, has been added; and Chapter 15, The Final Version: Writing and Rewriting, now features a new literary term paper as well as an historical term paper. To repeat what we have said of earlier shortened versions: the shorter edition is not intended to replace the larger, but to serve the instructor who requires less explanatory material and who prefers to choose his own readings.

In preparing the Shorter Third Edition we have not departed from the principles on which the earlier editions were based. We remain convinced that good writing is a natural expression of necessary modes of thought and not at all a matter of rules or tricks. We remain convinced, too, that the best and quickest way to learn to write well is not through a process of blind absorption, or trial and error, or automatic conditioning, but through the cultivation of an awareness of the underlying logical and psychological principles. We believe that the awareness to be developed involves a double process of constantly analyzing specific examples and constantly trying to write against a background of principle. To put the matter in a slightly different way: the student learns to write by coming to a deeper realization of the workings of his own mind and feelings, and of the way in which those workings are related to language.

We should like to repeat here the acknowledgments previously made to friends of this book. Though these friends are many and all merit our deep gratitude, we wish to make special mention of Mr. Lloyd Bruno, Mr. L. Morrill Burke of the University of Maine at Portland, Mr. Henry Cassady of Hartnell College, Mr. Edward Gordon of Yale University, Miss Mary K. Hill, Mr. Sanford Kahrmann, the Reverend Dennis B. McCarthy, O.P., Mr. Ernest Nagel of Columbia University, Mr. Gregory Smith Prince, Mr. George B. Rodman of the University of Wisconsin, Mr. Gerald A. Smith of the State University of New York at Geneseo, Mr. Marinus Swets of Grand Rapids Junior College, Mrs. Mildred Tackett, Mr. Morton A. Tenenbaum of West Los Angeles College, the late Richard M. Weaver, Mr. Rulon Wells of Yale University, and Mr. Harold Whitehall.

C. B.

R. P. W.

Contents

PART TWO

THE FORMS OF DISCOURSE

PART FOUR

THE RESEARCH PAPER

APPENDIX

PART ONE

MAKING A
BEGINNING

CHAPTER 1

Language, Thinking, Feeling, and Rhetoric

Man may be called the animal with language—the "symbol-making animal." By a little reflection we can see that only by means of language can man create and carry with him the body of concepts, attitudes, and skills that constitute civilization. Only by language can man carry the past with him, understand the present, and project the future. Only by language can he have a clear notion of himself as an individual: "I think, therefore I am," as the great philosopher Descartes put it. And only by language can men forge the bonds of a society—a society as distinguished from some sort of instinctual herd or tribal swarm.

Language and Thought

Ordinarily and superficially, we regard language as merely a convenient device for communicating preexisting ideas or attitudes. It is indeed hard to overestimate the value of language in communication, but it is even harder to overestimate its value in thinking. Language is tied to the very process of thought. This principle is affirmed in a time-worn joke about the old lady who, when asked to say what she meant, replied, "But how can I know what I mean till I say it?"

How often have we felt that we knew our own minds on something, only to find, when we started to talk, that we didn't know at all what we were talking about. When we frame even the simplest sentence, we are forced to establish a set of meaningful relations; that is, we are forced to think more clearly. We instinctively know this, and we imply as much when, in a moment of confusion or doubt, we say, "Let's talk this out."

"Writing things out"—which is the business of this course—is only a more rigorous way of trying to understand a subject and understand oneself in relation to that subject. "Talking out" and "writing out"—both are ways, fundamentally, of "thinking out."

Language and Feeling

We not only think things out, we feel things out too. And language is fundamental, too, to this "feeling out." A human being isn't merely a machine for logical thought. Thought shades off into feeling, and feeling shades off into thought. We cannot exclude feeling from our experience, nor should we wish to do so, but we do want our life of feeling and our life of thought to be consistent with each other, to make some kind of total sense. A person whose feelings run counter to his judgment is bound for disaster.

This is not to say that one's judgment is necessarily good and one's feelings are necessarily bad. It may well be the other way around. But if feelings and judgment are not more or less in tune, we will be constantly jangled and disorganized. We want some degree of unity in ourselves.

To gain this unity, we need not only to think straight but also to understand our own feelings and to see how they are related to each other, to our own general experience, and to the world around us. Our use of language involves our instinctive attempt to clarify our feelings, to come to grips with them. We say, "Now that I've talked about it, I feel better." In other words, the talking-out process not only helps us to make up our minds but to "make up our feelings" too.

Language is an instrument for discriminating and expressing shades of feeling. The poet's metaphor and the schoolboy's slang have this purpose in common—and the slang may sometimes serve the purpose better than the metaphor. Later on, we shall discuss how language discriminates feelings—by imagery, rhythm, tone, and so on—but for the moment we merely emphasize the fact that language helps us to understand feelings as well as ideas, and thus, in the end, helps us to understand ourselves.

The Immediate Practical Demand: And Beyond

We have been speaking of language in broad, sweeping terms. Let us come closer to home. You are beginning your college career, and no matter what your major interests are, much of your instruction will be in language, and you will be required to respond in language. And after college language will become more, not less, important. There are letters and reports to be written, conferences to be held, policies to be drawn up and debated, and many other forms of communication that require skill in language. Even for a person who has great aptitude in one of the occupations in which thinking seems to be nonverbal—even if he is a born musician, painter, physicist, or businessman—there remain those aspects of life outside that occupation, the part of life that involves a person's relation to society and the part of life that is purely inward and personal. Whatever a person's practical success, he will, if he lacks competence in language, spend much of his life fumbling in a kind of twilight world in which ideas, facts, and feelings are perceived only dimly and often in distorted shapes.

So we have come back to our starting point, the notion that through language man discovers his world and himself. This idea is nowhere better put than in Helen Keller's account of her introduction to language. She had been blind and deaf almost from birth, and had never learned to speak. When she was seven, a gifted and imaginative teacher began her education:

> We walked down the path to the well-house, attracted by the fragrance of the honeysuckle with which it was covered. Someone was drawing water and my teacher placed my hand under the spout. As the cool stream gushed over one hand she spelled into the other the word water, first slowly and then rapidly. I stood still, my whole attention fixed upon the motions of her fingers. Suddenly I felt a misty consciousness as of something forgotten—a thrill of returning thought; and somehow the mystery of language was revealed to me. I knew then that "w-a-t-e-r" meant the wonderful cool something that was flowing over my hand. That living word awakened my soul, gave it light, hope, joy, set it free! There were barriers still, it is true, but barriers that could in time be swept away.
>
> I left the well-house eager to learn. Everything had a name, and each name gave birth to a new thought. As we returned to the house every object which I touched seemed to quiver with life. That was because I saw everything with the strange, new sight that had come to me.
>
> —HELEN KELLER: *The Story of My Life.*

A note about this course: rhetoric

What is this course about? Is it concerned with punctuation, figures of speech, and participial phrases? Does it have to do with outlining themes, constructing topic sentences, and studying the principles of unity, coherence, and emphasis? Obviously, the answer to these questions is yes. But such matters are not studied for their own sake. They are studied because they contribute to the effective use of language.

Rhetoric is the art of using language effectively.

A note about you

We have said that language is at the very center of the life of thought and the life of feeling. This sounds very grand and impressive—and may seem to cast an awesome shadow over the day-to-day business of studying exposition or narration and the rules of punctuation, or of writing themes.

But you should realize that you are not beginning at the beginning. You began to learn language when you were an infant, and you are still learning. Books have helped you toward an effective use of language, and now they will help you even more, but remember that what books can give is not something separate from what life can give. What books can give is, rather, an extension and refinement of life.

■ APPLICATIONS

The exercises offered below are to suggest some of the questions involved in writing. They may give you a chance to feel your way into the work you will be required to do—or better, to feel your way into the state of mind that will enable you to do that work. Your acquaintance with the types of questions involved here is of more importance than the particular answers you may give. But, of course, you will become fully acquainted with the questions only if you conscientiously struggle to find satisfactory answers.

I Here you are to deal with the meanings of individual words. Choose the word in the column that, in your opinion, comes closest to the meaning of the word to the left. Some of the words, of course, are not close, and even in the word you choose you may see important shades of difference in meaning. After you have made your choice, try to state whatever differences in meaning you find. (When you have completed the exercise, consult a dictionary to see what words appearing in the column are regarded as *synonymous* with the word to the left.)

1	inscrutable	dark	2	spite	irritability
		unknown			rancor
		arcane			detestation
		mysterious			hate
		indistinct			mercilessness
		abysmal			revenge
3	subversion	craftiness	4	despair	resignation
		treason			stoicism
		substitution			failure
		dishonesty			timidity
		overthrow			hopelessness
		defalcation			defeat

II Read the passage below very carefully several times. Try to sense the overall meaning. Now from Group 1, choose the word that will best fit into the first blank space. And from Group 2, the best word for the second blank space. Be prepared to defend your choices. Remember that you are trying to choose the words that will fit best into the passage taken as a whole. Use a dictionary for the meanings of words you are not absolutely sure of.

It was a situation so full of shadows, uncertainty, and
_____(1)_____ that it gave no firm _____(2)_____ on which to
base a lever of decision.

	(1)			(2)	
chagrin	mistrust		point	middle
turpitude	nihilism		basis	fulcrum
distress	assiduity		relation	wedge
ambiguity	melancholy		idea	aspiration
confusion	ambition		religion	intention
solace	mercilessness		hope	morality

In making your choices, you no doubt have determined that for Space 1
you need a word closely related to *shadows* and *uncertainty*, but a word that
does something more than merely repeat those notions. You may have vaguely
considered the words *nihilism, melancholy,* and *mercilessness*, because they
do have a negative quality bearing some relation to *shadows* and *uncertainty*.
But *ambiguity* and *confusion* have closer relations. *Confusion* perhaps seems
too close to *uncertainty*. So *ambiguity*, which adds a new dimension but one
that extends what is already there, seems the best choice of all.

When you come to Space 2, your sense of the overall meaning tells you
that the space should be filled with something related to the metaphor of the
lever. You may have considered such words as *religion* or *hope,* but they are
too general. *Point, basis,* and *wedge* might have some merit. But *fulcrum* is
the most precise.

III Here are two passages, one the work of an eminent writer [1] and the other
a garbled version. The context of the scene described is the walk in Venice
of a middle-aged man who suddenly finds himself involved in a shameful
infatuation that he cannot break out of. With this information as a background,
try to decide which is the original version.

A   There was a hateful sultriness in the narrow street. The air was so heavy that
all the manifold smells wafted out of houses, shops, and cook-shops—the
smells of oil, perfumery, and so forth—hung low, like exhalations, not
dissipating. Cigarette smoke seemed to stand in the air, it drifted so slowly
away.

B   In the city, there was, now that morning had passed, an uncomfortable heat.
As he passed down a narrow street, he found that all the manifold smells
wafted out of houses, shops, and cook-shops—smells of oil, perfumery, and
so forth—hung in the air, because now there was no wind off the Adriatic
to relieve the heat, which grew more intense every day. Even cigarette smoke
hung in the air a moment before it began to drift off, beautifully blue in the
sunlight.

IV Here again we are dealing with two passages, one the original [2] and the
other a garbled version. Our concern now is with logical order. Which passage do you regard as more satisfactory?

---

[1] *Death in Venice*, by Thomas Mann.
[2] From *The Hero in History*, by Sidney Hook. Reprinted by permission of Humanities Press
Inc.

A   In our own time interest in the words and acts of outstanding individuals has flared up to a point never reached before. There is a perennial interest in heroes even when we outgrow the hero worship of youth. The sources of this interest are many and deep. One is that what outstanding people do makes interesting copy for the newspapers, TV, and radio, and this is the age of communications. But laying that aside as not really relevant, the special reasons for this passionate concern vary in intensity from one historic period to another. The passionate concern in our age has reasons which are quite apparent, because we think that what important people do may affect our society. But, as I pointed out, they make good reading or "viewing," in any case.

B   There is a perennial interest in heroes even when we outgrow the hero worship of youth. The sources of this interest are many and deep. But they vary in intensity and character from one historic period to another. In our own time interest in the words and acts of outstanding individuals has flared up to a point never reached before. The special reasons for this passionate concern in the ideas and deeds of the uncrowned heroes of our age are quite apparent. During a period of wars and revolutions, the fate of peoples seems to hang visibly on what one person, perhaps a few, decide.

CHAPTER 2

The Problem of Making a Beginning

In the preceding chapter we have tried to answer the question: "What is the ultimate purpose of the study of writing?" The next question is: "Where should the study of writing begin?" Should it begin with the medium—that is, with a study of words? With the subject—that is, with the ideas that one wishes to express? Or with the occasion—that is, with the situation in which the writer finds himself with respect to a particular audience? It is impossible to say that any one of these considerations is more important than the other two, and it is also impossible to say that one of the three should logically precede the others, since they are all intimately related.

We might argue that we should begin with the medium, with the study of words, and then move by easy stages from diction through the next larger units, the sentence and the paragraph, and then on to the general problems of organization to be met in the whole theme.

But we might say that when we choose words, we choose them in relation to other words, in relation to the general subject about which we mean to write, and in relation to our attitude toward our reader (that is, in relation to the occasion). In the same way, we could argue that the study of the sentence, important as it is, should not necessarily precede the study of general organization. For it is the pattern of sentences, the relation of sentences to one another, that defines the progression of our ideas. In writing, we are first concerned—just as we are finally concerned—with our complete utterance, our overall idea, our main purpose. There is something to be said, therefore, for beginning, as we do here, with problems of general organization. Other problems usually take specific form only when the writer attempts to come to grips with his subject.

Finding a Subject

Sometimes a subject will be assigned to you, but often in this course you will have to choose one from a range of suggestions or find one of your own. What kind of subject is likely to draw forth your best work?

Beginnings are always hard, and this beginning of the very beginning of a piece of writing is often the hardest of all. You may find some help, however, in asking yourself two questions:

What do I know about?

What am I interested in?

We have said that all your life up to this point has been a preparation for this course, and in the question of choosing a subject this is obviously true. You know about many things at first-hand: dressmaking, movies, people, carpentry, gardening, fishing, jobs, chess or checkers or bridge, football, friendship, family life, pains and pleasures. And you know about many other things through reading, for instance, the Antarctic or George Washington. Your experience has been rich—far richer than you ordinarily realize.

What makes that experience rich is that it represents your life, your reactions, your evaluations, your interests. Trust those interests. If you are interested in something you can probably make it interesting to others.

When you set out to choose a subject, you are, then, engaged in self-scrutiny, self-exploration, self-evaluation. So we return to the thought that writing is, ultimately, an extension of your own life process.

Finding a true subject: focus

Suppose, out of your experience and your interests, you have settled on a subject, perhaps tennis, your grandmother, rose gardens, or George Washington. Now that you think you have a subject, what do you really have? What, for instance, are you ready to say about tennis?

You are a good tennis player, have followed the game, know a great deal about many high-ranking players, and even know some good competition players personally. So you begin:

> I have played tennis since I could hold a racket, and before that my father made me do strokes with a badminton racket and a light ball. My father was a very good player. He once had a national ranking, and if he had not broken his wrist he might have made a name for himself. Not that he grieves about that, for he has a full life, and as a hobby still follows the game and knows a lot of players. In any case, I have always had my tennis heroes, and I have known——

You stop, suddenly realizing that you are lost. There is no clear line of development here, no control, no forward thrust on which you can depend. You simply don't know where you are going. And certainly your reader would not know.

The trouble is that your subject—tennis—is too inclusive, too shifting.

You must try, therefore, to be more specific, to find more manageable topics drawn from the general subject matter of tennis. You may even scribble them down:

Why I like tennis.
The strategy of doubles.
History of the game.

Then you look at the last sentence of your trial beginning, and put down another topic:

Players I have known.

That, you decide, may have more general interest than the previous topics, and so you linger on it. Suddenly an idea hits you. What do tennis players—really good tennis players—have in common? What background? What training? What characteristics? What temperament?

You write down another topic:

The tennis temperament.

This is specific. It involves, directly or indirectly, all you know about tennis, but it sharpens that knowledge to a point. It is a topic brought to focus. It is a true subject.

You may not yet be ready to write, but you have a question to control your thinking: What is the tennis temperament? It is conceivable that, after reflection, you may decide that there is no such thing as the "tennis temperament"—that you have no true subject after all. But your question was a real one, and you have at least learned to isolate and explore a topic.

Too bad it did not turn out.

The true subject and the proposition

Let us suppose, however, that it does turn out. On further reflection you decide that, after all, in spite of all the differences among tennis players, there is a similarity of temperament that sets them apart from other athletes. Your struggle to convince yourself that you have a true subject is, you suddenly realize, a great blessing to you. The fact that other people may resist the idea that there is a "tennis temperament" means that you have a controversial proposition for your theme: There is a tennis temperament.

You know now that you have to meet objections. You have to prove your point. You have, therefore, a motive and a direction for your theme.

THE PROPOSITION: WHAT IT IS

A proposition is an assertion that may be believed, disbelieved, or doubted. It is, in itself, clear-cut. It can be dealt with.

The proposition is what gives the hard core of your intention. It is what you must demonstrate, or exhibit, to your reader. It is your governing idea—your thesis.[1]

---

[1] We shall return to the nature of the proposition in considerable detail when we come to the subject of Argument (pp. 127–32).

It embodies your fundamental belief about, or attitude toward, your true subject.

Do not be disturbed if the proposition you arrive at is debatable. A proposition that is universally acceptable will probably result in a very dull theme. Remember that it is easier to overcome resistance than to overcome lack of interest.

A writer is, in one way, like a judo expert. He uses the reader's resistance to throw the reader.

● CAUTION: LOOK TWICE AT HIGHFALUTIN SUBJECTS

There is always a temptation to choose grand, high-sounding, highfalutin, general subjects, such as patriotism, democracy, religion, justice, and education. Such subjects are, at first glance, attractive because they seem easy—easy because they have accumulated around themselves a body of generally accepted and conventionally approved interpretations and arguments, and a set of respectable and pious attitudes. The writer thinks that he can merely rehash the interpretations, arguments, and attitudes and have his theme.

He is wrong, and on three counts.

First, such topics are usually so sweeping and general that the writer—certainly the beginner—has trouble getting down to a true subject, down to specifics, down to a sense of experience, down to concrete illustrations.

Second, a topic of this kind tends to encourage dependence on abstract words, which stand for general qualities, relations, ideas, and concepts. We are not implying that such words should be struck from the language; they are essential for thought. But dependence on such words makes for vagueness, dullness, and irrelevance. The interplay of the abstract and the concrete is the very life of language and thought. (See pp. 287–89.)

Third, the writer who takes refuge in grand, highfalutin subjects is wrong because such subjects, having accumulated around them generally accepted ideas and respectable attitudes, are usually lacking in the dramatic resistance spoken of above. The reader knows what to expect. He is bored before he begins.

There is, however, a way to beat the game of the dull, abstract subject, to awaken the reader to the reality that has been lost in the mossy growth of conventional ideas and attitudes. You have to scrape off the moss, break the crust. The reader must be shocked into rethinking his attitudes, into sorting out the conventional from the vital aspects of the subject.

When Samuel Johnson, the famous eighteenth-century writer, said that "patriotism is the last refuge of the scoundrel," he was not denying the value and nobility of patriotism, but paradoxically, he was shocking the reader into contrasting true patriotism with the shabby, self-serving substitutes. James Russell Lowell once said that "democracy is nothing more than an experiment in government . . . which must stand or fall on its own merits as others have done before it." Johnson and Lowell are scraping off the moss. They force us to take another look at patriotism, at the sanctity of democracy.

A theme that begins with a statement like that of Johnson or Lowell would wake the reader up.

■ APPLICATIONS

I Here is a list of general subjects. Select five from the list, and frame three true subjects for each.

Marijuana	Space exploration	Morality in the year 2000
The jury system	A professional army	Robert E. Lee
Military service	Wiretapping	Abraham Lincoln

II For each of five of the true subjects you have framed, write a proposition that you think would lead to an interesting theme.

The Discourse: Main Divisions

Once you have found your true subject and have framed your proposition, you must consider the organization of your theme. You know that there will be an introduction, a discussion, and a conclusion—that is, a beginning, a middle, and an end. Very probably, in trying to settle on your true subject and frame the proposition, you have already been thinking of these divisions. They are, in fact, the natural divisions for the treatment of any subject; they represent the way the mind works.

Now you should try to think your whole scheme through, to firm up the structure and flesh out each division with the main points involved in it. Some writers find that the best way to start is to jot down ideas almost at random, letting the mind wander over the subject, jumping here and there, if necessary, without trying to state all the logical connections. What comes out of this process will look like a hodgepodge, but the process may catch on the wing certain things that might have eluded a more systematic approach.

You cannot, of course, leave the ideas caught in this free fashion in the order in which they came. You must sort them out under the three main divisions. Having done this, you should try to arrange in logical order the ideas in each division. To guide you in this process, you will find in Chapter 14 a discussion of the Outline. After consulting this, you are prepared to make a more or less complete projection of what you now think your theme will be—a topic outline or a sentence outline.

Example of preparation for a theme

A student who had chosen from the previous Application "Morality in the year 2000" as a general subject came up with a true subject in the form of the following proposition: The change of forms of morality will not change the essential basis of morality. Here are his running notes:

RUNNING NOTES ON "MORALITY IN THE YEAR 2000"

Bible—revealed morality.
 Other religions had revealed morality too.
 Social values of morality vs. idea of revealed values.
 Hemingway: "Morality is what you feel good after."

Idea that morality of a society is what that society needs for survival—raise children, defend economy, defend country, etc. This means family, whatever economic system, and patriotism.

Overpopulation example of conflict between social morality (birth control) and revealed morality. Attitude of Roman Catholic Church.

Patriotism changing. A hundred years back a person here was patriotic about his state, like Robert E. Lee about Virginia, etc. Nobody thinks much of the state now. People move about too much. United Nations. What will mobility do for patriotism by 2000?

Property sense and business attitudes changing. More of feeling that business has to pay its way, socially speaking. Business in ghettos, etc.

Sexual morality changing. Divorce more acceptable. Effect of pill.

Morality will always have to satisfy human needs or it will not survive—family, patriotism, the profit motive will continue to exist even though changed in form.

The notes above are simply a random set of ideas, put down as they came into the student's head. Here is the next stage in his preparation, in which he sorted out the running notes according to the major divisions:

Beginning [Introduction]
Definition of morality [two views]

Middle [Discussion]
1. Changes in sex morality based on changing family needs.
 Overpopulation
 Divorce
 The pill
2. Patriotism. Change of focus from state to nation.
3. Business morality—social obligation of business; profit alone not enough.

End [Conclusion]
Same needs will continue for individual and group in spite of change in forms.

The last stage of preparation was to make a sentence outline, which is here offered. Observe that certain items in the running notes are dropped, and that certain things are added. The points of support for the basic proposition, too, are developed in the outline. Observe, also, that the divisions of the outline follow the three divisions of the second stage.

OUTLINE OF THEME ON "MORALITY IN THE YEAR 2000"

Proposition: The change of forms of morality will not change the essential basis of morality.

I. We should begin by defining morality.
   A. There are two views: revealed morality vs. morality as an outgrowth of social needs.
      1. Revealed morality, as seen in Old Testament and Koran, came from a divine source.
      2. Morality as an outgrowth of social needs is seen in the practices that help a society survive: raise family, promote economic system, defend country.
   B. To predict morality in the year 2000 we must see how the definition will change with changing social needs.
II. Changes in morality reflect changes in society.
   A. Changes in the nature of the family have changed sexual morality.
      1. Overpopulation is making birth control more acceptable.
      2. Divorce is becoming more common and more accepted.
      3. The pill has increased sexual freedom among the young.
      4. Children often no longer accept parents' values.
   B. Patriotism has broadened because of social mobility.
      1. Loyalty to the state, paramount before the Civil War (Robert E. Lee and Virginia), has been replaced by loyalty to the country as a whole.
      2. Next may be the spread of loyalty beyond the nation to a supranational organization.
   C. Class and race unrest have changed our property sense and business morality.
      1. Business must "pay its way" socially speaking, having an obligation to the ghetto, etc.
      2. Mere profit is not enough for business; it must help society or there will not be any profit.
III. In spite of changes in forms, the morality of the future will have to serve the same human needs.
   A. In one form or another, the family will survive through affection for children and mate, common experiences, fear of loneliness.
   B. People need loyalties for a new "patriotism" even if the base is broader.
   C. New business morality will be based on more enlightened view of profit, not on death of profit motive.

■ APPLICATION

Do you think that you could tighten this outline? Do you have any different ideas on the subject of morality? This outline might lead you to do a theme on the same topic, especially if you disagree with the present writer.

● CAUTION

Never feel bound to an outline. The actual process of writing may give you something much better than what the outline promises. Though your outline is a useful guide, you must submit it to the process of thinking things through, word by word, as you begin the actual writing. And this sort of thinking a subject through may result in a thorough reorganization of the structure.

The outline is only a step in your thinking.

The introduction

An introduction must really introduce.

The reader is entitled to know what you are going to write about. Your title tells him something, but in the introduction, you must fix the subject more precisely. You must at least suggest your proposition, and it is good to indicate how you intend to present your discussion.

Here is the introduction of a student theme:

> Everyone knows the importance of jet propulsion today, but not everyone knows the history of how it was developed. That history is a good example of how important and complicated inventions can be worked out from the simplest of ideas. We can start by stating the simple idea from which jet propulsion developed.

Whatever its shortcomings, this introduction does state the subject (the history of jet propulsion), gives hints of a context that may be developed to make the subject interesting, and indicates the method the writer will follow in tracing the germ idea, stage by stage, to the modern mechanism. The introduction is simple and downright, and does not compare too unfavorably with the introduction to an article called "Causation of Ice Ages," written by two research scientists:

> Beneath the oceans lie clues to many basic questions regarding not only the earth's dominant features, the continents and ocean basins, but also the evolution of life, the climatic history and chronology of the Pleistocene, and one of the most tantalizing of all geological problems, the cause of the ice ages. —DAVID B. ERICSON AND GOESTA WOLLIN:
> in the *Columbia Forum* (Winter 1968).

The two scientists, like the student writing on jet propulsion, are setting out to give a direct, objective account of the subject (the relation of oceanographic data to the problem of the ice ages), which they place in the context of clues to other important questions. In both introductions the subject treated demands little more than the bare statement and the minimum of context because the author is giving a report. Even if a report involves vast information, the fact that it is objective means that certain demands are not made on the writer in his introduction. In other words, the nature of the introduction is modified by the subject and the occasion.

For instance, examine the following introduction:

> Contrary to current fears, there is little evidence, I believe, to support the notion that man is simply the passive creature of technology. Moreover, there is considerable unclarity as to how technology got to be the way it is in the first place. —SEYMOUR MELMAN: "Who Decides Technology?" *Columbia Forum* (Winter 1968).

Here the writer is going to present a body of objective facts, but his motive is not merely to give a report. He is going to try to persuade his reader, who may be subject to "current fears," that he should adopt a certain attitude based on those objective facts; the proposition that he wishes the reader to accept is that man is not "the passive creature of technology." The fact that the author is going to offer an argument against immediate and significant fears means that here the proposition—what he is specifically trying to establish—comes to the fore. It is the chief concern of the introduction, as of the whole article.

With the following introduction, again from a student theme, we encounter another concern:

> The textbook says that you write best about something you are interested in, and I am more interested in drag-racing than in anything else except my girl, who right here shall be nameless. So, since I cannot write about her, I'll write about drag-racing. To be more specific, and state my true subject, as the textbook advises, I am going to write about why I am interested in drag-racing—though *interested* is a very weak word for what I feel when I drop into the old bucket, latch the belt, and inhale that first dizzy whiff of burned high octane.

Our previous examples have been objective and impersonal. This last is intensely personal. It is effective, in fact, only insofar as we get some feeling for the author's personality—that of a vigorous, extroverted, happy-go-lucky lad, wrapped up in his girl, speed, and machinery, with a bright mind and a sense of humor. He even makes a sort of high-spirited game of writing his theme. He has a relish for the immediate experience of things; one manifestation of this is the concreteness with which he writes. He does not say, "when I get ready to begin a race," but says, "drop into the old bucket" and "inhale that first dizzy whiff of burned high octane."

The specific, the concrete, the immediate, the flavor of the moment come naturally to him, and these qualities are what catch us and remind us that the theme is about *him* and why *he* likes drag-racing. It is not merely about drag-racing objectively considered.

"Specifics"—of the concrete and the particular—are not confined, however, to themes that are strongly personal in tone. In objective factual accounts they may also appear, and appear most effectively, to give vividness and immediacy. For instance, here is the introductory paragraph of a news report in *Time* (March 21, 1969) about the relief flights over the Nigerian blockade of Biafra, sponsored by various charitable organizations.

COME ON DOWN AND GET KILLED

> By day, Sao Tomé Island drowses in tropic torpor. Toward evening, however, the diminutive Portuguese colony off West Africa's under-

belly in the Gulf of Guinea suddenly rouses. Along its single airport's runway can be seen a motley squadron of DC-6s, a C-46, a Super Constellation, and lately bigger but nonetheless obsolete C-97 stratofreighters, wheezing into readiness. Trucks dash up, hauling crates of food and medicines. Eventually, crews as varied as their airplanes—Swedes, Finns, Americans, a stolid Yorkshireman, a not so dour Scot—screech up in cars and climb aboard. One by one, at 20 minute intervals, the cargo planes lumber down the runway, turn northward toward the Nigerian coast. Late afternoon sunlight splashes on little blue and gold fish, the fuselage emblems of the interfaith airlift organized by the World Council of Churches and the Catholic relief organization Caritas to shuttle food to starving Biafra.[2]

The reporter does not want merely to give us the facts; he wants us to have some of the "feel," the atmosphere, of the island waking from the "tropic torpor" of daylight to the bustle of the preparations, the excitement and danger. Notice, too, how a piece of mere information, the names of the sponsoring organizations, is presented visually—as though we had seen the little symbols and had inquired for their meaning.

● CAUTION

Do not think that we have listed all the ways of writing an introduction. Indeed, a mere list would be useless. What you must do is get the feel of the process. Ask yourself the question: What kind of introduction does my subject demand? How long should it be? One paragraph or more?

■ APPLICATIONS

I Skim through several current magazines, reading the introductory sections of articles. Select two that strike you as especially effective, copy them out, and bring them to class. Be prepared to explain your choice.

II Turn to the discussion of the Paragraph (Chapter 10). Now write an introductory paragraph (or paragraphs, if necessary) for one of the true subjects you have framed in the Application on p. 13.

INTRODUCTION: TO WHOM?

We have been discussing the introduction primarily in relation to what it introduces, but inevitably we have had to suggest, at certain moments, the presence of the reader. Let us turn more specifically to that question. Here we are concerned with what we may call the *occasion:* the kind of reader you are writing for, his attitude toward your subject and toward you, and, naturally, your attitude toward him.[3]

---

[2] Reprinted by permission; Copyright Time Inc. 1969.
[3] With regard to audience, see Tone, pp. 332–38.

Before you set down your first word, you should ask yourself some questions about the occasion, questions that will serve not only as a guide for the introduction but for the development of the whole theme:

1 Does the reader have any interest in my subject, or must I try to attract his attention?
2 If I have to attract his attention, how do I do it?
3 How ignorant is he of my subject? How much do I have to explain to give him a background for my discussion?
4 Am I merely trying to present something to him, or am I trying to convince him of something? If, in other words, he has a resistance to the view I am presenting, what attitude shall I take toward him?

Here is the introduction to a theme entitled "The Nature and Use of the Spinnaker," written by a student with a passionate interest in sailing.

> Anybody who has never sailed couldn't possibly be interested in what I am going to say about spinnakers, and in fact, probably wouldn't even know what one is. Anybody who has sailed at all, however, knows what a spinnaker is, and knows the thrill that comes when it first snaps out and bellies with wind and you hear the new hiss of water at the bow. That person will know, too, that there is a lot to know about the spinnaker, and will know that it is worth discussing and investigating. I am writing for him. Let landlubbers sheer off.

The writer here has put his cards on the table. He is writing strictly for readers who have some interest in sailing and who are willing to dwell on its finer points. He is humorous about his warning to landlubbers—but he means it.

Consider this example from an essay "Wordsworth in the Tropics," in which much more subtly the author warns off certain readers:

> In the neighbourhood of latitude fifty north, and for the last hundred years or thereabouts, it has been an axiom that Nature is divine and morally uplifting. For good Wordsworthians—and most serious-minded people are now Wordsworthians, either by direct inspiration or at second hand—a walk in the country is the equivalent of going to church, a tour through Westmorland is as good as a pilgrimage to Jerusalem. To commune with the fields and waters, the woodlands and the hills, is to commune, according to our modern and northern ideas, with the visible manifestations of the "Wisdom and Spirit of the Universe."
> —ALDOUS HUXLEY: *Do What You Will.*

Readers who don't know anything about Wordsworth, or what a "good Wordsworthian" is, need not apply for admittance to this essay. For those who have some acquaintance, however, this introduction does some well-mannered coaching: to commune with nature is to commune "with the visible manifestations of the 'Wisdom and Spirit of the Universe.'" The coaching is politely unobtrusive, a gentle nudge as it were, and the reader says to himself, "Yes, of course, I knew that all the time."

Aldous Huxley, like the young sailor in his introduction, has warned off certain readers. But the problem is different when the writer can assume that any reasonably intelligent reader may take an interest in a topic, even though he has no general background for it. In a theme entitled "Jet Pilots Are Human, and Space Men Too," a student deals with that problem:

> As new planes fly higher and faster every day, and as men take off for the moon, we begin to feel that there is no limit to what the designers and engineers can do. But we tend to forget one thing. There are no new designs for the human body, and there are no new models being built in the hush-hush atmosphere of the experimental shop. The pilot is the old model, and we have to think of what speed and altitude do to his "liver and lights" and how much sloshing around he can stand. And spacemen are old models too.

What has the writer done in this paragraph? He has corrected a misconception that the general reader may well have—the idea that design and engineering are the only important factors in the future of aviation and space exploration. And he has given a preliminary statement of the problem of the human body in flight, the central idea he intends to develop. He has built his introduction around an important fact that the reader, however intelligent, may have failed to consider. The assumption here is that the reader, once he has the fact pointed out to him, will want to pursue the topic.

The Uninterested Reader   Up to this point we have been assuming readers with special interests (sailors, Wordsworthians) or readers with general curiosity who merely need some special information. But what about the reader who brings no predisposition at all to your subject?

On many occasions you yourself have been the uninterested reader who, idly thumbing through a magazine, has been caught by the first few sentences of an article and has gone on to read the whole piece. The author of the following paragraph is making a bid for the reader's attention by showing how his subject, "The Aleutian Islands," might affect the personal life of his reader:

> There was a time when I thought that geography was the boring subject that happened in the first period after the noon recess or that it was the pictures in the old *National Geographic* magazines in the dentist's office which you thumbed through while you were waiting for a new filling. But now I know that what the Arabs eat in Mecca or the Burmese get as take-home pay affects our national security and our tax bill. This fact was brought home to me last summer when I went to Alaska and had the good fortune to be asked to go on a ten-day cruise through the Aleutian Islands in a private boat. Those islands are steppingstones between America and Asia, and you know that you can go two ways on steppingstones.

Having challenged the reader to accept his point of view about geography, the writer concludes his paragraph with what will become the chief point to be developed in his theme: the military importance of the Aleutians.

If we turn to the actual theme written by the tennis enthusiast mentioned earlier in this chapter (pp. 10–11), entitled "A Different Breed of Cats," we find another kind of appeal:

> Have you ever thought of a bear playing tennis? Or an elephant? Or a horse? Or a dog? If you ever did think of one of these whacking a ball, it would be strictly for laughs. Even a chimpanzee playing tennis—in spite of his resemblance to humans or perhaps because of it—would seem funny. But somehow it isn't funny to think of a cat playing tennis. At least, it isn't funny long, for the cat—I mean any member of what the biologists call the genus *felis*—has certain qualities that really do make us think of tennis players. They have the speed, terrific coordination, the power in grace, the timing, and the hard, honed-up, self-sufficient loneliness that a really good tennis player has. They have what I'll call the tennis temperament, and I'll try to explain what I mean.

Here the author is trying to appeal to readers beyond the world of tennis, to anyone interested in human psychology. He uses a startling, fantastic, humorous approach and a play on the slang meaning of the word *cat* in the title to catch the reader's attention. As in the theme on drag-racing, the appeal here also lies in the personality and fresh point of view of the writer.

The Hostile Reader   The best long-range method for dealing with the hostile reader is to find a common ground with him, to show that, in the end, you and he have sounder reasons for agreement than for disagreement. Later in this book you will find a discussion of this method, and a look at it now would be helpful (pp. 123–26). Another effective approach is to establish that the hostile reader's position actually works against his self-interest or is inconsistent with some other of his more deeply held convictions. In all of these methods the reasonable, friendly tone is extremely important—more important, perhaps, than any logical argument that could be mentioned in an introduction.

The student who wrote the following introduction was trying to win over a hostile reader.

> In my senior year in high school I was what is known as a "student leader," and one thing I led was the nearest thing to a riot that Silas Morton High School ever had—and I hope ever will have. I am giving this information not as a way of boasting or as a horror story in which I beat my breast and explain how my experience made me decide to "go straight"—that is, suck up to anybody who happens to be running the show. I simply want anybody who reads this to know that I have had a real experience with what for most college freshmen is purely theoretical and that I do understand what it means to be in a school as full of faults as Swiss cheese is of holes and Limburger is of perfume. Our grievances were really real, and I sympathize with any student who feels powerless against a situation like that. It is not that "bad" people have ganged up on you. It is that there is a kind of gray, greasy, smothering fog over everything, and you can't do anything about it. It is nobody's responsibility any more than the weather is, it just happens. I know what that feeling is, and I am all in favor of doing something about it. The "what" is what I am writing about.

The tone of the introduction above is soothing. But shock can also be a method for dealing with the hostile reader—the assumption being that only through shock, through making him fully aware of his hostility, can he be brought to reconsider his position. An excellent example is in this introduction to a magazine article on the race question in America, entitled "Black-White: Can We Bridge the Gap?" (Patricia Coffin, *Look,* January 7, 1969). Here are the first few sentences of the opening paragraph:

> Black Power is Beautiful! Does that shock you? If so, you are one of millions of Americans, black and white, who haven't a clue to what is happening here. Does it puzzle you? Then you do not comprehend that the black man inherited the American dream with Lincoln's Emancipation Proclamation. . . .

NO FORMULA

There is no formula for the introduction of a theme. Certainly, keep your eyes open as you read to see various possibilities. The main thing, however, is to cultivate your common sense and imagination. Try to put yourself in the reader's place. Ask yourself what information you would need to follow the discussion. Ask yourself how you would respond if some deep conviction of yours were being affronted by a theme. Ask what would make you reconsider—give a second thought to—a long-held belief.

INTRODUCTION: DELAY IT?

We have given a good deal of space to discussing the introduction, and it is of extreme importance. But sometimes the way to write a good introduction is not to begin the actual process of writing with the introduction. It may be a good idea to plunge straight into the body of the theme and follow through to the end. Then ask yourself what you have accomplished, what needs to be said in the introduction to give the reader his bearings for what you have already put down. As we saw earlier in Chapter 1, often it occurs that we know what we want to say only after we have tried to express it in words.

This introduction-in-reverse process should not be used regularly, but it may help give you a better sense of the relation between the introduction and the body of the theme. When the introduction is written before the rest of the theme, it may be well to reconsider it after the body of the theme has been completed. In the light of the completed theme, you may be able to make very useful revisions.

■ APPLICATION

Write an introduction of 75 to 100 words addressed to a hostile reader. Be careful to choose a subject that would offer some real provocation.

The body of the discussion and the conclusion

For the present, we shall take very little space to discuss the body of the discourse and the conclusion. There is a good reason for this, for, from this point on, everything we shall be doing in this course will be a way of studying how to develop the main body of the discussion. Suffice it to say here that the body of the discussion should not betray the promise of the introduction. You have promised the reader to develop a fixed and limited subject along a certain line. Having made this promise, keep it.

There are one or two things that ought to be said about the conclusion. A short theme often does not need a formal conclusion. The paragraph making the last important point, or the climactic point, may constitute a thoroughly adequate conclusion, provided always that the theme has a sound general organization.

But whether your concluding paragraph is elaborate or simple, it occupies one of the two naturally emphatic positions in the composition. Moreover, it constitutes your last chance at your reader. Failure at this point may well mean failure for the whole piece of writing. You must avoid two things: (1) merely trailing off or (2) taking refuge in vague generalities and repetitious summaries. The conclusion must really "conclude" the discussion. Put your finger on your main point, on what you want to bring to focus. Then write your conclusion on that point.

CHAPTER **3**

Organizing the Composition

The introduction, body, and conclusion—or, if you like, the beginning, middle, and end—are the natural divisions of a discourse. But there is another threefold set of terms natural to any process of composition. They are unity, coherence, and emphasis.

Unity

Common sense tells us that the basic interest determining the writer's subject must permeate the whole composition. The composition must be *one* thing—not a hodgepodge. We have, of course, already encountered the demands of unity in the problem of fixing on a true subject—that is, of limiting our interest to a single dominant topic—and in organizing a theme through notes or an outline.

But unity is not a limitation imposed from the outside. It is inherent in the subject. If we decide that "George Washington" is too general and vague to give us a true subject for a theme—that is, that it lacks unity—and settle on "What the Frontier Taught George Washington," we can do this only because the frontier *did* teach Washington something, and because, no matter how deeply related this fact is to Washington's whole career, it can be thought about as separate; it has a natural unity.

● CAUTION

We recognize unity. We do not impose it.

How to recognize unity: three tests

Unity, however, is not always easy to recognize. If you are scatter-brained, you will not recognize it. To recognize it you must put your powers of logic to work. You must be able to do three things:

1 Define your dominant topic—that is, your true subject.
2 Distinguish what is relevant to the main topic from what is irrelevant to it.
3 Keep the minor topics subordinated to the main topic, and do not allow any one of them a disproportionate amount of space.

A bad example

This theme, written on an assigned topic, is by an intelligent and serious-minded student, but it is defective in several respects, chiefly in regard to unity. The teacher's comments accompany the theme:

WHAT DO I WANT OUT OF COLLEGE?

The subject assigned for this theme is, I know, one of the standard ones for generations of freshmen. It is as old as the hills, and when I saw the assignment, I was tempted to adapt the standard joke, and say: "Yes, old as the hills and not half as grassy," for there didn't seem to be anything fresh and green about it. Then it occurred to me that maybe it was fresh. What I mean is, fresh to me, fresh because I was the one trying to answer the question: "What do I want out of college?"

> Unity: I applaud what you are trying to do here—an easy, humorous way into a stodgy subject, but I fear that this is distracting—and wordy. I don't know the joke, I confess. But even so?

To break down and confess, this is a question that has never really crossed my mind. I have been a kind of day-to-day fellow, doing what came my way, whether it was play or work. But I never had much tendency to see the overall scheme of things, and that means, I suppose, that I am sort of average, for I have noticed that a large number of people tend to lead their lives this way, hacking along as best they can or happen to. I hadn't even bothered to notice this fact until I went to the funeral last spring of my Uncle Gilbert. He had been a fine athelete, a pro baseball player, until he sprung his knee and had what you might call an inforced retirement. He had just enjoyed things as they came and had made no plans for his life after baseball. He stumbled into a good job given him in the business of one of his fans, but it didn't last, he went steadily downhill, and died before his time, broke, beat-up, and suffering from alcoholism.

> Unity: Is the idea of your "averageness" relevant to the main idea?

> Unity: Does the account of Uncle Gilbert belong in the theme? True, it prepares you to look at things with a new seriousness, but wouldn't your basic point be as forcefully put without him here? In any case, if you do keep him, this should be a new paragraph.

> Spelling

> Wordy: Why not simply say alcoholic?

So I am ready to try to think about the question which is the subject of this theme and see what it means to me. And I have an answer. I know it will sound either trite or flip or what they call hedeonistic, but I do not mean it exactly any of those ways. I have really thought about it. For what it is worth, here it is, "I want happiness out of college."

Wordy: Cut it!

See below!

Spelling

I have said "trite" about the answer because anybody will say they want to be happy. And I have said "flip," because saying this can be taken as a way of just being offhand. I have said "hedeonistic," because it might sound like I was just out to have a good time in college. But, to begin with, the assignment says "out of college" and not "in college"—which I take to mean what you have got to take away when you finish, and which means that I want the happiness I can take with me afterwards, so it is not just the good times I may happen to have in college, even remembering them the way Uncle Gilbert would remember his hell-raising days. The question is to find out while I am in college what will make me happy later.

Wordy: Why be apologetic? You have a good idea.

Repetition: Here you repeat a good deal from the previous paragraph. Furthermore, are these explanations necessary? Perhaps you might cut the bit in the previous paragraph and keep the idea of hedonism here, which is directly related to your word "happiness." Unity, again!

Sentence structure: This has a broken back. Try again.

Unity: Uncle Gilbert again!

But now I do not know what kind of work I want to do for my lifework. So one thing I want out of college is to try to decide. I like math, and I have even thought of being a mathematician, but I now think of business administration to get some action in the real world—and some money too. I want to shop around in courses. This may sound like I just want to dabble, but I know that if I don't work reasonably hard at a course, I won't know what the subject might have to offer me for a decision. My father has the habit of saying that you get out of a thing what you put into it. I have heard that often enough to begin to believe it, especially when I see how much my father has put out for his success.

Repetition

Unity: Is this on the main line of thought?

Diction: Is know the right word here? Isn't it arrive at, work out, achieve—or something like that?

There is another thing I want out of college. You do not live just in your job, and I want to know a general sense of values. I don't mean this to sound like Sunday School, which, to tell the truth, I never got much out of. I mean I want to find out what might satisfy a man beyond just making money and providing for his family, and going fishing now and then. One of my friends teaches in a slum school, and he says this makes him feel he is connected with something bigger than he is. My brother, who is a whiz at languages and has a big scholarship to Columbia University, was in the student strikes there. He is getting more and more interested in politics, and is about to give up the idea of being a professor of Romantic Languages. He says in politics you have a

Unity: Is this paying its way?

Repetition: You have been overworking this word throughout, sometimes unnecessarily. Check back!

Diction: The word is Romance. Check your dictionary.

chance to mold society into more decent forms and make idealism pay off. I do not know what I want, but I intend to experiment and find out.

A person has one life to lead and he can't take anybody's word. He has to experiment and try to find out. What I want out of college is a chance to do that.

General remarks: You have a sound idea, but there are serious faults in execution, all connected, I think. (1) *Proportion:* You take three—really four—paragraphs for the introduction. It seems that you feel you will not have enough to say and so pad out as much as possible. Or have you merely failed to think your subject through before beginning? (2) *Unity:* This defect may spring from the same impulse to pad, or again, from a failure to plan ahead. In any case, it gives an impression of being scatterbrained. You simply do not stay on the main line of thought, and you keep bringing in competing interests. (3) *Wordiness:* This, again, is padding, but padding in a merely local way. Try to think what you really mean to say. It is better to be accurate than graceful—if that hard choice arises. But don't think that multiplying words means grace.

The theme is basically good but badly needs rewriting. This means rethinking. Outline the whole thing from scratch to clarify your line of thought. In this process think about proportion. Use a sentence outline, for this will help you discard the irrelevant—though often interesting—things. By the way, the theme is far longer than the assignment. Rewrite it and reduce to essentials.

■ APPLICATION

After carefully studying the theme above, follow the teacher's suggestion. Make a sentence outline of what you think the theme should be, and then rewrite it in about 400 words.

Coherence

As an effective discourse must have unity, it must have coherence; that is, the elements of the discourse must stick together. This may seem to be simply another way of saying that a discourse must have unity. Unity and coherence are, indeed, related, but it is worth making a distinction between them.

Let us take the example of a "hashed" paragraph—one in which the order of sentences is shuffled.

The second is the slowness of its operation even when he believes the majority is right. But sooner or later he finds himself straining against two features of the democratic process. The hero in a democratic community—the potentially event-making man—may sincerely believe that he accepts its underlying philosophy. The first is the principle of majority rule, especially when he is convinced that the majority is wrong on a matter of great import.[1]

From even a casual reading, it is clear that this paragraph has a kind of unity: every sentence either mentions the word *democratic* or refers to the question of majority rule. But the paragraph lacks coherence. With the very first sentence we are in a fog, for we don't know what the "second" referred to is or what the antecedent of "he" is. In the second sentence, we don't know to what the "but" stands in opposition, and though we assume that the "he" is the same as the "he" in the first sentence, we still don't have an antecedent. Worse, we see no connection between this sentence and the first. In the third sentence we feel that the "hero" is the antecedent of the "he," but this sentence has no demonstrable continuity with the previous sentences. In the last sentence we suspect that the "first" refers to one of the "two features" of the second sentence and are fairly certain, again, that the antecedent of "he" is, as throughout, the "hero."

Even though we begin to sense a continuous line of thought, it is because we are fumbling at a reconstruction of the paragraph, not because there is coherence in the present form. The paragraph lacks logical order.

The word *order* is the key to the distinction between unity and coherence. In unity, the emphasis is on the relation of the various elements of a discourse to the dominant topic. In coherence, the emphasis is on the order—the continuity—of the elements.

■ APPLICATION

Put the four sentences of the "hashed" paragraph above into their logical order. To do this, you will merely have to push a little further into the process we have outlined in the discussion.

Kinds of order

The kind of order that will give coherence to the description of, say, a woman's face would not serve for giving an account of a baseball game, for arguing for the abolition of Greek-letter fraternities, or for explaining the causes of the Russian Revolution. Different subjects demand different principles of order.[2] In a broad general way, we may say that there are four

---

[1] Drawn from *The Hero in History,* by Sidney Hook. Reprinted by permission of Humanities Press Inc.

[2] We must not confuse these kinds of order with the four modes of discourse—exposition, argument, description, and narration—that we shall later be studying. The kinds of order involved here flow into and interpenetrate the modes of discourse. For example, though it is true that the order of logic is most obviously fundamental to exposition and argument, it is also found in all but the most rudimentary form of narration—that of mere sequence. See p. 31 and Chapter 9, Narration.

kinds of order that may, singly or in combination, be involved in establishing coherence:

1 order of logic   3 order of space
2 order of time   4 order of feeling[3]

ORDER OF LOGIC

Logic is, the dictionary says, the science of reasoning. At the very center of the reasoning process is the order in which relations are established between one thing and another: one thing is connected with or leads to another. We inspect cause and effect, evidence and conclusion.

The coherence established by logical order depends, fundamentally, on the clarity with which (1) the steps in the reasoning process are distinguished from each other and (2) the interrelations are established among the steps. To put it simply, one thing must lead to another; each "thing" must be recognizably "one"; and the process of "leading" must be convincingly indicated. Later we shall study this process in considerable detail, but for the moment, in a rough-and-ready way, we can dwell on the fact that the language itself offers many connective words and phrases with the function of indicating structure. If we can recognize the function of such "controls," we have gone a long way toward understanding how to achieve coherence in a discourse.

Below is a section from a theme by a student defending his choice of a profession; he intends to take a teacher's certificate after college and teach in a slum high school. In this section we have underscored the "controls" —the words or phrases that help us grasp the relations involved in the discourse.

> I know that there are objections to my choice of a lifework. Specifically, there is the big one my father points out: money. I know, of course, that a man has to make a living, that money makes the mare go, to use the old saying; but, as I tell him, a man doesn't need more than his tastes require. He says, in good nature, that I don't know how expensive my tastes are, that I have had lots of privileges I don't even recognize as such, for example, coming to this kind of college. It doesn't do much good to reply that, even though I have had it easy, I want something beyond that easiness of life. You see, he cuts me off here, and says that I have a good hard logical mind and a man isn't happy unless he is using his best talents, and that, consequently, I should go into law or something like that to use mine. Undoubtedly, my father is right, generally speaking. He himself, in fact, has used his talents; for he is one hell of a good corporation lawyer, and is happy in his business. But I am me.

Let us list the underscored items and state the function of each:

specifically: introduces an illustration, one of the "objections."
of course: makes a concession, here to the general idea the father proposes.

---

[3] The discussion of this question will be postponed. See chapters on Description, Narration, Metaphor, and Tone.

but: introduces a contradiction, here of the father's general proposition as applied in particular cases.

for example: introduces an illustration.

even though: admits a concession that is to be reversed.

consequently: announces the conclusion of a line of reasoning, here about the use of a man's best talents.

undoubtedly: admits a concession, the father is right.

generally speaking: modifies the concession.

in fact: introduces an illustration of the father's proposition, here working as an additional concession.

but: makes a contradiction of the father's proposition.

Logical Order: Other "Controls"   The section of the theme presented above is basically an argument: the student is arguing in defense of his choice of profession. But many of the controls merely indicate the structure of thought and do not refer to the process of reasoning, which is the moving from evidence to conclusion or from cause to effect. We notice that only one control does that: *consequently.* But there are available other controls that pinpoint reasoning, and a list of them may be helpful. Since reasoning may be presented as going forward or backward (evidence-conclusion, cause-effect; conclusion-evidence, effect-cause), we shall divide the controls into two groups.

Controls that announce a conclusion (effect) after evidence (cause) has been given:

thus	implies that
hence	leads one to conclude that
proves that	therefore

Controls that announce evidence (cause) after a conclusion (effect) has been given:

because	as shown by
since	for [4]
as	

Such a list need not be memorized, but you should familiarize yourself with it; and in your reading, you should be constantly aware of the words and phrases that indicate relations.

■ APPLICATION

In the excerpt from the theme above, the author, working hard to give his work coherence, may have put in unnecessary controls. Read the excerpt, omitting all the underscored items. Is the line of thought clear without the controls? If it is not, which do you think should be restored?

---

[4] The control *for* may be used *only* after the conclusion or result has been given. It should be observed that we refer here to *for* used as a conjunction and not as a preposition.

The order of logic depends on the way the mind works in moving from a cause to an effect, a piece of evidence to a conclusion—that is, in establishing a certain kind of connection between the two things. The order of time depends on our natural perception of sequence in our experience. We perceive that one thing simply comes after another thing. That is the only relation with which we are concerned in simple perception—not cause and effect, not evidence and conclusion. We may, of course, add such ideas to the sequence to interpret it, but they are not necessary to the fact of sequence. Look at this passage of pure sequence:

> Lying on the bed, in the dark room, he heard the flow of the strange language from the street below. He heard footsteps in the hall, outside his door. Somebody was going down into the street. He lay on the cot and felt the hard lumps in the mattress. Somewhere in the hotel, a phonograph was playing American jazz. He tried not to hear it. He began reciting the multiplication table. Then he saw, against the purple sky of the night, the first long finger, far off, of a searchlight, moving majestically. He shut his eyes. He tried not to listen to the phonograph. The phonograph stopped. It was in the middle of a record.

This is in pure sequence. Nothing is explained or interpreted. We do not know who the man is, where he is, what he is doing there. But the next paragraph runs:

> The *alerte* came. He began to sweat. He knew he would have to vomit soon. At least, he had last night. He shut his eyes and waited for the first explosion.

We now have an interpretation grafted onto the sequence. We now know that the man has been clinging to the mere fact of sequence, even to reciting the multiplication table (a mechanical sequence), in order to overcome his fear of an impending air raid. We can guess that if he tries not to listen to the jazz, it is because the association may divert him from the sequence in which he takes refuge. Even with the addition of this explanation and interpretation the time order remains the basic order of the passage.

Here are some common controls of time:

since	afterwards	the following day (or whatever)
when	after	having completed that (or whatever)
while	before	(so and so) being begun
as	then	having met success (or failure)

■ APPLICATIONS

I What are the meanings of the word *as*? Use the dictionary, then make up a sentence exhibiting each meaning.

II Discriminate between the meanings of *when* and *while*.

The order of space, like that of time, is based on the way we perceive the world in which we live. When the eye moves we are aware of a spatial sequence—left to right, near to far, or whatever the case may be. If we recount the sequence in which the eye perceives objects, we have a principle of coherence that the reader instinctively recognizes and accepts. In its simplest form, such a principle of organization may be found in the literal movement of the eye from one object to another, as in the following passage:

> The train toils slowly round the mountain grades, the short and powerful blasts of its squat funnel sound harsh and metallic against the sides of rocky cuts. One looks out the window and sees cut, bank, and gorge slide slowly past, the old rock wet and gleaming with the water of some buried mountain spring. The train goes slowly over the perilous and dizzy height of a wooden trestle; far below, the traveller can see and hear the clean foaming clamors of rock-bright mountain water; beside the track, before his little hut, a switchman stands looking at the train with the slow wondering gaze of the mountaineer. The little shack in which he lives is stuck to the very edge of the track above the steep and perilous ravine. His wife, a slattern with a hank of tight drawn hair, a snuff-stick in her mouth, and the same gaunt, slow wondering stare her husband has, stands in the doorway of the shack, holding a dirty little baby in her arms.
>
> —THOMAS WOLFE: *Of Time and the River.*[5]

There are, of course, many patterns more subtle, complex, and imaginative that can be derived from spatial order. We shall come to study these in the section on Description, but meanwhile, as need arises, you should try to develop your own variations from the simple, literal pattern.

■ APPLICATIONS

I Assume that, on coming into a strange room, your eye fixes on some single striking or interesting particular and then discovers other things in relation to that. Write a paragraph of description, of 100 words, using this principle. Or write a paragraph based on some other principle of perception.

II Make a short list of controls for the order of space.

OTHER CONTROLS

We have made some fairly sharp distinctions among kinds of controls in terms of cause and effect and evidence and conclusion, time, and space. But there are many others that somewhat less specifically indicate relationships. For example, for adding or continuing we have such controls as the following: *and, or, but, moreover, likewise, also, in fact, indeed.* For oppo-

---

[5] Reprinted with the permission of Charles Scribner's Sons from *Of Time and the River* by Thomas Wolfe. Copyright 1935 Charles Scribner's Sons; renewal copyright © 1963 Paul Gitlin, Administrator C.T.A. Reprinted by permission of William Heinemann Ltd.

sition and contrast we have, for example: *but, nevertheless, still, notwithstanding.* For concession: *although, whereas.* Then there are all sorts of words and phrases of reference that give lines of connection through a discourse. For instance, pronouns that cast back to antecedents, including relative and demonstrative pronouns, and phrases like *all of them, some of them, as we have said, as we have pointed out, as will be seen, as will be clear in the sequel, that is to say, that is, to anticipate,* and *remembering that.*

Equally important, and even more flexible and subtle, are the controls that an author may develop for logical, temporal, spatial, or other relations. Let us glance at a few examples, chosen almost at random:

> . . . When you read what New England intellectuals were saying about the common people early in the nineteenth century you are reminded of what British and French colonial officials were saying about the natives when the clamor for independence rose after the last war: "Wait and see what a mess these savages will make of things."
>
> A resemblance between intellectuals and colonial officials strikes us at first sight as incongruous . . .   —ERIC HOFFER: *The Temper of Our Time.*[6]

Observe that the second paragraph begins with a restatement in different words ("resemblance") of the comparison between the New England intellectuals and the colonial officials, this restatement as preparation for the development of the discussion.

> . . . it is a literature of combat because it assumes responsibility, and because it is the will to liberty expressed in terms of time and space.
>
> On another level, the oral tradition—stories, epics, and songs of the people—which formerly were filed away as set pieces are now beginning to change.   —FRANTZ FANON: *The Wretched of the Earth.*

Here the "binder" is a phrase, "on another level," which introduces another example of the idea of the previous paragraph, the effect on literature of a revolutionary situation.

> . . . I threw off an overcoat, took an armchair by the crackling logs, and awaited patiently the arrival of my hosts.
>
> Soon after dark they arrived, and gave me a most cordial welcome . . .
> —EDGAR ALLAN POE: "The Gold-Bug."

This is an example of continuity by pure sequence: "Soon after dark . . ."

> . . . He caught her eyes only as she went, on which he thought them pretty and touching.
>
> Why especially touching at that instant he could certainly scarcely have said; it was involved, it was lost in the sense of her wishing to oblige him . . .   —HENRY JAMES: *The Wings of the Dove.*

The repetition of a single word here provides the continuity: the word *touching* leads to the development in the second paragraph of the idea that brings the former paragraph into focus.

---

[6] From pp. 74–75 in *The Temper of Our Time* (Hardbound Ed.) by Eric Hoffer (Harper & Row, 1965). Reprinted by permission of Harper & Row, Publishers.

No Formula There is no formula for using such transitions to give coherence. But you should observe constantly the variations you encounter and stock your mind with them. The point of this is not so much to repeat accepted devices as to master the principle—the necessity for maintaining continuity while indicating shifts in meaning and emphasis. You can then develop devices of your own that carry the impression of spontaneity.

● CAUTION

You should not depend merely on controls and devices of transition to establish coherence. You should aim at a continuity embodied as fully as possible in the actual writing—continuity from sentence to sentence, paragraph to paragraph, and division to division. Then, when such intrinsic continuity is not immediately obvious, you may resort to the controls.

■ APPLICATION

In the following passage fill in the controls that you feel appropriate to estab-. lish the coherence.

_____ we had come out of the gorge, the snow stopped, and now, as a _____, we could see the great opening out of the prairie beyond. _____ the sun was near setting, we could see with great clarity, in the distance _____ the expanse of new snow, the Indian village in the cottonwood grove at the bend of the river. _____ there was no wind, the smoke from the tepees stood straight up, gray-blue in the gold light of sunset. We looked to our firearms, _____ there was no way to know of what tribe they were. _____ we were thus engaged, François, the trapper, was peering across the distance. "Blackfeet!" he suddenly exclaimed. My heart sank, _____ I knew that he was rarely mistaken in such matters. I gave the order to proceed across the prairie toward the village, hoping, _____ against my better judgment, that a bold show was the best policy.

Emphasis

A piece of writing may be unified and coherent and still not be effective if it does not observe the principle of emphasis. When this principle is properly observed, the intended scale of importance of elements in the discourse is clear to the reader. All cats are black in the dark, but all things should not look alike in the light of a reasonable writer's interest in his subject. To change our metaphor, there is a foreground and a background of interest, and the writer should be careful to place each item in its proper location. Like unity and coherence, emphasis is a principle of organization.

Emphasis by flat statement

How does the writer emphasize an element in a piece of writing?

The most obvious way is to make a flat statement of his own view on the importance of a matter. In an article by the editors of *Time,* the first sentence reads "Crime in the U.S. is a national disgrace." In the *New York Times Magazine* ("The Great Society Is a Sick Society," August 20, 1967), Senator J. W. Fulbright concludes an article by writing:

> If I had to bet my money on what is going to happen, I would bet on this younger generation—this generation of young men and women who reject the inhumanity of war in a poor and distant land, who reject the poverty and sham in their own country, who are telling their elders what their elders ought to have known—that the price of empire is America's soul and that the price is too high.

The editors of *Time* and Senator Fulbright have insisted on the importance of what they have to say. The editors start with their proposition and proceed to develop it in detail. Senator Fulbright moves toward his through the body of discussion. But in both instances the cards are on the table. There is no question as to the focus of importance.

The statement is the most obvious device of emphasis. But if the statement is unsupported, it will not achieve its purpose. You must be sure, when you resort to stating the emphasis outright, that the statement proceeds from, or will be justified by, the line of thought you have developed.

Be sure you really believe your own statement.

Emphasis by position

A second way to emphasize is by position. "First or last" is a fairly sound rule for emphasis by position. This rule corresponds to two general methods for treating a subject. The main idea can be presented and then discussed or proved, or discussion or proof can lead up to the main idea. Ordinarily the second method is better, and the end is the most emphatic position, for the last impression a reader receives is what counts most. But some rather conventionalized forms of writing, such as news stories, put the most important material first.

Emphasis by proportion

Proportion in itself is a means of emphasis. The most important topic in a discussion reasonably receives fullest treatment. This principle, however, is more flexible than the preceding statement would indicate. In some writing the last and most important topic may have been so well prepared for by the foregoing discussion that it does not require elaborate treatment. The writer must decide each case on its own merits and be sure that he is not indulging in elaboration merely for the sake of elaboration.

Other devices of emphasis

Flat statement, order of importance, proportion, and style (to be discussed in Chapter 13) are major means of expressing emphasis, but there are certain minor ones. For instance, repetition of an idea can give it prominence. The danger here is that the repetition may become merely mechanical and therefore dull. To be effective, repetition must be combined with some variety and some progression in the treatment of the subject. Then there is the device of the short, isolated paragraph. The idea set off by itself strikes the eye. But not all short paragraphs are in themselves emphatic. The content and the phrasing of the short paragraph must make it appear worthy of special presentation. Obviously if many paragraphs are short, all emphasis disappears.

Faulty devices of emphasis

Certain common devices of emphasis are worse than useless. Irresponsible exaggeration always repels the reader. Catchwords and hackneyed phrases, such as *awfully, terribly, tremendously, the most wonderful thing I ever saw, you never saw anything like it, I can't begin to tell you*—these make a claim on the reader's attention that he is rarely prepared to grant. Random underlining and italicizing and the use of capitals and exclamation points usually defeat their own purpose. Writers use these devices when they are not sure that what they have to say will stand on its own merits. To insist that what you have to say is important does not prove the point. As the writer, you must prove it.

In applying any of the means of emphasis the writer must first of all be sure that the thing emphasized is worth emphasizing. Common sense must help him here. Nothing else can.

A student theme

A student was assigned to write a theme on the standard topic "An Interesting Person." Wisely enough, he thought over people he knew well and settled on a member of the family, his uncle, for whom he had affection and respect. But Uncle Conroy, if taken in the lump, would, he knew, be too general and uncontrolled a subject, and so he set about trying to define for himself the reasons for his feelings about the old man. Having arrived at a fairly clear notion, he focused his subject in the title "The Person I Admire Most." He jotted down some of the things he could remember about his uncle, and some of the reasons for his feelings about him. Then he tried to organize them in an outline. His outline ran as follows:

Statement of the Subject   Why I admire my Uncle Conroy
Introduction
    I. My uncle as he now appears—apparent failure and real success
Body
    II. The background of my uncle's achievement
       A. His worldly success and ruin
       B. His illness and despair

III. The nature of my uncle's achievements
    A. His practical achievements
        1. Help with the children
        2. Help with my father's business
        3. Help with my mother's illness
    B. His achievement in self-control
        1. Naturalness of his actions
        2. Cheerfulness in the face of pain
    C. His greatest achievement, an example to others—the summary of his other achievements

Conclusion

IV. My uncle as a type of success and my admiration for him

When he had written the note for the conclusion, he decided that the title was too vague and did not really suit the theme. So now he scratched it out and substituted "Success and Uncle Conroy."

SUCCESS AND UNCLE CONROY

1 I suppose that my Uncle Conroy is the person I admire most in the world. This statement would probably seem strange to anyone who happened to visit our home and see the old man sitting, hunched over and shabbily dressed, at a corner of the hearth, not saying much, with his old meerschaum pipe left over from his early days stuck in his mouth, but not lit, probably. He looks like the complete failure, and by ordinary standards he is. He has no money. He has no children. He is old and sick. But he has made his own kind of success, and I think he is happy.

2 At one time in his life he was a success by ordinary standards. He was the son of a poor Methodist minister (my mother's father), but he ran away from home in Illinois to Oklahoma, back in the days when things were beginning to boom out there. He had a fine house in Oklahoma City and a ranch. He was hail-fellow-well-met, and men and women liked him. He was a sportsman, kept good horses, and took long hunting trips to Mexico and Canada. Then one day, on his own ranch, his horse stumbled in a gopher hole and threw him. He was in the hospital for two years. While he was there, a partner, either through dishonesty or stupidity (my uncle would never discuss this), ran everything into the ground and broke it off. So he came back to Illinois, and my mother and father took him in.

3 It must have been awful for a man like that to be living on charity. But the worst was to come, for he developed arthritis in a very painful form, and he could never work again. I remember the first year or so, even though I was a very small child. He even tried to commit suicide with gas from the stove. But my mother saved him, and after that he began to change.

4 The first thing was that he began to take an interest in us children. He would read to us. He helped us with lessons. That relieved mother and made her life easier. My father was an insurance man and had a lot of paper work to do. My uncle took an interest in that, and before long he was helping my father by doing reports and writing letters. Then when my mother was ill for a long time, he learned to do the housework, as much as his strength would permit, and even dressed the two smaller children.

5   What he did was important, but more important was the way he did things. He was so natural about it. You never got the impression he was making any effort or sacrifice. We all got so we didn't notice what he did, and I am sure that that was what he wanted.

6   As I look back now, or when I go home and see Uncle Conroy, his biggest achievement, however, seems to be the kind of example he gave us all. He was often in pain, but he was always cheerful. If he felt too bad, he simply hid away from the family for a while in his room—what he called his "mope-room." He even made a joke out of that. And he didn't act like a man who had failed. He acted like a man who had found what he could do and was a success at it. And I think that he is a success. We all admire success, and that is why I admire my Uncle Conroy.

This theme is unified and coherent, and builds to an effective emphasis in the summarizing conclusion. Let us examine the general pattern.

First, by way of introduction, the author gives a brief sketch of the uncle as he now appears—the man who is to be interpreted by the theme. The appearance of failure (even the detail of the burned-out pipe) in contrast to the reality of success excites the reader's curiosity. The introduction implies a proposition, a leading idea: This man embodies a success beyond his practical failure. The proposition is expressed in the image of the old man in his failure, and this image suggests a question that leads into the body of the theme: How can this old man be a success? In other words, the proposition gives the focus for the unity of the theme, and the question provides the principle of coherence: the whole theme demonstrates the proposition, but the process of answering the question is what carries us from point to point. It must be remembered, to be sure, that the unity and coherence here, as always, are intimately related. The student achieves emphasis by putting his main interpretation at the very end of Paragraph 6, where it serves as the climax of the whole composition. Thus, the theme has a sound structure, which was developed in the outline before the actual writing was begun.

■ APPLICATIONS

I   In the theme "Success and Uncle Conroy," indicate the kinds of controls used to maintain coherence. Explain the function of each. Indicate the devices of emphasis, and explain them.

II   You are now ready to write your longest theme to date, a theme of some 750 words about yourself. Remember that you have a particular audience, the instructor. That person is almost a stranger to you, but he is friendly and interested. He wants to know you better. For one thing, he wants to know the basic facts of your life. These facts are bound to be part of your story. But he wants to know a good deal more, something of the inside "you," your character, your training, your ambitions, your view of yourself.

But "yourself" is a big topic. Begin by thinking about it, by exploring it. Try to answer honestly, in your own mind, such questions as the following:

1   To what extent have circumstances (heredity, family situation, certain per-
    sons, and experience) made me what I am?
2   To what extent do I feel myself responsible for what I am?
3   How do I assess my character, personality, and possibilities at this moment?
4   What do I want to do with myself?

When you have a subject, begin to jot down notes, almost at random,
trying to feel your way into your theme. Next, try to sort out what you have
assembled, establishing relations to the main idea. But—and perhaps fortunately—you may have struck on another idea. If so, inspect it. Don't feel
wedded to the first one.

Your next stage is to make an outline, a topic outline to start with. Then
you should convert your outline into a sentence outline, using sentences that
really say something, that indicate content and stages of development.

Now write. But when you actually begin composition, keep an open mind.
If new ideas come, as they almost certainly will, think them over on their
merits, even if this means a change in your plan.

After you have finished the first draft of your theme, check it by the outline. If the theme seems good and systematic but does not match the outline,
revise the outline to conform to the theme. But if the theme does not seem
satisfactory and the outline does, revise the theme to conform to the outline.
Attach your rough notes and the outlines to the theme before you hand it in.

PART TWO

THE FORMS
OF DISCOURSE

CHAPTER 4

The Main Intention

Thus far we have discussed three key topics: (1) the true subject and how to arrive at it; (2) the divisions of a discourse, and their special functions and interrelations; and (3) unity, coherence, and emphasis, what they are and how to achieve them. Looking back on these topics, we see that they are closely related, and that the discussion of each represents a stage in a larger, continuing discussion that is concerned with a deep, general question—the relationship between form and function, shape and point.

Form and Function

A piece of writing has, presumably, been composed to accomplish some purpose, perform some function, make some point. All the elements in a composition should contribute, directly or indirectly, to fulfilling that function, making that point. The form is determined by the function, the shape by the point. But function, too, is determined by form, point by shape. This idea lies behind everything that you will be studying in this book.

The reciprocal relationship between form and function, shape and point, appears in the very process of composition. Certainly, your purpose—the function you wished to see fulfilled—conditions what you put down on paper. But in the process of putting ideas into words, the words themselves tend to generate new ideas, and so the function intended may be constantly modified in the very act of embodying it in a form.

The Main Intention

The reciprocal modification of form and function in the process of composition is, however, limited by what we may call the main intention appropriate to the occasion. When a lawyer sits down to write a brief, he may well come on new points that will enrich his thought or new objections that will deflect it into new channels. But he is not likely to drift off into writing a poem, a short story, or even a letter to his aged mother. There may be other occasions on which he writes a poem or a letter to his aged mother, but not on this one. Now he will stick to his main intention. In the same way, a fiction writer at work on a novel may change his characters and plot a half dozen times along the way, and what had started as a comedy may end as a tragedy, or vice versa, but it is highly improbable that this writer will drift off into a legal brief, a poem, or even a letter to his own aged mother.

The main, the underlying, purpose of the lawyer is to write the brief. That of the novelist is to write a novel. The purpose underlies and conditions the process of the writing. It determines the kind of form and the kind of force appropriate in each instance. The form and force of a brief are different from those of a novel. The form and force of the brief are those appropriate to an argument. The form and force of the novel are those appropriate to a narrative.

The Four Kinds of Discourse

There are four basic natural needs that are fulfilled in discourse. We want to explain or inform about something. We want to convince somebody. We want to tell what a thing looked like—or sounded like, or felt like. We want to tell what happened.[1] These natural needs determine the four forms of discourse. Each need represents, then, an intention that is fulfilled in a particular kind of discourse.

The four kinds of discourse are exposition, argument, description, and narration.[2] Let us linger a little longer on the kind of intention that each represents.

In the first of these, exposition, the intention is to explain something, for instance, to make some idea clear to the reader, to analyze a situation, to define a term, to give directions. The intention, in short, is to inform.

---

[1] Somebody may well object that there are more than four natural needs—that when you hit your finger with a hammer you cry "ouch" or swear. But your exclamation is not discourse, it is an utterance. To look at the question from another angle, a discourse aims at communication; the utterance aims at mere expression. When you cry "ouch," you blow off steam without necessary reference to an audience.

[2] Persuasion, to which a separate chapter is given in this book, is commonly thought of under the mode of argument.

In argument, the intention is to make somebody change his mind, his attitude, his point of view, or his feelings.[3]

In description, the intention is to make the reader as vividly aware as possible of what the writer has perceived through his senses (or in his imagination), to give him the "feel" of things described, the quality of a direct experience. The thing described may be anything that we can grasp through the senses, a natural scene, a city street, a cat or a racehorse, the face of a person, the sound of a voice, the odor of an attic, a piece of music.

In narration, the intention is to present an event to the reader—what happened and how it happened. The event itself may be grand or trivial, a battle or a ball game, a presidential campaign or a picnic; but whatever it is, the intention is to give the impression of movement in time, to give some immediate impression of the event, the sense of witnessing an action.

Mixture of the kinds of discourse

We have commented on the four kinds of discourse as traditionally described in their pure form. We do, now and then, encounter an example in a relatively pure form. The excerpt from the theme whose author plans to be a teacher in a slum high school (p. 29) is primarily an argument, an argument between the student and his father. But more often we find the forms mixed, for instance, in the theme "Success and Uncle Conroy." There paragraph 1 is chiefly description, giving a picture of the old man as he now is. Paragraphs 2, 3, and 4 are primarily narration, and bits of narration appear even in paragraph 6, the conclusion. But is the main intention descriptive or narrative?

No, it is neither. If we look at paragraph 1, we find a question implied: Why should I admire the apparent failure, Uncle Conroy? The body of the theme answers that question, and the intention of doing so is what controls the description and narration. When we get to the conclusion, we find that the author admires Uncle Conroy because he is a "success," but further, we find that the theme has been concerned with a distinction between what we may call a false success and a true success, the kind that Uncle Conroy has attained in the midst of his worldly failure.

In other words, the main intention of the theme is expository, and the descriptive and narrative elements are subordinate to that intention.

At this point the student may well ask: "What becomes of the notion of a kind of discourse as the main intention if the kinds are so mixed up in ordinary practice?" This is a reasonable question, and the answer to it is fundamental. In a good piece of writing the mixing of the kinds of discourse is never irresponsible. The class report will always be, by its very nature, a piece of exposition. The novel, no matter how much exposition, description, or argument it may contain, will always be primarily an example of narration. Certain instances, it is true, may not be as clear-cut as these. A magazine article on international affairs may seem to be primarily exposi-

---

[3] But see also Chapter 7, Persuasion.

tory, but it may, in the end, aim to convince the reader of the need for a certain policy—and thus, by the main intention, be an argument. In fact, exposition and argument easily blend. Exposition is often the best argument, or exposition may resort to the kind of reasoning characteristic of argument, the reasoning from cause to effect or from evidence to conclusion.[4]

Method of study

Though most writing does involve a mixture of the kinds of discourse, we can best study them in isolation, one by one, as we shall do in the five succeeding chapters.[5] We will analyze relatively pure examples in order to observe the types of organization appropriate to each kind of discourse. It is only after one understands the kinds of discourse in pure form that one can make them work effectively together in unity in a larger composition.

■ APPLICATIONS

I Try to label the dominant kind of discourse in each of the following selections. When there are intentions subordinate to the main intention, try to label them too.

A How can there fail to be unity in the achievement of all life, as there is in its chemical basis? Flowers have evolved their perfection of color, shape, and scent, insects their brilliance and intricacy of bodily form, birds their plumage and song, animals their strength and grace. Man has evolved his noble cultures and his troubled, imperfect soul, nourishing them upon the rest of creation. If, as I believe, evolution has a purpose to achieve in the sense that the acorn is purposeful, then clearly there is an underlying power behind it of which all these manifestations are related parts. In the total picture there can be no absolute division between the feathers put out by a bird of paradise and the canvases filled in by painters; all are equally reactions of life expressing itself through the finest organizations of matter. I am certainly not inclined to minimize the importance of the human mind and its creative power; for me it is supreme so far as this small planet is concerned; but there is no impassable barrier between it and the rest of existence . . .

               —Jacquetta Hawkes: *Man on Earth*.[6]

B Another, more ingenious theory, is that before the progenitor of man became a hunting ape, the original ape that had left the forests went through a long phase as an aquatic ape. He is envisaged as moving to the tropical sea-shores in search of food. There he will have found shellfish and other sea-shore creatures in comparative abundance, a food supply much richer and more attractive than that on the open plains. At first he will have groped around in the rock pools and the shallow water, but gradually he will have started to swim out to greater depths and dive for food. During this process, it is argued, he

---

[4] As we shall see, description and narration also naturally flow together.
[5] Argument and persuasion are usually lumped together as one form of discourse, but they are treated here in separate chapters.
[6] From *Man on Earth*, by Jacquetta Hawkes. Reprinted by permission of A. D. Peters & Co.

will have lost his hair like other mammals that have returned to the sea. Only his head, protruding from the surface of the water, would retain the hairy coat to protect him from the direct glare of the sun. Then, later on, when his tools (originally developed for cracking open shells) became sufficiently advanced, he will have spread away from the cradle of the sea-shore and out into the open land spaces as an emerging hunter.

—Desmond Morris: *The Naked Ape*.[7]

C   This sea-marsh stretched for miles. Seaward, a grayness merging into sky had altogether rubbed out the line of dunes which bounded it that way: inland, another and darker blurred grayness was all you could see of the solid Welsh hills. But near by loomed a solitary gate, where the path crossed a footbridge and humped over the big dyke, and here in a sodden tangle of brambles the scent of a fox hung, too heavy today to rise or dissipate.

The gate clicked sharply and shed its cascade as two men passed through. Both were heavily loaded in oilskins. The elder and more tattered one carried two shotguns, negligently, and a brace of golden plover were tied to the bit of old rope he wore knotted about his middle: Glimpses of a sharp-featured weather-beaten face showed from within his bonneted sou'wester, but mouth and even chin were hidden in a long weeping mustache. The younger man was springy and tall and well-built and carried over his shoulder the body of a dead child. Her thin muddy legs dangled against his chest, her head and arms hung down his back; and at his heels walked a black dog—disciplined, saturated, and eager.   —Richard Hughes: *The Fox in the Attic*.[8]

[7] From *The Naked Ape* by Desmond Morris. Copyright 1968. Used with permission of McGraw-Hill Book Company. Reprinted by permission of Jonathan Cape Ltd.
[8] Reprinted from *The Fox in the Attic*, by Richard Hughes, by permission of David Higham.

CHAPTER **5**

The Methods of Exposition

The word *exposition* quite literally means to set forth a subject. It appeals to the understanding. Argument also appeals to the understanding, but it does so, not to explain, but to convince the reader of the truth or desirability of something. Description and narration may, of course, lead to understanding, but their special appeal is to the imagination, to the reader's capacity for re-creating the immediate qualities of an object or event.

Exposition is the most common kind of writing, for it is applicable to any task that challenges the understanding—the definition of a word, the way to a street address, the structure of a plant, the mechanism of a watch, the cause of a historical event, the meaning of a philosophy.

When we study the methods of exposition, we are studying some of the ways our minds naturally work. We are not following an arbitrary scheme; we are following the ways in which we ordinarily observe and reason about our world. We are doing systematically something that ordinary living, in its hit-or-miss fashion, forces on us, quite naturally, all the time.

Interest

A piece of exposition may be regarded as the answer to a question. If a specific question has been asked—"Why are you majoring in chemistry?" or "What were the causes of the American Revolution?"—it is rather easy to frame an answer that does not waver too badly from the point. The question controls the answer.

If, however, we set out to write a piece of exposition simply because we feel that a subject is engrossing or important, we are likely to give a wandering and confused account. Much in the way we went about locating a "true subject" in a general one (pp. 10–11), we must decide what specific question may be taken as our concern. The question sharpens to a focus the *interest* the subject holds for us and will govern our answer.

Let us draw up an informal list to suggest at least some of the kinds of interests that exposition may satisfy:

1   What is it?
2   What does it mean?
3   What does it do?
4   How is it put together?
5   How does it work?
6   What was it intended to do?
7   How did it come to be this way?
8   When did it occur, or exist?
9   Why, or how, did it occur, or exist?
10   What is it good for?
11   What is its importance?
12   How well does it fulfill its function, or purpose?

Naturally, not all of these questions would be appropriate for the same subject. If we are trying to define a triangle, we would scarcely ask when it occurred, since the nature of a triangle—what makes a figure a triangle and not something else—has no reference to time at all. Or if we are discussing a railroad wreck, we would scarcely ask how well it fulfilled its purpose. It would be appropriate, however, to ask how or why it occurred.

At first glance, some of these questions may seem too obvious or trivial to provide the basis for a discussion. For instance, the questions "What is it?" and "When did it occur?" ordinarily demand only the briefest answer. But if we ask the former question with reference to a complicated concept such as democracy, we may wind up with a book. Or if we ask the latter question with reference to the existence of the dinosaur, we may well have to go into an elaborate account of methods of geological dating.

Question and proposition

In a discussion of any length we commonly find more than one question involved. There is the main question, which represents the main interest, but to get a satisfactory answer to that, perhaps other questions must be asked and answered along the way. So we encounter again the problems of unity and coherence.

The main question must govern the whole. And we may think of the answer to the main question as giving the proposition, the thesis, the governing idea of the discussion. For instance, a historian, in answering the question "Why did it occur?" about the American Revolution, might come up with this answer to serve as his proposition: "The causes of the American Revolution were primarily economic." He might proceed to do a book offering a very elaborate analysis of the background of the event, but this proposition would control the whole book.

● CAUTION

The list of questions offered above must not be taken as complete. It merely suggests the kinds of interest that exposition may be used to satisfy—or, to put it differently—the kinds of question that a "thing," anything, an idea, an object, an event, may provoke in our minds.

More emphatically, these questions are not to be taken as necessarily corresponding to particular methods of exposition that we shall now study —though some of them may happen to do so.

The purpose of the list is to suggest ways in which you may regard a general subject and bring it into focus.

■ APPLICATIONS

I   Can you add to the list of guiding questions given above?

II   Below is a list of general subjects. What questions, including, if relevant, some from your additional list, would you think appropriate for any three of these subjects:

Going steady	Fraternities
College reformers	The honor system
Drinking	Abraham Lincoln
The Catholic (or other) Church	The "new mathematics"
The concept of justice	Dogs

An example: dogs

A student who is particularly fond of dogs takes that subject as one to frame questions about. His questions are:

1   What is a dog?
2   How did it come to be as it is today?
3   What is it good for?

When he comes to write a theme, he toys with the idea of making the first question his topic, thinking that he might use a zoological classification as the basis of his work. But this seems too dull. Then he thinks he might answer the question with some such title as "Man's Best Friend," but this strikes him as even duller. The second question appears more promising. He is really a fanatic about dogs and has read everything he can get his hands on; so he considers the possibility of writing on the evolution of the dog and the development of the two basic types, the wolf-dog and the jackal-dog. But he decides that this would not give him much opportunity for originality, for any personal touches. The third question leads him to consider the various kinds of work that dogs may be bred or trained to do. He is about to drop this subject when suddenly he gets his idea. He will write on training. He begins to jot down his ideas as a basis for an outline.

His preliminary jottings begin like this:

> where start—name, come, stand, heel, sit, wait
> time factor—when puppy—repetition—patience—

The word *patience* gives him another idea. He sees how boring a theme would be that merely lists the methods of teaching a dog, for there would be little variety in the actual process of teaching. But with the idea of patience, interest switches to the teacher. He now jots down:

> patience—imagination—put self in dog's place—be fair—be consistent—

He knows that he now has the true subject for his theme: the qualities necessary to a good trainer. He sets up a scratch outline:

I. *Introduction*
II. *Body*
   A. Sympathy—friendliness—start early to gain his confidence
   B. Patience—dog learns only by repetition—not lose temper
   C. Imagination—put self in dog's place
   D. Consistency—signal always same—never change mind—firmness in demands
   E. Fairness—most important—dog wants appreciation most of all— not bribery—no irrational punishment—*never lose temper*
III. *Conclusion*
   Training brings out best in dog

The student has no idea for the introduction and therefore starts with the main discussion. Having finished that to his satisfaction, he returns to the introduction. After several false starts, he decides simply to give a personal background for the theme. He writes that introduction, then jumps to the end and flings down his one-sentence conclusion. So we have:

TRAINING A DOG

I have always liked dogs. I come by this naturally, for my father is crazy about them too, not only his hunting dogs, but other kinds as well. We have always had a half dozen or so around the house, and my father and I like nothing better than talking about dogs, or reading about them, or going to dog shows. Dogs are a fascinating subject to us. One of the most fascinating things is to raise and train a dog. You really feel, then, that it is yours.

For the best results you have to start to train a dog young. I always feel, as a matter of fact, that you ought to start when the dog is only a puppy. It is true that the puppy can't learn, but you set up some kind of confidence, and the puppy gets to recognize and like you. This makes things easier later.

To train a dog you need several qualities. You must be patient. You must put yourself in the dog's place. You must be consistent. You must be fair.

A dog can learn only by repetition. It is boring for a human being to go over and over the same simple thing, but you have to realize that this boredom is the price you pay for a good dog. You have to be patient and never let your boredom show. And you must never lose your temper.

This leads to the second thing, putting yourself in the dog's place. You have to sympathize with him. If you do, you will feel how hard it is for the animal to understand your wishes and how dependent he is on you.

It is obvious why you have to be consistent. The dog understands you only when your word or signal is exactly the same as before. If you are inconsistent, he gets confused. For the same reason you must never change your mind. Once you give an order, stick to it, even if it was a bad order. Your word must be law, or you are wasting your breath.

Fairness is important always, but especially in training. You have to show the dog that you appreciate him, and once he gets this point, he wants nothing more than to please you. There is no use bribing a dog to obey. You have to make him want to please you, and the only way is by fairness. As for punishment, there is no use in punishing the dog if he doesn't know why he is being punished. You should always punish him immediately after the misbehavior, and always use the same punishment for the same kind of misbehavior. But don't lose your temper.

Training brings out the best in a dog and is worth all the time it takes.

On reflection, the student finds the conclusion skimpy and graceless. He wants something rather similar in tone to the introduction, which he now looks at again. The word *father* in the first sentence reminds him of something else his father has said and suggests his conclusion. The new conclusion is personal; it balances the introduction and is directly tied to the introduction by the reference to the father. The conclusion now reads:

Training brings out the best in a dog and is worth all the time it takes. But my father says something else in addition. He says that when you train a dog you are training yourself, too. My father says that you cannot learn too much patience and sympathy, consistency and fair play, and so you ought always to be training a dog just to learn to control yourself.

The theme has some repetitiousness, the phrasing is occasionally vague, and the organization in the next to last paragraph is a little fuzzy. But the writer has intelligently located his true subject, which gives his theme unity; he has a clear system of organization for the main body (the listing and discussion of the qualities of the trainer), which gives his theme coherence; and he has a sensible conclusion, which carries a little agreeable surprise with it (not the dog but the man learns most from the training process).

● CAUTION: MULTIPLE INTERESTS

The author of the theme on the training of dogs located and followed through one interest in his theme about dogs. This *main interest* gave him his subject. A writer may, however, appeal to more than one interest in the same composition, and in any extended discussion he is almost certain to do so. But in so doing he must be careful to keep the interests distinct. He must develop each interest at a different stage in his overall treatment. He must be sure that all the interests to which he appeals are related to the main interest of the composition and are subordinated to it. He must be sure that the main interest dominates and permeates the whole.

■ APPLICATION

Below is a list of general subjects. Select three that seem fruitful to you (or take three of your own), and for each state an interest that might give you a true subject. Then take one of the true subjects you have prepared and work out the pattern for a theme with the true subject as the main interest and other subjects as subsidiary interests. Specify the relations the subsidiary interests would bear to the main interest. Prepare a full sentence outline.

Space exploration	The variety of religious beliefs
Television	Cooking: art or science?
Camping	Newspapers
The crisis in the cities	Women's fashions

The methods of exposition

We shall now study the methods of exposition: identification, comparison and contrast, illustration, classification, definition, and analysis. These are the ways in which we go about answering questions that demand exposition. But as we have pointed out above, this statement does not mean that there is a method to correspond to each question on our list. Some methods may be used in answering more than one question, and the answer to a single question may sometimes be arrived at by a combination of methods.

Almost any discourse—for example, an editorial, an essay, a theme, a chapter in a textbook—will use more than one method. We rarely find a method in its pure state. But here, to understand the nature of each method, we shall be concerned with relatively pure examples.

The First Method: Identification

Identification is the simplest way of answering the question: "What is it?" It is a kind of pointing by means of language. "Who is Mrs. Bertrand Smith?" somebody asks, and the answer is, "Oh, she is the blond woman in the black dress, sitting to the right of the white-haired old man." The reply has in effect pointed a finger at Mrs. Smith. But perhaps Mrs. Smith is not there to be pointed at. In that case, the answer may be, "She is the woman who won the city golf tournament last year and then married the son of old Jason Smith, the banker." In either case the answer places the subject, Mrs. Smith, in a context so that she can be identified.

We constantly use such casual forms of identification in conversation. But we can use the same method in writing. For example, we can begin an article on the Carmel Mission by writing: "The Carmel Mission stands just outside the village of Monterey, California. It was founded by Padre Junipero Serra, who had come up from San Diego in the year 1770." We have thus identified the subject. Such a method might be considerably elaborated, though in this process it would tend to absorb, or be absorbed by, other methods of exposition. The main thing to remember is that in using identification the writer makes a kind of frame or chart in which to locate the item that needs to be identified.

The Second Method: Comparison and Contrast

It is natural for us, in confronting an unfamiliar object, to set it against the familiar. We instinctively want to know in what ways it is like the familiar and in what ways different. This is a simple, and essential, way of sorting out our experience of the world.[1]

A child asks, "What is a zebra?" We reply, "Oh, a zebra—it's an animal sort of like a mule, but it's not as big as a mule. And it has stripes like a tiger, black and white stripes all over. But you remember that a tiger's stripes are black and orange." Here we have compared the shape of the zebra to that of the mule, but have contrasted the two animals in size. And we have compared the stripes of the zebra to the stripes of a tiger, but have contrasted them in color. If the child knows what mules and tigers are like, he now has some idea of a zebra.

The informal, instinctive use of comparison and contrast, as in the answer to the child's question, is useful; but we can make the method infinitely more useful in thinking and expressing ourselves, if we are systematic.

Kinds of purpose

To be systematic means, first of all, to understand the kinds of purpose for which comparison or contrast may be made.

We may distinguish three types of purpose. First, we may wish to pre-

---

[1] Here we are speaking of comparison and contrast strictly as a method of exposition, but we should recognize that the instinctive need to make comparisons reaches in many other directions. For example, a poet making a comparison in a poem or a painter contrasting two forms in planning the composition of a picture would not be concerned at all with exposition as we are discussing it here. He would be acting from an appreciative or artistic motivation, as compared with an expository or scientific one. Again comparison and contrast are rich sources of humor. For these and related matters, see Chapter 12, Metaphor, and Chapter 13, Tone.

sent information about one item and may do so by relating it to another item with which our audience is familiar. For example, if we wish to explain the British Parliament to a fellow American, we may do so by comparing it with our Congress, which he does know about.

Second, we may wish to inform about both items, and proceed to do so by treating them in relation to some general principle that would apply to both and with which our audience is presumably familiar. For example, if we are reviewing two novels, neither of which our audience is acquainted with, we may compare and contrast them by reference to what we assume our audience knows about the principles of fiction.

Third, we may compare and contrast items with which our audience is familiar for the purpose of informing about some general principle or idea. For instance, if we want to give a notion of what religion is, we may compare and contrast several kinds, say Protestantism, Catholicism, Buddhism, and the religion of the Aztecs, to show what elements they have in common. In fulfilling this last purpose, we are, of course, using comparison and contrast as a way of proceeding from our examples to a general description of the class to which these examples belong. (See Argument, pp. 152–57.)

Area of interest: class

There is an amusing little scene (III, 2) in Shakespeare's play *Hamlet* in which the Prince baits the foolish old Polonius:

HAMLET: Do you see yonder cloud that's almost in shape like a camel?

POLONIUS: By the mass, and 'tis like a camel, indeed.

HAMLET: Methinks it is like a weasel.

POLONIUS: It is backed like a weasel.

HAMLET: Or like a whale?

POLONIUS: Very like a whale.

Part of the humor of the little scene comes from the fact that the comparisons Hamlet suggests and that the old simpleton accepts so seriously are meaningless and random. And this leads to our point that random similarities and differences are not very instructive. Our minds, in the casual making of comparisons, do throw off many merely fanciful notions of resemblance or difference, and such notions may be humorous or poetic, but we learn no more from them than we learn about clouds, camels, weasels, and whales from Hamlet's baiting of Polonius.

We have said that comparison, to be useful, must be systematic. To be systematic, a comparison or contrast must be between two or more items within a special area of interest—members, that is, of a group or class that is defined by a special interest brought to the material.[2] A zoologist, for example, may profitably compare and contrast a hawk and a garter snake,

---

[2] The idea of *class* in this sense will recur throughout this chapter, for we shall find thinking by classes a basic method in exposition.

for he can place them both in the significant class of living creatures. An aeronautical engineer may compare the hawk and an airplane by putting them in the class of things that fly. But it isn't likely that he would find much profit in putting an airplane and a garter snake together, even for contrast.

Contrast, like comparison, is significant only when some common ground is recognized between the things contrasted—when they belong to the same significant class, the class depending upon the purpose of the contrast. For instance, it is not instructive to say that John's dog is wicked, and in contrast to John, who is virtuous. The dog, unlike John, does not belong to the class of morally responsible creatures in which such a contrast would be significant. It would be nonsense to contrast them on this basis, for, in fact, a dog cannot be said to be wicked. But we can make sense of the contrast between the virtuous John and his wicked brother James.

Let us look at this as a picture:

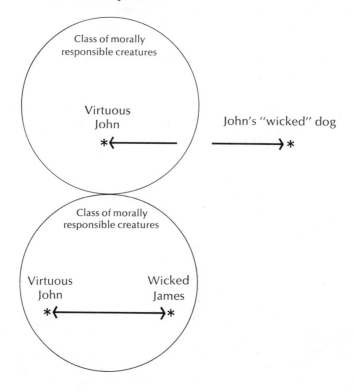

INTEREST AND SIGNIFICANT CLASS

The nature of a class used for a comparison or contrast is determined, we must always remember, by some interest we ourselves bring. Our interest defines the class. A farmer looking at a field thinks of the quality of the soil, the drainage, the exposure, and so on. That is, he puts the field in the class *arable land* and, on this basis, compares or contrasts it with other tracts he is acquainted with. But suppose that an infantry officer comes along and looks at the same field. He may well think of how a defensible position might be found there. That is, he would put the field in the class *defensible position*—a class determined by his special interest—and set it against other "positions" in the class.

We bring an interest to bear on an object or situation, but interests, of course, are variable. The military man, for example, may also be a farmer, and one moment he may regard the field as in the class *defensible position,* and the next, as in the class *arable land.* Or he may also be interested in painting, and at a particular moment, may think neither of crops nor of machine-gun emplacements, but of the color relations of the landscape.

Kinds of method

When we come to use comparison and contrast in extended form, we find that there are, broadly speaking, four ways of presenting material.

By the first method, we may fully present one item and then fully present the other, making continuous reference to the points of comparison or contrast. This method is, in general, appropriate when the points to be set against each other are fairly broad and obvious. By the second method, we present a part of one item and then a part of the second in relation to the corresponding part of the first item, until we have touched on all relevant parts. When a great many details are involved, this method is likely to be more useful than the first. By the third method, we present one item fully, and then, in presenting the second, refer, part by part, to the first item. Finally, by the fourth method, when a general principle is involved (as in the second and third of the types of general purpose mentioned on page 54), we can move from a statement of the principle to the process of comparison or contrast, or reversing the method, move through the process toward the principle. Sometimes, as we shall see, there may be a mixture of the methods.

■ APPLICATIONS

I   Put three of the following sets of items into one or more significant classes, and give a few points of comparison or contrast for each set.

> Chess, bridge, and poker
> Carpentry and writing verse
> The pictures an artist may see under the influence of drugs and those he paints on his canvas
> Martin Luther King and John F. Kennedy
> New York and ancient Rome
> The poet and the advertising man

II   Give five different sets of items for comparison or contrast and state your reasons for making each grouping.

Examples of methods of organization

Here is a student theme written according to the first method:

MY CHILDHOOD

My father died when I was a small child, and I was raised by my mother and my maternal grandfather, in whose home we lived until I came to college. My mother loved her father, and I have no reason to think he did not love her, but they were so different that I was aware from the first of a conflict between them. Or, if it was not a direct conflict between them, it was a conflict between what they stood for. And both of them exerted a strong influence over me. Therefore, as I grow up, I think more and more about their contrasting personalities and try to detect in myself the traces of each of them. I do this because I am trying to understand myself.

My grandfather, whose name was Carruthers McKenzie, was of Scotch-Irish blood and belonged to the Presbyterian Church. He had a long, bony face, sunken cheeks, and a straggly beard. He was a man with an iron will if I ever saw one, and all of his way of life was one long discipline for himself and everybody about him. But it was a discipline chiefly for himself. He never spent a day in bed in his life until his last illness, and yet he was probably ill a good part of his life. After he died—and he died of a cancer of the stomach—the doctor told us that he could not understand how any man could keep on his feet so long without giving in to the pain.

There was discipline enough left over for my mother and me and the two hired hands who worked about the place. We had morning prayers and evening prayers. I had to read the Bible an hour a day. My grandfather was a prosperous man, but I never had a nickel to spend which I had not earned, and his rates of payment for my chores were not generous. From the time I was eight, I had to study three hours in the afternoon and at least two hours at night, except for weekends. My grandfather never uttered a word of praise to me except now and then the statement, "You have done your duty." As one could guess, my grandfather never told jokes, was scrupulous about all kinds of obligations, never touched an alcoholic beverage or even soft drinks, and wore sober black, winter and summer.

My mother must have taken after her own mother, who was of South-German parentage and a Catholic by training. My mother's mother had given up her religion to marry my grandfather and had taken on his way of life, but she died very young. My mother was rather short in stature and had a rather full but graceful figure, the kind they call "partridge-y." She had round, pink cheeks and a complexion like a child's. She had blue eyes, very large. She loved to laugh and joke. My mother was a good mother, as the phrase goes; she loved me and she was careful of all my wants. But she also liked idleness. She would sit on the veranda half the afternoon and look across the yard, just rocking in her chair and enjoying the sunshine. And she went to bridge parties and even took an occasional glass of wine or, as I imagine, a highball. She was made for a good time and noise and people, and when my grandfather was out of the house, she used to romp and play with me or take me on long walks in the country back of our place.

When I was eighteen and went off to college, she got married. She married the kind of man you would expect her to pick. He is big and strong-looking, with a heavy, black mustache with a little gray in it. He smokes cigars and he likes fine whisky. He has a Cadillac agency in the city, and he keeps a little plane out at the airport. He loves sports and a good time. My mother has married exactly the man for her, I think, and I am enough like my mother to think he is fine, too. But as I look back on my grandfather—he died three years ago, when I was seventeen—I have a great admiration for him and a sneaking affection.

Here, in an excerpt from a discussion of English and American sportsmanship, is an example of the second method, which proceeds by a series of contrasts on different points of the items under discussion:

> Thanks to this universality of athletic sports, English training is briefer and less severe. The American makes, and is forced to make, a long and tedious business of getting fit, whereas an Englishman has merely to exercise and sleep a trifle more than usual, and this only for a brief period. Our oarsmen work daily from January to July, about six months, or did so before Mr. Lehmann brought English ideas among us; the English varsity crews row together nine or ten weeks. Our football players slog daily for six or seven weeks; English teams seldom or never "practice" and play at most two matches a week. Our track athletes are in training at frequent intervals throughout the college year and are often at the training table six weeks; in England six weeks is the maximum period of training, and the men as a rule are given only three days a week on the cinder track. To an American training is an abnormal condition; to an Englishman it is the consummation of the normal.
>
> —JOHN CORBIN: *An American at Oxford.*

The third method of organization appears in the following selection. First, one item of the comparison, General Grant, is given in full. Then General Lee is compared and contrasted, point by point, with Grant.

> Grant was, judged by modern standards, the greatest general of the Civil War. He was head and shoulders above any general on either side as an over-all strategist, as a master of what in later wars would be called global strategy. His Operation Crusher plan, the product of a mind which had received little formal instruction in the higher art of war, would have done credit to the most finished student of a series of modern staff and command schools. He was a brilliant theater strategist, as evidenced by the Vicksburg campaign, which was a classic field and siege operation. He was a better than average tactician, although, like even the best generals of both sides, he did not appreciate the destruction that the increasing firepower of modern armies could visit on troops advancing across open spaces.
>
> Lee is usually ranked as the greatest Civil War general, but this evaluation has been made without placing Lee and Grant in the perspective of military developments since the war. Lee was interested hardly at all in "global" strategy, and what few suggestions he did make to his government about operations in other theaters than his own indicate that he had little aptitude for grand planning. As a theater strategist, Lee often demonstrated more brilliance and apparent originality than Grant, but his most audacious plans were as much the product of the Confederacy's inferior

military position as of his own fine mind. In war, the weaker side has to improvise brilliantly. It must strike quickly, daringly, and include a dangerous element of risk in its plans. Had Lee been a Northern general with Northern resources behind him, he would have improvised less and seemed less bold. Had Grant been a Southern general, he would have fought as Lee did.

Fundamentally Grant was superior to Lee because in a modern total war he had a modern mind, and Lee did not. Lee looked to the past in war as the Confederacy did in spirit. The staffs of the two men illustrate their outlooks. It would not be accurate to say that Lee's general staff were glorified clerks, but the statement would not be too wide of the mark. Certainly his staff was not, in the modern sense, a planning staff, which was why Lee was often a tired general. He performed labors that no general can do in a big modern army—work that should have fallen to his staff, but that Lee did because it was traditional for the commanding general to do it in older armies. Most of Lee's staff officers were lieutenant-colonels. Some of the men on Grant's general staff, as well as on the staffs of other Northern generals, were major and brigadier generals, officers who were capable of leading corps. Grant's staff was an organization of experts in the various phases of strategic planning. The modernity of Grant's mind was most apparent in his grasp of the concept that war was becoming total and that the destruction of the enemy's economic resources was as effective and legitimate a form of warfare as the destruction of his armies. What was realism to Grant was barbarism to Lee. Lee thought of war in the old way as a conflict between armies and refused to view it for what it had become— a struggle between societies. To him, economic war was needless cruelty to civilians. Lee was the last of the great old-fashioned generals; Grant, the first of the great moderns.

—T. HARRY WILLIAMS: *Lincoln and His Generals.*[3]

Following is another example of the various methods of organization, in an extended contrast between two types into which the author would divide humanity, the "Red-bloods" and the "Mollycoddles."

We have divided men into Red-bloods and Mollycoddles. "A Red-blood man" is a phrase which explains itself; "Mollycoddle" is its opposite. We have adopted it from a famous speech by Mr. Roosevelt [Theodore Roosevelt], and redeemed it—perverted it, if you will—to other uses. A few examples will make the notion clear. Shakespeare's Henry V is a typical Red-blood; so was Bismarck; so was Palmerston; so is almost any businessman. On the other hand, typical Mollycoddles were Socrates, Voltaire, and Shelley. The terms, you will observe, are comprehensive and the types very broad. Generally speaking, men of action are Red-bloods. Not but what the Mollycoddles may act, and act efficiently. But, if so, the Mollycoddle acts from principle, not from the instinct for action. The Red-blood, on the other hand, acts as the stone falls, and does indiscriminately anything that comes to hand. It is thus that he carries on the business of the world. He steps without reflection into the first place offered him and

---

[3] From *Lincoln and His Generals,* by T. Harry Williams. Copyright 1952 by Alfred A. Knopf, Inc. Reprinted by permission of the publisher. Reprinted by permission of Hamish Hamilton, London.

goes to work like a machine. The ideals and standards of his family, his class, his city, his country, his age, he swallows as naturally as he swallows food and drink. He is therefore always "in the swim"; and he is bound to "arrive," because he has set before him the attainable. You will find him everywhere in all the prominent positions. In a military age he is a soldier, in a commercial age a businessman. He hates his enemies, and he may love his friends; but he does not require friends to love. A wife and children he does require, for the instinct to propagate the race is as strong in him as all other instincts. His domestic life, however, is not always happy; for he can seldom understand his wife. This is part of his general incapacity to understand any point of view but his own. He is incapable of an idea and contemptuous of a principle. He is the Samson, the blind force, dearest to Nature of her children. He neither looks back nor looks ahead. He lives in present action. And when he can no longer act, he loses his reasons for existence. The Red-blood is happiest if he dies in the prime of life; otherwise, he may easily end with suicide. For he has no inner life; and when the outer life fails, he dies too. Nature, who has blown through him, blows elsewhere. His steps are numb; he is dead wood on the shore.

The Mollycoddle, on the other hand, is all inner life. He may indeed act, as I said, but he acts, so to speak, by accident; just as the Red-blood may reflect, but reflects by accident. The Mollycoddle in action is the Crank; it is he who accomplishes reforms; who abolished slavery, for example, and revolutionized prisons and lunatic asylums. Still, primarily, the Mollycoddle is a critic, not a man of action. He challenges all standards and all facts. If an institution is established, that is a reason why he will not accept it; if an idea is current, that is a reason why he should repudiate it. He questions everything, including life and the universe. And for that reason Nature hates him. On the Red-blood she heaps her favors; she gives him a good digestion, a clear complexion, and sound nerves. But to the Mollycoddle she apportions dyspepsia and black bile. In the universe and in society the Mollycoddle is "out of it" as inevitably as the Red-blood is "in it." At school, he is a "smug" or a "swat," while the Red-blood is captain of the Eleven. At college, he is an "intellectual," while the Red-blood is in the "best set." In the world, he courts failure while the Red-blood achieves success. The Red-blood sees nothing; but the Mollycoddle sees through everything. The Red-blood joins societies; the Mollycoddle is a non-joiner. Individualist of individualists, he can stand alone, while the Red-blood requires the support of a crowd. The Mollycoddle engenders ideas, and the Red-blood invents. The whole structure of civilization rests on foundations laid by Mollycoddles; but all the building is done by Red-bloods. The Red-blood despises the Mollycoddle, but, in the long run, he does what the Mollycoddle tells him. The Mollycoddle also despises the Red-blood, but he cannot do without him. Each thinks he is master of the other, and, in a sense, each is right. In his lifetime the Mollycoddle may be the slave of the Red-blood; but after his death, he is his master, though the Red-blood may know it not.

Nations, like men, may be classified roughly as Red-blood and Mollycoddle. To the latter class belong clearly the ancient Greeks, the Italians, the French and probably the Russians; to the former the Romans, the Germans, and the English. But the Red-blood nation *par excellence* is the American; so that in comparison with them, Europe as a whole might almost be called Mollycoddle. This characteristic of Americans is reflected in the predominant physical type—the great jaw and chin, the huge teeth, the predatory mouth; in their speech, where beauty and distinction are sacrificed to force; in their need to live and feel and act in masses. To be born a Mollycoddle in America is to be born to a hard fate. You must either emigrate or succumb. This, at least hitherto, has been the alternative practiced. Whether a Mollycoddle will ever be produced strong enough to breathe the American atmosphere and live, is a crucial question for the future. It is the question whether America will ever be civilized. For civilization, you will have perceived, depends on a just balance of Red-bloods and Mollycoddles. Without the Red-blood there would be no life at all, no stuff, so to speak, for the Mollycoddle to work upon; without the Mollycoddle, the stuff would remain shapeless and chaotic. The Red-blood is the matter, the Mollycoddle the form; the Red-blood the dough, the Mollycoddle the yeast. On these two poles turns the orb of human society. And if, at this point, you choose to say that the poles are points and have no dimensions, that strictly neither the Mollycoddle nor the Red-blood exists, and that real men contain elements of both mixed in different proportions, I have no quarrel with you except such as one has with the man who states the obvious. I am satisfied to have distinguished the ideal extremes between which the Actual vibrates. The detailed application of the conception I must leave to more patient researchers.

—G. LOWES DICKINSON: "Red-bloods and Mollycoddles," *Appearances*.[4]

■ APPLICATIONS

I   We have distinguished the various methods of organization for comparison and contrast (p. 57). In the selection that discusses "Red-bloods" and "Mollycoddles," we find that the first two paragraphs offer fairly clear examples of different methods. Specify the methods used. But how is the third paragraph organized? Do you think that the third paragraph is an example of clear organization, or do you find it somewhat confused?

II   Take two of the comparisons or contrasts you worked out for the Application on p. 57 and expand them into full sentence outlines.

III   In a single paragraph not shorter than 150 words, develop each of the outlines you have prepared. In each use a different method of presentation.

The Third Method: Illustration

Our conversation is full of phrases like "for example" and "for instance" and "for illustration." Our use of illustration is as instinctive as that of

[4] From *Appearances* by G. Lowes Dickinson. Copyright 1914 by G. Lowes Dickinson. Reprinted by permission of Doubleday & Company, Inc.

comparison and contrast. But in illustration the mind operates somewhat differently. Both comparison and illustration, it is true, involve thinking in terms of class and particular items, but the characteristic relations are different. In comparison and contrast, as we have seen, two or more particular items in a significant class are set against each other. In illustration, we cite the particular item (or items) to clarify the nature of a class in which it is included.

Here, "for example," is how the method works:

> If anyone wants to exemplify the meaning of the word "fish," he cannot choose a better animal than a herring. The body, tapering to each end, is covered with thin, flexible scales, which are very easily rubbed off. The taper head, with its underhung jaw, is smooth and scaleless on the top; the large eye is partly covered by two folds of transparent skin, like eyelids—only immovable and with the slit between them vertical instead of horizontal; the cleft behind the gill-cover is very wide, and, when the cover is raised, the large red gills which lie underneath it are freely exposed. The rounded back bears the single moderately long dorsal fin about its middle. —THOMAS HENRY HUXLEY: "The Herring."

We may indicate by a diagram what Huxley has done:

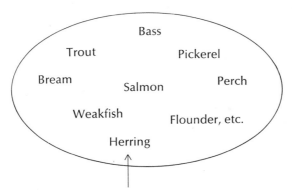

"to exemplify the meaning of the word 'fish,'
he cannot choose a better animal than a herring"

We have said that the relation of the particular to the class is fundamental to the process of illustration. But what of the fact that here the species *herring* (which of course is a group, or class, of fish) appears as a particular? The point is that though *herring* is a class, it is being used to explain a more inclusive class *fish:* the characteristic movement from the particular to the general, to the class, is observed. What is important is that the particular—be it individual or group—must be truly included in the class and must truly represent the relevant qualities of that class. To sum up:

1 The nature of the general governs the nature of the particular.
2 The particular must really belong to the class in question.

The particular and its irrelevant qualities: interest

When Huxley uses a species as his particular, it is implied that any individual herring would possess the relevant qualities. Certainly, there are differences among individual herring—size, weight, and so forth—but these differences are not among the essential characteristics that set off the species herring from other species of fish. So Huxley, for all practical purposes, is referring to any herring.

But let us jump from fish to men. We think of the class *man,* but we also recognize the individuality of any member of that class we encounter—the postman, our sister, a stranger on the street, anybody. In addition to the qualities any individual member of the class *man* must have in order to be a member of that class, he has an infinite number of other qualities that are irrelevant to the class but constitute aspects of his individuality.

If, then, we are to use Mr. Jones as an illustration of the class *banker,* we have to think of him as Mr. Jones—the individual—at the same time that we think of him as a typical banker. Otherwise we are not using Mr. Jones as an example; we are merely using an abstract scheme that we happen to label Mr. Jones. The individualizing—and irrelevant—qualities contribute essentially to what we may call the dramatic tension at the heart of the intellectual act of illustration. The interest of an illustration lies in a tension between the relevant and the irrelevant. As writer or reader, we may become enthralled with the particular for its very particularity, but at the same time we must maintain our concern for the relations of the particular to the class.

● CAUTION

Writing a good piece of illustration is like walking a tightrope. You can fall on either side.

Notice how the author of the following selection about the great Western gunman Billy the Kid has balanced relevant and irrelevant qualities:

> The secret of Billy the Kid's greatness as a desperado—and by connoisseurs in such matters he was rated as an approach to the ideal desperado type—lay in a marvellous coordination between mind and body. He had not only the will but the skill to kill. Daring, coolness, and quick thinking would not have served unless they had been combined with physical quickness and a marksmanship which enabled him to pink a man neatly between the eyes with a bullet, at, say, thirty paces. He was not pitted against six-shooter amateurs but against experienced fighters themselves adept in the handling of weapons. The men he killed would have killed him if he had not been their master in a swifter deadliness. In times of danger, his mind was not only calm but singularly clear and nimble, watching like a hawk for an advantage and seizing it with incredible celerity. He was able to translate an impulse into action with the suave rapidity of a flash of light. While certain other men were a fair match for

him in target practice, no man in the Southwest, it is said, could equal him in the lightning-like quickness with which he could draw a six-shooter from its holster and with the same movement fire with deadly accuracy. It may be remarked incidentally that shooting at a target is one thing and shooting at a man who happens to be blazing away at you is something entirely different; and Billy the Kid did both kinds of shooting equally well.

His appearance was not unprepossessing. He had youth, health, good nature, and a smile—a combination which usually results in a certain sort of good looks. His face was long and colorless except for the deep tan with which it had been tinted by sun, wind, and weather and was of an asymmetry that was not unattractive. His hair was light brown, worn usually rather long and inclined to waviness. His eyes were gray, clear, and steady. His upper front teeth were large and slightly prominent and to an extent disfigured the expression of a well-formed mouth. His hands and feet were remarkably small. He was five feet eight inches tall, slender and well proportioned. He was unusually strong for his inches, having for a small man quite powerful arms and shoulders. He weighed, in condition, one hundred and forty pounds. When out on the range, he was as rough looking as any other cowboy. In towns, among the quality folk of the frontier, he dressed neatly and took not a little care in making himself personable. Many persons, especially women, thought him handsome. He was a great beau at fandangos and was considered a good dancer.

He had an air of easy, unstudied, devil-may-care insouciance which gave no hint of his dynamic energy. His movements were ordinarily deliberate and unhurried. But there was a certain element of calculation in everything he did. Like a billiardist who "plays a position," he figured on what he might possibly have to do next. This foresightedness and forehandedness even in inconsequential matters provided him with a sort of subconscious mail armor. He was forearmed even when not forewarned; forever on guard.

Like all the noted killers of the West, Billy the Kid was of the blond type. Wild Bill Hickok, Ben Thompson, King Fisher, Henry Plummer, Clay Allison, Wyatt Earp, Doc Holliday, Frank and Jesse James, the Youngers, the Daltons—the list of others is long—were all blond. There was not a pair of brown eyes among them. It was the gray and blue eyes that flashed death in the days when the six-shooter ruled the frontier. This blondness of desperados is a curious fact, contrary to popular imagination and the traditions of art and the stage. The theater immemorially has portrayed its unpleasant characters as black-haired and black-eyed. The popular mind associates swarthiness with villainy. Blue eyes and golden hair are, in the artistic canon, a sort of heavenly hallmark. No artist has yet been so daring as to paint a winged cherub with raven tresses, and a search of the world's canvases would discover no brown-eyed angel. It may be remarked further, as a matter of incidental interest, that the West's bad men were never heavy, stolid, lowering brutes. Most of them were good-looking, some remarkably so. Wild Bill Hickok, beau ideal of desperadoes, was considered the handsomest man of his day on the frontier, and with his blue eyes and yellow hair falling on his shoulders, he moved through his life of tragedies with something of the beauty of a Greek god.

So much for the fact versus fancy. Cold deadliness in Western history
seems to have run to frosty coloring in the eyes, hair, and complexion.
—WALTER NOBLE BURNS: *The Saga of Billy the Kid.*[5]

Method of presentation

Although illustration is, in its main intention, expository, we observe
that in actual presentation other forms of discourse may be used. For
instance, description appears in both the illustration of the herring and of
Billy the Kid.

In the following selection, which illustrates the concept of "neighborliness," narration is the basic method. But note that the narrative elements
are clearly subordinate to the main intention, which is expository.

> A good neighbor, as the term was understood in the days when as a little
> girl I lived on a farm in Southern Michigan, meant all that nowadays is
> combined in corner store, telephone, daily newspaper, and radio. But your
> neighbor was also your conscience. You had to behave yourself on account
> of what the neighbors would think.
>
> A good neighbor knew everything there was to know about you—and
> liked you anyway. He never let you down—as long as you deserved his
> good opinion. Even when you failed in that, if you were in trouble he
> would come to your rescue. If one of the family was taken sick in the
> night, you ran over to the neighbor's to get someone to sit up until the
> doctor arrived. Only instead of sending for the doctor, you went for him.
> Or one of the neighbors did.
>
> The Bouldrys were that kind of neighbors. Lem Bouldry was a good
> farmer and a good provider. Mis' Bouldry kept a hired girl and Lem had
> two men the year round. They even had a piano while the most the other
> neighbors boasted was an organ or a melodeon. Mis' Bouldry changed her
> dress every afternoon (my mother did too; she said she thought more of
> herself when she did), and they kept the front yard mowed.
>
> But the Covells were just the opposite—the most shiftless family the
> Lord ever let set foot on land. How they got along my father said he didn't
> know, unless it was by the grace of God. Covell himself was ten years
> younger than my father, yet everybody called him "Old Covell." His face
> and hands were like sole leather and if his hair had ever been washed, it
> was only when he got caught in a rainstorm. Father said Old Covell would
> borrow the shirt off your back, then bring it around to have it mended;
> Mother said, well, one thing certain, he wouldn't bring it around to be
> washed.
>
> Yet the time Mis' Covell almost died with her last baby—and the baby
> did die—Mis' Bouldry took care of her; took care of the rest of the children
> too—four of them. She stayed right there in the Covell house, just going
> home to catch a little sleep now and then. She had to do that, for there
> wasn't so much as an extra sheet in the house, much less an extra bed.
> And Mis' Bouldry wasn't afraid to use her hands even if she did keep a
> hired girl—she did all the Covells' washing herself.

---

[5] From *The Saga of Billy the Kid* by Walter Noble Burns. Copyright 1925, 1926 by Doubleday & Company, Inc.

But even Old Covell, despite his shiftlessness, was a good neighbor in one way: he was a master hand at laying out the dead. Of course, he wasn't worth a cent to sit up with the sick, for if it was Summer he'd go outside to smoke his pipe and sleep; and if it was Winter he'd go into the kitchen and stick his feet in the oven to warm them and go to sleep there. But a dead man seemed to rouse some kind of pride and responsibility in him. There was no real undertaker nearer than ten miles, and often the roads were impassable. Folks sent for my mother when a child or woman died, but Old Covell handled all the men. Though he never wore a necktie himself, he kept on hand a supply of celluloid collars and little black bow ties for the dead. When he had a body to lay out, he'd call for the deceased's best pants and object strenuously if he found a hole in the socks. Next, he'd polish the boots and put on a white shirt, and fasten one of his black ties to the collar button. All in all, he would do a masterly job.

Of course, nobody paid Old Covell for this. Nobody ever thought of paying for just being neighborly. If anybody had offered to, they'd have been snubbed for fair. It was just the way everybody did in those half-forgotten times. —DELLA T. LUTES: "Are Neighbors Necessary?"

■ APPLICATIONS

I What touches in the illustration of neighborliness give vividness? Which of these touches are "irrelevant" (that is, are there merely for vividness), and which also indicate some relation to the class being illustrated?

II In the Lutes selection, why do you think that the most worthless fellow in the community is used as the chief illustration of the idea of neighborliness?

III Make a diagram of the method used in the illustration of neighborliness.

IV You are now to write a theme of 500 words using the method of illustration. You have two obligations: your particular example must truly represent the class, and it must be in itself as interesting and vivid as you can make it.

In fulfilling the first requirement, you must be sure you know what the essential qualities of the class really are, as contrasted with the merely individual qualities of your particular item. If the qualities of the class are fairly numerous and complicated, be sure that you are systematic in establishing the relation between your example and those qualities. Here an outline can be useful.

In fulfilling the second requirement, hunt for details that catch the attention. Use your imagination. Visualize the illustration. What you want are details like the scales of the herring, Billy the Kid's crooked teeth, the little black ties Old Covell kept on hand.

There are various ways of organizing such a theme, as you have no doubt observed, but two obvious ones should be mentioned. You can set up a generalized presentation of your subject, say the "Campus Go-getter," and then introduce your example. Or you can present an individual "go-getter" and indicate, one by one, how the qualities of the class are embodied in him. Go back to the examples given earlier and see what method has been used in each.

Be sure that your theme has a shape.

If none of the following topics attracts you, use one of your own.

The Campus Reformer	Laziness Pays
The Campus Go-getter	The American Town
The Campus Beauty Queen	Honor
The Campus Rebel	The Young Executive

Write a funny theme if you like.

The Fourth Method: Classification

Like comparison and contrast and illustration, classification is a natural process, and like them, it is a process of bringing order out of experience. Like them, too, it is concerned with the relation of a class to a particular item (or particular items, as the case may be). Classification, however, is concerned with systems of classes, ranging from the least inclusive class up to the most inclusive. When we place a particular item in any given class in the system, we can immediately know its relation up and down the system. Classification is a fundamental way of organizing knowledge. It is a filing system. It is also a method for arriving at new knowledge.

Let us linger a moment to say what is at stake here. A class is not a mere sum of the items that fall within the class. It is, rather, the idea, the concept, of the qualities that any particular item must have in order to fall within the class. If we think of the class *cat* we do not think of an endless parade of particular cats. We think of what qualities a creature—any cat— must have in order to be termed a cat. A cat is not a cat because it is black or white, big or little, long-haired or short-haired. A cat is a cat because of its "catness." The qualities that constitute "catness" define the class *cat*.

A class, to state matters more technically, is determined by a complex of significant characteristics shared by all members of the class.[6]

Significant characteristics: interest

When we say "significant characteristics," we must ask the question, "Significant to whom?" What constitutes a significant characteristic *may* vary according to the person and his special interest. For example, a maker of cosmetics may think of women in classes determined by complexion, and the secretary of the YWCA, in classes determined by religious affiliation. The registrar of a college and the gymnasium instructor would classify the same body of students according to different systems—one by grades, the other by athletic ability.

The maker of cosmetics and the other classifiers are all dealing with the

---

[6] See Analysis, Classification, and Structure, p. 95.

human race. They have been subdividing the class *man* according to their special interests. But how do we set the class *man* in a larger system of classes? A zoologist would do this by treating man as a subclass far down in a system based on the interpretation of life forms.

ANIMAL KINGDOM

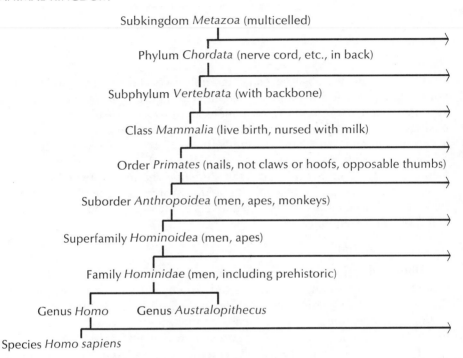

Subkingdom *Metazoa* (multicelled)

Phylum *Chordata* (nerve cord, etc., in back)

Subphylum *Vertebrata* (with backbone)

Class *Mammalia* (live birth, nursed with milk)

Order *Primates* (nails, not claws or hoofs, opposable thumbs)

Suborder *Anthropoidea* (men, apes, monkeys)

Superfamily *Hominoidea* (men, apes)

Family *Hominidae* (men, including prehistoric)

Genus *Homo*   Genus *Australopithecus*

Species *Homo sapiens*

● CAUTION

Because the same group of items may be classified according to different interests, and because the classifier chooses the basis on which a classification is to be made, do not think that classification is arbitrary or whimsical. To approach the matter negatively: if you merely break up a group of one hundred persons into groups of ten, you are not classifying, you are merely dividing. No individual will be in any particular group because of any qualities he possesses; he merely counts as one of the ten. But if you divide the group of one hundred persons by religious affiliations or by complexion, then you have a classification. It is a classification because the quality that provides the basis of the classification inheres *objectively* in the items—the particular persons—being classified.

It is true that the basis of a classification is subjectively chosen, as when the maker of cosmetics decides to classify ladies on the basis of complexion. But his choice is significant only insofar as differences in complexion actually exist.

Keep this distinction in mind.

The president of the Young Republican Club in college makes the following classification of the student body:

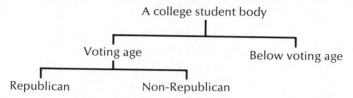

This system, we observe, indicates only two classes at any one stage: voting age and below voting age, Republican and non-Republican. Such a system, called *dichotomous,* is a method of splitting each group into a positive and a negative—those who have as against those who do not have a certain characteristic. In its simplicity, this system is well adapted to certain purposes. For instance, it is suitable to the purpose of the Young Republican Club in that it isolates the students who may vote and who may be expected to vote Republican. But such a system has one obvious limitation. It tells nothing about the "negative" groups—those below voting age and those non-Republican.

COMPLEX SYSTEM

At the opposite end of the spectrum from this simple system is, for example, the enormously complicated zoological classification that, in theory, aims at indicating the relationships of all forms of animal life. Or to think of something somewhat less complex, there is the classification of the books of a great library, which, presumably, would hold all types.

The most obvious difference between the simple system above and these systems is the fact that at no stage is there simple splitting. For instance, the class *voting age* is merely split into Republicans and non-Republicans, as contrasted with the treatment of *suborder* **Anthropoidea** (monkeys, apes, and men) in the zoological classification.

Or if we subdivide the class *history* in a library classification, we do not simply split it into American history and non-American history. Instead, we would get a very complicated breakdown like this:

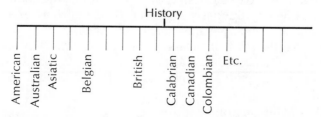

The point is that in such complex classifications, all distinguishable subgroups are, at each stage, accounted for specifically.

● CAUTION: CROSS-RANKING

The great trap in making a classification is what is called cross-ranking. Suppose you need to work out a classification with reference to more than one interest. You are a member of the Young Republican Club who has been assigned the task of finding out how many Republican coeds have done volunteer teaching in the slums. There are, obviously, three interests to be considered in the classification: (1) political affiliation, (2) sex, and (3) volunteer teaching in slums. Each interest must be confined to a single stage. A moment ago, we reduced the classification to "Republican" and "non-Republican." And now, under "Republican" we can distinguish "male" and "female." Having done that, we can distinguish the "teachers" from the "nonteachers." In this acceptable classification, each stage deals with one, and only one, principle of division. So we have:

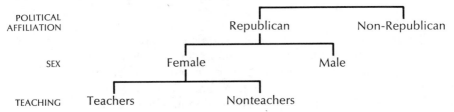

But here is an example of absurd classification in sorting out a student body:

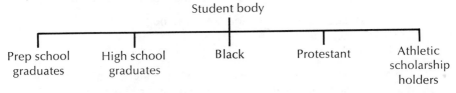

This example of what is called "cross-ranking" in classification is absurd because the groups involved (prep school graduates, high school graduates, blacks, Protestants, and athletic scholarship holders) are not mutually exclusive. That is, a prep school graduate might also be a black Protestant who holds an athletic scholarship. How, then, could you proceed to place him in this scheme? It would be impossible.

■ APPLICATIONS

I Construct a classification that would locate the prep school graduates who are black, Roman Catholic, and athletic scholarship holders.

II Here is a classification from the first sentence of a student theme: "The people connected with this college fall into the following groups: the board of trustees; the officers of the administration; the staff, meaning clerical workers, maintenance personnel, and so forth; the faculty; the boys; and the coeds."

What is wrong with this?

Classification: how you use it

Classification helps us organize things, ideas, experiences. It is a way of coming to grips with a subject. Classification places a subject in relation to a system. It gives it a logical context.

You may ask, however, of what use are such things as the zoological classification or the library classification in writing ordinary exposition? They are only rarely of direct use, but they are often of great indirect use because they show the principle of classification in a highly elaborated and precise form. If you have grasped the principle they illustrate, you are ready to adapt it to your special purposes.

PURPOSE

Classification, in many instances, serves the purpose of increasing your understanding of a subject, but such an understanding is only a preparation for writing a piece of exposition. A chart, in short, is not a theme. However, a classification may serve as an outline, and often can provide the structure of a discussion. Furthermore, a classification may need explanation, and the placing of any particular item in the scheme may need justification; thus the classification itself becomes subject matter.

Classification, then, serves three distinguishable, but related, purposes:

1 It may serve as preparation for a theme.
2 It may provide the structure of a theme.
3 It may contribute to the subject matter of a theme.

In the following example, an essay from a college magazine, we can easily detect the scheme of classification underlying the discussion and at the same time see that without the discussion the scheme would not be very interesting.

FOR WOMEN MOSTLY

With all the controversy about the relative uselessness of Penn men and Penn women, there seems to be a need for a certain amount of field work in the subject. Apparently each side is judged by the most objectionable of its kind, so—girls—here is submitted a carefully compiled report on Penn Men You Need to Avoid. If referred to before you accept dates, it may save you a lot of bitterness and gnashing of teeth.

Type 1. The Party-Boy. This one simply isn't himself until he gets outside of a little alcohol. Then he manages to be so much himself that you are bored to death. His conversation is either quiet or loud; when quiet, it consists of long accounts of drinking bouts, in which he took part: and when loud, it is usually carried on with his buddy across the room who wants everybody to sing the "Whiffenpoof Song," while our joyboy favors "Roll Me Over in the Clover." For these occasions he is conveniently equipped with a foghorn voice that makes everybody turn around and look. If you happen to be sitting next to him you cringe and wilt and feel about two inches high. You gaze up at him with a sick smile that you hope will make everybody think you're having as much fun as he is.

There may be occasions in the course of the evening when he feels like dancing. Dancing, to him, consists of zooming around ricocheting off walls, other couples, moose heads, etc. They ought to jail him for flying low.

Then the fire-eater creeps up on him and he commences to be morose. In the life of every party-boy there is an unrequited love; and furthermore given even less than half a chance, he will tell you all about it. It sounds vaguely like *True Confessions*. But because you have nothing better to do at the moment, you listen, and sympathize—outwardly, with him; inwardly, with the girl.

Finally he quietly passes out, wrapped comfortably around a chandelier or something, and one of his less enthusiastic brothers takes you home. All this is very interesting, provided you can hold him up long enough to get through the party. And he really isn't useless; he always makes a good bar rag.

Type 2. The Lover. He is a ball of fire with the women—the sultry, slow-burning kind, of course. He overwhelms you with attentions. He leans so close to you when you talk that you get the impression he is concerned about the condition of your wisdom teeth. He has a special hungry sick-dog look which he uses for gazing deeply into eyes. When you go away and talk to somebody else, he sulks. He may even follow you and turn you around to face him, and look silently at you. He is hurt. You have crushed him. You are ashamed. You monster.

An evening with him is like a nice quiet session with a boa constrictor. No amount of hinting around that, as far as he's concerned, you are of the let's-just-be-friends school of thought, will do; you have to pick up a bottle or something and slug him before he gets the idea. Then, kid, you're washed up. Your name is mud. Not only are you nasty, ungrateful, and a terrible date—but to top it all off, you're an icebox—and this is the sin unforgivable.

Type 3. The Great Mind. You have to prepare ahead of time for a date with one of these. If you're not read up on your Nietzsche and Schopenhauer, you've got two strikes against you before you start. You and Junior will sit down together, cozy-like, in a corner and solve world problems. Then for the sake of variety you might go on to metaphysics. You toss Absolutes and Causes and Effects back and forth for a whole evening. I won't say any more on this subject. There's nothing more to say.

Type 4. The Bohemian. This one's theme song is "I Don't Care." He dreams of a garret for two on the Left Bank and a Jug of Wine, a Loaf of Bread—and Thou; and if Thou isn't crazy about the idea, Thou is inhibited, repressed, suppressed, a slave to convention, a conformist, and a louse. The boy knows he's a genius, but just because he dyes his hair pale green and wears a purple satin shoestring for a necktie, people don't appreciate him.

He has moods. Blue moods, black moods, red moods—all kinds. If he's having mood number 157E, keep away from him. Keep away from him anyway. Unless you've reserved a bunk at Byberry, that is.

Type 5. The Dud. He gives you a fleeting impression of a horrible, sticky, gray nothingness. He doesn't smoke, drink, dance, drive, stay out late, or raise his voice. He isn't funny—he isn't interesting—he isn't clever. You talk into a vacuum. He is probably very good to his mother, but every time he comes out with that slightly hysterical giggle you feel like slapping him. He sits there like a rock in mid-stream and the party eddies around him. He has a wonderful time. You go home and get a nice big ax and go hunting for the person who got you the date.

Watch the aftereffects of this. He'll call you up, sure as next week. He'll call you again. He'll call you nine or ten times more. If you happen to be wandering around on campus with somebody whom you'd like to impress, he'll pop up out of his hole in the lawn and greet you like a long-lost sister. He's the world's best argument for mercy killing.

Type 6. The Missing Link. Not that we object to muscles, but there is a type that has too much of a good thing. He has an amazing supply of every kind of matter but gray. He looks like something out of the Old Stone Age—and talks surprisingly like it, too. His knuckles drag on the ground. He grunts occasionally to show he's alive. You expect him to stand up and hammer on his chest at any minute. He majors in-duh-phys ed, and takes Advanced Pencil Sharpening on the side.

He's a charming date if you're taking anthropology. Or if you have to write a criticism of *The Man with the Hoe* or *Of Mice and Men*. You couldn't find a better case study.

Of course you have to watch these creatures. If he gets playful you're liable to end up mashed into dog food. It's best to take along a whip and a light metal chair and be able to say "Back, Sultan," in an authoritative voice. Once your nerve fails, you're done.

Well, there they are. Now the object of the game is to go out and find one that doesn't fall into one of these categories. Then, if it's got blood and skin and if it moves around, you're set. Hang onto it. It must be a man.

—BARBARA JONES.[7]

The general purpose of the college coed who wrote "For Women Mostly" was not to do a sociological survey or a term paper for a psychology course, or even a handy guide to dating. She was having fun, and part of the fun lies in taking a method usually reserved for sober-sided purposes and using it for something considerably less pretentious.

● CAUTION

Notice that even in the article "For Women Mostly," which contains a classification made with a humorous intention, the classification is real. The divisions are not mere divisions, they are not arbitrary. They are made with reference to a principle.

Exhaustive classification

We have said that dichotomous classification (p. 70), though limited in its usefulness, does, by the very nature of its formula of division by x and

---

[7] From *Penn Pics,* a Franklin Society publication of the University of Pennsylvania.

non-x, give an exhaustive scheme. We have also said that complex schemes such as that made by the zoologist or used in the great library aim to be exhaustive. But what about exhaustiveness when you are settling down to the practical business of writing a theme?

Let us examine a theme:

TEACHERS I HAVE KNOWN

In my thirteen and a half years at school, I have, of course, known many teachers; I have made rather a hobby of studying my teachers because I hope one day to become a teacher myself. There are many kinds of teachers, but they can all be classified under one of two headings—good and bad. Fortunately for students there are many more teachers under the first heading than under the second.

Actually, it does not mean much to say that teachers are good or bad—the same can be said of people in any profession. A better way of separating the teachers that really teach from those that just stand up in front of a class is to ask how they got to be teachers in the first place. Did they become teachers because they were really interested in their subject and in young people, or did they just drift into the profession through indifference or necessity?

I should like to dispose of the second category first. There is little need to say much about such teachers; every student has known a few of them. Either they are indifferent toward their job, in which case the class is terribly boring, and the students fool around; or they actively hate teaching. Then watch out! The best thing to do in a class like that is to keep quiet and do only as much work as necessary to avoid the teacher's notice.

The other teachers are much more interesting, and there are many more kinds of them. Some become teachers because of an intense interest in their subject. They may be great teachers or well-known researchers; particularly in college, they may be outstanding men in their field. Some of them do not have the ghost of a notion how to put their subject across; they may not even try particularly, for students simply don't exist for them. All that matters is the subject. Even so, the student can get a lot out of his courses if he puts some effort into understanding them. Other teachers in this category do have a gift for organizing and communicating their subject. Their classes are a constant challenge—the teacher is not likely to make his subject easy!—and a delight.

Another variety of teacher with a purpose is the kind who is interested in his students. He is not a

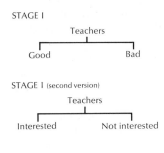

STAGE I

Teachers

Good — Bad

STAGE I (second version)

Teachers

Interested — Not interested

STAGE II

Not interested

Indifferent — Hateful

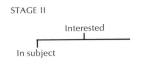

STAGE II

Interested

In subject

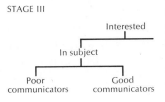

STAGE III

Interested

In subject

Poor communicators — Good communicators

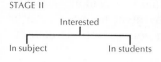

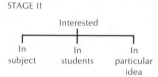

scholar; his main motivation is to help students. That is his mission in life. At the college level you probably find fewer of these teachers than in elementary or high school. I remember particularly my seventh-grade arithmetic teacher. It was a bad year for me; more than once I got into trouble with the school authorities. But this teacher was so decent to me that I became better, and I even learned some arithmetic. Miss Jones may not have been a great mathematician, but she did me some good and taught me more than many other teachers I have had.

I should mention one other kind of interested teacher, a kind to be careful of. That is the teacher who wants to indoctrinate his students about something. He believes fanatically that all automobile engines should be limited to 60 horsepower, and he wants you to believe that, too. He is apt to spend lots of time preaching about this *idée fixe,* and that time will be largely wasted for you. But otherwise he may be a good teacher. Be tolerant of the bee in his bonnet, and remember that the teacher is human, too.

This theme is based on a classification, as we have indicated along the left margin. If we assemble these notes, we find a scheme like this:

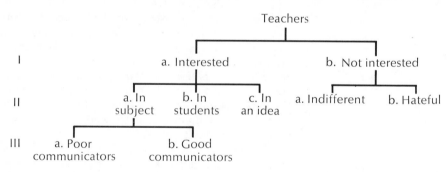

Is this scheme adequate for the student's purpose? Does it exhaust the kinds of teachers he has known? Doesn't common sense suggest some types that are not mentioned? Or does the author mean to imply that, though he knows other kinds exist, he is dealing only with types that he has actually observed in the classroom?

There is still another problem with the classification in this theme: in the first paragraph the author says that he expects to be a teacher himself, and we therefore expect that at the end of the theme he will present some type of "good" teacher whom he will take as a model. A classification should be governed by the purpose for which it is undertaken, but we are never quite sure of this writer's purpose.

The writer's uncertainty about his purpose accounts, no doubt, for some of the fuzziness in the classification. In Stage I, the classification is dichotomous, and therefore exhaustive; it might be argued that Stage III is also exhaustive insofar as it develops IIa. But Stage II is not developed according to a clear-cut principle, and as we have said, we don't know whether it is supposed to be exhaustive.

It may be objected that the theme "For Women Mostly" is not exhaustive either, that there are many other types of dates. But for the writer's purpose, which is to write a light-hearted piece of satire, her classification is adequate. She has chosen her types shrewdly and with enough variety. They give good targets for her fun—and ours. What more should we ask?

The kind of classification—that is, the criteria by which the sorting out is made—and the degree of exhaustiveness are determined by purpose. Your first step in making a classification is to know what your purpose is.

■ APPLICATION

Write a theme of some 500 words based on classification. Make it funny, whimsical, satirical, serious—whatever tone you wish. Do not feel limited to the following topics:

Trout Flies	Wives
Classmates	Saturday Night on Campus
College Reformers	Sensitive Souls

The Fifth Method: Definition

A dictionary will give you two different definitions of the word *definition:* (1) "a statement of what a thing is" and (2) "a statement or explanation of what a word or phrase means or has meant." In the strict sense, a definition, as we shall use the word here, is not of a thing but of a word.[8]

If we define *cat,* we are telling how to use the word *cat.* A definition sets the limits or bounds within which a term can be used, as the derivation of the word *definition* implies (it comes from two Latin words: *de,* meaning "with relation to," and *finis,* meaning "limit").

This sense of the word *definition* is quite natural to us, for we speak of "looking up a word in the dictionary," we talk of the "precise definition of a word," and we say to the opponent in an argument, "define your terms"— a term being any key word or phrase that constitutes a unit of meaning in his argument.

---

[8] The dictionary tells the generally accepted usage of a word. For a word in common use the dictionary reports as a standard what is acceptable among educated people. For a word of some specialized use, such as a technical term, it reports what is acceptable among the specialists who use the word—say, engineers or zoologists. The dictionary may give other information too, but this is basic: to report usage within a certain "linguistic community."

The process of making a definition is not, however, a mere game of words. It is clear that we cannot make a useful definition without knowledge of the thing (that is, object, event, idea, etc.) to which the word (or term) refers. And it is equally clear that the definition of a word communicates knowledge about the thing. A definition does give knowledge of "what a thing is," and equally important, may lead the maker of a definition to clarify his own thoughts on the nature of the "thing."

In fact, a description can often serve as a definition: by enlightening us about a thing, it enlightens us about the use of the term that refers to the thing. For example, we find later in this chapter (pp. 100–01) a theme describing the mechanism used to make maple syrup, and when we have finished reading that, we know how to define the term *syrup cooker*. But for the moment, we are not concerned with description as a form of definition, nor concerned with certain other kinds of definition (for instance, what is known as *recursive definition* in arithmetic and grammar). We are, instead, concerned with traditional, or classic, definition, which goes back as far as Aristotle. Our discussion is confined to that form.

● CAUTION

A definition is not a synonym. If, in the dictionary, you find the word *sacred* after the entry *holy,* this does not mean that *sacred* is a definition of the word *holy*. It is merely a word with approximately the same meaning as *holy*. This fact becomes immediately clear if you do not know the meaning of *sacred*. You must have a definition, after all.

Parts of a definition: convertibility

A definition has two parts, two terms: the *to-be-defined (definiendum)* and the *definer (definiens)*. The terms appear as an equation. For example, if we define *slave* as a human being who is the legal property of another, then we can set up the equation:

| Slave | is | human being who is the legal property of another |
| The *to-be-defined* | = | the *definer* |

We know that the terms of an equation are interchangeable. So if we make a statement using the word that is the *to-be-defined,* we may substitute the *definer* for that word without any change of sense. The statement "To be a slave is worse than death" has exactly the same meaning as the statement "To be a human being who is the legal property of another is worse than death." The terms are, as we say, *convertible*.

DEFECTS OF DEFINITION: TOO BROAD AND TOO NARROW

Let us take another proposition: "A slave is a man." This statement is, clearly, true. But is it a definition? Let us consider the question by thinking of two classes, *slave* and *man*. The class *man* is, clearly, a larger group than the class *slave;* that is, there are men who are not slaves. Our original proposition, "A slave is a man," affirms that the class *slave* will be included in the class *man*.

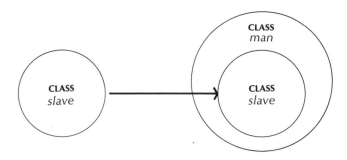

It is obvious that any statement we make about man as a class (that is, any statement that is true of all men) will necessarily be true of slaves, for the class *slave* is included in the class *man*. But no statement about slaves is *necessarily* true of all men. It may be true (as when we say, "Slaves have two legs"), but there are many reasonable statements about slaves (such as our statement above, "To be a slave is worse than death") that are not applicable to all men (for we can scarcely substitute *man* for *slave* in our last statement and say, "To be a man is worse than death"). In other words, our proposition, "A slave is a man," does not have convertible terms (pp. 152–54). The *definer* is larger than the *to-be-defined* and includes it. The definition is, we say, too broad.

We can also go wrong in the other direction. We can have a *definer* that is smaller than the *to-be-defined*. We make that error, for instance, if we say that a table is a piece of furniture on which we serve meals. The *definer* ("a piece of furniture on which we serve meals") is too small, because it will not cover the many other classes of tables—study tables, bedside tables, sewing tables, billiard tables, and so on. Here the definition is too narrow. So we get the following picture:

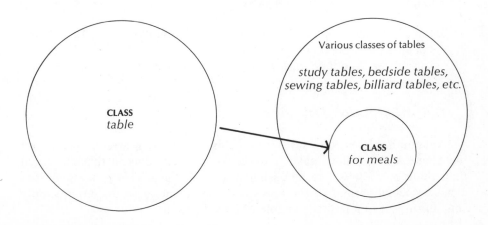

To sum up, the *to-be-defined* and the *definer* must, if we think of them graphically as one superimposed on the other, be the same size; they must be *coterminous*.

Definer   To-be-defined   Definition

And this, of course, is only another way of saying that the terms of a definition are convertible.

■ APPLICATION

None of the following statements is a correct definition. Some are too broad and some are too narrow. For example, if we say "A belt is what a man puts around his waist to hold his trousers up," our *definer* is too narrow. There are, of course, belts not worn by men. Furthermore, belts may be used for purposes other than holding up trousers: women use them to hold up skirts. Some belts are used for carrying weapons. Some are purely ornamental. And so on. Or suppose we say, "Lacrosse is a game played with a ball and a kind of racket." Our definer here is too broad. Tennis, too, is played with a ball and racket. So is squash. If we modify "racket" by saying "a kind of racket laced with thong and called a stick," we begin to narrow the definer, although such a statement may not yet be an adequate definition of lacrosse. But making an adequate definition is not your present problem. You are to determine only whether each definition given here is too broad or too narrow or perhaps both.

1 Baseball is a game played with a clublike wooden instrument called a bat, and a rather small, leather-covered ball.
2 A hero is a man who is useful to society.
3 Democracy is the form of government we have in the United States.
4 A collar is the thing a man wears around his neck.
5 Leisure is that free time during which you can rest.

The structure of definition

A definition locates its subject in a class and then proceeds to point out the characteristics that make it differ from other items in that class and that, therefore, allow it to be assigned to a subclass. This process is, it is clear, a special variant of the process of classification. A definition simply sets its subject in a limited scheme of classification.

The process of definition is, like classification, a natural way the mind works. It is no more arbitrary than other methods of exposition we have studied. We make definitions constantly, and instinctively. Let us examine a very simple example of how the process works.

A small child who has never seen a cat receives one as a pet. The father tells the child that the animal is a cat—a kitty. The proud parent now assumes that the child knows what the word *cat* means. But he is surprised one day to find the child going up to a Pekingese and saying "Kitty, kitty." It is obvious that the child is using the word to mean any small, furry animal. When the father takes him to the park, the child is very likely to call a squirrel a kitty, too.

The father now undertakes to give the child a definition of *cat*. To do so, he must instruct the child in the differences between a cat, a Pekingese, and a squirrel. In other words, he undertakes to break up the class, or group, that the child has made (all small, furry animals) into certain subgroups (cats, Pekingese, squirrels) by focusing attention upon the differences (the differentiae) that distinguish one subgroup from another.

If the child understands his father, he can then give a questioner a definition of the word *cat*—an inadequate definition, of course, but nevertheless one arrived at by the proper method and exhibiting the characteristic structure.

QUESTIONER: What does *cat* mean?
CHILD: It's a little animal, and it's got fur.
QUESTIONER: But dogs have fur, too, and dogs aren't cats.
CHILD: Yes, but dogs bark. Cats don't bark. Cats meow. And cats climb trees.
QUESTIONER: But squirrels have fur, and they climb trees and are little.
CHILD: Yes, but squirrels don't just *climb* trees like cats. They live in trees. And they don't meow like cats.

The child has put *cat* into a class or group (small, furry animals), and then has distinguished the subgroup *cat* from the other subgroups, *dog* and *squirrel*.

If we chart the child's reasoning, we get a diagram like this:

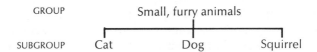

GROUP   Small, furry animals

SUBGROUP   Cat   Dog   Squirrel

Whenever we make a definition, we go through the same process as the child trying to tell what a kitty is. We locate the *to-be-defined* as a species in relation to a group (genus) that includes several different species and then try to say what quality or qualities (differentia or differentiae) distinguish the *to-be-defined* from the other species in the genus. So we get the formula:

$$\text{Definition of species} \quad = \quad \textit{genus} + \textit{differentiae}$$
$$\text{The } \textit{to-be-defined} \quad = \quad \text{the } \textit{definer}$$

The pattern of the child's attempt to define *cat* is the pattern of all definition of the classic type, but the definition that the child gives will not serve us in our adult world. It will not serve us, because the genus and differentiae that the child adopts are not significantly distinguished for our adult purposes.

A zoologist, for instance, would go about the business very differently. He might begin by saying: "A cat—*Felis domestica,* we call it—is a digitigrade, carnivorous mammal of the genus *Felis,* which includes the species tiger (*Felis tigris*), the species ocelot (*Felis pardalis*), the species lion (*Felis leo*), the species cougar (*Felis concolor*), and several other species. All the species of the genus *Felis* have lithe, graceful, long bodies, relatively short legs, with soft, padded feet, strong claws, which are retracted into sheaths when not in use, powerful jaws with sharp teeth, and soft, beautifully marked fur. The cat is the smallest of the genus, usually measuring so-and-so. It is the only species easily domesticated. . . ."

Like the child, the zoologist has set up a group, which he calls a genus, and has given the characteristics of the group. Then he has broken up the group into several subgroups, each of which he calls a species. Last, he has set about pointing out the differences between the species *cat* and the other species of the same genus.

Diagrammed, his thinking has this form:

The form used by the zoologist is, we see, the same as that used by the child. The difference is that the zoologist thinks in *significant* classes. We should note, too, that the zoologist uses the words *genus* and *species* with somewhat different meanings from ours. For him the word *genus* means not only a group including smaller groups called species but also a group of species closely related structurally and by origin; and the word *species* means a subgroup whose members possess numerous characteristics in common and interbreed to preserve those characteristics. In other words, the zoologist has a specialized significance for the words *genus* and *species,* a significance dictated by the materials he is dealing with—living forms. But he uses the words in his pattern of definition just as we do, for instance, in setting up the formal scheme for the definition of *bungalow:*

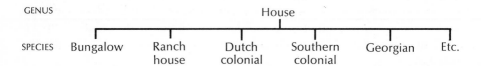

Though genus and species are part of all definition, we do not ordinarily use technical language in giving a casual definition. For *bungalow* we are likely to say: "Oh, it's a kind of house. It differs from Dutch colonial, Southern colonial, Georgian, and some other styles in that it has only one story. The best way to distinguish the bungalow from other one-story houses is by the floor plan. For instance, if we compare it with a ranch house, we find . . ." Here, in an informal way, we are giving the differentiae.

Let us analyze a dictionary definition:

> *hammer,* "a tool for pounding, usually consisting of a metal head and a handle." [9]

Here "tool" is clearly the genus and "for pounding" is a differentia. But on a moment's reflection we see that the single differentia "for pounding" would be too broad: there are tools other than the hammer that are used for pounding, for instance, pestles and tampers. So we should know what distinguishes a hammer from a pestle or tamper. To help us here the dictionary adds "usually consisting of a metal head and a handle." Set up as a scheme this runs:

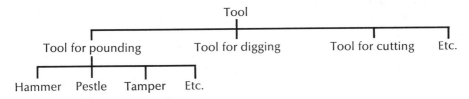

differentia: metal head and handle [10]

The dictionary definition has compressed three stages of classification, but the experienced reader of dictionaries learns to sort out the various stages in question. The dictionary gives a kind of shorthand.

■ APPLICATION

Below are a group of definitions drawn from the same dictionary as that of *hammer*. Set up each in the following form. For example, here is the definition of a triangle ("A triangle is a geometrical figure having three angles and three sides."):

To-be-defined	genus	differentiae
Triangle	geometrical figure	three angles and three sides

---

[9] *Webster's New World Dictionary of the American Language,* College Edition, 1953.

[10] A student may well object that "usually consisting of a metal head and a handle" does not really distinguish a hammer from a tamper or a pestle. He would be right. He might also object that the metal head would not indicate the class *hammer,* but a subclass under *hammer,* for there are hammers with stone heads and, even, rubber heads. Again he would be right. For further discussion see pp. 84–85.

The main problem is to be sure you have the genus right. Here is the dictionary's definition of *hammock:* "a length of netting, canvas, etc., swung from ropes at both ends and used as a bed or couch." Which is the genus—"length of netting, canvas, etc." or "bed or couch"? This question would, in all likelihood, never arise if you were framing your own definition. Almost certainly the first thing to pop into your head about a hammock is that you lie in it. Your response would be correct: a hammock is something you lie in, made in a certain way. Set up the scheme.

1 *chasm:* "a deep crack in the earth's surface; abyss; crevasse; narrow gorge."
2 *ravine:* "a long, deep hollow in the earth's surface, worn by the action of a stream."
3 *lend:* "to let another use or have (a thing) temporarily and on condition that it, or its equivalent, is to be returned."
4 *ax:* "a tool for chopping trees and splitting wood: it has a long wooden handle and a metal head with a blade usually on only one side."
5 *hatchet:* "a small ax with a short handle for use with one hand."
6 *fog:* "a large mass of water vapor condensed to fine particles, at or just above the earth's surface."

Necessary and sufficient characteristics

We have seen from our formula that the definer specifies at least two conditions, that of the genus and that of the differentia (or differentiae) determining the species. The definition will not apply, that is, to something that satisfies merely the requirement of the genus or merely that of the species. To state it another way, a characteristic may be necessary and yet not sufficient to fulfill the requirement of a definition.

Let us look at what is probably the most famous definition ever made, Aristotle's definition of *man:*

Man is a rational animal.

The formula might be set up as:

To-be-defined	genus	differentia
man	animal	rational

Being an animal is the condition specified in the genus, and being rational, that in the species. Both are *necessary* characteristics for qualifying as a member of the class *man.* For example, there are numberless species of animals that are nonrational (all nonmen). And there are creatures conceived as rational but nonanimal—like the gods of Greece or the angels of Christian theology.

Neither of the necessary characteristics is, taken alone, *sufficient.* Taken together they are sufficient. They fulfill all the conditions of the definition.

Only two conditions are proposed in Aristotle's definition of *man,* but in some cases several may be involved. Looking back at our discussion of the definition of *hammer* (p. 83), we see that, though being a tool and being for pounding (the requirements proposed by genus and species) are necessary conditions for fulfilling the definition of *hammer,* they are not, strictly speaking, sufficient. There are, of course, tools for pounding that are not hammers. To distinguish hammers from such tools we should have to add the characteristics of having a heavy head and a handle, and perhaps that of having a certain relation between the handle and the head. Then we should have *all* the necessary conditions—and, as we have seen, we must have *all* the necessary conditions if we are to have a sufficient definition.

Definition and generalization: supportive characteristics

It is clear that if we have a definition of *hammer* we want it to be good for all hammers. That is, the definition must be a general statement, applicable to all members of the class tagged by the word being defined. In dictionaries, however, we often find definitions like the one we have quoted for *hammer:* "a tool for pounding, usually consisting of a metal head and a handle." What is the word *usually* doing here?

When the dictionary-maker adds the *usually,* he is getting away from a truly generalized definition: there are, for instance, stone hammers in museums, and perhaps some are still being used in, say, New Guinea. But the dictionary-maker's aim is not necessarily to give a universal definition; he simply tries to provide a helpful description of a common type of modern hammer, one that most people have seen. He is trying to be helpful, again, when he adds (as he does in the rest of the definition): "one end of the head may be a pronged claw for pulling nails."

Having a metal head, or a claw on one end of the head, or a magnetized head for tacks—none of these attributes, let us insist, is necessary to the basic quality of "hammerness," but they may be incidentally useful in identifying the object. We shall call such characteristics *supportive,* in contrast to those that are necessary or sufficient. Some such distinction is what the dictionary-maker has in mind when he says "usually," or, as in connection with the claw hammer, "may be."

Supportive characteristics may be helpful in a definition, even if they are not strictly a part of it, not only in that they remind us of relevant examples we are likely to have seen and so pinpoint the application of the definition, but in that they indicate a subgroup, or subgroups, under the species. Under the species *hammer,* the reference to the metal head sets up a subgroup, the reference to the claw head sets up another, subsumed under "metal head." Thus a supportive characteristic boxes in the definition, as it were; by extending the classification, it broadens the base of information. In fact, an understanding of the relation of supportive characteristics to the necessary and the sufficient will help us to frame a definition.

I In each of the following "definitions" indicate necessary and sufficient characteristics and those that are merely supportive. The question is not whether a definition is acceptable or not. Simply try to follow the instruction as best you can.

1 *electron:* an elementary particle that is a fundamental constituent of matter, having a negative charge of 1.602×10^{-19} coulombs, a mass of 9.108×10^{-31} kilograms, and spin of $\frac{1}{2}$, existing independently or as the component outside the nucleus of an atom.
2 Man is a featherless biped.
3 Faith is the evidence of things not seen.
4 *lugsail:* a four-cornered sail, with no boom or lower yard, suspended from an upper yard hung obliquely on the mast: the name probably in reference to the lugging, or hauling, of the sail around the mast in order to change course.
5 War is legalized murder on a large scale, without, it may be added, the usual rational justifications for murder.

II Develop a definition of a word chosen from the list below. Hand in all your notes along with the finished definition.

freedom	capitalism
lassitude	tyranny
conscience	administrator
sport	psychiatrist

● CAUTION: DEFINITION AND THE COMMON GROUND

We shall soon discuss the more complex kind of definition known as extended definition, but before we embark on that, there are two important cautions to be given, one concerning the common ground and one concerning what is called circular definition.

Suppose, history and language permitting, that we try to give our definition of *bungalow* to an American Indian of the old days. He probably would not let us get past the first sentence, "Oh, it's a kind of house," for he would immediately want to know what a house is. In other words, if we give a definition, we assume that our audience knows the genus we are going to work in. If the audience does not know the genus, we must go back to a more inclusive group, a group including our genus as a subgroup, and try again, hoping now to have a common ground. So, if our Indian does not understand what a house is, we may try again and begin by saying, "A house is a kind of shelter—but a shelter you make, and so on." Our Indian knows what a shelter is, and he can get a notion of manmade shelter, for he has a tepee or lodge or hogan. We now have a common ground.

What we have developed by implication is a scheme something like this:

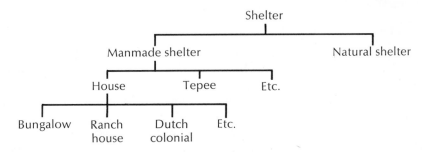

The Indian has pushed us back a couple of stages, and we now have a common ground and can define *house*. It is not likely that we'll get down to *bungalow,* for the Indian probably will not understand our necessary differentiae under the now-established genus *house.*

Not only with our Indian but with everyone, a common ground is necessary for an effective definition. This principle of the common ground is very important, for it implies that a definition is not only *of some term* but is *for somebody.* The giver of the definition can define only by reference to what his particular audience already knows or is willing to learn for the purpose at hand.

This necessary knowledge must be of two kinds: of words and of things. It must be of words, for a definition is in words. The giver of the definition must use words that his audience can understand or can readily become acquainted with. For instance, when the zoologist refers to the cat as a "digitigrade mammal," he is using a word that most of us would not know. For the general reader, the zoologist would need to explain further that *digitigrade* means "walking on the toes," as a cat does, as opposed to "walking on the whole foot" (*plantigrade*), as a man does. In this way the zoologist would provide the common ground of language.

The second kind of knowledge is, as we have said, of things. For instance, there is no use in trying to define the color beige to a man blind from birth. If you say that beige is a light, brownish color, the natural color of wool, you have really said nothing to him, for he has had no experience of color. If you go on and give the physicist's definition of color, referring to wavelengths of light, you run into the same difficulty. He can grasp the notion of wavelength, but he has no basis for knowing what light is. You run into a defect in his experience, in his knowledge. There is always the possibility of running into some defects in our audience's knowledge, and, insofar as possible, we must work with what is known.

● CAUTION: METAPHORICAL LANGUAGE

The language of definition should be as logically precise as possible. The purpose of a definition is, as the derivation indicates, to limit the meaning of a word in an acceptable way. For this purpose metaphorical language is especially dangerous, for the essence of metaphor is not to limit meaning but to extend meaning by developing new and complex ranges implicit in the literal base.[11]

● A STRONG CAUTION: CIRCULAR DEFINITION

We cannot define a word by repeating the word itself in the definition. If we define the word *statistician* by saying that it means anybody who makes a profession of compiling and studying statistics, we have committed this error. The real question: "What kind of thing does a statistician do?" is left unanswered. The pretended definition does not enlarge anybody's knowledge; it merely repeats the term to be defined: *statistics, statistician*. It is also possible to make the error of circular definition without repeating a word, but merely by repeating an idea, as, "The causes of war are the several factors that result in armed conflict." (Observe that here we have, in another form, a definition by synonym. See p. 78.)

■ APPLICATIONS

I   None of the following statements is an acceptable definition. What is wrong with each? Is it too broad, too narrow, circular? Or what? If you lack the information necessary to judge some of the statements, use a dictionary or some other reference work. For example, Number 8 uses the word *anthropology*. If you do not know what anthropology is, find out. If it studies more than morality, then the statement here is not acceptable.

1   A god is a divinity.
2   Poetry is what is written by poets.
3   A soiree is a social function that does not take place in the afternoon.
4   The French word *cheval* means "horse."
5   A protuberance is a thing that protrudes.
6   To inhume is to put something into the ground.
7   To inhume is to inter.
8   Anthropology is the science that studies morality.
9   Cricket is a game played with a wooden instrument called a bat and a rather small, leather-covered ball.

II   Amend as many as possible of the above statements to make acceptable definitions. For instance, you cannot well amend a mere synonym given as a "definition." You would have to start over. Confine your efforts to the statements that are definitions, however inadequate.

Extended definition

Thus far we have been dealing with relatively brief definitions of the kind that commonly appear in themes of exposition. We might, for instance,

---

[11] See Metaphor, Chapter 12.

begin a theme on drag-racing by defining the term for the uninformed reader. Sometimes, however, particularly when we are thinking seriously about a complicated concept, such as democracy, we use a definition as the basis for an entire theme; that is, we write what may be called an *extended definition.*

The basic problem with a word such as *democracy* is that no commonly available short definition is sufficient to give us an understanding of the full implications of the word. For such understanding we would have to go into the history lying behind the word and into the complex systems of ideas involved in it. For instance, as a basis for understanding the term *democracy,* we might find ourselves not only referring to the origin of the word in Ancient Greek, but also using the history of Athens, even including the development of techniques and crafts that preceded the rise of popular government. Or we might find ourselves using the beginnings of Christianity, with its idea of the worth of the individual human soul, in relation to the democratic impulses in subsequent history. We would have to feel our way along, trying out different ideas to see where they lead us, discarding some and trying again. We can use whatever will help us, including other forms of exposition or other modes of discourse—description, narration, or argument.

This sort of treatment may seem to lead us far from the purpose of definition—which is to limit the meaning of a term. It may, that is, seem to confuse the mere explanation of the meaning of a word for some "linguistic community" (or communities) with the explanation of when, how, and why the term came to be so used. True, both purposes may be present in an extended definition, but there will be no confusion if we can clearly use the second purpose to support the first—that is, if all the material concerning when, how, and why is directed toward giving a fuller understanding of the term in question. We shall soon be dealing with certain examples that make this process clear, for instance, an extended definition of *wealth,* to which we now come, and a student theme in extended definition.

The formula of definition as frame

The most obvious way to organize an extended definition is to use the standard formula as a frame, taking genus, species, and differentiae as a basis for the development of a discussion. Here an economist sets out to define *wealth* by this method:

> There is a certain desirable thing which is and must be the subject of political economy. Whether avowed or not, a definite conception is, in reality, under discussion in every treatise on this science. For this conception the term *wealth,* if used in accordance with history and etymology, is an accurate designation. The Saxon *weal* indicated a condition of relative well-being, the state of having one's wants well supplied as compared with a prevailing standard. No possession common to all men can constitute such relative well-being. The limitless gifts of nature do not produce it, since they are indiscriminate in their ministrations; air and sunlight make no differences among men and, though creating absolute well-being, can-

not create that social condition indicated by the term *wealth*. This relative condition can be produced only by that which, besides satisfying wants, is capable of appropriation.

It is by a transfer of meaning that the term which primarily designated a condition of life has been applied to the things which produce the condition. But not all causes of comparative happiness are included in the meaning of the word. Wealth, as historically used, signified the well-being resulting from outward rather than inward causes. Health and contentment may make a shepherd happier than the owner of flocks; yet the owner only is "well off." Reserving a broader term to designate well-being in general, usage has employed the word *wealth* to signify, first, the comparative welfare resulting from material possession and, second, and by a transfer, the possessions themselves.

Wealth then consists in the relative weal-constituting elements in man's material environment. It is objective to the user, material, useful, and appropriable. . . .   —JOHN B. CLARK: *The Philosophy of Wealth.*

Here the author starts with the derivation of the word, just as a dictionary might do, and then shows how the meaning has become specialized by the addition of differentiae that distinguish wealth from other kinds of weal, or well-being. Since the differentiae are somewhat complicated, he does not simply list them, but explains each one.

The following is a student theme of extended definition:

WHAT IS A GOOD COACH?

Ever since I went to high school, I have wanted to be an athletic coach for my life work—I mean a good coach. A coach is a trainer, but he is a special kind of trainer, not like the trainer who gets a squad in condition. The coach assumes that the squad is in good condition before he begins his special work. What he does, it seems to me, has two parts, one concerning the body, the other the mind.

For the first part, he has to bring the body into the proper relation to the particular sport involved. This means that he has to analyze the various factors of a peak performance for each boy on the team, on one hand things like speed and timing in general, and on the other, special aspects of the action belonging to the sport, such as passing, line backing, broken field running. For the requirements of the game (and the position the boy is to play) the coach has to analyze the elements and then weld them back together in a fluid performance.

I have been talking about the requirements of the sport, whatever sport it is, but even if a coach has a group perfectly prepared in this respect, he has to do another welding job along the way; he has to weld the individuals together into a team, and that means to make them all understand the overall purpose of the game, how every individual player, and every individual act, is part of a pattern that is pointed like a pistol at the goal line or basket or whatever. He has to make each boy realize that no matter how great he is, he is expendable. That is, the game doesn't exist just to make him shine. The purpose is to punch the ball over.

For the second part, the mind. A coach has to instill the fighting spirit, sure. But to make this mean anything, he has to be able to inspire confidence of two kinds. The first is confidence in him, not just as a guy who is expert at the game, but as a guy who understands every fellow and has his good at heart. Then he has to inspire the fellows with confidence in themselves. Each fellow has to know that he has something to give, but more important, he has got to feel that he stands a little above winning or losing. If a fellow can't stand losing one Saturday, for instance, he probably won't have the bounce to come back and win the next time. Sure, it feels good to be winning, to be the guy who pushed the ball over and got the cheers, to feel tuned up and with a skill you can depend on. But there's something more in knowing how to live a sport without reference to winning or losing, to feel that the sport has its own value somehow. A coach has to get this across. Call it character-building, like they do in the college catalogue. Even that won't spoil it.

It is what made our team at school carry Coach Hadley around the field on their shoulders after we lost the championship—on our own field. The poor old guy looked as though he were going to cry.

Here the author has made a real effort to think through his definition, and he has tried to be systematic in the same way as Clark in his definition of *wealth*. He has moved through a number of distinctions, setting up the differentiae for each, trying to close in on his subject. This theme has two features not found in the example by Clark, for here the author gives a specific setting to explain the need for definition, and in the last paragraph he deserts the method of definition for that of illustration, using the illustration to sum up all he has been talking about. Let us notice, too, that the illustration is not simply exposition; it contains a hint of narrative.

■ APPLICATIONS

I   Outline the method of extended definition in "What Is a Good Coach?" For example, in the first paragraph the author begins with the class *trainer,* which he subdivides into two smaller classes, one of which indicates what he means by *coach.* Then he makes another kind of distinction between the two kinds of things, generally considered, that the coach must work on: body, mind. Proceed with the analysis of the theme. Use diagrams if you find them useful. Do you find any blurs or confusions? If so, comment on them. Another point: Is the title accurate for this theme? When you make a definition of *nail,* are you thinking about bad nails, or nails characteristically considered? Ponder this awhile.

II   Analyze the structure of the following definition. How is the method of genus and differentiae used? Indicate the distinctions made. Are there any merely descriptive elements here? Any supportive characteristics?

Chemistry is that branch of science which has the task of investigating the materials out of which the universe is made. It is not concerned with the forms into which they may be fashioned. Such objects as chairs, tables, vases, bottles, or wires are of no significance in chemistry; but such substances as glass, wool, iron, sulfur, and clay, as the materials out of which they are made, are what it studies. Chemistry is concerned not only with the composition of such substances, but also with their inner structure. Further, these materials are constantly undergoing change in nature: iron rusts, wood decays, sugar ferments, coal burns, limestone rock is eaten away by water, and living organisms digest their foods and build up their structures. Chemistry investigates such changes—the conditions under which they occur, the mechanism by which they take place, the new substances that are formed as their result, and the energy that is liberated or absorbed by them. Chemistry also studies the way in which these and similar changes can be carried out in the laboratory or on a larger scale in the chemical plant. As a result of investigations along these lines, chemistry has found how metals can be extracted from their ores; how impoverished fields can be made fertile again; and how the materials that are found in nature can be converted into thousands of new substances to help feed the race, to cure the sick, and to provide such comfort and even luxury for the common man as was not enjoyed by the wealthy of an earlier generation.

—John Arrend Timm: *General Chemistry.*

III Write a theme of extended definition of 300 to 400 words. The list below may suggest a subject to you:

Political Equality	Student Power
The Hippie	The Good Citizen
Sportsmanship	Physics

You may find it necessary to investigate your subject before writing. Use the library.

VARIETY IN EXTENDED DEFINITION

We have seen how the author of the theme about coaching leaves, at the end, the ordinary method of definition and resorts to illustration. The purpose of a definition is, after all, elucidation, explanation, and clarification, and so in extended definition we often find a great variety of methods. The writer uses any tool necessary to make us know what the limits of his term are. For instance, the contrast of "Red-bloods" and "Mollycoddles" (pp. 60–62) amounts to an extended definition of both, and the short essay on "Neighborliness" (pp. 66–67) amounts to a definition by means of illustrations that in themselves employ description and narration. By the same token, definition, in either a strict or a broad form, is often a useful device to lead to or support other forms of exposition, or other modes of discourse. For instance, the definition of *wealth* given above is merely preliminary to a long study of economics that involves argument as well as exposition.

If definition may be used so loosely, why, you may ask, have we dwelt in such detail on definition in the strict sense?

We have done so, because a grasp of that process is the greatest help possible to clarity in free-flowing discussion in which the formal structure of definition is absorbed and blended with other methods. For instance, look at the following selection as an example of such absorption or of methods other than definition used for the purposes of definition.

> I think it is legitimate to say . . . that the Beat Generation's worship of primitivism and spontaneity is more than a cover for hostility to intelligence; it arises from a pathetic poverty of feeling as well. The hipsters and hipster-lovers of the Beat Generation are rebels, all right, but not against anything so sociological and historical as the middle class or capitalism or even respectability. This is the revolt of the spiritually underprivileged and the crippled of soul—young men who can't think straight and hate anyone who can; young men who can't get outside of the morass of self. . . .
> —NORMAN PODHORETZ: "The Know-Nothing Bohemians,"
> *Doings and Undoings: The Fifties and After in American Writing.*[12]

■ APPLICATIONS

I Here are six statements about religion. Some are definitions that are too narrow or too broad. Perhaps you might interpret one or more as acceptable. The point here is for you to discuss these "definitions" as thoughtfully as you can. Do indicate what limitations you find. But also try to see which of these statements might be drawn into a proper definition of religion—that is, into one that you yourself would accept. Furthermore, try to see what led the maker of each statement to say what he did.

For this exercise, as for many other exercises in this book, there is no clear-cut right or wrong, yes or no, with the answer in the back of the book. Simply try to reflect seriously on what is at stake here.

A Religion, after trying to see as best I could what various religions and religious people had in common, I felt impelled to define as the reaction of the personality as a whole to its experience of the Universe as a whole.
—Sir Julian Huxley.

B Religion is 'morality tinged with emotion.' —Matthew Arnold.

C Religion is the 'belief in spiritual beings.' —E. B. Tylor.

D Religion is 'a propitiation or conciliation of powers superior to man which are believed to direct or control the course of nature and of human life.'
—Sir James Frazer.

E Pure religion and undefiled before God is this, to visit the fatherless and widows in their affliction, and to keep himself unspotted from the world.
—Saint James.

F Being religious means asking passionately the question of the meaning of our existence and being willing to receive answers, even if the answers hurt.
—Paul Tillich: "The Lost Dimension in Religion,"
Adventures of the Mind.

II You are now to write a long theme (at least 800 words) of extended definition. This will differ from your earlier theme of definition not only in length, for here you should aim to use a variety of methods, including straight descrip-

---

[12] Reprinted from "The Know-Nothing Bohemians," from *Doings and Undoings: The Fifties and After in American Writing,* by Norman Podhoretz, by permission of Norman Podhoretz. This essay first appeared in *Partisan Review,* vol. 25, no. 2 (Spring 1958).

tion or even narration. In preparing for the actual writing, you might use the following questions to guide you, making notes as you go along:

1 Derivation of the word—does the origin enlighten us?
2 History of the application of the word—do earlier applications differ from the present application?
3 Genus and differentiae in present application—how can the species be distinguished from other significant species?
4 Analysis of species—does it have any "subspecies," and if so, how are they to be distinguished from one another?
5 Application of the definition to individual instances—does the definition really meet this test, and does it enlighten us about the individual instances?
6 Can you think of any contrasts or comparisons that would help pinpoint the subject?
7 Looking back over your notes, do you feel that your major interest is to frame a definition or to use the method of definition (in the broad sense) as a way to control a discussion?

The topics below may serve as suggestions. You will notice that some are similar to topics that have appeared before. You may even have written a theme on one. Do not let that keep you from using it again; this will be a different theme. It should be the most ambitious and interesting one you have done.

How I Define Personal Liberty
Leisure: Fun or Fulfillment?
Black Power
Sexual Freedom
The Duty of the Individual to Society
War

Love
The Role of a Parent
Tragedy (in the literary sense)
Comedy (in the literary sense)
Education
Patriotism

The Sixth Method: Analysis

In studying the methods of exposition thus far, we have been often concerned with the relation of the particular to the general, of the individual item to the class. Now, when we turn to analysis, we treat the individual item, whatever it may be, not in relation to something more general or inclusive, but in relation to its own parts.

Analysis is the method of dividing into component parts. (The word *analysis* actually means "loosening into parts.") It can be applied to anything that can be thought of as having parts. We can analyze an object, such as a dog, a house, a tree, a picture. We can analyze an intangible, such as the character of a person, or an idea, such as "goodness." We can analyze an organization, such as a church or a corporation. We can analyze a process, such as baking bread, or an event, such as the French Revolution.

Analysis, classification, and structure

You may ask how analysis differs from classification. A class may, it is true, be said to include the items in that class, but a class, as ordinarily conceived, has no structure in relation to the particular items that fall within it. That is, particular items are not *parts* of the class.[13]

A thing (object, mechanism, idea, or whatever) is an analyzable structure when its components are organized and have a mutually supporting function in determining the nature of the structure. A brick wall is a structure, for the individual bricks supporting one another are necessary to one another and to the wall. The human body is a structure, for the parts are mutually necessary and necessary to the whole.

A class does not have such characteristics. A class exists as the *idea* of the qualities shared by a number of individual items. But no one item or set of items belonging to the class is necessary for the existence of the class. We can destroy one individual book, or a million, and the class *book,* the idea of what constitutes a book, is not impaired. But we cannot knock many bricks from a wall or do much cutting on a human body. Nor can we omit an act from a play or a logical step from an argument. For here, too, we are dealing with structures—as common usage recognizes, for we refer to the structure of a play or the structure of an argument.

An analysis cannot take place except in accordance with the principle of the structure of the thing being analyzed. A small boy beating on an alarm clock with a hammer is not analyzing the mechanism, no matter how many things get knocked loose. Even if he carefully takes the clock apart with a screwdriver and not a hammer, he is still not making an analysis— unless he grasps the principle of the relation among the parts.

Interest and method

Analysis represents a rational interest of the person making the analysis. Therefore it must be conducted by some method, not hit-or-miss. The method used depends on the nature of the structure under consideration.

But here we must remember that the same object may, according to the different kinds of interest brought to bear on it, be regarded as more than one kind of structure. The botanist would regard an apple as a botanical structure and therefore would analyze it into stem, skin, flesh, seeds, and so forth; whereas a chemist would regard it as a chemical structure and would analyze it into certain elements, or a painter would regard it as an aesthetic structure and would analyze it into a pattern of form and color. Each man would perform his analysis in terms of a particular interest, and the interest prompting his analysis would decide the kind of structure that he took the object to represent. The kind of structure would in turn determine what might be regarded as the parts of the structure.

In illustrating the fact that a particular object may be regarded as hav-

---

[13] There are "ordered classes," for instance, in mathematics, but they do not concern us here.

ing different kinds of structure, we have used an example having physical existence, an apple. But what we said may also apply to something with no physical existence, say a short story. We may regard it as a grammatical structure, for it is made up of words. Or we may regard it as a fictional structure, that is, as being composed of plot, of characters, of theme—elements that we can think of and discuss separately. An institution may also be regarded as having different kinds of structure. For instance, we may regard the family as a biological structure, or as an economic structure, or as a moral structure. Each of these structures focuses attention on different kinds of relationships among the members of a family.

● CAUTION

Do not confuse analysis with classification. For example, in the exercise that follows it is not relevant for you to place your mother in a religious, ethnic, or financial classification. But you could regard her as, for instance, a chemical structure. What other structures would be applicable to her? Or suppose love were an item on our list. It is not relevant to place it among the emotions or sentiments. It would be relevant, however, to try to discriminate what motives or feelings merge to give us what we call love. For instance, William Wordsworth was said, by his friend Coleridge, to regard love as a mixture of lust and esteem. Wordsworth had performed an analysis of love—good or bad, that is not the point.

■ APPLICATION

Can you think of more than one kind of interest by which an analysis of the following items might be executed? Be specific. List the kinds of interest, and indicate certain parts that might appear in each kind of analysis.

Your mother	Generosity
A poem	The human heart
A helicopter	A corporation
A picture	The American party system

Analysis and technical (or expository) description

Analysis is the form of description achieved by distinguishing the parts of the thing described. This kind of description, which we shall presently contrast with ordinary description, is called *technical* (or *expository*) *description*.

We can contrast technical description and ordinary description by considering the different types of occasion from which each arises. Technical description arises from the demand for *information about* the thing described; ordinary description, from the demand for an *immediate sense impression* of the thing described. The first kind of description is expository in that it attempts to enlarge the understanding. The second kind, ordinary description, aims to give us an experience of the object through imagination. (See Description, pp. 196–99.) We shall call it *suggestive description*.

Let us take two examples and contrast them:

TECHNICAL DESCRIPTION:

For Quick Sale

Attractive Cape Cod cottage, lge. liv. rm., 13 x 25, knotty pine, stone fireplace; din. rm., sunny, 12 x 14; small den or libr., fireplace; kitchen, modern, elec. stove, lge. refrig., dishwasher, all practically new; med.-size, concrete basement, gas furn., ht. water; 2 bedrms., 14 x 16, 15 x 18; 2 baths, lge. and small; roof white oak shingle. Lot well planted, landscaped, brook, 2 acres; heated garage, 2 cars; small greenhouse. Built by owner, 1936. Excellent condition. Take reasonable offer. Call: BE–1632.

SUGGESTIVE DESCRIPTION:

Dear Mother:

We have found a place at last, and we love it, Jack just as much as I. I must tell you about it, so you can have some notion before you come to see us here. Well, you don't see it from the highway, for there is a high hedge with just a little gap that lets you into the lane, a winding lane among a grove of white oaks, like a lane going down to a pasture on somebody's farm, a million miles away from town. When you pass the oaks, you see a dip down to a brook, lined with willows, a stone bridge, and just beyond the bridge the house on a slight rise. The house is white and trim, two stories, but rather low, just seeming to crop out of the ground. You have the feeling that once you cross that bridge and enter that door you'll be safe and sound and the world will never come to bother you.

When you do enter, you know that your feeling is right. There is a long room with a big fireplace, and windows to the east for the morning sun. It is a perfect room for the furniture that Grandmother left me, just the sort of room she would have loved, peaceful and old-fashioned. The instant you come in, you think of a fire crackling on the hearth, and a kettle humming to heat water for tea, and you see the copper glinting on the andirons. . . .

The motives behind the two pieces of description are very different. The seller of the house wants to give information about the house. The buyer of the house, writing to her mother, wants to give the feel, the atmosphere, of the house. (Note that we are here using the method of contrast, with illustrations, to drive home the difference between the two kinds of descriptions.)

The advertisement, which is an analysis of the house, is an instance of technical description. Except insofar as we know the general type of Cape Cod cottage, we have no basis for visualizing the actual house. The writer of the advertisement has not been concerned that we should get a direct impression of the house; the only attempt in this direction is his use of the word *sunny* about the dining room. But if the writer has not been concerned with giving us the picture and atmosphere of his house, he has been greatly concerned with giving us a fairly complete body of information about the house considered, from a technical point of view, as a shelter and a mechanism for living.

We should find the same motive behind a naturalist's description of a species of bird, a mechanic's description of the ignition system of an automobile, or a physiologist's description of the structure of the human brain. In none of these examples would there be any attempt to make us perceive the thing described except insofar as that attempt would enlarge our understanding of the object's structure.

In the excerpt from the letter above, however, the situation is reversed. The writer is concerned with making an appeal to her reader's senses in order to establish the impression of the house, its quietness and isolation, its old-fashioned charm. The details she has selected all contribute to this impression. The suggestive description does not, as does the technical, give a systematic and relatively complete body of information concerning the subject: it does not analyze the subject. Instead, it simply presents the details that support the sensory and emotional effect the writer wishes to communicate. The technical description *tends* to be enumerative; the suggestive description *tends* to be selective and impressionistic.

TECHNICAL DESCRIPTION AND INTERPRETATION

There is another and very important distinction between technical and suggestive description. In strictly technical description there is no place for interpretation by the writer. The description is concerned only with the facts about the object, facts that can be observed by anyone. For example, when the writer of the advertisement of the Cape Cod cottage lists six rooms or says that the living room is of knotty pine, he is stating a fact, something objective and beyond dispute. He is being strictly technical. But when he says that the cottage is "attractive," he is not being technical, but subjective; that is, he is interpreting the object according to his personal tastes. The letter of the buyer, though it lists certain objective facts about the house, is primarily subjective; she is trying to explain why she finds the house charming. The subjective bias becomes clear when we think that to another person the house might be depressing rather than charming.

GENERALIZED DESCRIPTION

In the above example of technical description a specific house has been the subject. Often, however, technical description analyzes the characteristics of a *type,* a class, and not of a specific thing. For instance, here is a technical description that is generalized:

> Chestnut oak is the big tough-looking tree with bark in heavy ridges. At the bottom of the furrows between ridges, bark is cinnamon-red. Chestnut oak has the largest acorns known on oaks—$1\frac{1}{2}$ or even 2 inches. This is the acorn to roast and eat. It's the sweetest of all the northern oaks. Look for orange-brown twigs that are not round but angled in an interesting way. Name comes from resemblance to chestnut leaves—large ovals with wavy edges; one of the most beautiful of oak leaves.
>
> —RUTHERFORD PLATT: *A Pocket Guide to the Trees.*

This description gives the characteristics of a species of oak, not of a particular tree one has known—the tree at the corner of the yard that once sheltered childhood play, or the tree on the ridge blasted by lightning to a peculiar shape, weird in moonlight.

THE DEVELOPED ANALYSIS

The two examples of technical description, the advertisement for the Cape Cod cottage and the description of the species of oak, are very brief. They are little more than listings of parts. But many occasions for analysis demand more development. For one thing, we want to indicate the relation among the parts, to give an overall concept of the thing analyzed. In a book on fly-fishing, the following paragraph introduces an analysis of that sport:

> Fly-fishing has three elements: equipment, knowledge of stream life, and presentation. The equipment centers on the artificial fly; the knowledge of stream life encompasses insects and trout; presentation is skill, acquired and magical, in presenting the fly to the trout. Fly-fishing argument, which is fabulous, revolves around the comparative values of these elements.
> —JOHN MC DONALD: Introduction to *The Complete Fly Fisherman, The Notes and Letters of Theodore Gordon.*

This example differs, as we can readily see, from the two previous examples in that it systematically indicates the relation among the elements and thereby gives the basis for a detailed discussion. We shall never be at a loss to fit any detail into the overall structure here outlined.

Not only should we establish the relation among the parts, but we should, to make understanding easier for our reader or listener, settle on some single governing idea by reference to which, for the purpose of the description, the parts can be charted. In the following passage the comparison of the heart to a pump gives us the basis for understanding the relation among the parts:

> The heart is a complicated mechanism. Essentially it is a muscular pump composed of four chambers and their incoming and outgoing blood vessels. The action of these chambers is coordinated and controlled by an intricate nervous mechanism. The chambers are paired into a right half and a left half. The upper chamber on each side is called the auricle; the lower, the ventricle. Each auricle is separated from its ventricle by a muscular valve which permits the flow of blood downward but prevents the leakage of blood backward.
> —LOUIS I. DUBLIN: *The Problem of Heart Disease.*

■ APPLICATION

Write a short theme (250 words) of generalized description, being sure to bring your subject to focus by a single governing idea, or image. Avoid a merely random list of parts. Indicate the relation among the parts of the thing you are analyzing.

Functional analysis

The kind of analysis we have been discussing answers the question: "How is it put together?" A tree, we say, is composed of roots, trunk, branches, and leaves, attached to each other in a certain way. A radar set is composed of a modulator, a radio-frequency oscillator, an antenna with scanning mechanism, a receiver, and an indicator. But with the tree or the radar set, as soon as we begin to explore the idea of the relation among parts, we come to another question: "How does it work?" It is not merely the parts, but the function of the parts in relation to a characteristic function of the whole that now concerns us. The explanation of how the parts of anything relate to one another in action we may call functional analysis.[14]

Here is a student theme analyzing the parts of an apparatus in relation to function:

COOKING SYRUP

There is one mechanical contraption that I know well—that for making maple syrup. I ought to know it well, for I was raised on a farm in Vermont, the last one in the neighborhood that made syrup. The season for syrup-making was for us kids, all five of us, about as fine as Christmas, and I think it was that way for our parents and grandparents, too.

To describe the mechanism, I'll have to explain the process. Maple sap as it comes out of the tree is very clear, weakly sweet in taste, and as thin as water. People used to call it "sugar water," in fact. To get syrup this sap has to be boiled down at about a ratio of forty to one. You can, if you want to, just boil some down in a pot on the stove, and get syrup. And the early settlers used a big "cauldron" over a wood fire. The process is so simple that the Indians did it, and they didn't have metal for cooking, just threw hot rocks in a container of wood or bark.

But the paleface gave up the cauldron system as soon as he had learned to tap the trees on a large scale and had a sled to haul sap. So the evaporator was developed. That is the key to the syrup set-up—a big flat container where the syrup can spread thin and get the most even heat. In the old days the evaporator, just a big metal pan, was set on a brick arch that held the fire. That was the kind my grandfather, who liked old things, had.

The pan of the modern evaporator is of galvanized iron, tin sheet, or copper. The size depends on the size of the "sugar-bush," as you call the grove, allowing about ten square feet of pan for every hundred good trees. The evaporator is divided into two sections, the front and the back, the back getting more heat. In our sugar house the back pan is eight-and-a-half feet long, and the front is five feet and two inches, and both are five-and-a-

---

[14] We may, strictly speaking, distinguish between function and purpose. If we are discussing a university, we can treat the subject in terms of purpose, for it is an institution created by men to achieve certain ends. But if we are discussing the circulation of the blood, we can treat the subject only in terms of a characteristic function. We cannot say that purpose is involved. In both instances, however, we observe a relation of parts in terms of a characteristic action, and for the present purpose we use the term *functional analysis* for either. The distinction can be important, however, when it comes to understanding what sort of structure is involved in a particular case.

half feet wide. The rim is seven-and-a-half inches high. The back pan has a corrugated bottom, for this exposes the sap to more heat, and you want the heat at the back where the sap enters. The front pan has a flat bottom. At one corner of the back pan is a door for letting the sap in, and at each front corner of the front pan is a "draw-off" door. You can take your choice of draw-off door according to which settling pan is full. But I'll be coming to that. The pans have partitions to maintain an even flow.

Under the pans is the firebox, made of galvanized iron sheets lined with firebrick and protected with brick. It is still called the "arch" in memory of the time when it was just that. Inside, it has a grating for the wood (you use hardwood to build the heat) and a slope backward toward the chimney for draft.

There are two other basic parts to the set-up, one leading in, the other out. The "in" is a storage tank, ours being outside the sugar house on the north wall, with a pipe and automatic control for the evaporator. You have to have a storage tank, for the syrup in the pan should be about one inch deep always, and you have to be ahead of the game to keep it so.

The "out" apparatus consists of one or more settling tanks, made of galvanized iron and equipped with felt filters for their outlet pipes. Our tanks have three filters each. Below the filters is the lead for filling cans or bottles. We never use bottles. My father has fine fresh new cans that have bright labels on them, with a picture of our sugar house and the name "Joshua Millbank," and under that: "If you want the best." Then comes the grade of the syrup. I forgot to say that there are several grades, with the best grade called "fancy."

So you see we have come a long way from the poor Indian.

The author of the theme has thought out the mechanism. He might have been tempted to describe the mechanism and build in the comment on function as he went along, but he is probably right in stating the principle underlying the process before embarking on the analysis of the structure. It is not as clear, however, that the arrangement of the rest of the theme is the best possible. Having set up the principle, the author might have started with the storage tank, the lead pipe, and the automatic control, and then proceeded step by step to explain the rest of the apparatus. This organization might have been more economical and achieved a tighter composition. Even so, the present system is acceptable.

As for faults, perhaps there is some disproportion between the part of the theme that deals with the evaporator proper and the parts concerned with the storage tank, settling tanks, and firebox. The lack of proportion is not so much a matter of length (after all, the evaporator is the central part of the mechanism), as a failure to give a few relevant details in treating the subsidiary parts. How big should a storage tank be? How does the automatic control work? What, in fact, is a sugar house like? He merely mentions one. Adding such details would not necessarily have made the theme too long, for some close revision could reduce what we now have.

The next to the last paragraph is rather miscellaneous, and throughout the sentence structure tends to be loose.

Write a theme of 500 words, or more, analyzing a mechanism, organization, or institution. In doing so, consider the following points:

1 Identify or define the structure to be analyzed.
2 Explain the basic function or purpose of the structure.
3 Specify what principle of structure determines the characteristic operation.
4 Indicate the parts, relating each to its characteristic operation as a part.
5 Be sure that all parts are clearly related to the overall structure and the basic function or purpose.

Remember that these points are *not* to be taken as an outline of your theme. You must develop what you consider an appropriate way of presenting your material.

The following list may suggest a topic:

A newspaper office	An insurance company
A tank corps	A poem
A political party	A hospital
A church	An athletic team
A bank	A television set

FUNCTIONAL ANALYSIS AND PROCESS

Thus far we have been putting the emphasis on the parts of a structure as explained by their characteristic function. That is, we have been concerned, by and large, with mechanism. But we may switch the emphasis to the analysis of a process. A process may involve a mechanism—the human heart or a legislature—but our chief concern here is with the stages of the process and not with the parts of the mechanism. The parts, then, are interesting only insofar as they help explain the stages.

Functional analysis is the method by which we distinguish the stages in a process that may be regarded as having a characteristic function or purpose.

EXPOSITORY NARRATION

Once we are concerned with the stages of a process, we are dealing with a sequence of events in time. That is, we have narration, but narration used for an expository purpose.

As we can make a distinction between technical (or expository) description and ordinary description (pp. 96–98), so can we make one between expository narration and ordinary narration. Ordinary narration, as we shall see when we come to discuss it as a basic kind of discourse (in Chapter 9), is concerned with presenting an action. It aims to give the sense of the event as experienced, and it involves an appeal to the imagination. But expository narration merely gives information to enlarge the understanding. If we give directions as to how to build a boat or make a cake, we are treating a sequence of events in time, and we are forced to use a form of narration. If we tell how radar works, we are again using a kind of narration. An instructor in military history lecturing on the First Battle of the Marne in World War I is concerned with making his class understand the stages of the event and the problems of tactics, but he is not necessarily concerned with bringing the event into the imagination of his audience. So he, too, is using expository narration.

GENERALIZED NARRATION

By analogy with generalized description, we can see that when expository narration deals with a type of process or type of event, instead of a unique and particular event, we call it generalized narration. For example, if we give the steps that we went through in baking our first pie, we are writing expository narration; we are dealing with the stages of a particular event. But if we are giving directions for making apple pie, we are dealing with stages in a type of process, and hence with generalized narration.

Let us glance at a section from a book on repairing antique furniture:

GLUING FELT TO WOOD

You may occasionally wish to glue thin felt to wood, as when replacing it on an old desk top. Other occasions are applying felt to a lamp base or to the bottom of legs of heavy furniture so that floors will not be scratched.

Thin felt for such purposes may usually be purchased in a variety of colors at department stores. The most popular colors are green and brown. Measure the size needed and buy a piece larger than required, as it may shrink somewhat when applied and the glue dries.

Use either the "Synthetic Resin Waterproof Glue" mixed a bit thick or "Old Fashioned Glue" as it comes from the container.

Proceed as follows:

1. When the surface is prepared, by removing any old glue, scratch or roughen it with coarse abrasive paper and clean off. Then apply a generous and even coat of the glue. Allow this to dry until it becomes very sticky and is not too liquid. Otherwise, it might soak through the felt.

2. Apply an oversize piece of felt to the surface, starting on one side and laying it carefully in correct position with no wrinkles. The felt must overlap on all sides. The hands must be clean and free from dust.

3. The felt must now be rolled or patted into the glue. This is best done with a photographer's roller. If a roller is not available, hold a lintless clean cloth around a small wood block and pat the entire surface. It is best not to rub it for fear of moving or stretching the felt.

4. Allow to dry for 24 to 48 hours in a warm room.

5. If the felt goes beyond the edges, trim off closely with sharp scissors. Should it be used on a piece such as a desk top which has a wood border around the surface to which it is applied, the excess felt material is best cut off with a safety razor blade against a straight edge as a guide. (A carpenter's large steel square is good for this purpose.)

—RALPH KINNEY: *The Complete Book of Furniture Repair and Refinishing.*[15]

[15] Reprinted with the permission of Charles Scribner's Sons from *The Complete Book of Furniture Repair and Refinishing* by Ralph Kinney. Copyright 1950 Charles Scribner's Sons.

This is a very clear and systematic account of a simple process. It has a single point—to tell us how felt is glued—and it never wavers from that intention. It is complete; it tells us everything we can reasonably want to know, assuming nothing on our part, not even that we know where to get the felt or what kind of glue is best. And it uses very simple language. Technical terms known only to expert cabinetmakers are not used; any amateur of furniture repairing can understand the directions given.

The organization is systematic. It falls into three sections, which correspond to the order in which questions will arise:

I   Type of situation that demands gluing felt to wood

II   Identification of materials

III   The process—"proceed as follows" with stages in strict chronological order, and numbered. Notice that there are certain interpolated cautions and suggestions, but that these appear at points where they may be needed in the process.

We see that the directions are little more than an expanded outline, a skeleton that is to be fleshed out, not by words but by the actual doing. But often we are concerned with the explanation of a process, not in order to carry it out, but merely to satisfy curiosity and to enlarge the understanding. In such instances the strict schematic method used for giving directions will scarcely satisfy us or our readers.

Here is an account of the method of planting dark tobacco in Tennessee and Kentucky, written as part of an introduction to an American novel translated into French. The account is thus intended for a reader who knows nothing of farming in those states and has only the casual interest provoked by the novel itself, and certainly no intention of raising a crop.

> The work begins in January, when winter breaks a little and the soil thaws. On the sunny side of a patch of woodland, where the soil is thick and rich, the farmer piles up some dry wood, mixed with a little green, on a space about twenty feet wide by fifty to a hundred feet long. At evening he sets fire to his big woodpile, and sometimes in a sort of ritual picnic all the family comes down to watch, for this is the beginning of a new year of work and hope. Next day the soil, mixed with the ashes of the bonfire, is turned up, pulverized and raked to prepare a bed for the little seeds of tobacco which the farmer then treads into the soil and ashes. Long ago the farmers used to place boughs over the bed to protect it, but in later times they stretch over the bed, on a frame, a cheap white cloth, very light, called canvas, light enough to allow sun and rain to come through. In this protected bed the fragile plant of tobacco develops until the time when it will be replanted in the open field.
>
> The time of setting out the plants comes in May or June. The farmer has prepared his field. He has plowed and harrowed the soil to pulverize it as perfectly as possible, and he has laid it out in squares. When the rain comes and the soil is well soaked—that is to say, when the farmer gets what he calls a "season"—the tender plants are drawn from the bed. Now every available person turns out, women and children, to carry the plants in baskets across the field, letting one fall at the exact center of each square. Behind the "droppers," the women and children with the baskets

of plants, come the men, the "setters," who with one hand pick up the plant and with the other drive a sharpened stake of wood, called a "dibble," into the earth to make a hole for the plant. The setter presses down the damp earth around the plant, and without straightening up, takes another step forward, to the next square and the next plant. This setting out process is grinding work; in May or June, the sun of Kentucky is already powerful, and you can't interrupt yourself, even to straighten an aching back, for every moment is precious as long as the soil is damp enough to receive the plants.

Here the writer has tried to fill out the skeleton of the exposition with just enough material—the family coming down to watch the fire, the heat of the sun, the aching back, and so on—to make the French reader have some immediate sense of the process. In other words, there are certain elements in the passage that belong to suggestive narration or description. But the intention here is primarily expository—to analyze the process of tobacco setting for the French reader.

■ APPLICATION

Below is a list of possible subjects for themes, some that may well be treated as directions, some more properly adapted to the account of a process to satisfy curiosity. Select one of the subjects that interests you (or think up one of your own). First decide whether your subject suggests a particular or generalized form of narration. The two examples given above are generalized; the directions for gluing felt are, of course, supposed to be applicable in general, as is the account of setting tobacco. But if you take the last football game at your school, you will be explaining a specific event.

If you are giving a generalized treatment, you must remember that you are trying to present the essential pattern that never varies significantly from one instance to another. If you are giving an explanation of an event—for instance, the last football game—you are concerned with its particularity and must make clear why your team won or lost under the special circumstances.

Having decided whether you are concerned with a particular or general treatment, make your outline, breaking the process or event down into its stages, in chronological order. Then write a short theme, say about 500 words, to develop the outline. Remember that you are supposed to be giving information to a person relatively ignorant of the subject, that you should leave nothing of consequence to his surmise, and remember, too, if you are writing directions, to include any appropriate cautions or suggestions. But always stick to your main point; do not let your cautions or suggestions lead you away from it.

How the news story gets to the front page	A chemical experiment
	Baking a deep-dish apple pie
How to lay out a vegetable garden	How to organize a charity drive
	The Battle of ——
Space exploration	Slalom racing

Causal analysis

In dealing with processes we often want to go beyond the mere account of the stages in time sequence. In fact, in expository narration we naturally find ourselves concerned with what makes one stage lead to the next. In other words, we find ourselves making a causal analysis.

Causal analysis concerns two questions:

1. What caused this?
2. Given this set of circumstances, what effect will follow?

In answering the first question we must reason from effect back to cause, and in answering the second, from cause forward to effect.

CAUSE

We all have a rough-and-ready notion of what cause is. We must in order to get through the day. The burnt child who doesn't shun the fire may well get incinerated, and even the stupidest cat does not make a habit of sitting on hot stove lids.

Indeed, the cat that has once sat on a hot stove lid will probably give up the idea of sitting on *any* stove lid. The cat has achieved a notion of cause and effect, but the notion is too rough-and-ready to be useful except in a negative way: no stove lid to be sat on. The cat has not gone far enough in causal analysis to see that it is not stove lids as such that are unsittable, but stove lids that have, or have recently had, fire under them.

The cat has made a connection between events: stove lid and hot behind, but the connection has not been fully analyzed.[16]

RULES OF CONNECTION

Cause is the kind of connection between events that conforms to the following rules:

I   Without event *A*, event *B* would not have come about.
II   Whenever there is *A* there will be *B*.

Keep these rules firmly in mind.

CONDITIONS: REMOTE AND IMMEDIATE

No event takes place in isolation. It always involves a complicated set of circumstances spreading in all directions. Tennyson, in the poem "Flower in the Crannied Wall," states the notion:

---

[16] The use here of the word *event* may be objected to. It may be said that the word *thing* is more appropriate, at least in some circumstances. But suppose, for example, we say that a nail is the cause of the fact that a picture hangs on the wall. A nail is, of course, a thing, but it is not the nail as a *thing* that sustains the picture. It is the nail's state of being in the wall that causes the picture to be sustained, and being in the wall is an event. Things must exist, of course, for events to exist, but the event is what we are concerned with. The state of a thing is an event in our meaning of the word.

Flower in the crannied wall,
I pluck you out of the crannies,
I hold you here, root and all, in my hand,
Little flower—but *if* I could understand
What you are, root and all, and all in all,
I should know what God and man is.

Since there is in the world an almost infinitely extended texture of relations, if the poet could know the complete "cause" of the flower—all the conditions determining its existence—then he would know the universe.

In a passage from Tolstoy's novel *War and Peace,* we find the same principle more elaborately stated and carried over into human behavior:

> When an apple has ripened and falls, why does it fall? Because of its attraction to the earth, because its stalk withers, because it is dried by the sun, because it grows heavier, because the wind shakes it, or because the boy standing below wants to eat it?
>
> Nothing is the cause. All this is only the coincidence of conditions in which all vital organic and elemental events occur. And the botanist who finds that the apple falls because the cellular tissue decays and so forth is equally right with the child who stands under the tree and says the apple fell because he wanted to eat it and prayed for it. Equally right and wrong is he who says that Napoleon went to Moscow because he wanted to, and perished because Alexander desired his destruction, and he who says that an undermined hill weighing a million tons fell because the last navvy struck it for the last time with his mattock. In historic events, the so-called great men are labels giving names to events, and like labels they have but the smallest connection with the event itself.
>
> Every act of theirs, which appears to them an act of their own will, is in an historical sense involuntary and is related to the whole course of history and predestined from eternity.   —LEO TOLSTOY: *War and Peace.*

Clearly, when we are making a causal analysis, we cannot be concerned with the notion of cause in the way Tennyson and Tolstoy have referred to it. We must be concerned with the more or less *immediate* connection between an event and its conditions. We need a workaday, usable conception.

Let us look at a simple experiment. To a rod is attached a little bell. The rod, in turn, is attached to an electric mechanism that will make it sway back and forth when a button is pushed. The whole affair, except the control button, is rigged up in a hermetically sealed jar connected with a vacuum pump. Somebody pushes the button, the rod sways, the bell rings. We hear the sound of the bell. What is the cause of the sound?

One person says it is caused by the clapper striking the inside of the bell. Another says it is caused by the movement of the rod. Another says: "No, Jack pushed the button." And common sense tells us that everybody is right and everybody is wrong. In each case the person answering has fixed on some particular factor and assumed the other factors.

We can see more clearly how much assumption is involved in our talk about cause if we pump the air entirely out of the jar and then push the button. The mechanism works, the bell clapper strikes metal, but there is no sound. We know why. For sound to exist, there must be a medium, in this instance air, in which the sound waves can travel.

The first three people who specified a cause for the sound forgot all about the necessity for a medium for the sound waves. But now a fourth person says: "Ah, it was the air that caused the sound." Again, he is both right and wrong. The air is a "cause" in the sense that without air there is no sound, but the air is only one of several factors that must be present: the bell, the clapper striking it, the person pushing the button, and the air for the sound waves. All these factors are necessary. *A necessary factor is called a condition.*

● CAUTION

In considering the problem of cause in any situation, it is essential to distinguish between the *necessary factors*—the *conditions*—and the *incidental factors*. In our experiment here, for example, the bell may be brass or steel, the insulation on the wire may be silk or rubber, the person who pushes the button may be male or female, red-haired or black-haired. None of these factors is crucial—that is, none is a condition.

In thinking of causality we are concerned with conditions.

CAUSE AND INTEREST

Since there is a necessary interrelation among the conditions of an event, we may, strictly speaking, maintain that cause is always complex, and we shall return to this idea. But for the moment, let us ask in what sense can we say that a particular condition is *the* cause of an event?

The choice of any particular condition as *the* cause is always *provisional* and *selective*. The choice is determined by a special interest brought to bear on the event.

Let us take the instance of the death of a small child. We must confine ourselves, we remember, to conditions having a more or less immediate connection with the event: we rule out as too remote, for example, the birth of a certain grandfather, even though that birth is necessary to the existence of the child. Among the immediate conditions, various choices might be made. A neighbor telling the news says, "Little Willie got killed from falling off a stepladder." The bereaved mother takes her own carelessness as the cause: she had left the ladder standing on the edge of the back porch instead of putting it in the closet where it belonged. The doctor, making out the death certificate, records that death was the result of a skull fracture.

Each person has brought a special interest to bear on the event, a special interpretation, and each statement is, in itself, true. At the same time, each is incomplete. The point is to be aware of what we are about when we select a particular condition in the light of a special interest. We must know what conditions are being rejected, and why.[17]

The fallacy of post hoc, ergo propter hoc Let us turn again to *War and Peace:*

> Whenever I see the movement of a locomotive I hear the whistle and see the valves opening and wheels turning; but I have no right to conclude that the whistling and the turning of wheels are the cause of the movement of the engine.
>
> The peasants say that a cold wind blows in late spring because the oaks are budding, and really every spring cold winds do blow when the oak is budding. But I do not know what causes the cold winds to blow when the oak buds unfold. I cannot agree with the peasants that the unfolding of the oak buds is the cause of the cold wind, for the force of the wind is beyond the influence of the buds. I see only a coincidence of occurrences such as happens with all the phenomena of life, and I see that however much and however carefully I observe . . . the valves and wheels of the engine, and the oak, I shall not discover the cause of . . . the engine moving, or of the winds of spring. To do that I must entirely change my point of view and study the laws of the movement of steam . . . and of the wind.
>
> —LEO TOLSTOY: *War and Peace.*

Here the peasant who thinks that the cold wind comes because the oak leaves are out is committing one of the most common errors in thinking about cause, the fallacy of *post hoc, ergo propter hoc*—"after this, therefore because of this."

The trouble here is that the peasant has in his mind a false generalization about cause. He ties event *A* and event *B* together in time sequence and then, because sequence is a *necessary* feature in causality, assumes that it is a *sufficient* feature.

The mind of the peasant, however, is not unsimilar to that of the modern educated citizen. This fallacy, for instance, is the stock in trade of most politicians on the hustings and of many historians when they take pen in hand. If it could be abolished, there would be vast stretches of silence on the airwaves at election time, and the shelves of libraries would be decimated. Needless to add, among advertising agencies bankruptcy would set in like the Black Death. (See Chapter 7, Persuasion.)

---

[17] You may well ask how selection of *the* cause from among a set of conditions squares with the Rules of Connection for causality with which we started.

Since by definition a condition is a necessary factor, Rule I is fulfilled. Restating the rule, we have: without the "necessary factor" *A,* event *B* would not have come about. No argument is possible here.

Rule II is fulfilled *only* if we are properly aware of the limitation of the act of selection. Restating the rule, we would say: whenever there is the "necessary factor" *A* (in conjunction, of course, with the complex of other, unspecified conditions), there will be *B*. Here the awareness of the nature of the act of selection is crucial. Thus, the fact that the mother left the stepladder on the porch is a necessary factor only because little Willie climbed the ladder and fell on his head.

■ APPLICATION

The following statements are among the clichés of our time. Study them.

1 If Abraham Lincoln had not been assassinated, a peaceful and just Reconstruction would have ensued in the South.
2 If President Kennedy had not been assassinated, there would have been no escalation of the war in Vietnam.
3 Student unrest can be traced back to the bomb, ultimately.
4 America beat Japan by dropping the bomb on Hiroshima.
5 The pill is destroying old-time American sexual morality.

Having studied these statements, try to say how each might be discussed as an example of reasoning about cause and effect.

There is no yes-or-no answer here. Use your common sense, your acquaintance with logic, and whatever information you possess.

Generalization and Uniformity   We have remarked that Tolstoy's peasant was guilty of a false generalization. What generalization should he have made?

When we say that *A* is the cause of *B*, we are not merely referring to the particular case of a particular *A* and a particular *B*. We are implying that a general principle exists, that under the same circumstances any *A* would cause a *B*. We imply a principle of uniformity behind the particular case. To arrive at a true principle of uniformity, Tolstoy's peasant should have studied the "laws of the movement . . . of the wind."

In other words, the peasant should have studied what we call the laws of nature.

The Laws of Nature   The principle of uniformity is most clearly seen in what we call a law of nature. A chemist says that when we ignite hydrogen in the presence of oxygen, we will get water (H_2O). Under specified conditions the element hydrogen and the element oxygen always behave in the same way. At least, as far as we know, they have always behaved that way in the past. We appeal to experience and to a number of instances for our principle. We assume that there will be no exceptions.

Here we must emphasize the word *assume*. We base our scientific operations, as well as our decisions of ordinary life, on this assumption. But, as the eminent philosopher and mathematician Bertrand Russell put it, we have, even in science, only a probability:

> It must be conceded . . . that the fact that two things have often been found together and never apart does not, by itself, suffice to *prove* demonstratively that they will be found together in the next case we examine. The most we can hope is that the oftener things are found together, the more probable it becomes that they will be found together another time, and that, if they have been found together often enough, the probability will amount *almost* to a certainty.
>
> —BERTRAND RUSSELL: *The Problems of Philosophy.*

● CAUTION: ESSENTIAL CHARACTERISTICS

The principle of uniformity, we must remember, refers only to the essential characteristics of a situation. For instance, it does not matter whether the laboratory worker igniting hydrogen in the presence of oxygen is a Catholic or a Jew, a Republican or a Democrat, a Chinese or a Greek. The boy who, in Charles Lamb's essay, accidentally discovered how to roast a pig by burning down a house, had not isolated the essential characteristic of the situation: he had not learned that he did not need to burn down a house every time he wanted roast pig. He had not recognized, as we have earlier put the same idea, the incidental factors, and then discarded them.

Never appeal to the principle of uniformity without analyzing the circumstances to determine the relevance of characteristics involved.

Controlled Circumstances   In the laboratory a scientist can control the circumstances of his experiments and repeat them at will, without variation. But outside the laboratory it is difficult to control circumstances with any certainty, and many events that we want to explain—for instance, a political election—cannot be repeated at will and identically. When we want to understand the causes of an event that we cannot repeat, we must examine similar events, that is, the various political elections we know about, and try to make sense of them. In other words, we must try to see what is uniform in them in the hope that this process will lead to the discovery of a cause. We look for uniformities beyond the particular situation.

An Example from the Ordinary World   Let us take an example, applying the principle of uniformity, not from a laboratory, but from the ordinary world:

TOM: Why did Jane speak so curtly at dinner last night?

JACK: Because she was angry with her husband.

TOM: How do you know?

JACK: That's the way she always behaves when she's angry with him.

TOM: You must have been around the family a lot.

JACK: Sure. I lived in the house for a year.

When Jack says that the cause of Jane's conduct was her anger with her husband, he is not merely commenting on the particular instance. And Tom's further question elicits the fact that a principle of uniformity is involved: Jane behaves this way *every* time she gets angry with her husband. The principle here may not be one we can depend on with any great degree of certainty. On some future occasion she may not be short with her husband at dinner but may kick the cat, get a divorce, or shoot her husband. But past observation gives us some degree of probability that when Jane is angry with her husband, she usually behaves in a certain way at dinner— that is, a principle of uniformity is involved. In fact, a second and broader principle of uniformity is involved: not only do we have a generalization that when Jane becomes angry with her husband, she displays a bad temper and forgets her manners; we have another generalization that any person who becomes angry with a spouse may then display a bad temper in general and forget his manners, simply because temper and anger tend to spill over.

Hypothesis In answering Tom's question, Jack has offered what is known as a hypothesis. He confronts a problem—"What made Jane curt last night?" He assembles evidence in terms of a principle of uniformity. Then he asserts that the question at hand is to be regarded as an instance of a general principle.

■ APPLICATION

Write a short theme, say 250 words, illustrating the principle of hypothesis. It may be an episode treated in dialogue, as in the discussion of Jane's manners, or it may be a description of an experiment. Or you may devise some other form of presentation. But it must involve a particular case, an illustration of the principle.

Samples When Tom says to Jack that he must have been around Jane's house a lot, he is implying that, to establish a principle of uniformity, you must have a certain number of relevant samples in agreement. Jack gets this point, for he immediately says that he has lived in Jane's house for a year—that is, he has many samples of her conduct.

Certainly a year is better than a month for observing Jane and her husband, but as we have suggested, no matter how many samples are obtained, they can lead only to an assumption about cause, not a certainty.

Negative Instances and Control Suppose that often when Jane quarrels with her husband she does not lose her manners, and that Bill, who hears the conversation between Jack and Tom, is aware of this fact. That is, Bill knows negative cases that impair the generalization Jack has made.

To go further, let us take it that Bill, who is often in Jane's house, has observed that Jane loses her manners after a quarrel *only* when these circumstances occur: (1) when she has quarreled with her husband because the husband insists that Jack remain as a guest in the house; and (2) when, at dinner after the quarrel, Jack is at the table.

Here Bill knows what we may call control instances—that is, that Jane does not lose her manners merely from quarreling with her husband. These instances suggest that there must be another factor—Jane's dislike for Jack's presence.

Competing Hypothesis Let us assume that Jane does not dislike Jack, and assume that another person, Sam not Bill, is listening to the original conversation. Sam is Jane's physician, and he thinks that Jack's hypothesis is wrong. He knows that Jane is a secret drinker and always sneaks a few extras before dinner, and that she has come to him worrying about her habit. His hypothesis is that the drinking, with associated guilt and self-contempt, accounts for Jane's bad manners at dinner. Of course, his professional ethics forbid him to offer his hypothesis to Jack and Tom, but it may be preferable to either of theirs.

When possible, consider competing hypotheses.

Assessing Hypotheses: Simplicity and Statistics   How do we choose between competing hypotheses? There is no rule of thumb. But within limits, certain principles are useful.

For instance, there is the principle that the simple explanation is to be preferred to the complex. The idea that Oswald independently assassinated President Kennedy has the appeal of simplicity over the theories that invoke conspiracy as an explanation. But the appeal of simplicity is never decisive in the face of contrary evidence. It is merely a starting point.

There is, also, the principle of statistical frequency—the simple notion that the more frequently a certain kind of event occurs the more likely it is to occur again. For instance, the night watchman of a bank finds a man wandering around in the basement of the building where the vaults are at about 3 A.M. He puts in an alarm, and the police arrive. The man is taken to the station house and rigorously questioned. He has no identification and is not entirely coherent, but he claims that he had been passing the bank, had been taken by a fit of dizziness, had entered and gone down to the wash rooms, had fainted, and had only come to in the dark. He explains that he must have lost his wallet and papers when he fell.

The police, acting on the principle of statistical frequency (most people caught in the vault section of banks at 3 A.M. are up to no good), regard him with suspicion. But statistical frequency can be misleading: investigation absolves the unfortunate man. The wallet is found. He is a respected clergyman, has recently had fainting fits because of ear trouble, and had been seen in a dazed condition on the street just outside the bank, toward closing time.

Nature of the Observer   To return to the competing hypotheses of Jack, Bill, and Sam, we may mention another factor that may influence us to accept Sam's version of Jane's behavior. He is a doctor. The relevance of this is not merely that, as a doctor, he has had access to certain information (Jane drinks and is worried), but also that, as a doctor, he has been trained to make certain kinds of observation. By reason of such training, he is, we assume, prepared to work out the psychological generalization (drinkers tend to suffer from guilt and self-contempt) that he theorizes is applicable to Jane.

Remember that the nature of the reporter may affect the weight to be given his evidence (pp. 145–47).

■ APPLICATION

How would you assess the reasoning about causality in the following instances?

1   James knows that Jack is allergic to ham. After they have dined out together, Jack gets sick. James says: "There must have been ham in that meat loaf."
  The wife of Jack, who is with them, says: "Yes, I think you are right."

2   Bill says: "All the best shots have light eyes. Billy the Kid had them, and Wild Bill Hickock, Wyatt Earp, and Jesse James."
Ralph says: "But my Uncle Josh is a great shot, and he has brown eyes."

3   Isaac says: "Poetry is written by people who simply can't deal with the world."
Jim: "What makes you think that? You haven't studied literature."
Isaac: "Good Lord, look at a guy like Shelley, the mess he was always in, or Hart Crane committing suicide."

4   Louise: "I have always said that it is the lowering of moral standards in the family that causes so much juvenile delinquency in the slums."
Lucy: "What makes you think that?"
Louise: "My aunt was a social worker for years, and she ought to know."
Lucy: "I didn't know she ever had a job."
Louise: "Well, it wasn't exactly a job. She was a volunteer when she had time."

5   The treachery of the Japanese caused the United States to get into World War II.

Complex Cause   Even in a simple event—the bell ringing in the jar, say—we find a number of conditions, necessary factors as we have called them; and we have discussed what is at stake when, in terms of a special interest, we select one of the necessary factors as *the* cause. We know that the event takes place as the result of a number of factors (the clapper striking the bell, Jack pushing the button, the presence of air in the jar, etc.), and that none of these factors, though *necessary,* can be taken as *sufficient.* Knowing this, we often wish to analyze a number of the conditions involved in an event; we wish to get, in other words, as full and rounded a picture as possible of the "causes," or, if we wish to put it another way, of the complex cause. Many events, if they are to be understood at all, must be considered in this way. For instance, how can we have any notion of the meaning of World War II if we do not try to sort out a number of factors in the context of the event and try to understand insofar as possible, their interrelations? We know that it is idiotic to say "Hitler caused the war" or "The Treaty of Versailles caused the war." Or, "The fact that Germany was allowed to occupy the Ruhr caused the war." Or, "The British caused the war by the appeasement at Munich." All these factors have a place in the picture, along with a number of others. For a century—or for centuries—historians will be trying to assess them, and there will never be an easy and definitive answer to the problem of what caused World War II.

Events involving human behavior—even relatively simple events—are always difficult to treat in terms of cause and effect, but we are all committed to the attempt. Many occupations and professions—advertising, teaching, psychiatry, politics, poker playing, fiction writing, sociology, history—are fundamentally concerned with cause and effect. Aside from such special and highly organized instances, we are all inevitably involved in trying to understand the causes of human behavior. If we don't try to understand the people we live among, and don't try to understand ourselves, we are very likely to make a mess of our lives, and the only rug under which to sweep such messes is usually the turf. The turf in the cemetery.

● CAUTION

There is no easy rule for determining causes in the tangled situations of life—in society, in history, in medicine, in politics, and so forth. But we can begin to think constructively about cause if we steadfastly refuse to accept simplistic solutions and try to discriminate between necessary factors (conditions) and incidental factors, and between what is necessary and what is sufficient. For instance, when someone says "The Treaty of Versailles caused World War II," he is taking as sufficient what is, at the most, only necessary. If an event is the result of a set of conditions, no single condition, much less an incidental factor, can be taken as sufficient. And of course an incidental factor can never be a cause. Yet attributing cause to one condition or incidental factor is one of the commonest of errors.

Here are two handy rules of thumb to apply in order to distinguish between conditions and incidental factors:

1   A cannot be the cause of B if A is ever absent when B is present.
2   A cannot be the cause of B if B is ever absent when A is present.

These rules are relatively easy to apply in a laboratory. They are very far from easy to apply out in the world. But you must try to apply them.

● A LAST CAUTION

In the foregoing discussion of cause many of the principles involved have struck you as familiar. You have been making judgments of cause and effect all your life—in fishing and hunting, in games, in laboratory work, in crossing the street. Being acquainted with the principles, however, is not quite enough. You must make a practice of applying them systematically, as occasions demand. If you can think straight about a problem of cause and effect, it will be easy for you to write well about it. And to think straight, you must be systematic in analyzing events and in applying principles.

■ APPLICATION

You are going to be asked to write a theme in causal analysis, but before you begin, here is a student theme to consider. It is not complete; it is only the first part of a long research theme for late in the course. But the writer has chosen a subject involving causal analysis. (The footnotes proper to a research theme are dropped here. We will take up the problems of the research paper in Chapters 14 and 15.)

CAUSES OF THE TEXAS REVOLUTION

In this paper, I intend to do three things: First, to list the causes of the Texas revolution and define each one. Second, to show how these causes combined to bring about the revolution. Third, to sort out the causes in some order of importance. It is all a little bit like trying to keep three Indian clubs in the air at one time. But since I can't do everything at once, I shall list and define the causes first, then try to tell the story, and then, by way of a conclusion, line them up in importance, or what to me seems to be their importance.

The first cause was simply the difference in civilization between the Mexicans who owned Texas and the Americans who came there. I don't mean in the amount of civilization; I mean in the kind of civilization they had. The Mexicans had a Spanish and Catholic civilization, and they believed in power and authority and tradition. The Americans believed in democracy and self-reliance. You might say that this difference was the thing underlying all the trouble that followed. But perhaps it would not have been enough of a thing to make the revolution if certain other things had not been the way they were.

The second cause was the fact that the Mexicans couldn't get rid of a fear of American adventurers coming in to seize Texas. There had been a lot of adventurers coming in to filibuster far back in the Spanish times, and the Mexicans didn't really trust the Americans that they themselves invited in and who took out citizenship and honestly tried to be good and loyal Mexicans.

The third cause is related to the second. There were many adventurers in Texas, and you might go so far as to say that some of the leaders, like Sam Houston, were adventurers seeking to take Texas from Mexico.

The fourth cause was bad Mexican policy and administration. After they had called in American settlers to develop the country they couldn't develop and fight off the Indians they hadn't been able to control, the Mexican government turned around and tried to block the prosperity of these people. They used heavy custom duties, passed laws to prevent further immigration, and failed to establish coastwise trade with Mexico proper.

The fifth cause was violation of civil rights when a dictatorship was set up, the sending in of troops to hold down the people, sometimes convict troops, and Santa Anna's flinging Austin into jail.

Another cause was the United States policy in trying to buy Texas. The United States government had very bad judgment in the choice of diplomats. A man like Butler tried to bribe high Mexican officials and wrote anonymous letters to stir up rebellion.

It was the big financial panic of 1819 that drove so many Americans to Texas, especially frontiersmen of Kentucky and Tennessee. The self-reliance of the frontiersman was . . .

This theme is written in a dull style. But the writer has tried to be systematic, and his concern with being systematic makes this theme one for the student to analyze. He can see another writer wrestling with the problem of organization. Basically the way the writer of the theme solves his problem is sensible. The difficulty is that he is somewhat awkward in applying the solution.

For your own theme in causal analysis you may take some historical event that you already know something about or an event that you have observed or experienced. You should try to make your theme more than an expanded outline, such as we find in the theme above. Try to apply the principles of reasoning about cause that we have been studying. For instance, when you sort out conditions, distinguish them clearly from incidental factors, and at the same time indicate, when possible, the interrelations among the conditions. The line of reasoning must be constantly available to your reader, but remember that you are analyzing a process in life and should try to make the account lively. Flesh out your discussion of cause with illustrations and with vivid detail. Your subject is, in one sense, a narrative, and so try to give it the suspense of narrative. It deals with human experience. How did the human beings feel who were involved?

Here is a list of topics that may be suggestive:

Why I Failed to Make the Grade
What Caused the Vietnamese War?
Why Did Benedict Arnold Become a Traitor?
Was It Good Luck or Bad?
My Aunt's Character
Why _____ Lost the Election
A Triumph of Character over Circumstance
If Stonewall Jackson Had Not Been Killed, Then What?
What Forces Made Your Home Town What It Is?

CHAPTER **6**

Argument

We commonly think of argument as arising in conflict. "Why did Mr. Smith shoot Mr. Jones?" we ask. And somebody answers, "Oh, they had an argument." We think of formal debate between two college teams as a sporting event, of the confrontation on television between two presidential candidates as something akin to a gladiatorial combat, and of the encounter of two lawyers before a jury as, to use the phrase lawyers themselves often use, a joust.

Much of our time is spent, in fact, in listening to, or participating in, arguments that do arise, quite obviously, in conflict. It is only natural, then, that when we try to prove a point to a stupid or recalcitrant friend, or try to justify an opinion in class, we should think in terms of attack and defense. We think in terms of "winning" and "losing."

Argument and Doubt

When we think of argument between two persons, the element of conflict is very often clear. Even when we think of it as between two ideas, or two points of view, the element of conflict is present, as is indicated in the phrase "a conflict of opinions" or "a conflict of values." But once we shift the emphasis from persons to views, we introduce another factor.

Look at it this way. A person, we say, wins an argument. How does he win? He wins in that his opponent says, "I was wrong, you are right," or that a third party (or parties), in the role of judge, says, "You win, you are right." In short, at the inception of the argument somebody (a participant, a judge, a mere bystander) has had the option of two opposing views. There had been a doubt as to which was "right."

Argument may, and frequently does, arise in conflict. But underlying this notion is another notion—the notion of doubt. A party to the conflict is thus merely supporting a view of the matter that hangs in doubt.

This is not to say that a person in an argument may not be passionately certain of being right. His passionate certainty is not, however, a guarantee that his view is not false, and some of the greatest errors in history have been the most ardently defended. When we say that argument arises in doubt, we refer, not to the depth of commitment of the participants, but to the fact that if one were *obviously* right, there could be no argument.

Antagonists, in fact, are not even necessary to argument. This is clearly indicated by the fact that when you are in doubt about something you will probably say that you are "arguing" with yourself, or that you are "debating" your decision. In your own mind, you are, it is true, alternately playing two roles, now defending one option, now the other; but the key fact of this process is your doubt about which is the right one.

Doubt may often be the dynamic of argument.

The appeal to reason

Thus far we have been primarily concerned with the situations—those of conflict or doubt—in which argument ordinarily develops, those in which we most commonly feel the need to argue. We have been concerned, that is, with what we may call the *psychological context* of argument.

A little reflection shows us, however, that there are kinds of occasions other than those of conflict or doubt that involve argument. For instance, even though we may not be in conflict or doubt concerning a certain theorem of geometry, we may be interested in the process by which the theorem was established. We may even want to see, as students not infrequently do, if a theorem can be proved by a process not given in the textbook. Here we would be concerned to analyze and evaluate the reasoning involved in the proof, or to construct a new and different line of reasoning to make a proof. In such a situation we have turned from the *psychological context* to the *logical process*—that is, to the nature of the argument.

To approach the matter in another way, we may ask how conflict or doubt may be resolved.

A conflict between persons may be settled by threats, deception, cajolery, or force. Doubt may be settled by an act of faith, an instinctive decision, or a desperate leap in the dark. But either conflict or doubt may, sometimes, be settled by argument.

To settle a matter by argument means to settle it by the appeal to reason.

By reason we mean the mental operation by which we move from what we take as the starting point—the *data,* the *premises,* the *evidence* [1]—to the conviction that, with such a starting point, a certain *conclusion* will follow. To state it differently, to reason is to make an *inference*—to accept the conclusion as a consequence of having accepted the particular starting point.

The end of reason is to reach a conclusion which we can accept, which is dependable, or which we can, at least, gamble on. Through reason we seek "truth." Ideally, since argument implies the appeal to reason, it also implies that the parties involved will accept the findings of reason.

When a person is "arguing with himself," he will presumably accept the findings of reason—if he can override, that is, whatever irrational preferences he may consciously, or unconsciously, have. Similarly, men of good will, seriously bent on finding truth, will seek to resolve by reason whatever differences divide them. But there are "arguments" that are purely situations of conflict, and in such cases, to win, not to find truth, is the object. A lawyer defending a man accused of murder has not been hired to seek the truth, he has been hired to save his client's neck. A debating team is not seeking truth, it is trying to score points. A congressman may not be seeking truth, either; he may be trying to satisfy a lobby, consolidate his constituency, or attract enough national attention to be put on the ticket for vice president. What, in such cases, happens to the appeal to reason?

The lawyer, the debater, the congressman *may,* in fact, be distorting reason, trying to confuse issues, and appealing to emotion or prejudices, but they all *claim* to be offering an argument—that is, they *claim* to be following the dictates of reason.

Even though reasoning may be used to defeat the natural end of reason, truth, the *claim* to reasonableness, defines a discourse as belonging to the category of argument. Reason, however distorted, dubious, or devious, remains the crucial substance of argument.

SUMMARY

Argument is the form of discourse characterized by the claim that one thing (the conclusion) merits belief because certain other things (data, premises, evidence) merit belief.

Argument: emotion and reason

If argument implies the appeal to reason, what, then, of the appeal to emotion that we find in the course of many arguments?

This question can be answered only by pointing out that in it the word *argument* is used in two quite different senses. The first time it appears it is

---

[1] The *data* is, literally, what is given. It is all the relevant material available at the inception of the argument. It is a broad, general term, including the *premises* and the *evidence.* In the strict sense of the word, in deductive reasoning, a *premise* is a proposition which is assumed to be true and on which the argument is based (pp. 124 and 128–29). *Premise* is also used with the wider meaning of whatever the parties to a dispute take as an assumption they share and can use as a basis for the argument. *Evidence* is whatever can be used to support an argument (pp. 142–47).

used in a very restricted and technical sense: the form of discourse with the intention of convincing by the appeal to reason. By definition, *argument* in this sense would leave no room for the appeal to emotion. The second time the word appears it is used quite loosely to indicate a discourse seeking to gain assent by a combination of logical and other appeals.

Here we shall use the word *argument* in the more limited sense. But this usage is not merely arbitrary. We often say quite spontaneously, "He didn't really have an argument (that is, an appeal to reason), he merely carried the audience by appealing to their emotions." And quite commonly, too, we make a distinction between argument (as strictly considered) and persuasion (as an emotional appeal). What the question we started with is really asking is: What is the relation between *argument* and *persuasion?*

This is a question of great importance and great complexity, and we cannot tackle it until we have clearly limited the nature of argument. When we come to the question of persuasion, we come to the question of argument in its human context, and that is where trouble and fascination inextricably intertwine. (See Chapter 7, Persuasion.)

Argument, exposition, and logic

Despite distortions of reasoning that often appear in argument[2] and the intrusion of emotional appeals, the study of argument is, at root, the study of the principles of reasoning—that is, of logic. We are already familiar with many of these principles, for the study of exposition, too, involves them—as we have seen in classification, definition, and analysis.

What, then, is the difference between exposition and argument?

The act of inference accounts for the crucial difference. In exposition, the nature of a thing—whatever the "thing" may be, object, mechanism, process, idea—is set forth in certain logical forms. In argument, particular starting points are set forth and a particular conclusion is drawn from them.

Here it may be objected that we have treated causal analysis as a form of exposition, even though a discussion of cause involves inferences. True, but the primary intention in making a causal analysis is to set forth the order and structure of the situation involving causality. The motive, the intention, makes the difference.

But exposition and argument are often, and characteristically, intertwined. For example, the statement of a premise may well involve definition. You state your premise, and somebody asks, "What do you mean by that?" You have to tell him before the argument can proceed, and to do so you may have to resort to the process of definition. Or determining what elements in a situation may be taken as evidence may well involve analysis. It is important in a discourse to distinguish between the elements of exposition and argument, for to fail to do so may mean blurring and confusion; and it is also important to keep firmly in mind the dominant intention of a discourse, for it is the intention that determines the overall organization.

---

[2] Such distortions are called fallacies; we have already considered one (p. 109), and others will be considered later (pp. 165–69).

Are any of the following examples pure argument or pure exposition, or are they mixed? In any examples that are mixed, distinguish the elements of exposition from those of argument.

Let us examine such an example:

> A great many of the kids now looking at the Vietnam war and having just confronted the reality of the bomb for the first time are acting the way English schoolboys behaved in the last days of World War I. The war was taking a terrific death toll then, and the boys who were just under military age all expected to be killed. There are quite a few young people who are doing that now, saying there is no use in going to class, we'll all get drafted and we'll all be killed. So you get this behavior of dancing on the eve of Waterloo, except that now the young men are not dancing.
>
> —Margaret Mead and Irene Neves: "We Must Learn
> to See What's Really New," *Life.*[3]

In the first sentence Margaret Mead announces a comparison between the way young Americans confronting the bomb behave and the way "English schoolboys behaved in the last days of World War I." We take the main intention to be expository—the making of the comparison to clarify the present situation. The next two sentences develop the parallel, the behavior of the two different groups of young people in the face of the expectation of death. But in these two sentences, there is, too, an argument partly stated and partly implied: ". . . there is no use in going to class, we'll all get drafted and we'll all be killed." If we develop this argument, we see something like this:

> The only reason for going to class is to get ready for the future.
> But there isn't going to be any future.
> So I'm not going to class.

Then in the last sentence of the excerpt we get a new element in the argument, the dancing instead of class attendance. This implies another development of the argument, which we may state as follows (though this is not the only way to state it):

> If there isn't any future, then I'm going to enjoy the present.
> There isn't going to be any future.
> So I'm going to enjoy the present (that is, dance).

But another element has entered with the last sentence. The reference to the ball before Waterloo implies another comparison (young people now, young people in World War I, and young people at the time of Napoleon—perhaps with the implication of "young people always in the face of great danger"). Then, in the second half of the last sentence we find a contrast developed from the comparison: the young now do not resort to dancing. We may ask, then, what do they resort to? The unstated answer is "protest." Let us make one

---

[3] From "We Must Learn to See What's Really New," by Margaret Mead and Irene Neves, *Life* Magazine, August 23, 1968 © 1968 Time Inc.

more observation on the last sentence. It returns us to the main intention, the expository intention that underlies the argument.

In analyzing the following examples, remember that you are not dealing with something as simple as the yes-or-no answer of a problem in arithmetic. There may be discussable margins. There will certainly be different ways of stating things. Furthermore, in handling the methods of argument, you are, in a sense, on your own; you have not yet studied this chapter. But you have argued all your life. Bring to bear now what you have in the way of logical capacity and training. This will be one way for you to approach the study of this chapter.

A   AIR–RIDE PROTECTS YOUR POSSESSIONS ON ANY ROAD

> We have replaced stiff, hard springs with Air-Suspension on our Mayflower long-distance moving vans. Now we float your fragile, delicate belongings over any road on big, soft cushions of air. It's our million dollar difference that gives your goods *a ride that's twice as gentle,* yet costs you not a nickel more.
> Mayflower takes no chances with your belongings.
> That's why we have pioneered the major improvements in long-distance moving: the first complete drivers' school . . . the first standardized quality packing service . . . first to remove tailgates from every van . . . the first exclusive, qualified agents' organization to help you. These are just a few, and we're always trying to come up with more. Let *your* nearby Mayflower agent give you the complete Mayflower story next time you move long distance. He'll take the load off your mind! He's listed in the telephone Yellow Pages.   —An advertisement.

B   Because he was such a firm democrat, Thomas [Norman Thomas] found no interest or enchantment in Soviet-style Communism. "The thing which is happening in Russia," he said after a visit during the 1930s, "is not socialism, and it is not the thing which we hope to bring about in America, or in any other land." On another occasion, he noted: "I daresay I have denied Communism, fought against it, more than most people, because at my end of the political spectrum one must make it clear that standing for democratic socialism is quite another thing from standing for Communism."[4]

C   There are two methods of curing the mischiefs of faction: the one, by destroying its causes; the other, by controlling its effects.
    There are again two methods of removing the causes of faction: the one, by destroying the liberty which is essential to its existence; the other, by giving to every citizen the same opinions, the same passions, and the same interests.
           —James Madison: *The Federalist* (no. 10).

Argument and the Common Ground

We have said that argument, in the strict sense, represents an appeal to reason. The willingness to accept the dictates of reason is, ideally, the com-

[4] From "An American Crusade," *Time,* December 27, 1968. Reprinted by permission; Copyright Time Inc. 1968.

mon ground on which the parties to an argument meet—just as it is the implied promise to the self when you argue with yourself and try to make a "reasonable" decision. The appeal to reason is the broadest and deepest assumption made for argument. It underlies the whole process.

The question of common ground may, however, be considered somewhat more narrowly. Though the parties to an argument accept the standard of reason, they still need to accept (consciously or unconsciously) other things in common on which to erect the structure of reason.[5] If they cannot find some such basis, then they cannot, in any true sense of the word, argue.

Let us take an example:

> Suppose that a Mr. Brown has strong anti-Semitic views and a Mr. Smith is arguing with him. Now the fact that they are arguing at all indicates, as we have said, that they accept, momentarily anyway, a common ground in reason. But clearly, in the conversation below, Mr. Smith is trying to find a more specific common ground to work from. If there is no starting point possible, argument is not possible.

SMITH: Look here, I know how you feel, but I'm just curious to know how it squares with your other views. It just doesn't seem consistent with what I know about you.

BROWN: What do you mean?

SMITH: Well, just the way you manage your affairs, the way you treat people.

BROWN: What's that got to do with it?

SMITH: Well, nobody ever said you aren't a straight shooter, or don't believe in justice, or any of these things. Like that time when you——

BROWN: That hasn't got anything to do with it.

SMITH: You don't deny that you believe in people getting justice.

BROWN: Sure, I don't deny that, but——

---

[5] We have already mentioned data, premises, and evidence as things from which an argument starts, and we have tried to indicate what they are (p. 120). The common ground is, as we have been saying, a thing that must also exist if argument is to exist. How do we distinguish it from the other things? Particular assumptions on which an argument *immediately* depends, we call *premises*. On the basis of immediacy we may also distinguish data and evidence from common ground in our sense. Common ground refers to the more remote and general assumptions.

The willingness to rest on the dictates of reason is the most general assumption for argument, the thing that is usually assumed more or less unconsciously. But there are always other assumptions more or less remote and general. Often we proceed in argument without specifying, or even thinking about, such assumptions. Sometimes, however, we are forced to go back to find a common ground, and to specify it, in much the same way that we had to go back several stages when we tried to define the word *bungalow* for the Indian (pp. 86–87).

When you do have to go back stage by stage in an argument, what was remote and general becomes immediate and can be regarded as a premise. In the example of Smith and Brown, in the argument about anti-Semitism that we are about to explore, we see Smith, under pressure from Brown, trying to find a common ground. When he does find the common ground ("the question just boils down to what a man's interests are"), the common ground can then serve as a premise for a stage in the argument.

We have to think, in other words, what we mean by a term like *common ground,* and in what context it comes.

Smith has tried to locate the more specific common ground in the notion of justice. He has made Brown admit that he has a notion of justice. Now he has the job of making Brown see what justice would mean in a given situation. That may be a hard job, but at least there is a starting point in the common agreement that justice is desirable. But suppose that Brown denies that he is interested in justice:

BROWN: Look here, I know justice is all right, by and large. But, buddy, this is a tough world, and a man's got to look out for himself. He's got to watch his interests.

SMITH: O.K., let's forget that justice stuff. A man's got to watch his own interests. That's right. It's a good practical point of view.

BROWN: I'm a practical man.

SMITH: Well, the question just boils down to what a man's interests are, doesn't it?

BROWN: Sure.

SMITH: Now on the Jewish question, maybe our interests aren't as simple as they sometimes seem——

Smith has here dropped the common ground of justice and accepted the common ground of practical self-interest. Now his job is to show that in the light of self-interest, anti-Semitism may be a shortsighted policy. Again, he may not convince his friend, but he has a starting point.

When we are sure about our common ground, we can say to our readers or listeners: "We disagree about the question before us, but we really agree on a more important question than this one, on something that lies deeper. And since we do agree on that deeper question, I can show you that we ought reasonably to agree on the present question." We may not say this in so many words, but it is what we mean to convey.

● CAUTION

This same principle applies when you are writing a theme. Although you do not face an actual person, such as Mr. Brown, whom you wish to convince, you must try to imagine what that unseen audience would accept in common with you. If there is no common ground, your work will be in vain.

This does not mean that you must, in your theme, go back and back, and trace every stage. It does mean that, at the least, you should try to know what unspecified things you yourself are assuming, and should think of these assumptions in the context of the theme you are writing and the audience you are writing for.

The necessity for this becomes obvious with a highly controversial topic. For instance, if you are writing on the population explosion, you (whatever your own religious beliefs) would not assume that a conservative Catholic, a liberal Catholic, a Baptist, and an atheist would share the same common ground. If you are writing about foreign policy, you cannot readily assume the same common ground with both a pacifist and a nonpacifist.

This is nothing but common sense. Look before you leap. Think before you write.

What Argument Cannot Profitably Be About

Argument represents an appeal to reason, but in a given context, certain matters cannot be settled by reason alone. To illustrate:

> John comes upon a group obviously engaged in a heated argument and asks: "What are you arguing about?"
>
> JACK: Football!
>
> JOHN: What about football?
>
> JACK: About who won the Army-Navy game in 1962.
>
> JOHN (*laughs*): You idiots, what are you wasting your breath for? Why don't you telephone the information bureau at the newspaper and find out?

John is saying, in substance, that the resort to verification rather than to argument is appropriate when reliable evidence is available. But an argument may well arise about the reliability of the evidence appealed to for verification. For instance, a man puts up a large bet to back his memory that Navy won the Army-Navy game in 1962. Would he accept the statement by an anonymous voice on the telephone that Army had won? Might not the person who answers the telephone, even assuming that he is actually in the reference department of a newspaper, misread the record of the game? Might not a printer's error have crept into the record? The man with the money at stake might call for further investigation.

But let us be clear on the general point. If there is readily available an *acceptable* means of verification, the resort to argument is not, to say the least, grounded in common sense. If you have a ruler handy, why argue about the length of a piece of string?

The question of what constitutes acceptability may, however, remain. The parties to the argument about a piece of string may well accept the resort to a ruler. But we can imagine a situation in which a party to a dispute about measurement might refuse the ruler as too gross and call for a machinist's calipers. In general, the situation—the nature of the question at stake—determines the nature of acceptability. But of course the parties to a dispute may agree beforehand on the means of verification; then their agreement, not the degree of reliability of the evidence, is what is crucial.

Let us turn to another example of what argument cannot profitably be about. Suppose, again, that John comes upon the group and asks the same question, and Jack again replies, "Football!"

> JOHN: What about football?
>
> JACK: Which is the better game, football or basketball?

JOHN (*laughs*):   For the Lord's sake, what are you wasting your breath for? You can't settle that. A guy just likes the game he likes. Take me, I like tennis better than either of them.

John is right again. An argument about a matter of mere taste is useless, and insofar as the word *better*[6] in the above conversation merely means what one happens to like, there is no proper matter for argument.

In other words, a matter of absolute taste is not a matter for argument; only a judgment about matters concerning which one may be mistaken is a subject for argument.

We must remember, however, that there is no single hard and fast line between matters of taste and matters of judgment. Between the obvious extremes are a vast number of questions about which it is difficult to be sure. Each such question must be examined on its own merits.

Let us take, for example, an argument about whether Wordsworth or Longfellow is the finer poet. Are we concerned with taste or judgment?

If one person says, "I don't care what other people think, I just like Longfellow better," he is treating the question as a matter of taste. He is making no appeal to reason. But if another person tries to set up a standard for poetic excellence and tests the poets by it, he is appealing to judgment. He may say, for instance, that Wordsworth has greater originality in subject matter, has more serious ideas, and uses fresher and more suggestive metaphors. He may not win agreement, but he is at least using the method of argument; he is trying to appeal to reason in terms of an objective standard, and the argument is now about what constitutes such a standard. The fact that such an objective standard for literary excellence is difficult to devise does not alter the nature of his intention.

The Proposition

We have decided that, ordinarily, argument cannot be about a readily verifiable matter or a mere matter of taste. But before we say what it can be

---

[6] In ordinary usage, expressions such as *better, more desirable, to be preferred, greater, good, acceptable,* and so forth may indicate mere preference, an unarguable question of taste. When dealing with such an expression in an argument, one should ask questions that will determine whether or not the word has an objective content. Take the simple statement: "That is a good horse." We immediately have to ask, "Good for what?" For draying, for racing, for the bridle path, for the show ring, for the range? Or does the speaker merely mean that the horse is gentle, responsive, and affectionate, a sort of pet? By forcing the question we may discover the real meaning behind the original statement. Sometimes there is no meaning beyond the question of taste. Somebody says, "Jake is a good guy." If you force the question here and get the reply, "Oh, he's just regular. I like to be around him," you discover that the statement has no objective content. It tells you nothing about Jake. As the philosopher Spinoza would put it, Paul's opinion about Peter tells more about Paul than about Peter.

Useful forcing questions to apply to such expressions are: What is it good, desirable, useful for? What is it good in relation to? Is the standard invoked objective and therefore worth discussing?

about, let us go back to the "argument" about football. When Jack says that he and his friends are arguing about football, John quite naturally asks: "What about football?"

So we have the following dialogue:

JACK: Oh, about the Michigan-Purdue game last Saturday.
JOHN: Gosh, but you are thickheaded. What *about* the game?
JACK: About Randall and Bolewiensky.
JOHN: Well, I give up!

John is outdone by his friend's stupidity because he knows that one cannot reasonably argue about something just in general—about the game, for instance, or *about* Randall and Bolewiensky. So John now says: "What about Randall and Bolewiensky?"

JACK: About which is the more useful player. I think Randall is.
JOHN: Well it's sure time you were telling me.

John's thickheaded friend has finally managed to state what the argument is about. Jack is prepared to declare: "Randall is a more useful player than Bolewiensky." Somebody denies this, and the argument ensues. The argument is, then, about Jack's declaration. That declaration is *the* proposition of the argument.

A proposition is the declaration of a judgment. As such, it may be believed, doubted, or disbelieved. It is the only thing an argument can be about, for the end of argument is to establish belief or disbelief—or, we may add as a third possibility, to define the ground of continuing doubt.

● CAUTION: THE PROPOSITION

When we use the phrase "the proposition of the argument," we are using the term *proposition* in a special sense: the statement of what is to be established by the argument. This is perfectly clear in formal debate, where the proposition is embodied in a resolution. For example: *Resolved,* That the Electoral College should be abolished. Or: *Resolved,* That the language requirements for the B.A. degree should be abolished.

We must, however, distinguish this restricted use of the term from its more general use: any declaration of a judgment is a proposition. In other words, a proposition may be used for many purposes other than that of stating what is to be established by an argument. For instance, a proposition may be the premise of an argument, or the conclusion. Let us go back to the argument about football—or rather, about the proposition that, according to Jack's judgment, Randall is a more useful player than Bolewiensky. This judgment is disbelieved by John. So we have the following interchange:

JOHN: I don't believe that.
JACK: Well, why not, he made that great run?
JOHN: Sure he made a great run, but you said he was more useful.
JACK: Well, a great run is always useful.

JOHN: It sure is. But if we're going to argue about being useful, we ought to know what useful means. Well, here is what I take it to mean. It means being really good and dependable in more than one department. Will you accept that idea?

Here John has offered a proposition about what constitutes usefulness. If Jack accepts this statement as John intends it, they have a premise for their argument; for, clearly, to decide which of the two players is more useful, the arguers must settle on some notion of what usefulness is. Suppose that Jack does accept John's proposition as a premise, and, then, after some discussion, says: "OK, John, you win. Even if Randall is a great runner, he isn't more useful than Bolewiensky." So the conclusion of the argument is that Randall is not more useful than Bolewiensky, and this conclusion is also a proposition.

In other forms of discourse, and indeed in argument itself, propositions may appear with many different functions, but we must distinguish from all others *the* proposition, which asserts what is to be established in argument.

To look at matters another way, an argument is provoked by a proposition, it proceeds with the affirmation of a premise (or premises), and ends with an affirmation about the original proposition (belief, disbelief). This affirmation, consequent upon the appeal to reason, is the conclusion.

Locating the proposition

Formal debate, as we have said, clearly presents a proposition. But formal debate makes up a very small fraction of all argument, and ordinarily the proposition underlying argument is not formally stated—and, in fact, may not be stated at all. If we want to think straight, however, and want to be effective in argument, we ought to be able to state whatever proposition underlies our argument. We must know what is at stake, and the best way to know that is to frame the proposition, at least for ourselves.

When we come to writing a theme in argumentation, we find that the proposition provides our subject. If we don't know what the proposition is, we shall be floundering; the theme will lack point and unity; it will have poor organization. Even if argument is only a subordinate part of a theme that is primarily expository, descriptive, or narrative, we should make sure that we can state the proposition relevant to that part of the theme.

■ APPLICATIONS

I   What proposition do you think is involved in each of the following excerpts? What premises?

A   I would like first to point out that it is not right to suppose that all the poor live miserable, scarred lives. I don't hold any romantic notions about the poor, but I once was poor myself, and I believe there is a kind of subculture that they live in; they have a kind of confidence in themselves, a kind of completeness, as long as they are not driven to the bare edge of subsistence. My family was not very poor while I was growing up; it had been previously. In any case, I would say we lived a comparatively happy life.

—Paul Weiss and Jonathan Weiss: *Right and Wrong*.[7]

B   A modest but original Frenchman, Cagniard de la Tour, in 1837 poked around in beer vats of breweries. He dredged up a few foamy drops from such a vat and looked at them through a microscope and noticed that the tiny globules of the yeasts he found in them sprouted buds from their sides, buds like seeds sprouting. "They are alive, then, these yeasts, they multiply like other creatures," he cried.   —Paul de Kruif: *Microbe Hunters*.[8]

II   State three propositions. (Look carefully again at the definition of a proposition.) For each try to state what premises you think would be necessary for an argument about it. Now for one of the propositions write a short theme (250 words) embodying your argument. (You are undertaking this without having studied the principles of logic in this chapter. Do the best you can.)

The proposition: two kinds

For present purposes, as we have indicated (p. 128), we will refer only to the proposition that states what is to be established in argument. This proposition may take either of two forms.[9] The first states that something is a fact. The second states that something should be done. Even if we state a proposition negatively and say that something is *not* a fact, or that something should *not* be done, the basic type remains. We have merely turned it upside down.

Let us illustrate. When a lawyer states that his client has an alibi, he is dealing with a proposition of fact: his client *was* at a certain place, at a certain time—or so the lawyer declares. When a car salesman tries to sell a car, he presents a proposition of action: the prospect *should* buy that car. These are the propositions that the lawyer and the car salesman must, respectively, argue.

There is an important distinction between the kinds of argument that are appropriate for these propositions. For the proposition of fact, you have *only* to establish the key fact. For the proposition of action, you have to work from facts ("this car will save you money," etc.) to the need for action.

● CAUTION

There is a temptation to blur the distinction between the proposition of fact and that of action by saying that a fact leads to action. A fact often does lead to action, but this does not affect the distinction.

---

[7] From *Right and Wrong* by Paul Weiss and Jonathan Weiss, Basic Books, Inc., Publishers, New York, 1967. Reprinted by permission of Basic Books, Inc., Publishers.

[8] From *Microbe Hunters*, by Paul de Kruif. Reprinted by permission of Harcourt Brace Jovanovich, Inc.

[9] For other purposes, propositions may, of course, be treated according to other classifications. For instance, as singular, general, affirmative, negative, and so on.

For example, I am looking at poor John lying abed. I say: "That fellow has typhoid fever." This is a proposition of fact. It says no more than what it says: "The fact is that John has typhoid fever."

Now it is quite likely that if I announce to alarmed relatives that John has typhoid, somebody is likely to exclaim: "Call a doctor!" The exclamation, if put into the form of a proposition, would be: "A doctor should be called." This is a proposition of action: it recommends a certain action.

Let us grant that this second proposition does flow from the first. We set up a logical connection when we say: "John is sick, therefore a doctor should be called." But they are distinct, as we can see even from the foregoing statement, in which the first is given as ground for the second.

This may become clear if we point out that though the second does flow from the first as we have narrated the event, this logical connection is not a *necessary* one. We can have either proposition without the other. A certain fact may indeed lead to action. But to what action? Circumstances alter cases, and the context determines the action. The fact and the action are clearly distinguishable. For argument they must be treated separately.

■ APPLICATION

Which of the following propositions are of fact and which of action? (We are not talking about truth or falsity, merely about the type.)

1 You should vote in every election.
2 Tom Brown did not vote for a Republican in the last election.
3 Leisure is the basis of culture.
4 The capacity for work distinguishes the civilized man from the savage.
5 The civilized man should seek to recapture the sense of the wholeness of life that characterized earlier periods of man's development.
6 If you are going to be an engineer, you do not need to study history.

The clear proposition

A proposition should state clearly what is at stake. But it is not always easy to state matters clearly. For one thing, most words, as we ordinarily use them, do not have very precise limits. Even words that refer to an objective, physical situation may be vague. How "tall" is a tall man? Five feet eleven? Six feet? Six feet three? Any of these men is well above average height, but should all be considered "tall"? We may use "tallish," "tall," and "very tall" to indicate the scale, but even then we might hesitate about the choice of a word. Or take the word bald. How much hair must be lacking before we can say that a man is bald? The word does not fix an objective standard, although it does refer to an objective situation.

The problem is even more complicated when we come to such words as *good, cute,* or *progressive,* which do not refer to measurable attributes. If we hear, "Mr. Black is a progressive citizen," what are we to understand?

That Black works hard, pays his taxes, treats his family decently, and stays out of jail? Or that he is interested in bringing new factories to town and planting flowers in the park? Or that he has a certain political philosophy? The word seems to indicate some general approval on the part of the speaker, but we do not know exactly what, and the odds are that he does not know either. The word is vague.

Let us take another example of vagueness: "Soviet Russia is more democratic than England." A person defending this proposition might argue that Russia is more democratic because in its system there are no hereditary titles, because great fortunes cannot be accumulated, and because the worker is glorified. A person attacking the proposition might argue that England is more democratic because political power is in the hands of leaders chosen by the majority of voters in free elections, because there is freedom of speech, and because a man can choose his occupation.

The word *democratic* is vague. It is also ambiguous in that the two disputants are using it in different senses—and ambiguity, like vagueness, is an enemy of clarity. In any case, the disputants can have no argument on the original proposition until they have agreed on a definition of *democracy*. And this, of course, may mean that the argument will shift to a new proposition: "Democracy is so-and-so." To proceed they must find a common ground in a definition.

● CAUTION

We cannot expect a proposition to be clear in the same way a good argument is clear. We may very well make such a proposition as "Soviet Russia is more democratic than England," if we know what is at stake in the statement. The meaning of the word *democratic* is at stake, for the first thing. The concept is complex and requires a great deal of defining. In fact, there is no generally accepted definition, and so we should have to scout the various definitions. The problem is that there would be no way to put the content of our process of definition into the proposition. Sometimes we have to accept what we may call a *clue term* in the proposition—a term that points to the line of investigation but does not solve it. The word *democratic* in the proposition about Russia and England is such a clue term. We cannot make that proposition clearer. We simply have to recognize two things: the unsatisfactoriness of its meaning and the direction in which it points. Then we can proceed to clarify the proposition.

Though we often have to accept the inevitability of certain kinds of vagueness, this does not imply that we can accept *any* kind of vagueness. For instance, the proposition, "People should be good," is rather idiotic. That is, it is both obvious and vague. Certainly the word *democratic* is vague, too. But it is a much more effective clue than the word *good* to a line of fruitful discussion.

HISTORY OF THE QUESTION AND OCCASION OF THE DISCUSSION

Thus far we have been discussing the clarity of a proposition by thinking of the meaning of the words that compose it. Sometimes, however, we need to go beyond this and try to see the meaning of the proposition in some general context. One of the best ways to do this is to investigate what handbooks of debating call the *history of the question*. To do this is to inform ourselves about the circumstances that brought the argument about. For example, if we are arguing that such-and-such a bill to raise tariffs should be passed, we cannot know what is at stake in the proposition unless we know something of how tariffs have affected our economy in the past and what situations, and motives, generally lead to the raising of tariffs. And it is equally important, of course, to investigate the particular situation behind the present bill—what we may call the *occasion of the discussion*.

For almost any truly important subject some knowledge of the history and of the occasion is essential if we are to grasp what is at stake. Topics do not exist in a vacuum.

■ APPLICATIONS

I Are any of the following propositions not to be profitably argued—for instance, are any mere matters of taste? Are any vague? If so, discuss the nature of the vagueness.

1 The dog is man's best friend.
2 A good book is the best friend a man can have.
3 No good Democrat will vote for a Republican.
4 No good citizen will be a slave to his party.
5 The atomic bomb is the most useful invention since the steam engine.

II Frame an unclear proposition and a proposition you consider acceptable for six of the following topics:

Religion	Tennis
United Nations	Patriotism
War	Education
Motherhood	Democracy
Black Power	Illegitimacy

The single proposition

An argument must have a main point if it is to make sense. That main point is what the proposition of the argument should state, and the proposition should state only the *main* point. In other words, the proposition behind an argument should be single.

Let us take an example. A college student named George is very depressed, lacks energy, has headaches and poor digestion, and doesn't seem to be able to study. A friend says: "You should see a doctor."

There are many factors in the situation behind the proposition—George's depression, lack of energy, and so forth—but the proposition is single. It involves a single decision, a single act: to go or not to go to the doctor.

George does go to a doctor, who says: "You ought to take more exercise and study harder." This, clearly, is two propositions, and the fact that they occur in the same sentence doesn't make any difference. True, the reasons that make the doctor decide on more exercise and the reasons that make him decide on more study may be intimately related. They must be intimately related, for they have to do with George's total condition and the causes of that condition. But there are two independent propositions: (1) exercise more and (2) study harder.

We see this fact immediately if we think of George going to another doctor, who says that George should get a job on a pick-and-shovel gang to build up his strength and should, for the time being, forget study altogether. And another doctor may say: "Take no exercise at all, for your heart is very bad, but try to develop an interest in your studies."

We don't know anything about George, and we don't know which doctor is right, but we do see, by common sense, that to accept one of the ideas, that about exercise, doesn't necessarily mean that we have to accept the other one, that about study. They are independent propositions; we may accept one and not the other. And if they are independent, then two arguments, not one, are involved.

● CAUTION

1   The fact that two ideas appear in one sentence does not mean that they are one proposition. They are still two.
2   The fact that two ideas relate to the same situation (such as George's ill health) does not mean that they are one proposition. They are still two.
3   If there are two (or more) propositions, each has to be argued individually.

The main proposition and supporting points

To say that an argument must have a main point, a main proposition, is not to say that more than one idea may not well appear in the course of the argument. In support of the main proposition the arguer may make a number of different individual points, and each point will, in itself, represent a proposition and will have to be argued individually. But if the argument is to have unity and coherence, such supporting points must be subordinated to the main proposition and have a significant relation to it.

Below is a student theme arguing for coed dormitories. In order to make clear the line of argument, the instructor requested that the student include a marginal commentary indicating the relation of minor propositions to the main proposition.

WHY I AM FOR JOINT DORMITORIES

Our college has not yet gone coed, but it is certain that, in the face of the local pressure from students and with the example of places like Princeton and

1st Minor Proposition:
Arguments for coeducation support joint dormitories.

Main Proposition:
Joint dormitories are desirable; implication that they prepare for life.

2nd Minor Proposition:
Purpose of education is to prepare for life.

3rd Minor Proposition:
Part of preparation is to get knowledge.

4th Minor Proposition:
Nonintellectual preparation also important.

5th Minor Proposition:
Part of nonintellectual preparation is to know women.

6th Minor Proposition:
Presence of girls helps intellectual preparation: illustration.

7th Minor Proposition:
Generational objection to coeducation based on past experience, not now relevant; distraction.

8th Minor Proposition:
Presence of girls gives the student impression that what he learns is relevant.

9th Minor Proposition:
Acquaintance with girls as "people" prepares for world.

10th Minor Proposition:
Friendships with girl companions make for more intelligent marriages.

11th Minor Proposition:
Divorces come from romantic notions not based on real acquaintance with opposite sex.

Repeat: 1st Minor Proposition.

7A: Repeat 7th Minor Proposition in reference to joint dormitories.

12th Minor Proposition:
Objection on moral grounds not consistent with present rules.

Yale, the day is not far off. The arguments for coeducation are well known, and it would be old hat to go into them now except for one thing. If those arguments are worth considering at all, they point beyond the simple fact of coeducation to joint dormitories as well.

I am going to review some of the old arguments for coeducation to make myself clear on my main point: joint dormitories. As everyone agrees, the main purpose of education is to prepare for life. Now a big part of that preparation is to get knowledge and skills in a systematic way, but intellectual equipment alone is not enough. It is equally important to learn to live with people, and half of them are female.

This idea leads to two points: One is that having girls around actually helps the intellectual side of things. They look at the world differently and open up new ideas and perspectives. With girls in a class, the play *Othello* would always look different. Girls can help to educate boys just as boys help to educate them. When older people like my father object to coeducation because they think girls will be a distraction, they forget that the distraction in their day came from the fact that boys and girls only saw each other once a term at a prom. If you see girls every day, it's not such a big deal, and they will make you feel that what you are learning belongs to the real world outside.

My other big point is that the regular presence of girls makes you look at them as people, and so helps prepare you for life. With girls around, you can have genuine friendships and get to know them as people. Then if two people happen to fall in love, they are able to judge each other on a sounder basis. I have recently read an article by a psychologist who says that most divorces are the result of disillusionment about some childish idea of romance.

I have gone over these old arguments to show that they lead to joint dormitories. I know what the objections are, and I'll say that if any of them makes sense, I lose the game. But I don't think I will.

First, there is the old objection about distraction. I think I have proved in my argument above that once a college goes coed, girls are no longer a distraction, and everyone just gets on with his work.

The second big objection is morality. I will begin to answer that by asking a question: Right now girls are allowed in our rooms till ten o'clock two nights a week and till eleven-thirty on Saturday. Would there be any moral difference if girls lived in the dormitory and visited in our rooms? Can morality be measured by the

13th Minor Proposition: Morality in joint dorms would derive from general social morality.

14th Minor Proposition: Rules by college can control behavior no better than rules by parents.

15th Minor Proposition: Values of the individual are crucial.

clock? Joint dorms would not create a new morality; their moral standards would reflect the morality of society in general.

This reminds me of another objection. The administration says that parents would object, that they want the college to stand *in loco parentis*. That may be true, but college students, in the end, are going to behave according to the moral values they bring with them to college. What parents need to do is to help the child build his values. If he hasn't got decent ones by the time he is in college, his parents have flunked the course.

ANALYSIS OF THEME

Here we have the main proposition and fifteen minor propositions (two repeated). Each minor proposition can be discussed independently; taken together they support the main proposition, they constitute the discussion.

Some of the minor propositions are directly supportive of the main proposition, for instance, (1), which affirms that the arguments for coeducation support joint dormitories, and (2). Other minor propositions indirectly support the main proposition in various ways. The following chart will illustrate the relationships.

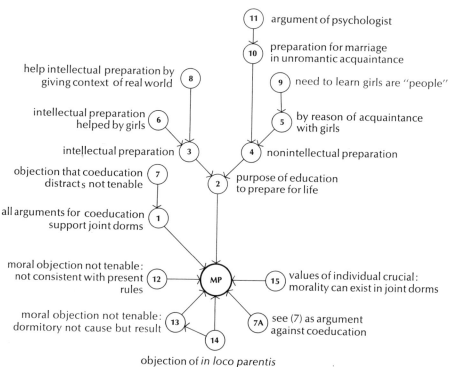

11 argument of psychologist

10 preparation for marriage in unromantic acquaintance

help intellectual preparation by giving context of real world — 8

9 need to learn girls are "people"

intellectual preparation helped by girls — 6

5 by reason of acquaintance with girls

intellectual preparation — 3

4 nonintellectual preparation

objection that coeducation distracts not tenable — 7

2 purpose of education to prepare for life

all arguments for coeducation support joint dorms — 1

moral objection not tenable: not consistent with present rules — 12 — MP — 15 values of individual crucial: morality can exist in joint dorms

moral objection not tenable: dormitory not cause but result — 13

7A see (7) as argument against coeducation

14

objection of *in loco parentis* untenable: no rules really work

Observe that this chart is *not* concerned with a chain of cause and effect. It is, instead, concerned with a chain of reasons for having made a statement. For instance, (1) points to (MP), not because (1) causes (MP), but because (1) is a reason for holding (MP); that is, one should believe in joint dormitories (says the author) as a consequence of having accepted the arguments for coeducation. Or we could read back from (MP) through (2) to (3) and (4) as follows: we accept the joint dormitories, for, the purpose of education being to prepare for life, the joint system fulfills this requirement, in both intellectual and nonintellectual terms.

■ APPLICATIONS

I Examine carefully the points in the argument for joint dormitories. Can you think of any additional points that might have been made in favor of the arrangement? Can you think of any additional points against the arrangement that the author has not thought of? If so, can you answer such objections? Remember that the question here is not whether you yourself approve or disapprove of joint dormitories. It is to inspect the argument.

II Settle on some proposition you think may provide you with the subject of a theme later on. Work out a number of relevant minor propositions and embody them in a chart. Then make a sentence outline in which the logical connections are specified.

An issue

To treat the main proposition in an argument will, as we have seen (from the theme on joint dormitories), involve minor propositions that must be argued individually. When such a minor proposition *must* be proved in order to win the argument, that minor proposition is called an *issue*. An issue, then, is a proposition crucial to the argument: if you defeat it, you defeat the argument. If there happens to be more than one issue in an argument (as there usually is), the defeat of *only* one still spells defeat for the argument. For instance, in the theme on joint dormitories, the author accepts both the matter of distraction and the matter of morality as issues: if the situation distracts from work, the argument is lost, *or* if the situation entails immorality (to be defined), the argument is lost.

Let us take another, and simpler, example. The constitution of a certain college honor society, the Corinthians, specifies that to be eligible for membership a student must (1) have a scholastic average of B or above, (2) have won a letter in at least one college sport, (3) have made some substantial contribution to the general good of the college community, and (4) have conducted himself as a gentleman. William Smith is proposed for election. His sponsor argues that Smith has made an A average, has won the state junior championship in swimming, has brought about a reform of the student council system by his editorials in the college paper, and is a person of high character and good manners. Smith seems certain of election until one Corinthian refers to the constitution and regretfully points out that Smith cannot fulfill requirement 2. "But he is an excellent athlete," the sponsor retorts. "He can outswim anybody in this school."

"That's not the point," the other Corinthian replies. "The constitution explicitly states that to be eligible a student must have won a letter in at least one sport. Our college has no swimming team and therefore does not give a letter for swimming."

If the constitution is taken seriously, Smith's eligibility must be denied. The proposition is that Smith is eligible for membership in the Corinthians, and the constitution is the source of authority for the requirements for eligibility.

Each of the four requirements implies a proposition: "Smith has an average of B or above," for example. Each of those propositions is a minor one in the argument, the proposition of which is, "Smith should be elected to the Corinthians." Each is, also, an issue; that is, to fail one means that Smith is not eligible. But here we come to an important distinction. About three of the issues—1, 3, and 4—there is no debate. Such issues outside debate by general consent are called *admitted* issues. An issue (or issues) not admitted is *crucial*. In the case of the eligibility of Smith, the issue of the college letter is crucial: all hinges on this.

But suppose somebody says, "Well, Smith ought to be elected, and if a man like Smith can't get in, what's the meaning of the Corinthians?"

This remark may be true and just—in a general sense. Smith may be the sort of man the college would willingly honor. But—and here is the rub— eligibility isn't based on a general notion of suitability, but on the constitution. Perhaps someone else then says, "The constitution of the Corinthians ought to be changed." Maybe it should, but this is a new proposition and would start a new argument.

This situation is similar to that in certain cases at law in which one may feel that the letter of the law defeats justice. For example, a defending lawyer in a first-degree murder case may argue that his client had suffered intolerable provocation, that the victim had grievously slandered the defendant's wife, and that the defendant, a simple man, raised in rather primitive surroundings, had thought killing the slanderer to be the only course of honor. The prosecution argues that these facts are not issues in the case, because the legal definition of murder makes no recognition of the provocation of slander or of the personal background of the accused. The prosecution is, of course, right. The law defines the issues by which the proposition that the defendant is guilty of murder in the first degree must stand or fall. If the jury does acquit the defendant, it does so out of sentiment, prejudice, or some notion of justice that is inconsistent with the law.

We must keep firmly in mind the distinction between law (or rules, e.g., the constitution of the Corinthians) and justice. This question is perennial in all institutions of society; the most famous instance in our history arose from the legal status of slavery as opposed to the injustice of the institution. To turn to the ordinary workings of law, we know how, with a conviction, a jury may recommend clemency, or a judge may suspend sentence, or give a light one.

Analysis of the proposition

In the case of William Smith and the Corinthians, or of the murderer, the issues are handed us on a silver platter: in the first case the constitution of the society defines eligibility; in the second, the law defines murder. But ordinarily, things are not that simple, and we must locate the issues for ourselves. We must, in other words, analyze the proposition.

To analyze the proposition means simply to apply the method of analysis that we have discussed under the chapter on Exposition. We try to sort out the various elements involved in a situation. This is one of the more obvious instances in which the method of one mode of discourse, here exposition, is intertwined with another, here argument.

It is important, in this connection, to remember that there are, as we have seen, two kinds of proposition, the proposition of fact and that of action. The method for analyzing one is not the same as that for analyzing the other.

ANALYSIS AND PROPOSITIONS OF FACT

Let us take some propositions of fact and see how we should go about analyzing them to determine the issues.

We shall begin with a very simple instance, one in which there can be only a single issue. Two men in the wilderness wish to cross a stream. One of them proposes that they drop a tree across it, but the other objects that the available tree is too short. Though they can establish the height of the tree, they cannot establish the width of the stream. Therefore the proposition that the tree is long enough is a matter of judgment and is subject to argument. Several arguments, good or bad, may be offered on either side, but there is only one issue: Is the tree long enough? In such cases of simple fact, the proposition itself establishes the issue. But in other cases the fact may not be simple.

Let us take the proposition: "John did right in leaving his fortune to the Ashford Medical Foundation."

First, is this a proposition of fact? It may look like a proposition of action, for John did perform an action. Certainly this would be a proposition of action if it were stated: "John will do right to . . ." Or: "John should leave . . ." But in its original form, the proposition concerns an action that has *already* taken place and concerns a judgment of the value of the event. This becomes clear if we translate the proposition into the standard form: "John's conduct in leaving his fortune to the Ashford Medical Foundation *is* (or *was*) right."

Second, how can we establish the issues? To do so, we must decide what we mean by the word *right*—a vague word in the predicate of the proposition. Suppose the opponents agree that a deed is ethically right *only* if it fulfills *all* of the following requirements: (1) the doer is responsible; (2) the doer undertakes the deed for a laudable motive; and (3) the consequences of the deed are beneficial. The issues then become:

1 Was John of sound mind when he made his will?
2 Was his motive laudable?
3 Was the money to be used for a beneficial activity?

The affirmative must establish *all* of these issues in order to win the argument. Suppose that there is no doubt of John's sanity and no doubt that the money will be used for a good purpose. Suppose that these facts or issues are admitted. The second issue then becomes crucial. If the negative establishes that John, in a fit of fury at his daughter for making a marriage without his consent, changed his will to leave his money to the foundation, his motive is a bad one, and the proposition is lost.

Where a fact is complex, as in the proposition above, the locating of the issues becomes a matter of analyzing the fact. In practice this may mean defining the key word (or words) in the proposition, as *right* was defined above.

■ APPLICATION

Analyze three of the following propositions of fact into minor propositions and issues:

Big-time college football destroys sportsmanship.
Air travel is safer than automobile travel.
Christianity is the basis of American democracy.
The doctrine of state rights caused the defeat of the Confederacy.
Democracy makes for military inefficiency.

ANALYSIS AND PROPOSITIONS OF ACTION

To analyze a proposition of action, to be certain that we understand all sides of an argument and can answer positions taken by possible opponents, or simply to clear our own minds, we should systematically set up all the propositions we can think of on each side of the main proposition. The minor propositions will tend to go in pairs, one *for* and one *against*.

Then we should examine the propositions with these questions in mind:

1 Are the propositions all significant?
2 Do they cover the subject?
3 Do they overlap one another?
4 Does any proposition really include more than one idea?

Example A farmer wants to convince his wife to move to town. He jots down some reasons to give her.

1 Better income
2 Better schools
3 House on farm not convenient
4 Social life fuller

5   Better cultural facilities
6   Difficulty of getting farm labor
7   Susie's dental work

That evening he takes the matter up with his wife. On 1, she immediately counters by saying that in the country their expenses are much less than they would be in town, and adds that he will be coming into a nice inheritance, and therefore they don't need the extra income, anyway. On 2, the matter of schools, she replies that schools are not all of education, that getting acquainted with nature and developing one's own resources in solitude are important, too. She grants that the schools in town are better, but reminds him that he has agreed to send the children east to a prep school. So, by her argument, this question is, finally, not significant. As for 3, she admits that the house is not convenient, but says that it has great charm and the heating system can be fixed. For 4, she replies that they now have more guests than they really want, especially in the summer; then she brings in a new proposition, that they both love the outdoors, and horses and hunting. On the matter of cultural facilities, 5, she says she would like some of the concerts in Smithville, but can make do with radio and hi-fi. As for labor, 6, he can get more machinery to make up for the difficulty of finding labor. She agrees that the dental work for the girl, 7, is important, but she can drive to Smithville once a week to a good dentist there.

From the discussion, the husband now discovers that in 1 he had involved two ideas, not one, omitting to specify the question of need for added income, which in part would arise from the plan to send the children away to school in the East. This need would, in general, raise another subject for debate. He confesses to himself, too, that 2 puts forward a not very significant point, in the light of the plan for prep schools; and as for the matter of outdoor life, he had failed to consider the subject at all. On reflection, he agrees with his wife about social life and drops that topic.

But there are still points of disagreement. He does want more money. His farm is not suited to mechanization. So the systematic husband scribbles down a new summary of the problem.

Husband		*Wife*	
1	need more money	1	no—inheritance, lower expenses on farm
2	better income in town	2	admitted—but not significant
3	admitted	3	schools not relevant
4	house on farm not convenient	4	admitted—but charming
5	admitted	5	love of outdoor life
6	admitted	6	social life now satisfactory
7	admitted	7	cultural life satisfactory
8	farm not suited to machinery	8	buy machinery
9	Susie's dental work	9	will drive to town

Here we see two sorts of changes.

First, the husband has brought his list into better order. He has now divided his first minor proposition into two propositions. And he has better covered the subject, in that the love of outdoor life is considered.

For the second kind of change, we see that both parties have made certain admissions. The husband does not now see 6 and 7 as important. He admits 5, too; outdoor life is important to him, but in admitting this he merely indicates that he must weigh this value against other values. The wife makes admissions on 2 and 4, but with reservations; she does not think that what she admits is very important to her final position: that in 2 the increased income would be offset by added expenses, and in 4 the charm offsets inconvenience, to a degree anyway.

As things now stand, we cannot be sure how the couple will finally decide. But we can see that now the argument has been brought to sharper focus. The husband will, it would seem from the last summary, argue on the matter of money, 1 and 2, and on the matter of labor and mechanization, 8, with, no doubt, some deep thought on 5 as balanced against moving to town.

What we have been really doing thus far is to follow the process by which an argument might be brought to essential focus. We have been analyzing what is at stake in the proposition "We should move to town."

But suppose the husband suddenly confesses to his wife that he has not laid all the facts before her, that his doctor has just told him he has a bad heart and strongly advises him to reduce his physical activity. The husband's health would then become the crucial issue, and the family would probably move to town.

■ APPLICATION

In the Application on page 137 you were asked to settle on some topic that you thought might later be good for a theme, to state the main proposition and develop the minor ones, then to work out a chart and a sentence outline. Go back to that material, and in the light of what you have learned since, criticize it. If it is not acceptable, revise it. Now write a theme of 500 words.

Evidence

What we have been studying thus far is really preparatory to the joining of battle in argument. We have been deciding what kind of game we are to play—draw poker, stud, or seven-card stud—and have been deciding what the stakes will be. The next step is to assemble the evidence and start reasoning from it. Here we are playing our cards. Here we win or lose.

When you get into an argument, your opponent will be from Missouri. To him, seeing is believing, and what he wants to see is evidence. Without evidence, you can offer only your unsupported views, which you already know your opponent will not accept—for if they had been acceptable to him, there would have been no argument in the first place.

What constitutes evidence?

There are two kinds of evidence, of *fact* and of *opinion*.

The most obvious and natural appeal is to the facts. We appeal, we say, to the "facts of the case," and we take facts as hard and decisive.

But we also appeal to the opinion of other people who are supposed to have some special authority. In the courtroom "expert testimony" is called evidence—the testimony of the psychiatrist, the medical examiner, the ballistics expert, the handwriting expert, and so on. Presumably the expert bases his testimony on facts, but what the jury is asked to consider is his *opinion*—his judgment of the facts. An expert may be wrong, and experts often disagree among themselves, but what they disagree about is ordinarily not the facts themselves, but their interpretation of the facts.[10]

This expert opinion is not, however, the only kind that may appear as evidence. The law also recognizes, as does common sense, what is called the "character witness," an ordinary person who is called on to offer his opinion as to the character of the defendant.

What tests can we apply to evidence?

Fact as evidence

A fact must be a fact. Direct observation by a reliable witness (what constitutes reliability we shall come to) is a powerful indication of fact, but is not infallible. What is offered as observed fact may, on occasion, turn out to be merely a mistaken opinion. We well know this pattern from detective stories. A "fact" points to the guilt of a certain character, who is arrested by the stupid police sergeant. The clever detective proves that the "fact"—that Miss Perkins was observed near the scene of the crime at a certain hour—is not a fact at all: the true criminal, the beloved old butler, had taken Miss Perkins' hooded raincoat and worn it while committing the murder on the moor. But justice is done: Miss Perkins is exonerated and the murderer brought to book.

A fact must be (1) verified or (2) attested by a reliable source.

VERIFICATION

Sometimes observed "facts" may be established by reference to some mechanism of observation more accurate than human perception. For instance, the camera is a more dependable device than the human eye for determining which race horse's nose pokes first over the finish line. And many a football referee has been embarrassed by a camera.

Verification may come, however, not by the recording of an event, but by the appeal to some regularity in nature such as we have encountered in

---

[10] It may be held that there is no hard and fast distinction between evidence of fact and that of opinion—that what we take as fact (say, that ice melts at 32 degrees Fahrenheit, or that the Declaration of Independence was signed on July 4, 1776) is held to be fact by the assertion of a person (or persons) of special competence, that is, of an expert. By this line of thought the distinction between evidence of fact and that of opinion would become a distinction between items of evidence supported very persuasively and those supported less persuasively —that is, by "experts" of greater or lesser authority. A fact, then, is evidence about which there is no reasonable doubt and hence general agreement, while opinion signifies matters about which even admittedly competent and informed men *may* differ. The distinction, as originally given, is nevertheless useful for practical purposes, and is commonly made.

studying causal analysis: that a certain type of cord will not support a certain weight, that potassium permanganate will explode under certain conditions, that the robin's egg is a certain shade of blue with brown markings, that *rigor mortis* sets in at a certain time after death. Each such fact belongs to a pattern in nature that is observable, and to test a particular fact we refer it to the pattern. We have an example in a story of one of Abraham Lincoln's law cases. A witness testified that he had observed a certain event. Lincoln asked him how, and he replied that he had seen it by moonlight. Be producing an almanac, Lincoln showed that there had been no moon on the night in question. Lincoln tested the fact by referring it to a natural pattern.

FACT ESTABLISHED BY TESTIMONY

Suppose, however, that the testimony offered cannot be tested against such a natural pattern. What questions may be asked to determine the reliability of the evidence offered by the witness? Four questions are relevant in such a case:

1 Was there opportunity for the witness to observe the event?
2 Is the witness physically capable of observing the event?
3 Is the witness intellectually capable of understanding the event and reporting it accurately?
4 Is the witness honest?

The first question is clear enough, but the others are a little more complicated. For instance, if a blind newsman attests that Bill Sims was present in a railway station at such a time, how good is his evidence? Was he capable of observing the event? If it can be demonstrated that the blind man is capable of recognizing a familiar step and is acquainted with the step of Bill Sims, who stopped at this newsstand every day to buy cigarettes, then it can be assumed that the newsman is capable of recognizing Bill Sims' presence. If, furthermore, it can be accepted that the blind newsman has common sense, is not given to delusions, flights of fancy, or exaggeration, and has a good memory, then it can be assumed that he is intellectually able to understand and report the event. What remains is the question of honesty. If the blind newsman has no connection with the case, if no malice, profit, or other special interest is involved, then it can be assumed that his report is an honest one. But if some motive that might make him color or falsify the report can be established, then his report probably would not be readily accepted, especially by a person who is hostile or indifferent.

The case we have given here for reliability—the blind newsman's testimony—is a relatively simple one, but it illustrates the kind of questions that must be raised in all situations involving testimony. A historian trying to determine the truth about an event long past, a congressional committee conducting a hearing on an economic situation, a farmer shopping for a new tractor, all are engaged in assessing the reliability of testimony and must ask the same questions. And so must you, on occasion after occasion, in daily life as well as in your college reading and writing.

Never admit as fact what cannot be (1) verified or (2) reliably attested.

Opinion as evidence

Parallel to tests for the admission of fact as evidence, we can set up tests for the admission of opinion. Corresponding to verifiability—the first requirement for the admission of a fact—we find the authority for an opinion. There is no use in introducing an opinion to support an argument if the opinion will carry little or no weight. For instance, no lawyer would want to introduce as expert a witness who had no reputation for competence in his particular field. The manufacturer of athletic supplies wants a champion, not a dud, to endorse his tennis racket, and the manufacturer of cosmetics wants a lady of fashion or a famous actress to give a testimonial for his facial cream. We should be as sure as possible that an authority we invoke in an argument is a real authority: a second-rate navy is no navy, when the moment of combat comes, and a second-rate authority is no authority.

AUTHORITY AND THE TEST OF EXPERIENCE

How do we find out if an authority is a real authority? "Ask the man who owns one," a famous automobile advertising slogan suggests; and the maker of a washing machine shows the picture of a happy housewife standing by her prized appliance. The advertisers here appeal to authority on the principle that the proof of the pudding is in the eating: ask the eater, for he is an authority. This is a kind of rough-and-ready authority based on experience, useful but very limited in the degree of conviction that it can carry. Very probably the automobile buyer has not used many different makes of car, and the housewife has not used many different kinds of washing machine. The opinion of an impartial technical expert who had tested many makes of car or washing machine for efficiency, durability, and so forth, would carry much more authority. Here we appeal to experience, too, but to the experience of the expert. And here we are again concerned with principles we have met in studying causal analysis, that of a uniformity in nature and that of the number of samples from which one can reason (pp. 110–13). The expert knows the principles involved, and he has a wide acquaintance with "samples" of cars, washing machines, or whatever.

AUTHORITY AND THE APPEAL TO SUCCESS

Authority is very often based on an appeal to success. The rich man is supposed to know how to make money, the famous painter how to paint pictures, the heavyweight champion how to fight. Success carries prestige and predisposes us to accept the pronouncement of the successful man.

But we should still scrutinize success as a criterion for authority. Perhaps the rich man got rich by luck—he happened to get into business at a time of expansion and rising markets. No doubt he himself attributes his success to his own sterling character, shrewdness, and indefatigable industry, but we may be more inclined to trust the evidence of the economic situation of his time. Or, the famous painter may have been lucky enough to hit upon a popular fashion; history is littered with the carcasses of artists of all kinds whose success was the accident of the moment. The heavyweight gives us a better instance, for it is a simpler one—he merely had to square off with one man and slug it out. But perhaps a granite jaw, a fighting heart, and an explosive punch gave him the championship, and all that he has to say about training, footwork, and strategy may be wrong. He didn't succeed by luck, as did the businessman or the painter; he really did flatten his opponent—but he may give the wrong reasons for his success.

The fact of success doesn't mean that the successful man really knows the conditions of his success. And he can speak with authority only if he does know. Many successful people are like the man who lived to be a hundred and revealed his secret for long life: "I never read less than one chapter of the Holy Writ a day or drink more than three slugs of likker a night."

AUTHORITY AND TRANSFERENCE

Not infrequently we encounter an appeal to what, for lack of a better phrase, we may call authority by transference. Because a man is considered an authority in one field, it is assumed that he is an authority on anything. The famous musician is used as an authority on statesmanship, the great mathematician is appealed to as an authority on morality, and the great physicist on religion. This sort of reasoning is obviously nonsensical and often pernicious, for it is simply a means of exploiting the gullibility of the audience.

AUTHORITY AND TIME

Authority, too, may have some relation to time. What was acceptable as authority at one time may not be acceptable at another. In any field where the body of knowledge is constantly being enlarged, timeliness is very important. A book on chemistry written ten years ago may now lack authority, or a history of the American Civil War written in 1875 may now be misleading. Should George Washington's views on foreign policy influence us?

We want the best authority of *our* time.

CHOOSING AN AUTHORITY

Finding the man who knows is, of course, different from finding out for ourselves what he knows. If we are dealing with authority presumably based on experience, we can ask about the breadth of experience (one washing machine or ten?) and the intelligence and training of the person who has had the experience. If we are dealing with authority based on success, we may inquire into the nature of the success (how much was luck?) and into the capacity of the successful person for analyzing the means to success. And we should not forget to ask if the authority of the successful person is being used as authority by transference. Furthermore, we must ask if the authority is timely.

Let us suppose, for example, that we wish to find an authority on some point of American history. It will not do to go to the library and take down the first book on the subject. The mere fact of print bestows no authority, for every error is somewhere embalmed between boards. We have to find out something about the author. Is his book of recent date? (That is, would he have available the latest research on the subject?) Does he have any special bias or prejudice which must be discounted? Does he occupy a responsible position or has he had other professional recognition? (That is, is he on the faculty of some good college or university, have his works been favorably reviewed, and so forth?) How do his views compare with the views of other historians of recognized importance? To answer these questions means that we have to find out something about American history, even though we are not capable of settling the particular point in question by our own investigation.

AUTHORITY AND THE AUDIENCE

One more thing must be considered. The authority we use must convince a particular audience. Effective authority is authority that is acceptable to the particular audience. The Mohammedan *Koran* carries no authority to a Catholic, the Pope carries no authority to a Methodist, and the first chapter of Genesis carries no authority to a geologist. If we can use an authority that our audience already knows and respects, we have an initial advantage. If this is not possible, then we must establish the prestige of the authority. We can sometimes do this merely by informing the audience, but sometimes we must resort to persuasion. As we have said, the discussion of persuasion will be taken up in the next chapter.

■ APPLICATIONS

I   In the trial of the case described below, what elements would be taken as evidence? Which would be evidence of fact, and which of opinion? Which elements, without being evidence, might be used to influence a jury?

> Percival Jones, a young instructor in Sullivan College, while driving down an icy street at 1 A.M., got into a skid, struck a pedestrian, and killed him. The accident occurred in a 35-mile zone, and neither of two witnesses testified that Jones was going faster—or much faster—than that. But a block before the spot where the accident occurred there was a traffic sign warning against the pavement when wet. After the accident, Jones walked to an all-night diner and called the police.
>
> When they arrived, his manner was cool, detached, and apparently unconcerned. The police discovered that his driver's license, recently expired, had not been renewed. There was no indication of alcohol on his breath, but it developed that two years earlier he had been arrested for driving while intoxicated. With him in the car on the present occasion was a young woman,

a student of his, who was out of the girls' dormitory without permission, after hours. It developed that she was in possession of a pass key that Jones, some weeks earlier, had deviously procured.

At the college, Jones was regarded as a brilliant teacher, but a "trouble-maker," as the dean put it, and was irregular about turning in grades and attending faculty meetings. But he devoted a good deal of his own time to coaching the student dramatic club. He was the son of a respected Episcopal clergyman in an upstate parish, well known for his work among the poor.

The victim of the accident was identified as one Leo Morris, aged 69, of no certain address or employment. Autopsy showed that at the time of his death there was, in his blood, a concentration of alcohol of .10 percent. One of the two witnesses, both companions of Morris, testified that Jones had not sounded his horn and that when he inspected the body, he said, "Gee, I've cool-cocked the old twirp."

II Analyze the evidence you have offered in your last theme. Would you care to revise it now?

Reasoning

Once we have assembled our evidence and tested its acceptability, we need to find out for ourselves, and show to others, what the evidence means in relation to the argument, how the evidence will lead to our conclusion. This is not a new process for us. The whole business of living, from first to last, is a long education in the use of reason. Fire burns, cats scratch, pulling things off tables brings a frown or a spanking—we learn these great truths early. Later on we learn other truths—a stitch in time saves nine, honesty is the best policy, to be good is to be happy. We say we learn from experience (or from somebody else's experience), but that is not quite true. Experience would teach us nothing if we could not reason about it.

Reasoning is the process by which the mind moves from certain data (evidence) to a conclusion. We can make this progress to a conclusion— we make this inference—because we recognize some regularity in our world. We are back, in other words, to the principle of uniformity, which we talked about in connection with cause (see pp. 110–11).

This is the process by which we put the particular case up against the general principle to see whether it fits. By inspecting many green apples, we arrive at the conclusion that green apples are sour; therefore we do not eat green apples no matter how invitingly they hang on the bough before us. We know that heavy drinkers tend to have unsteady hands; therefore we don't want Dr. Lush to take out our tonsils.

Induction: generalization

The kind of reasoning by which we arrive at the conclusion that green apples are sour is called *induction*. Let us examine two examples of this kind of reasoning.

A businessman has, at different times, hired five boys from the Hawkins School and has found them all honest, well-mannered, and well-educated. Therefore, when the sixth boy comes along for a job, the man will be inclined to hire him. In other words, the man has generalized from the five instances to the conclusion that all boys from Hawkins School are honest, well-mannered, and well-educated. The man has made a generalization, moving from a number of particular instances to the general conclusion that all instances of the type investigated will be of this same sort.

To take a second example of generalization: after long observation men have concluded that water always freezes at a certain temperature, 32 degrees Fahrenheit. We assume that the same kind of event in nature always happens in the same way under the same conditions. Without this assumption of uniformity we could not accept the conclusions based on the examination of a number of individual instances. And, in fact, all science is based on this assumption.

But even if the same principle of uniformity is applied in reasoning about the boys of Hawkins School that is applied in reasoning about the freezing point of water, the two conclusions compel different degrees of assent. We scarcely doubt that the next pail of water we leave out will freeze at a certain temperature, but we do doubt that absolutely all graduates of Hawkins School are models of honesty. We recognize here that uniformity in human nature is scarcely as dependable as uniformity in nature.

THE INDUCTIVE LEAP

The conclusion about the boys of Hawkins School is offered, as we have said, as a generalization—that is, as a proposition presumably applicable to *all* the boys of the school. But again, the proposition is *only probable on the evidence.* When we argue by induction, our argument is not demonstrative; our conclusion does not *necessarily* follow from the premises, the premises being the number of instances considered. The fact that all the instances investigated—all the premises—agree in indicating a particular conclusion does not guarantee the truth of that conclusion.[11] We see this readily enough when we consider the proposition about the boys from Hawkins School, but logicians tell us that from a strictly logical standpoint the conclusion that water always freezes at 32 degrees Fahrenheit is also only probable on the evidence: no argument that moves from *some* to *all* can give more than probability. Undoubtedly millions of instances of water freezing at that temperature have been observed, but *all* instances —past, present, and future—have not been observed. After examining a certain number of instances, we take the leap from the some to the all, the inductive leap—another word for the process of *generalization.*

What tests can we apply to reduce the risk of error in making the inductive leap?

---

[11] For further discussion of argument that is demonstrative, see Deduction, pp. 152–57.

Suppose somebody says: "All Chinese are short and slender. Why, I used to know one out in Wyoming, and he wasn't more than five feet tall and I bet he didn't weigh more than a hundred pounds." We all know this type of reasoning and can see that it proves nothing. A fair number of instances have not been examined. Moreover, there is no way to determine with certainty what is a fair number of instances. We must consider all the evidence available in the given circumstances and remember that only the untrained mind is rash enough to leap without looking.

Second, the instances investigated must be typical. If it can be established that the samples being investigated are indeed typical, then very few are needed. Multiplicity would be superfluous. The problem, then, may often be to determine the typicality of samples. In a laboratory the scientist may be able to test a substance to be sure it is typical of its kind. He can, for example, detect alcohol in a sample of water and therefore will not use that sample in an experiment to demonstrate the freezing point of water.

But sometimes we have to assume, without testing, that the instances available are typical. For example, the businessman who has hired five boys from Hawkins School assumes that they are typical, that other boys from the school will be like them. At other times, however, when we can choose from among a number of instances, we must make choices on the basis of typicality. Let us consider the problem of a sociologist who, for some purpose, wishes to give a description of life in the southern Appalachians. The sociologist picks three settlements, investigates the pattern of life there, and concludes that life (in general) in the southern Appalachians is such-and-such. But a rival sociologist points out that the settlements are not typical, that the people in them, unlike most natives of Appalachia, are of Swiss descent and maintain certain Swiss attitudes. The first sociologist's generalization, then, may be worthless; his instances are not typical.

Third, if negative instances occur, they must be explained. Obviously, any negative instance among those we are using as a basis for generalization reduces the force of the generalization unless we find that the negative instance is *not* typical and therefore need not be considered. For example, if the businessman who has hired five Hawkins boys and found them all honest hires a sixth and finds that he is pilfering in the stockroom, he may decide that he must give up the generalization that the Hawkins graduates are desirable employees. But he may discover that the boy who did the pilfering is a very special case, that he is a kleptomaniac, and that consequently he cannot be taken as typical. So the businessman returns to his generalization that Hawkins graduates are desirable employees.

SUMMARY: TESTS FOR GENERALIZATION

1 A fair number of instances must be investigated.
2 The instances investigated must be typical.
3 All negative instances must be explained.

Induction by analogy is the type of reasoning based on the idea that if two instances are alike on a number of important points, they will be alike on the point in question. For example, a board of directors might argue that Jim Brown would make a good corporation executive because he has been a colonel in the army. The analogy here is between a good army officer and a good business executive. The points of similarity might be taken as the ability to deal with men, the ability to make and execute policy, the willingness to take responsibility. Thus, if Brown has been successful as a colonel, it is assumed that he will be successful as a business executive.

We can arrive at certain tests for analogy similar to those for generalization:

1 The two instances compared must be similar in important respects.
2 Differences between the two instances must be accounted for as being unimportant.

In addition to these tests, we must remember that increasing the number of similar instances tends to strengthen our argument. For example, if Brown, the man being considered for an executive position in the corporation, has been a successful division chief in a government bureau as well as a successful colonel, his case is strengthened in the eyes of the board. But with analogy, as with generalization, even true premises do not guarantee a true conclusion.

■ APPLICATIONS

I   Consider the following problems in the light of the principles of generalization and analogy:

1   You are in charge of hiring for a big industrial concern. You have to choose between a young engineering graduate with a college average of C and a young graduate who majored in history with an average of A—. Which would you take? How would you defend your decision?
2   I am not going to marry Susie; her mother is always sick and complaining. Look at what happened to Jack Carton after he married Elizabeth.
3   That man has had two accidents. I won't ride in his car. He's jinxed.
4   Our last three wars were entered into while we had a Democratic president. That proves that the Democratic party is certainly the war party.

II   Write a theme in argument (about 700 words), using in the course of your discussion both generalization and analogy. Indicate, however briefly, the "occasion of the question," and, if it seems necessary, the "history of the question." In other words, give an introductory setting for your argument. One of the following topics may suggest a subject to you:

There ought to be a required course in English composition (or in American history or some other subject).

College students should not have cars on campus.

Hemingway is a better novelist than Faulkner (or vice versa).

Despite modern appliances, housewives today are worse off than housewives of fifty years ago.

Television violence is a cause of juvenile delinquency.

Love makes the world go round.

Human nature can be changed.

Youth has (has not) a new role in society.

No revolution has ever achieved the end it sought.

What this college needs is a basic three-year degree, with additional time when required.

Deduction

In our discussion of induction, we say that in both generalization and analogy we do not get certainty, only probability. This is not to say that generalization and analogy are not useful. In fact, they are indispensable, for many important questions can be dealt with only in terms of probability. But there is a type of reasoning, deductive argument, that can be distinguished from induction on the basis of probability. It does not, indeed, guarantee the truth of its conclusion, but it does guarantee that *if* the premises are true, then the conclusion will necessarily be true. With a valid deductive argument, the one situation impossible to have is true premises and a false conclusion.[12]

We are already familiar with deduction from our study of geometry in high school. Geometry starts with certain axioms—self-evident statements that are accepted without discussion or demand for proof. For instance: "Things that are equal to the same thing are equal to each other." Or: "If equals are added to equals, the results are equal." Once having accepted the axioms, we use them as the basis for working out the first theorem. Then, from that we can prove—or deduce—the second, and so on through the whole system thus generated by the original axioms.

Once we have the axioms, the whole system will, *necessarily,* follow.

LIMITS OF CERTITUDE: PREMISE

The word *deduction* comes from two Latin words, *de*, meaning "from," and *ducere,* meaning "to lead." To deduce, then, is to lead from something to a conclusion. What is led from is, of course, the premise. A premise is a proposition that, for the purpose in hand, is accepted without demand for proof. The axioms are the premises of geometry.

---

[12] The situations that are possible are: (1) true premises and a true conclusion, (2) false premises and a true conclusion, and (3) false premises and a false conclusion. As for what is meant by validity, see p. 156.

We have said that "within proper limits," deduction gives "certitude." Those proper limits are always what the particular premises will permit. If, consciously or unconsciously, we accept bad premises, our conclusion may well be bad. *What we are concerned with here, however, is not the selection of premises, but the process of reasoning from them to their necessary conclusion.* (See p. 156.)

DEDUCTION AND REASONING BY CLASSES

What is the process by which we move deductively from premises? How do we think deductively?

One common form of deduction involves thinking by classes. We have already made some acquaintance with this process in studying certain methods of exposition, especially classification and definition. For instance, in discussing the notion of convertibility as a test for definition we found that the statement, "A slave is a man," is not a definition. It is a true statement, but that does not make it a definition. In a definition we must be able to substitute either term for the other in any form of the statement. We accepted the definition that a slave is a person who is legally held as the property of another because we can substitute the term *person legally held as property of another* in any context in which the term *slave* is acceptable. Take the statement, "To be a slave is worse than death." Here we can make the substitution—can *convert* the terms—and we get exactly the same sense: "To be a person legally held as the property of another is worse than death" (pp. 78–79).

We cannot, however, convert the terms of the statement, "A slave is a man." If we try it in the statement above, we get, "To be a man is worse than death," a notion that will find few takers.

Why are the terms *man* and *slave* not convertible, since they are linked in a true statement? The answer is simple: the term *man* indicates a class more inclusive than the term *slave*. In fact, *slave* is just one of many subclasses under the class *man*. We can indicate this by drawing a circle:

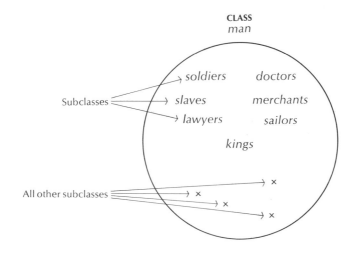

CLASS
man

Subclasses

soldiers   doctors
slaves   merchants
lawyers   sailors
kings

All other subclasses

It is clear that much we might say about the class slave is not necessarily true about the class *man;* that is, about men in general. But it is also clear that whatever we can say about the class *man* is necessarily true about the class *slave,* for the class *slave* is included in the class *man.* And what we say about the class *man* would be applicable, too, to doctors, lawyers, soldiers, and all other kinds of men. For instance, once we say, "God loves all men," we can clearly say, "God loves slaves." We have stated a premise, "God loves all men," and the other statement, the conclusion, necessarily follows from it. It follows necessarily because we accept as another premise the notion that slaves are men.

If we put these premises into circles, we will have a little circle, the class *slave,* which is in a larger circle, the class *men,* which we now have in a still larger circle, the class *what God loves,* which, of course, includes more than men.

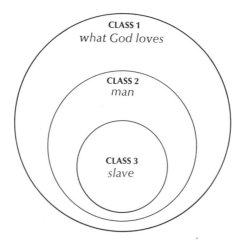

Behind the simple statement that God loves slaves, we have the reasoning indicated in our circles. This, then, is the process of deduction. There are two premises. The first, "God loves man," indicates the relation between Class 1 and Class 2. The second premise, "A slave is a man," indicates the relation between Class 2 and Class 3. From those two premises we deduce the conclusion, "God loves slaves." In other words, if Class 3 is in Class 2, and Class 2 is in Class 1, then Class 3 is in Class 1.

We may set this in the following scheme: [13]

(1st Premise)	God loves man.
(2nd Premise)	A slave is a man.
(Conclusion)	∴ God loves slaves.

Let us take another example, the statement "Even kings die." What argument would support the statement? We have the class *king* included in

---

[13] The form of argument embodied in this scheme is called the *syllogism.* It was first discussed by Aristotle.

the class *man*, and the class *man* included in the larger class *things that die*; and so we can attach the meaning (*to die*) of the biggest class to the smallest class (*king*), or to any member, to come down a stage, of that class. We can say, "No matter how proud King William is, he will die like the rest of us." Charted it looks this way:

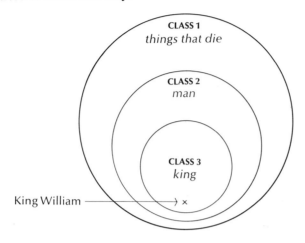

Let us look at another statement: "John simply cannot learn from experience, and anyone who cannot learn from experience is a fool." In this case, all we have given are the two premises, the relation between John and Class 2 (John is in the class of those who cannot learn by experience), and the relation between Class 2 and Class 1 (the class of those who cannot learn by experience is in the class *fool*). But we *necessarily* conclude that John is a fool (that John is in Class 1). If we chart it, we get this picture:

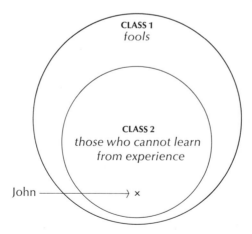

It does not matter whether we start with the conclusion (as in the statement "King William will die like the rest of us") and have to work back to the chain of reasoning, or whether we start with the premises (as in the statement "John simply cannot learn from experience, and anyone who cannot learn from experience is a fool"); the kind of picture we get is the same, a picture of the relation of classes, and in these two instances, of the relation of an individual to classes. The same is true if we are given the conclusion and one premise. For instance, suppose we say, "John is an awful fool; he cannot learn from experience." Here we have the conclusion and one premise, but we immediately know that the unstated premise is, "People who cannot learn from experience are awful fools." And again we have the picture above.[14]

Examine the following syllogism:

All men have green hair.
Your father is a man.
Therefore your father has green hair.

This is a valid syllogism. That is, it conforms to the process by which the mind moves from the premises to the conclusion. In this kind of argument *if* the premises are true, the conclusion will necessarily be true. Here the premise, "All men have green hair," is clearly false, and the conclusion is therefore false; but this does not affect the validity of the syllogism. This syllogism is as valid as the following one that does have true premises and therefore has a true conclusion:

Every man has a heart.
Your father is a man.
Therefore your father has a heart.

Truth refers to the premises of an argument, and its conclusion. *Validity* refers to the nature of the argument, as described above. Truth and validity must be distinguished. The assumption is that *true* premises and a *valid* argument will give a *true* conclusion.

● CAUTION

You may attack the last statement by saying that sometimes a bad argument does give truth. For instance, you may suggest the following:

Violence is bad.
War is bad.
Therefore war is violence.

The reasoning here is invalid, but the conclusion is true. It is true, how-ever, only by accident, as we can intuitively grasp by setting up another syllogism in the same way:

---

[14] When either a premise or the conclusion is not stated but left to be assumed, the form of syllogism is called an *enthymeme*. We have just been dealing with such instances, as: "John simply cannot learn from experience, and anyone who cannot learn from experience is a fool."

Men are living creatures.
Dogs are living creatures.
Therefore dogs are men.

Remember that what is at stake is truth *necessarily*, not accidentally, arrived at.[15]

■ APPLICATIONS

I Below you will find a list of statements. For each you are to decide whether you have a conclusion and a premise or two premises. Chart each item as a fully rendered piece of deductive reasoning. For a guide let us consider: "If you want to cut expenses, better buy an Acme typewriter." We have a general proposition, "You want to cut expenses," and a particular suggestion, "Buy an Acme typewriter." We can chart the statement by a circle with an X in it:

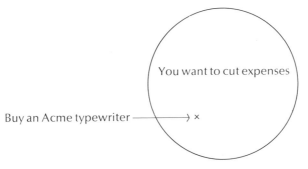

But on what grounds is the X placed in the circle? Obviously one premise is missing—which we may indicate by an intermediate circle that will be in the big one and will include the X. Of course, this circle would be, "Acme typewriters cut expenses." So we would have the picture:

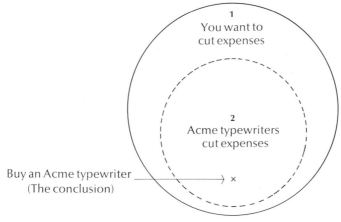

[15] In the two syllogisms just given we have been anticipating the discussion of *fallacy* (pp. 165–69). By way of further anticipation, make a chart of the syllogisms above. Do you see why the reasoning is not valid?

For another guiding illustration, consider: "Maybe people with lots of money can get by with dodging taxes, but you cannot." If we diagram the reasoning here, clearly we must draw a large circle for the class of people who have lots of money and a smaller circle for those who are able to dodge taxes with impunity. Our statement declares that the smaller circle falls within the larger, thus:

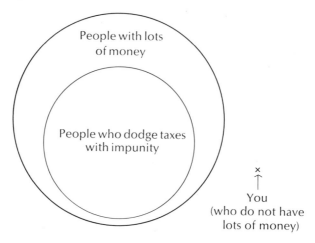

"You" would be represented by an X. The statement denies that X can be placed within the circle including people who dodge taxes with impunity, for it cannot be placed within the larger circle of people with lots of money.

Here is the list of statements to be analyzed:

1 One cannot afford to be careless of health forever. Sam has been careless a long time.
2 Why do you, who enjoy the citizenship of this country, think you should be exempt from the draft?
3 At the Battle of Gettysburg, an old woman called out to a detachment of Federal troops who were retreating: "What are you afraid for? They're only men!"
4 I am an aristocrat. I love justice and hate equality.   —John Randolph.
5 Fools say they learn from their own experience. I have always contrived to get my experience at the expense of others.   —Bismarck.
6 Nobody respects a boy who runs with the pack. No wonder you weren't elected to the Student Advisory Board.
7 You've missed another day's work. You'll be fired.

II In the Application above we have taken certain enthymemes (see footnote, p. 156) and tested them. Now you are to take a number of formal syllogisms and reduce them to enthymemes. Try to compose the enthymemes as they might appear in ordinary conversation or running argument.

1 All Southerners like hominy grits for breakfast.
   Jim Hathaway is a Southerner.
   Jim Hathaway likes hominy grits for breakfast.

2   You should give a guest what he likes.
    Jim Hathaway is going to be our guest.
    You should give Jim Hathaway hominy grits for breakfast.
3   Mortgagees who do not make the monthly payment by the 15th are fined.
    I have not made my payment by the 15th.
    I am going to be fined.
4   Boys who do not study fail this course.
    You have not studied.
    You fail this course.

III   Construct two syllogisms with true conclusions and faulty reasoning.

● CAUTION: STATEMENT OF PREMISES

Sometimes the form of the statement of a premise is confusing. The most ordinary cause of such confusion is the use of a restrictive or exclusive element in the proposition, an expression such as *all but, all except, none but*. For example, the proposition "None but the brave deserve the fair" seems at first glance to mean, "All the brave deserve the fair." But a little reflection shows that such is not the case, and that it really means, "All who deserve the fair are included in the class of the brave," and this does not exclude the possibility that "Some of the brave may not deserve the fair" for various reasons. In the picture we indicate that some of Class 1 (the brave) may not be in Class 2 (those who deserve the fair).

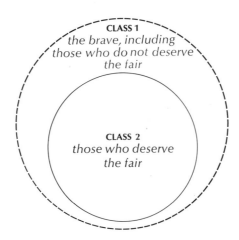

Or, to take another example: "Only students willing to work will pass this course." This does not mean, "All who work will pass this course." Rather, it means, "All who do pass this course will be in the class of those who are willing to work." So we have the picture:

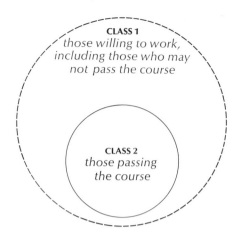

CLASS 1
*those willing to work,
including those who may
not pass the course*

CLASS 2
*those passing
the course*

In other words, it is quite possible that some students who work very hard will fail, because they are, let us say, badly prepared or stupid or in poor health.

■ APPLICATION

Interpret and draw the picture for each of the following propositions:

1   None but a fool fails to learn from experience.
2   Only the brave deserve the fair.
3   Only women bear children.
4   Democracies alone can afford mistakes.
5   All but the foolish seek to know God's will.

SLIPS IN REASONING

We have just seen that confusion may arise from misunderstanding the statement of a premise. But it can also arise from a slip in the process of reasoning itself.

Suppose that a lawyer defending a client accused of murder argues: "We know that all good men strive to provide well for their families. They work day after day for that purpose. All good men strive to be considerate and win the love and esteem of their families. They are beloved by their families. Well, I point out to you this man's long record of devotion to his family, and their devotion to him." What is the lawyer up to? He is clearly trying to indicate to his jury that Mr. X is a good man; that is, a man who could not commit murder. If we boil this argument down, it comes out like this:

Good men are devoted to their families, and so forth.
Mr. X is devoted to his family.
Mr. X is a good man, and so forth.

Let us start to draw our picture of this. Clearly, we get the class *good men* included in the larger class *men devoted to their families*. We can readily see this, for a criminal sometimes is a devoted family man, as for example, Jesse James, the notorious outlaw.

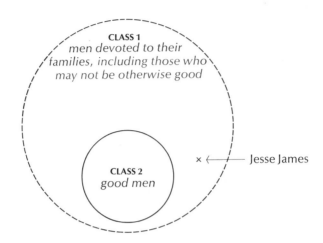

Now the lawyer wants us to put Mr. X in the class *good men*. But we see that we do not have to. All we have to do, according to our second premise, is to put him in the class *men devoted to their families*. Since that class may be larger than the class *good men,* we are able to put him there without putting him in the class *good men*—that is, men who could not commit murder. There is no *necessity* to put him in the class *good men,* and the necessity is what counts, not the possibility.

It is obvious that the chain of reasoning has slipped. In this case, we presume that the lawyer hoped the jury would not notice the slip and would vote for acquittal. But sometimes we slip without meaning to and deceive even ourselves.

Let us try another example. A political candidate says, "Every congressman who voted for the Jones-Higgins Bill betrayed this state. But I did not vote for it. I am no traitor to your interests, but would fight to the death for them."

We do not have to be impressed. The candidate has not offered any convincing reasoning that he is not a traitor to the public interest. Voting for the Jones-Higgins Bill would not be the only way a congressman could betray the public interest.

What the candidate *wants* his conclusion to look like is this picture:

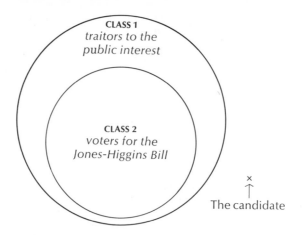

But all we are sure of is that the candidate belongs outside Class 2 (voters for the Jones-Higgins Bill). For all we know, he may still be inside Class 1 (traitors to the public interest). So our figure should indicate that he may fall either inside Class 1 or outside it:

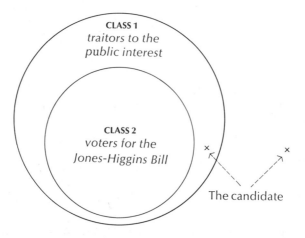

A good check on your own reasoning or on that of other people is to try to look behind the words and see what is *necessarily* included in what. The *maybe* or *perhaps* does not count. To be convincing, the conclusion *must* follow from the premises.

■ APPLICATIONS

I Which of the following arguments would you accept and which not? Draw a picture to show why.

1 No member of this fraternity has ever been expelled from college. No member has ever disgraced us.

2   We, like beasts, are the products of Nature. We are no better than beasts.
3   Everybody should seek virtue, because everybody wishes happiness.
4   The Stuart family has been distinguished in our history, and Joseph is a Stuart.
5   All members of the Stuart family are distinguished, and Joseph is a Stuart.

II Compose two examples of the slips in reasoning illustrated by the lawyer defending the murderer, and two of the slips illustrated by the politician's appeal to his constituency.

REASONING BY *EITHER–OR*

There are two other kinds of deductive reasoning, one of which is characterized by the use of the terms *either-or* and the other by *if-then*.

Let us set up an example of reasoning by *either-or* (the *disjunctive syllogism*). Upon going into the kitchen and finding the steak on the floor under the sink, we think that either the cat or the dog has pulled it down. Then we discover that the cat is locked in the barn to catch rats. Therefore the dog must have committed the crime. The formula is simple. We decide on two possibilities. We exclude one. Naturally the other becomes our conclusion.

To get a true conclusion, we must be sure, as with the usual process of deduction, that our starting point is dependable. The *either-or* premise must really cover the case. The alternatives must be exhaustive. In the example of the cat and dog, if the cat is locked in the barn and the dog is out chasing rabbits, the premise simply does not cover the case. We must investigate further to discover all the possibilities. We find that, after all, it was curly-headed little Willie who pulled the steak off the table and deserves the punishment.

In the example of the disjunctive syllogism just given, the pattern of reasoning may be described as follows: *A* or *B*, not *B*, therefore *A*. (The cat or dog was the culprit; the cat was not the culprit; therefore it was the dog that took the steak.) But can we also reason using this pattern: *A* or *B*, *B*, therefore not *A?* The validity of such reasoning will depend upon what we mean by *either-or*. We may mean (1) *A* or *B*, but not both (that is, *or* used exclusively), or (2) *A* or *B*, or both (that is, *or* used inclusively). If we are using *or* in an exclusive sense, the pattern represented by *A* or *B*, *B*, therefore not *A* yields a valid conclusion. If the cat or the dog, but not both, could have got the steak, and if we can be sure that the dog did get it, then it is valid to conclude that the cat did not. But suppose that we are using *or* in an inclusive sense; then the pattern of reasoning involved in *A* or *B*, *B*, therefore not *A* may yield a nonsensical conclusion. For example: "The man who said that is either a fool or a liar. Now I know that he is a liar; therefore he is not a fool." The truth of the matter may be that the man is foolish as well as guilty of false statement. (It is unlikely that we mean he is a fool or a liar but *not both*.) In a case so simple as the last, there is not much danger of our getting into trouble, but in more complicated cases we may very well get into trouble unless we check very carefully the sense in

which we are using *or*. There is a real opportunity for equivocation (p. 166).
But note that in the *negative* pattern of reasoning (*A* or *B*, *not B*, therefore
A) it does not matter whether we are using *or* in an exclusive or inclusive
sense. The negative pattern of reasoning is valid for both.

■ APPLICATIONS

I Discuss the following instances of reasoning by *either-or:*

1 What is not animal must be vegetable or mineral.
 This is not animal.
 Therefore this must be vegetable or mineral.

2 Bankruptcies are caused either by dishonesty or by idleness.
 John Sutter's bankruptcy was not caused by idleness.
 Therefore John Sutter must be dishonest.

3 If Williams revealed our plans, he is either a coward or a traitor.
 We know he is a coward.
 Therefore he is no traitor.

II From each of the following syllogisms construct an enthymeme:

1 Either you pay me now or I sue.
 So you won't pay me.
 Therefore I am going to sue.

2 You will either stop seeing that rat John or stop seeing me.
 You will stop seeing him.
 Therefore you need not stop seeing me.

REASONING BY *IF–THEN*

Reasoning by *if-then* (the *conditional syllogism*) deals with a condition
and a result. *If* the condition is fulfilled, *then* the result necessarily follows.

We constantly use reasoning of this kind, as in the statement, "You
haven't been watering the lawn; it will be awful for the party." Set out fully,
the argument would run:

> If you do not water the lawn, the grass will die.
> You did not water the lawn.
> Therefore the grass will die.

This reasoning is correct. We have affirmed the *if* (which is called the
antecedent), and therefore the result necessarily follows. But the reasoning
is also correct, if we deny the consequent, as we do below when we state
that the grass has not died:

> If you do not water the lawn, the grass will die.
> The grass has not died.
> Therefore you did water the lawn.

The following example does not, however, give us correct reasoning:

> If you do not water the lawn, the grass will die.
> The grass has died.
> Therefore you did not water the lawn.

The result here is not *necessarily* acceptable. The grass may have died, not because the lawn was not watered, but because grub worms are at the roots. For the reasoning in an example like the last to be valid, the *if* would have to mean *only if*. Most errors in reasoning of this type occur because we incorrectly interpret an *if* as an *only if*.

Of course, there are instances in which the *if* should legitimately be interpreted as *only if*. But this is a matter of the truth of the premise we start with, and if we mean *only if* we should say so in the premise.

■ APPLICATIONS

I Examine the pieces of reasoning below. Which are acceptable as they stand? Which could be accepted if the *if* were to be taken as *only if?*

1 If you leave bounds, you will be expelled from school.
  You have not been expelled from school.
  Therefore you did not leave bounds.
2 If you leave bounds, you will be expelled from school.
  You have not left bounds.
  Therefore you will not be expelled from school.
3 If you leave bounds, you will be expelled from school.
  You have been expelled from school.
  Therefore you did leave bounds.
4 If you do not catch this car, you will be late.
  You did not catch this car.
  Therefore you will be late.
5 If you do not catch this car, you will be late.
  You are late.
  Therefore you did not catch this car.

II Construct enthymemes of the syllogisms above that you consider valid.

III Compose two faulty examples of the conditional syllogism. Compose two acceptable examples of the conditional syllogism of the *only-if* type.

FALLACIES

We have already indicated certain characteristic errors in reasoning; for example, in induction a generalization based on too few instances or an analogy based on instances different in important respects, or in deduction the failure to relate classes properly. Such an error we call a fallacy. There are, however, other fallacies not yet touched on, at least not directly, that are common in argument. Those we shall discuss are equivocation, begging the question, ignoring the question, and *non sequitur*—Latin for "It does not follow." (Certain other fallacies appear in the chapter on Persuasion.

Equivocation   Equivocation is the fallacy of using the same term with different meanings. Here is a well-known example:

> Even scientists recognize a power beyond nature, for they speak of "natural law"; and if there is law, there must be a power to make the law; such a power beyond nature is called God; therefore scientists believe in God.

Here the word *law* is used equivocally, that is, in two meanings. In the sense in which scientists use it when they speak of "natural law," it means the recognition of regularity in natural process—the law of gravity, for example. Here the sense is descriptive. But in the second sense it means what is ordinarily meant in government, a command given by a superior authority. Here the sense is prescriptive. Since the whole argument is based on the word *law,* the argument does not make sense *as an argument* if the word shifts its meaning. It may be true that a number of scientists do believe in God, but that does not make this a good argument.

Begging the Question   Begging the question occurs when an arguer assumes as a premise the conclusion to be proved—or when he assumes as a premise a proposition that can be proved only with the help of the conclusion that he proposes to prove. Suppose that someone offers the proposition: "The unsanitary condition of the slaughter pens is detrimental to health." (See Circular Definition, p. 88.)

What we are supposed to argue, if there is to be an argument, is whether the condition of the slaughter pens is detrimental to health. But the word *unsanitary* means "detrimental to health," and that word has been put into the original proposition. The question that is supposed to be at stake has been begged. In the example above, the begging of the question is basically a matter of language in the proposition.

When we encounter such a proposition, we should restate it and try to see exactly what is being argued.

But the same principle may appear on a larger scale, as in this example of arguing in a circle.

A: I admire Rembrandt's painting "The Night Watch."
B: Why?
A: Because it is a great painting.
B: How do you know?
A: All the best critics say it is.
B: How do you know who the best critics are?
A: Why, the best critics are those who recognize great painting.

Here speaker A has given circular proof. He sets out to prove that the painting is great by appealing to the best critics and then identifies the best critics as those who recognize great painting. This instance is a very simple one, but sometimes the begging may be concealed in a very elaborate argument. We must always be on the watch for it, for such question-begging is an attempt to establish a thing *by itself.*

Ignoring the Question   An arguer ignores the question when he introduces any consideration that will distract from what is really at stake. There are numberless ways of doing this. A competing question may be used to shift the argument to new ground, or an appeal may be made to some emotional attitude having nothing to do with the logic of the case. For instance, a man arguing for a Republican candidate may shift the issue from the candidate's qualification to the praise of Lincoln, the great hero of the party. Or a Democrat may leave a present question of party policy and begin to discuss the glorious achievements of Thomas Jefferson. Or if a lawyer defending a man accused of murder merely argues that the victim was a wicked man or that the family of the accused is worthy of pity, he is ignoring the question.

One of the commonest forms of ignoring the question is to shift from the question to the character or personality of the opponent. For instance, a husband criticizes his wife, and she replies, "Well, you aren't so perfect yourself!" She has ignored the question, her own burnt bread or overbid at bridge, and has begun to discuss his shortcomings. We find another instance when we argue that we cannot endorse a certain political measure because the congressman who proposes it has been divorced or drinks whisky. We have shifted from the measure to the man. The Latin name of this famous and frequent fallacy is *argumentum ad hominem.*

Either-Or, All-or-Nothing   This fallacy is related to the disjunctive syllogism (pp. 163–64) in that it involves two possibilities that are presented as mutually exclusive. There are, of course, situations in which such an absolute dichotomy does exist and must be recognized. The surgeon says: "The choice lies between this operation and death." He may well be speaking the truth. Again, when you enter the polling booth, you have chosen one option in the absolute dichotomy of vote and nonvote. Once inside, you again face a clear-cut choice, with no middle ground, between voting for Jim Jones and not voting for Jim Jones. Life does present such yes-no decisions, and often such decisions cannot be postponed. The surgeon says the cancer cannot wait on your convenience.

But life is also full of situations in which thinking in dichotomies falsifies actuality. A situation may be very complex, with many different possibilities. When you look down at a chess board before your first move, you cannot think in dichotomies. But many people, facing the variables of life and its complexities of option and value, will do just that. For example:

SUSIE: It's too bad Jane is so impulsive; she does get herself and others into messes.

MARY: But I thought you were her friend.

SUSIE: Of course, I'm her friend! Whoever said I wasn't? I love her, and——

MARY: But you just said she is too impulsive.

SUSIE: Sure, she is, but she's warm-hearted and generous and loyal and intelligent. She has a hundred great qualities and I love her, and I'm her friend.

MARY: That's a funny kind of friend.

Here Mary is committing the fallacy of either-or, all-or-nothing. "People are either friends or not," she would say, and for her, friendship means a total blindness to any defects. She has no idea that friendship, affection, and love can accept defects in a person. This lack of realism on Mary's part means that she herself will make such absolute demands on friendship that she can never have a friend—except some bemused half-wit.

The fallacy of either-or is, too, a common device in propaganda. The revivalist, the reformer, and the politician know the value of what may be called crisis psychology. "Now is the time, this may be the last chance, tomorrow is too late, don't be a coward, stand up and be counted"—these are, in one form or another, the constant exhortations. There are, indeed, great moments of crisis, occasions when, without delay, a man should stand up and be counted. But there are also moments when to sit and think is of more value to all concerned. The fallacy occurs when the occasion does not warrant the urgency or when the options proposed are false.

Non Sequitur   *Non sequitur,* as we have said, means, "It does not follow." In one sense, any fallacy is a *non sequitur,* because by the very nature of the case the conclusion does not follow from fallacious reasoning. But here we shall use the term to cover certain more special kinds of argument.

For instance, it may be argued: "William Brown doesn't drink or smoke, and so he ought to make a good husband." But it is obvious that a man who does not drink or smoke may still make a poor husband. He may gamble, or loaf, or beat his wife. To take another example, it may be argued: "Harry Thompson would make a good governor because he belongs to the upper [or lower] class." We know, however, that belonging to a certain social class proves nothing about a man's ability or integrity. So the conclusion that Thompson would make a good governor does not follow.

A more complicated form of *non sequitur* appears in this piece of parental reasoning: "As soon as I increased Billie's allowance, his grades began to fall. Therefore we ought to reduce his allowance; having extra money makes him idle." But Billie may have been suffering from eyestrain or may now be beginning a subject for which he is badly prepared. Take another example: "Just after Herbert Hoover was elected President we had the greatest depression in history. How can you respect a man like that?"

In the argument about Billie and that about Hoover the same error occurs. It is argued that because A (an increase in Billie's allowance or the election of Hoover) precedes B (Billie's bad grades or the depression), A must necessarily be the cause of B. The arguer does not understand the nature of a cause or has not taken the trouble to analyze the situation. He simply assumes that if one thing precedes another, the first is the cause of the second. This is the fallacy of *post hoc, ergo propter hoc,* previously discussed (p. 109).

Fallacies and Refutation   Many people who have never heard the word *fallacy* can reason straight or locate defects in the reasoning of others. When we meet an example of a fallacy in cold type on the page of a textbook, we are inclined to say, "Nobody with common sense would commit such an error." But common sense is not, after all, so common, and sometimes we have to work for it. An understanding of fallacies is useful in helping us to reason straight, but it is also useful in helping us to locate defects in an opposing argument. If we can point out a fallacy in an opposing argument, we can refute that argument, and refutation is a powerful secondary weapon for maintaining our own position. Even when we are not engaged in a debate, but are simply writing a piece of argument, we often find that we have to refute certain arguments—arguments that we can anticipate in turning a question over in our minds.

■ APPLICATIONS

I   Identify the unacceptable premises or arguments in the following instances, and explain the fallacy, or fallacies, involved in each:

1   You should not read the poetry of Byron, because his private life was immoral.
2   Telegrams bring bad luck.
3   No man can live without faith. Faith is the mark of a good Christian. Therefore all men are inherently Christians.
4   After taking several bottles of Lightfoot's Liver Syrup, Mrs. Jones felt much better. So Mrs. Smith immediately bought a bottle.
5   This unjust tax should be repealed.

II   Compose two examples of each of the fallacies studied in this section.

III   Look back over editorials or articles in recent newspapers and magazines. Locate fallacious arguments, copy them down, analyze them, and bring them to class for discussion.

DEDUCTION AND EXTENDED ARGUMENT

When we finished discussing inductive reasoning, it was relatively easy and natural to set up an extended discussion embodying what had been learned. But often deductive reasoning seems limited and niggling, not suited to a full discussion of a subject. It seems useful only for hacking away at some small point.

Throughout the last several pages we have been hacking away at small points, which is the only way to illustrate what is involved in deductive reasoning. But once we have assimilated the principles, we constantly use them, without self-consciousness, in the development of a discussion.

In much ordinary argumentative prose, we find a series of limited bits of argumentation absorbed and used, step by step. We have seen how the full chain of inductive reasoning may be indicated by, say, one premise and the conclusion, or the two premises with the conclusion left to the logical sense of the audience—that is, by enthymemes. In this way much argument proceeds, without developing each piece of reasoning in full, with the basic lines embedded in the midst of incidental evidence, examples, and other material. Here, for example, is a paragraph from an editorial:

> Nobody denies that our tax situation is desperate and that we are facing a crisis, and nobody denies that there is great need for wise legislation in all matters affecting the business of the nation. We must scrutinize with redoubled attention every bill which comes before Congress and try to see what its effect will be in this sphere of activity. This is undoubtedly necessary with the present bill to lower taxes. If it is passed, it will have an inflationary effect. What attitude shall we take toward the present bill?

The main point here concerns a tax-reduction bill. It is assumed as background that the present situation is desperate and that good legislation is needed. The argument that follows can be divided into two chains of reasoning linked together:

> Tax reduction promotes inflation.
> The present bill would reduce taxes.
> Therefore the present bill would promote inflation.

The conclusion of this chain provides a premise for the next one, a link in the argument:

> Whatever promotes inflation is bad.
> The present bill would promote inflation.
> Therefore the present bill is bad.

The writer of the editorial feels that his reader knows that inflation is bad, and he says only that the present bill is inflationary. Nor does he bother to state the conclusion that this bill is, therefore, bad. He feels that the conclusion will strike the reader more powerfully if the reader is forced to come to it himself. The reader will himself answer the question: "What attitude shall we take toward the present bill?"

● CAUTION: THE WEAKEST LINK

When we are treating the stages of an extended argument, those stages, we readily see, are related, sometimes so closely related that they form what is called a chain of reasoning. Each stage is essential. A chain is not stronger than its weakest link.

The best insurance against using weak links is the habit of stating each individual piece of reasoning to ourselves, and then criticizing it.

Development of a Theme Below we shall follow the development of a theme in argument, step by step. The argument is a defense of manned space flights, against those who feel their cost is exorbitant. Its title is "Shoot the Moon."

First the student attempts to line up his arguments. The letter *F* before the number reference means "For," and the letter *A* means "Against." You will notice that *A–1*, which is the first argument offered "Against," is countered by a whole series of arguments "For," from *F–1A* to *F–1G*.

For	*Against*
F–1A. Money spent on space would not necessarily go for social reform.	*A–1*. Desperate need in society for social reform: space money could do this.
F–1B. No social program to justify money; unlike space programs, where there is great organization for planning and control.	
F–1C. Psychology of space: Toynbee and challenge: space most obvious challenge.	
F–1D. Importance of "man" in space.	
F–1E. Space as shot in arm to society: like Renaissance and America, new ideas.	
F–1F. Modern man said to be cut off from Nature: not in space.	
F–1G. Individual swamped in modern world, big organizations, etc.: space exploration puts emphasis back on individual, but in team.	
F–2. Don't know: some scientists say space can be habitable.	*A–2*. Space can bring no practical gains: not habitable, no resources.
F–3. See *1D*. Also scientific curiosity makes man want to "go and see." Science cannot progress by negative assumptions.	*A–3*. Scientific gains can be made with instrument flights: manned flights vastly more expensive.
F–4. Military objection not really relevant. Tensions already exist. Work on peace at central point, not at margin. Withdrawal from space no answer.	*A–4*. Space flights, because of military motivation, increase international tension.
F–5. Generation gap idea.	

When the student prepared his theme in the final form, he was requested to code it with his arguments for and against. He was also requested to outline in the margin the arguments used in the theme.

When you study the theme, you should work with both these sets of references in mind. Try to follow the process of the student's thinking. You will see, for one thing, that the order of the arguments above is not strictly an outline of the theme.

SHOOT THE MOON

For as long as I can remember I have been fascinated by space. Before I could really read, I was looking at comic books about Batman and Superman, which for a kid was space. Then space exploration was science fiction. Now it is not fiction at all. It is truth, and space is full of whizzing hardware with flesh-and-blood men dressed up like Buck Rogers. I have read that everything has to be a dream before it can be real, and so even those comic books were part of the dream. I will come back to this dream business later.

When I first realized that some people were against the space program, I was honestly shocked. It was like hearing that somebody was against chocolate malt shakes and football. As I got older, I began to understand the arguments of these people, but I still don't agree with them. In this paper I want to analyze and refute them.

A–1 The first objection is that our country is
in a desperate condition with the troubles of
poverty and race, and that all possible money
should be spent there. The second says that
A–2 there is no practical scientific value in space,
for space has no resources. Furthermore,
A–3 this objection holds that manned space
exploration is unnecessary and that instru-
A–4 ment exploration is equally good and cheaper.
A third and final objection is that because
space exploration has military potential, it
tends to increase international tensions.

F–1A To answer the first objection, I would like
to say that there is little likelihood the money
spent for space would go to social reform if
the space program were dropped. There is a
F–1B big difference between these two programs:
the space program has a sharp focus with
every dollar spent for the specific purpose of
putting a man on the moon, but social reform has no such clearly defined goal. Until
there is such a focus in the social programs,
there won't be big money for them.

But my main answer to this first objection
F–1C is that a country must have the will and the
imagination to respond to a challenge or it
will not long survive. Space is the most
obvious challenge of today: you look up and

1. If you are to argue, you must analyze.
I am going to argue.
* I must analyze.

2. Money should be spent where most needed.
Money is most needed for social reform.
* Money should be spent for social reform.

3. If there is no practical value in space, it should not be occupied.
There is no practical value.
* Therefore don't occupy.

4. If two methods equally effective, use cheaper.
Instrument exploration equally effective.
* Use instrument flight.

5. Military expansion increases tension.
Space exploration is military expansion
* Abandon space exploration.

6. If money saved from space would not go for social reform, this argument is not relevant.
The money would not go for social reform.
* This argument is not relevant.

7. If social reform does not offer a hard program, it cannot get big money like space.
It has not been able to offer hard program.
* It cannot get the money.

8. A civilization must expand or die.
We do not want death.
* Therefore choose space.

9. Toynbee uses induction: examine many civilizations to find principle.

F–1E

10. Argument by analogy: Renaissance and America in space age.

F–1D

11. You cannot suppress human curiosity.
Space exploration is human curiosity.
* You cannot suppress space exploration.

F–3

F–2

12. Modern man needs to regain touch with nature.
Space gives contact with nature.
* We need space exploration.

F–1F

13. Modern man needs sense of identity.
Space exploration gives this sense.
* Modern man needs space exploration.

F–1G

14. World permeated by military motives.
Space exploration of part of the world.
* Space exploration involves military motives.

F–4

15. If the problem of war is not attacked at root, peace will not be found.
Refusal of space is not an attack at root.
* Refusal of space does not give peace.

there it is. According to the historian Arnold Toynbee, who has studied many civilizations, all civilization depends on challenge and response. Just as the discovery of America helped bring about the Renaissance in Europe, the psychology of space can revitalize our civilization.

For this same reason, it is very important that we have manned space flights, and not just instrument exploration. When a man goes into space, our imagination becomes involved: man is accepting the challenge. The astronaut in the space suit is like a dream that reminds you of what people can be like. Human flight also satisfies one important human quality—curiosity, particularly scientific curiosity. Man wants to "go and see," and what a man sees is always a little different from what a machine records. This point also answers the objection that there are no practical gains in space, for the "go-see" philosophy requires an open mind. It does not make negative judgments. It assumes the possibility of a big breakthrough.

Also, there may be a practical side to space exploration. Some scientists say that certain planets may be habitable. If, as is often said, modern man is out of touch with nature, the space program certainly brings nature back to him. Again, it is said that the individual loses his identity in the complexity of the great modern world. But the space program proves that it is possible to have a big organization and not lose the individual in it. The space program may be the greatest organization ever assembled, but the astronauts remain individuals; they all know what they want to do and are willing to pay the price to do it. They are also team-spirited and know that a man just doesn't decide to grow wings and take off.

I have not yet spoken about the third objection, the one having to do with the military motive for space exploration. I admit that there is some military motivation. It would have to be so when we are living in a world of military motivation. Any sensible man knows we have to work toward reducing tensions, but I say "work" and not simply sit back. I don't have the particular answer, but I know it is not just to withdraw

16. To disarm unilaterally is not to gain peace.
To refuse space is to disarm.
* To refuse space is not to gain peace.

F–5

from space and watch the astronauts of other nations flying over. I say do anything to get to the root of the war question, but be sure that what you do is not an empty gesture.

One more general point: I will guess, from my own observation, that kids of the generation that has grown up with space don't have much objection to it. They may not want to turn space into a shooting gallery full of floating missile sites, but they still believe in occupying it. This generation accepts space exploration as natural. It is older people, judging from some I know, who feel shocked and left out by space development. They are afraid of the new world they cannot fit into.

Maybe I am prejudiced about all this. You see what I want to be is an astrophysicist. If I can make the grade. Well, back to the logarithms.[16]

■ APPLICATIONS

I Study the original line-up of arguments for and against space exploration. At this stage what arguments would you add to either column? Remember that you are not being asked to state your personal opinions. You are being asked to cover the case from both sides, in order to round out the argument. What matters would be issues in the new list?

II Criticize the pieces of reasoning that the author of the theme outlines in the left margin. Do you find any that are invalid? Be sure that you strictly interpret the word *invalid* (p. 156). Now make any general criticism you wish of the reasoning in the theme. Write a discussion embodying your criticism, including any material you think necessary to support your views. Observe that now, in the face of this theme, you are discussing your own views. If you agree with the author, you may develop further material in support of the position. If you disagree you will be systematically saying why.

III You are now to undertake your most ambitious theme up to this time. After choosing a topic, work out as full a survey of scratch notes as possible, on both sides of the question you are preparing to argue. Now sort out as systematically as you can the points you have raised, trying to pair them. (But, as the author of "Shoot the Moon" found out, you may find many particular points on one side related to one on the other.) What points raised do you regard as issues? Which are admitted, which crucial? Prepare a sentence outline, embodying the material you have assembled. Without concerning your-

---

[16] For another side of this argument see an article by the scientist and novelist C. P. Snow in *Look* (February 4, 1969).

self with an introduction or conclusion, compose the body of the theme. Do not be disturbed if you find you must abandon at some points the outline you have prepared. The body of the theme should run some 800 to 900 words. Finally, add an introduction and a conclusion. Turn in all your preliminary material with the theme.

As for your subject, you have had a large number of suggestions in earlier Applications. If none of these appeals to you, try to review your own convictions. What do you feel strongly about? It does not have to be a world-shaking subject, merely something that evokes a conviction in you. But be sure that your subject is one that is truly arguable.

Here are a few more suggestions:

1   This college should accept any high school graduate, on a first-come-first-served basis, without reference to grades.
2   All grading should be on a pass-fail basis.
3   In the junior and senior years all students in this college should be housed in coed dormitories.
4   Coed dormitories should be governed by a body of students elected by residents of the dormitory in question.
5   Athletic competition with other institutions should be abolished.
6   Between the ages of 17 and 21, all persons not physically incompetent should be required to serve one year in some nonprofit organization devoted to conservation, social service, medical assistance, or poverty relief.
7   The results of the Mexican War have, in the end, served civilization.
8   The Spanish-American War should not have been fought.
9   War is always a mistake.
10 Bar examinations, examinations for architectural licenses, and state medical examinations should take into account inequalities in educational opportunity.
11 Admission to the bar, to the practice of architecture, and to the practice of medicine should be on a basis of ethnic quota.
12 The United States should unilaterally disarm, except for such forces as might be needed for internal police.

CHAPTER 7

Persuasion

Persuasion is the art, primarily verbal, by which you get somebody to do what you want and make him, at the same time, think that this is what he had wanted to do all the time.

It may be objected that the person persuaded—the persuadee, shall we call him?—may not be persuaded actually to "do" anything, but merely to accept an opinion or adopt an attitude. Within certain limits this objection is reasonable, but there is no clear-cut line between belief, attitude, and feeling on the one side and an action on the other. Furthermore, as soon as we look at the characteristic occasions on which persuasion takes place, we see that the process is usually targeted, at short or long range, toward action. You persuade your friend to lend you five dollars until Saturday, you persuade the child to be good and go to bed, you persuade the policeman not to give you the ticket, you persuade the prospect to buy the car, you persuade the sinner to repent and join the church, you persuade the girl to marry you, you persuade the voter to vote for you.

The persuader wants something that can be granted by the persuadee, and if he is successful, it is granted and the persuadee is happy in the granting. Persuasion is the "engineering of consent." It is a way of exercising power without creating resentment.

Persuasion and Power

Persuasion represents power. Perhaps the highest compliment ever paid the power of oratory, the prime form of persuasion in the world of ancient

Greece and Rome, is embodied in the story of the death of Cicero. After Mark Antony had caused Cicero to be assassinated, and his head and hands were exposed in the Forum, Fulvia, Antony's wife, stuck a gold pin through the tongue of the dead man to take vengeance on its power.

In that world oratory was the instrument that swayed the Athenian electorate, the Senate of Republican Rome, or the street mob of the Roman Empire. Up to a few generations ago, even in this country the ambitious young man studied his Greek and Latin, and the halls of Congress rang with speeches imitated from Demosthenes or Cicero.

If the desire for power was once the spur that drove the young American to a study of the classics, it still remains the fundamental motive for the exercise of persuasion. In that earlier and less sophisticated America, the occasions of public persuasion—the sermon, the college oration, the speech on the hustings, the newspaper editorial, the debate in the state house or in the Capitol at Washington—were not numerous. Today such occasions are multiplied a thousandfold, but numerous as they are, they are lost in the more massive manifestations of persuasion that pour from printing presses, crowd the television screen, fill the airwaves, and blot out the landscape as our automobiles whirl down the highways. Demosthenes and Cicero have been replaced as the masters of persuasion by courses in salesmanship and psychology, charm schools, and other implementations of Dale Carnegie's famous formula "How to Win Friends and Influence People."

The engineering of consent is central to our democratic, industrial society. We live in the age of the advertising man, propaganda expert, and motivation analyst. What was once a limited exercise is now incessant and universal, and the stakes played for go higher every day. The political, psychological, social, and moral consequences are not yet fully clear. Even so, some observers are beginning to feel that there is serious cause for concern that the responsible forms of persuasion will be driven out by the irresponsible. That, however, is a question we shall come to later (pp. 191–94).

Differences Between Argument and Persuasion

Argument and persuasion are often lumped together, and their interrelation is indeed intimate. We cannot, however, understand this interrelation unless we sharply distinguish them. It is true that we sometimes say, "I am not persuaded of the truth of that argument." But in that case, we are using the word *persuade* (or the word *argument*) in a more general sense than is intended here (p. 120). The end of argument, strictly conceived, is truth—truth as determined by the operation of reason. The end of persuasion, on the other hand, is assent—assent to the will of the persuader.

This distinction between the end of argument and that of persuasion is crucial, but to profit fully from it we must realize another distinction. The end of argument is achieved in *only one way,* by the operation of reason;

but the end of persuasion may be achieved in a *number of ways,* sometimes used singly, but more often in combination. For instance, Aristotle, in his *Rhetoric,* remarks on three modes of persuasion, the first dependent on the character and credibility of the persuader, the second on the persuader's ability to stir the emotions of those whom he aims to persuade, and the third on the proof of "a truth or an apparent truth."

We may take these three modes as useful guidelines, even though they do not constitute a strict outline for our following discussion.

Identification

To return to the difference between argument and persuasion, we may say that the characteristic end of each implies a different germ situation.

The germ situation out of which argument grows is doubt, and argument usually involves some form of conflict. When conflict is involved in argument, the conflict cannot be resolved unless those contending share some common ground; and the minimal requirement for such a common ground is an agreement to accept the dictates of reason (pp. 123–25).

In persuasion, on the contrary, the persuader earnestly seeks to eliminate conflict from the germ situation, and if doubt exists he maintains that it must be shared and resolved in a joint effort marked by mutual good will. The persuader's characteristic assertion is that any difference between his point of view and that of the persuadee is the result of only a slight misunderstanding that can readily be cleared up by a little friendly discussion, for they are two persons of essentially identical interests.

In other words, what the persuader seeks is the broadest possible common ground with the persuadee, something far beyond the ground necessary for argument. What he seeks is much more, even, than an identity of interests objectively regarded. As the eminent critic Kenneth Burke has put it in *A Grammar of Motives:* "You persuade a man only in so far as you can talk his language by speech, gesture, tonality, order, image, attitude, idea, *identifying* your ways with his." *Identification,* not conflict, is what the persuader seeks. An attempt at identification is the key to his method.

The next time you go to a public meeting on a controversial issue try to heckle the speaker. If he is expert in his business, he will have diagnosed his audience and will know what attitude the majority will take to your attack. If he thinks you have support, or feels that he has not yet found a sympathetic relation with the audience, he will almost certainly say: "Now that is a very good question; let's try to think it through together." Or: "I'm glad you brought that up. Perhaps we can pool our efforts and . . ." Or: "That's an interesting way to go at the problem. I've been trying to state it, but you have done it so much better than I ever could."

Even when the speaker feels that he already has sympathetic relations with the audience, he may so value his role as a conciliator that he will pay you, the heckler, this deference. If, on the other hand, he is secure in his audience and chooses to answer your aggression with aggression of his own, trying wittily to make a monkey of you for the public delight, he is still seeking identification with his audience by provoking and entering into their sadistic pleasure in your humiliation.

To sum up, identification is the basic preparation for persuasion. One can go further and say: it is the first stage of persuasion, whether the main appeal is to be emotional or logical or some combination of these qualities.

The ground of identification: knowledge of the audience

Clearly the persuader cannot achieve identification or exploit the persuadee's relation to a group unless he knows the audience. From the time of Aristotle's *Rhetoric* on, writers on persuasion have tried to classify audiences with the hope of establishing basic appeals. Aristotle made a basic and very shrewd classification by age. The young, he said, are optimistic, energetic, brave, loyal, idealistic, quick to love or anger, but they lack calculation, are prey to fads, have no steady goals, and overestimate their own knowledge. The old are skeptical, suspicious, avaricious, dispassionate, comfort-loving, and doubtful of aspiration. But men in the prime may combine the best qualities of youth and age.

Since Aristotle's day, many other writers on persuasion have suggested many other classifications, and such classifications are essential to the operations of publishing, advertising, public relations, and politics. An advertising man makes classifications in relation to his product, and it is not likely that he will advertise mink coats in a magazine concerned with poetry. Politicians temper their speeches to their audiences: what gets applause in a silk-stocking congressional district in New York City might be suicide in the corn belt. Abraham Lincoln, in his famous debates with Stephen A. Douglas in 1858, altered his pronouncements about slavery according to the latitude of Illinois in which he was speaking.

Any persuader instinctively classifies audiences. You are not an advertising man or a politician, but in your themes, you, too, must think of the nature of the audience. In the very beginning of this course we have spoken, in general terms, about this matter (pp. 18–22). With persuasion, this principle demands special application.

Identification and the character of the persuader

We have pointed out that Aristotle bases the first mode of persuasion on the character and credibility of the persuader. The persuader may have, of course, a prestige that precedes his utterance and predisposes the audience to accept him; but there is also the immediate effect, the quality of the person on the platform, on the television screen, or behind the printed page. If the personality of the persuader is not acceptable, identification will be granted grudgingly, or not at all. The courses in salesmanship echo Aristotle with brutal simplicity: the first thing you have to sell is yourself.

Over the centuries, vats of ink have been spilt analyzing this process, but common sense remains the best guide. There are certain qualities that tend to detract from the appeal that the speaker might have for most listeners or readers. The man with little self-confidence can expect to win little confidence. The man eaten up by self-admiration can expect little admiration. The man who does not respect others can expect little respect. The man who does not know his own mind can scarcely control the minds of others. The man who cannot give sympathy rarely gets it—and certainly cannot arrive at identification with his audience. The man who has not thought through his subject cannot lead others into that subject. Nobody trusts a blunderer.

We see the face on the platform or on the television screen, the face of the insurance salesman courteously offering his fountain pen as he holds out the application form, or the face of a friend who wants us to go fishing with him. But what of the writer behind a page? We cannot see him. We cannot even hear his voice. How does his personality enter into persuasion?

We should realize, to begin with, that in a broad, general sense, the question of personality is involved in all kinds of writing, not merely in persuasion. We have touched on this very early in this text, for instance in discussing certain student themes (pp. 21–22). Style, in fact, has long been understood as an index of personality: the style is the man (p. 353). This whole book is, in a way, an attempt to develop the implications of that saying, but for the purpose of understanding persuasion, parts of the chapters on Diction and on Tone are especially important. At this point you should be sure that you have come to grips with the principles discussed there.

■ APPLICATIONS

I   In the light of your reading on Diction and Tone, go back to the themes you have written thus far. What impression do they give of your personality? Have you done yourself justice? What response would you expect from your readers? What kinds of readers have you been writing for?

II   Here is a sample of an introduction. Try to state what tone is characteristic, what attitude, in other words, the writer takes toward his audience. What does the writer reveal of his personality? Is he likely to be persuasive? Be sure that you consider questions of diction and rhythm.

> Dear Mary:
>   I have decided to start this book with a letter to you. You know that the idea came to me when I offered to help Johnny with his reading. It's really his book—or yours. So the only proper way to start it is with the words "Dear Mary."
>   You remember when I began to work with Johnny half a year ago. That was when he was twelve and they put him back into the sixth grade because he was unable to read and couldn't possibly keep up with the work in junior high. So I told you that I knew a way to teach reading that was altogether different from what . . .   —Rudolf Flesch: *Why Johnny Can't Read.*[1]

---

[1] Reprinted from *Why Johnny Can't Read,* by Rudolf Flesch, by permission of Harper & Row.

III Suppose that you are about to write a piece of persuasion—perhaps a letter or an editorial in the college newspaper. The occasion for this attempt at persuasion may be real or imaginary; but whatever it is, you are to establish clearly in your own mind the general situation, the nature of the audience you are to address, and the kind of attitude you think you should take toward them. You are to decide, in other words, what kind of an introduction would be appropriate. Now write the introduction. (The length may be from 150 to 200 words.)

Logic versus psychology in identification

We may further elaborate our discussion of the distinction between argument and persuasion by saying that the former is based on logic, the latter on psychology.[2] Persuasion begins, as we have said, with the persuader's act of identification and ends with the persuadee's act of assent, and both of these are psychological rather than logical events. That is, they involve the total man, not merely the mind working objectively and logically. The act of identification involves, as fully as possible, all the extralogical aspects of the persuader: he must, as Kenneth Burke puts it, take on all the "ways" of the persuadee. And the act of assent in persuasion requires far more than the logical conviction of the persuadee. As the old saying goes, "A man convinced against his will is of the same opinion still," but with the act of assent, the first thing the persuadee submits to the persuader is his will. His will is the determining fact of his being, of his identity, and when he *willingly* assents, the assent implies his total being.

What happens between the act of identification and the act of assent is a psychological event of fascinating complexity. It is a process of a paradoxical transformation: though by identification the persuader apparently surrenders his will to the persuadee, in the process he actually seizes the will of the persuadee. No, he does not seize the will of the persuadee; he lulls it, bemuses it, beguiles it, and he does so by appealing to the desires of the persuadee. And here we have another paradox: the persuadee, in the process of seeming to fulfill his own desires, surrenders his will.

When the target of the persuader is not an individual but a group, another psychological dimension develops. Merging with a group, the individual tends to slough off something of his identity—and often he does so with relief. The persuader fosters this process, in the expectation that insofar as the individual sheds the qualities that make him an individual, his willing submission to the persuader becomes more and more likely.

The most obvious example of this process is seen in mob action: we all know that a mob may commit acts of violence that no individual would commit if not caught up in the "mob spirit." But the same principle applies in certain religious services, patriotic meetings, political rallies, and protest

---

[2] This is true even when the persuader uses logic; the logic is presented in a "psychological context" (pp. 186–90).

demonstrations. The same psychological process may occur for either a good or a bad end.

Such persuasion of groups physically assembled together may seem very remote from your concerns in a chapter that has to do with the writing of themes embodying the principles of persuasion. But the same principles that govern the psychology of a group physically assembled have application to the individual privately reading words on a page.

An editorial in a college paper may suggest that "students" behave in a certain way, and the individual student, if he identifies himself with the writer's definition, is susceptible to the persuasion; that is, the individual student wants to "belong," and if certain attitudes and values are assumed to be necessary to belonging, then he may adopt those values. This principle is, of course, pervasive in advertising. For instance, a clothier runs an advertisement in a college paper with the heading "What the Student Will Wear This Fall." The implication is clear: Wear this if you wish to "belong."

■ APPLICATIONS

I Examine some newspapers and magazines to find examples, in editorials, articles, and advertisements, of the technique of persuasion that works by sinking the individual into a group.

II Write a short paragraph (150 words) that would serve as the opening of an editorial or article embodying this principle.

Persuasion and the Emotions

The second mode of persuasion according to Aristotle's analysis is through the emotions. Cicero, the master advocate, declared that all emotions "must be intimately known [by the orator], for all the force and art of speaking as a persuader must be employed in allaying or exciting the feelings of those who listen." This, clearly, is where the arts of the propagandist, politician, advertising man—and even the poet—intersect.

This is the point, too, that most radically distinguishes persuasion from strict argument (pp. 121 and 177–78). We have seen that, in the very first phase of the process of persuasion, the phase of identification, emotional attitudes rather than logic are essential, and are involved in the psychological maneuver by which an individual is reduced to a member of a group. But in the second mode of persuasion we move beyond those two preliminary considerations and consider emotion as the prime fact in the body of the persuader's discourse. Our key question, then, becomes: If assent is the end aimed at by the persuader, how does the mere stirring of emotion bring that about?

The answer lies in the psychological fact, long ago discovered, that an emotion, however aroused, seeks a justification and a target. The man who has an angry nature goes through life seeking excuses for his anger and targets on which to vent it. The man with a loving heart, likewise, goes about seeking justifications and targets. Furthermore, emotional agitation makes a person vulnerable to suggestion. "Emotional occasions," said William James, one of the founders of modern psychology, "especially violent ones, are extremely potent in precipitating mental rearrangements." And Freud later pointed out that we are not used to feeling strong emotions "without their having ideational content," and therefore, when content is lacking, "we seize as a substitute upon another content . . ." Thus the persuader, having worked up the emotion, of whatever nature, goes on to provide the content suitable to his intentions; and this content defines the target for the action he desires. Emotion always craves its appropriate fulfillment.

The persuader may work up a powerful particular emotion in his audience and manipulate it, as is done in the sermon of a revival preacher or in the harangue of the leader of a lynch mob. One famous example of such arousal, which we shall soon study, is in Winston Churchill's address to the House of Commons that focused the British will to win against Nazi Germany (p. 185).

But the persuader may also work, and sometimes most effectively, with long-term emotional attitudes that may represent desires and needs of which the persuadee may be scarcely conscious—or which he may even deny. The advertisement for the expensive Cadillac shows the vehicle against the background of a baronial establishment, and the gloating owners are, of course, a young, elegant, and beautiful couple, almost as much in love with each other as they are with the car. Thus all the hidden, unrealistic yearnings of some balding, no-longer-young but still minor executive—the yearnings for lost youth, good looks, fashion, social standing, ample means, sexual conquest, and true love, and the need to express aggressive impulses on the highway with 350 horsepower—all flow together to guide the hand that signs the contract for the convenient time-payment plan.

We are not concerned here with advertising for its own sake, but merely as a fairly simple illustration of the range and depth of attitudes that may be appealed to in persuasion. We have said "simple," for what is involved in selling cars is simple in comparison to the complexity of an even moderately successful literary work. And we say "literary work" because a poem (say "Ode to Autumn," by Keats, or a sonnet by Shakespeare) or novel (say *Bleak House,* by Dickens, or *War and Peace,* by Tolstoy) is as much a work of persuasion as a successful speech or an advertising campaign. The crucial difference—and the one on which the greater value of the literary work depends—is in the way the psychological factors are used.[3]

But what relation does all this have to you and your writing?

---

[3] A work of literature is not concerned with "selling" anything. It is concerned with an identification with other men and a sympathy with even the evil aspects of human nature—that is, with a knowledge of the human heart.

What is important for you is to cultivate your awareness of the psychological appeals of literature and to study its techniques of persuasion. You should constantly scrutinize your own responses, in your reading and in your daily life. You are your own best laboratory and reference library.

Slanting and suggestion

The evoking and manipulating of emotional attitudes that we have discussed often involve methods known as slanting and suggestion. By slanting we mean the method by which, without violating facts in any narrow sense, the persuader suggests such interpretations as are desired by the persuader. Slanting can be seen in its crudest form in single words or phrases used for connotative values. For example, Mr. X is, literally considered, a politician and a senator. The editorial in a newspaper supporting him refers to him as a "statesman" or a "dedicated public servant." But an editorial in an opposition newspaper prefers to call him a "party hack" or a "politico." The literal referent—Mr. X—is the same in both cases, but the aura of connotation is, clearly, not. (Read the section "How Associations Control Meanings" in Diction, pp. 298–99.)

This control of connotation is one of the devices determining the tone of any discourse, and tone, as we have pointed out, is of the greatest importance in persuasion. The instance of Senator X above is simple and obvious, but the principle can be applied with great complexity and subtlety. The "smuggling in" of emotion, as the critic I. A. Richards has called it, and the control of attitudes by this means are fundamental to all literature, especially to poetry. And this leads us from the general question of connotation in persuasion to that of metaphor; for metaphor, too, involves the smuggling in of emotion and the control of responses.

Let us take an example, the insult visited upon Edward Livingston, an extremely able politician of the early nineteenth century, by John Randolph of Roanoke, another politician and a famous wit. Livingston, said Randolph, "is a man of splendid qualities, but utterly corrupt. Like rotten mackerel in the moonlight, he shines and stinks." The insult converts Livingston's very reputation for brilliance into a liability. The brilliance becomes, in the metaphor, an index to the corruption: the same rotting fish that shines also stinks —the putrescence that it exudes adds to the glitter. And consider the use of the word *moonlight,* which implies that the rotting fish would not seem so brilliant by the light of day; then it would be recognized simply for what it is. The metaphor has condensed a range of meanings into the startling image, an image deep, paradoxical, and memorable.[4]

---

[4] The insult is sometimes reported, erroneously, to have been addressed to Henry Clay. For another famous insult (and a more complex one) see Whittier's poem on Daniel Webster called "Ichabod."

I What emotions are appealed to in the examples that follow? Does the speaker use the emotional appeal as a way of sinking the individual into a group? Does he insist on his own identification with the audience? Examine the language for elements that suggest unstated emotional appeals. Consider rhythm as a factor. In preparing to do this work, you might look over again the chapters on Diction, Metaphor, and Tone.

A The following passage is an excerpt from what is perhaps the most famous sermon ever preached in America, "Sinners in the Hands of an Angry God" (1741). The author was Jonathan Edwards, a Puritan minister famous for his piety and learning.

> O sinner! Consider the fearful danger you are in: it is a great furnace of wrath, a wide and bottomless pit, full of the fire of wrath, that you are held over in the hand of that God, whose wrath is provoked and incensed as much against you, as against many of the damned in hell. You hang by a slender thread, with the flames of divine wrath flashing about it, and ready every moment to singe it, and burn it asunder; and you have no interest in any Mediator, and nothing to lay hold of to save yourself, nothing to keep off the flames of wrath, nothing of your own, nothing that you ever have done, nothing that you can do, to induce God to spare you one moment.

B This passage occurs at the end of the speech made by Winston Churchill on June 4, 1940, to the House of Commons, after the defeat of the French and British armies and the evacuation of the remnant of the British forces from Dunkirk. The speech leading up to this conclusion is rather flat and factual, an account of events and an exposition of the desperate military situation.

> I am myself full of confidence that if all do their duty, if nothing is neglected, and if the best arrangements are made, as they are being made, we shall prove ourselves once again able to defend our island home, to ride out the storm of war, and to outlive the menace of tyranny, if necessary for years, if necessary alone. At any rate, that is what we are going to do. That is the resolve of His Majesty's Government—every man of them. That is the will of Parliament and the nation. The British Empire and the French Republic, linked together in their cause and their need, will defend to the death their native soil, aiding each other like good comrades to the utmost of their strength. Even though large tracts of Europe and many old and famous States have fallen or may fall into the grip of the Gestapo and all the odious apparatus of Nazi rule, we shall not flag or fail. We shall go on to the end. We shall fight in France, we shall fight on the seas and the oceans, we shall fight with growing confidence and growing strength in the air, we shall defend our island, whatever the cost may be. We shall fight on the beaches, we shall fight on the landing grounds, we shall fight in the fields and in the streets, we shall fight in the hills; we shall never surrender, and even if, which I do not for a moment believe, this island or a large part of it were subjugated and starving, then our Empire beyond the seas, armed and guarded by the British Fleet, would carry on the struggle, until, in God's good time, the New World, with all its power and might, steps forth to the rescue and the liberation of the old.

II In the first and second sets of Applications in this chapter (pp. 180–81 and 182) you were asked to write an introduction to a piece of persuasion. Return to those introductions and choose the one that you now consider more successful. What emotional appeals might be useful for developing the subject of the introduction you have chosen? Make an outline for such a development. Then write a section of the theme embodying these appeals (not less than 300 words).

Persuasion and logic: rationalization

We have been studying the relation of persuasion to emotion and certain methods of manipulating emotion. We now turn to Aristotle's third mode of persuasion, that of achieving assent by proving "a truth or an apparent truth."[5] The psychological phenomenon known as *rationalization* provides a sort of bridge between emotion in persuasion and logic in persuasion. Rationalization is the use of reason not to seek truth but to justify desires, attitudes, belief, decisions, or actions already determined on emotional grounds. In rationalization the forms of reason are used to work either or both of two kinds of deception: to deceive the self or to deceive others.

"Man cannot bear very much reality," the poet T. S. Eliot says in "Burnt Norton," and rationalization is man's built-in medicine against reality. We live by self-flattering illusions and self-exculpating alibis. When we catch the ball, we say: "Look, *I* caught the ball!" When we miss the ball, we say: "My *hand* slipped." Furthermore, we commonly live by decisions that we consider to be reasonably made and reasonably acted on, but that actually are determined by motives that are unconscious, or that we choose to avoid considering. The same is true of beliefs and attitudes. How much, for instance, does jealousy of the sexual vigor of the young contribute to the belief on the part of a number of the middle-aged that repressive measures in schools and colleges are essential to maintain law and order? How much does the "idealism" of the young spring from a desire for uninhibited sex and the automatic resentment against the authority of parents?

Although the rationalizer pretends otherwise, rationalization characteristically *follows* action, decision, attitude, or belief. Its function is to make the past comfortable to live with. Its role is not to initiate but to justify.

Not only the life history of an individual may reveal such rationalizations, but also the history of a nation. When the Nazis went to war, they went with Hitler's rationalization that Germany was being encircled and that they were acting in self-defense. When the Civil War in America is referred to as a crusade to free the slaves (which is very different from saying that slavery was a *necessary condition* of the war), some historians,

---

[5] We should clearly distinguish between two different relations of persuasion and logic. The first is the use of logic by the persuader in making his private preparation for the act of persuasion. For example, when the persuader analyzes his audience or the occasion, he is performing a logical operation, but one that is strictly for his own private use in preparing his discourse. The second relation between persuasion and logic appears in the discourse that is actually offered to the audience. It is with the use of logic in such a discourse that we are now concerned.

remembering Lincoln's statement that the war was to save the Union, are likely to detect here the sweet smell of rationalization. When slaveholders comforted themselves with the reflection that slavery brought the benighted African into contact with the Christian religion, the same odor began to rise. Europeans, and some Americans, remembering that the participation of the United States in World War I made us a rich and powerful country, look with suspicion on the slogan created to justify that war—"To Make the World Safe for Democracy."

Although it is true that much rationalization shows itself to be wildly illogical, illogicality is not the inevitable hallmark of rationalization. Rationalization, in fact, may express itself in what may seem to be very acceptable logic. To sum up, what distinguishes rationalization from valid reasoning is the *motive* from which it springs. Even a maniac may be faultlessly logical in argument, but we have to inspect his premises and his obsessions.

What use, you may ask, does an understanding of rationalization have for persuasion? The answer is that if you know the needs, desires, attitudes, and beliefs of the audience, then you know their most vulnerable points. A frequently successful stratagem is to provide the audience with an appropriate rationalization; in other words, the persuader may succeed by giving a mask of logic to the impulse of the audience that he wishes to exploit. Conversely, in order to defend yourself, you need to become aware of what rationalizations of your own a persuader may try to exploit.

To take an example from motivation research used in advertising:

> ... the producers of sugar-tooth items were confronting a public suffering from massive guilt feelings of another sort [different from the guilt feelings of cigarette smokers]. The public was starting to shun anything conspicuously sweet and sugary. Not only were Americans suffering their persistent guilt feelings about indulging themselves, but they were made doubly uneasy by all the publicity about the dangers of overweight and tooth decay, both widely attributed to rich, sugary foods. (Consumption of confectionery items fell more than 10 per cent from 1950 to 1955.) Much of the publicity, it should be added, was generated by the makers of low-calorie products and dentifrices. (Consumption of low-calorie soft drinks multiplied three hundred times from 1952 to 1955!) The candy manufacturers were reported losing customers in a "sticky market." Producers of sugary foods such as candy raised more than half a million dollars to tell their "story." More important, perhaps, the candymakers hired Dr. Dichter.
>
> He chided them for not countering blow for blow and for meekly accepting the role "imposed on candy by propaganda as being bad for the teeth and fattening instead of being widely known as a delightful, delicious, wholesome, and nourishing food . . . ." He mapped for them a strategy for getting us back to candy-munching on a mass basis in spite of all the propaganda. The real deep-down problem they had to cope with, he advised, was this guilt feeling about self-indulgence. One of the tactics he urged the candymakers to adopt was to emphasize bite-size pieces within the present large-size candy package. That, he advised, would appeal to us as self-indulgence in moderation. He confided: "You will be providing the excuse the consumer needs to buy a bar of candy—'After all, I don't have to eat

all of it, just a bite and then put the rest away.' Seriously, we doubt whether the rest will be put away. However, the consumer will be left with the feeling that candy manufacturers understand him and the bite-size piece will give him the 'permission' he needs to buy the candy because the manufacturers are going to 'permit' him to eat in moderation."

—VANCE PACKARD: *The Hidden Persuaders.*[6]

Fallacy

Persuasion, as Aristotle points out (p. 178), has not only to do with "truth," but with "apparent truth," and indeed the most obvious connection of persuasion with logic is its connection with the distortions of logic that we call fallacies. In studying persuasion, as in studying argument, one of the most fruitful fields to explore is that of fallacies. With one difference, however: in studying fallacies for argument, you study what you want to avoid in your own argument and to detect in that of others; in studying them for persuasion, you study what, unless you have moral scruples, you may sometimes profitably use. Certainly, if you want to study fallacies in persuasion, there are God's plenty of examples in advertising, political speeches, sermons, and commencement addresses.

Reasoning for Truth and Reasoning for Assent

We now turn to the relation between persuasion and valid reasoning.

The simplest examples of this relationship have either of two forms. The first is the persuasive appeal used merely as an introduction to an argument, or to the presentation of facts that are a basis for argument. Here the persuader is merely trying to gain fair attention; he trusts the force of the argument (or the facts) to achieve, by the logical process, the assent desired. The second form is the use of persuasion, after the argument or facts have been presented, to convert the logical conviction into emotional assent. A famous example of the latter form is to be found in the speech of Churchill after Dunkirk. The conclusion, which we have already seen above (p. 185), follows the low-keyed body of the speech, in which emphasis is not even on argument but on the exposition of the situation; and the conclusion comes all the more forcefully in that plain context, the emotional burst being, as it were, the answer to the question implied in the exposition: What, in such dire peril, shall we do?

The relations just discussed are, as we have said, simple. In more complicated instances, reasoning appears in the main body of the discourse, not as straight argument, but especially adapted to the demands of the persua-

---

[6] From *The Hidden Persuaders*, by Vance Packard. Reprinted by permission of David McKay Company. Reprinted by permission of Vance Packard and Longmans Green.

sive act. And this leads us to a distinction between *reasoning for truth* (as in straight argument) and *reasoning for assent* (as in persuasion). Reasoning for truth is directed to the subject, reasoning for assent to the audience—to the truth *about* the subject, to the assent *of* the audience. The first type of reasoning is characteristic of argument, the second, of persuasion.

Argument tends to the elaboration of reasoning; it aims to cover the case, to prove as much as possible. Persuasion tends to reason minimally, that is, only insofar as is necessary for assent; it aims to focus on one or more points, not to cover the whole case. Persuasion offers as little proof as necessary, for the simple reason that an elaboration of logical detail might, in the end, distract from the emotional commitment that persuasion seeks to evoke.

The amount of proof necessary for any particular instance varies according to the nature of the subject, the audience, and the occasion, but the accomplished persuader knows that even with the most logical audience you can "overargue." You can win the argument, but lose the audience. Therefore, when he resorts to logic, his problem is to be both minimal and effective. To be so, he must locate the *key point* (or *points*) to be argued and present them so that the argument *seems* to be definitive and comprehensive.

For a better understanding, we may regard this aspect of persuasion in relation to the issues of argument that we have discussed earlier (pp. 137–39). Logically considered, an issue is, as we have explained, a point that *must* be proved if the arguer is to win his case; there may, of course, be more than one issue involved, and when that is so, then to win the argument *all* issues must be proved.

With this in mind, let us look at the relation between an issue and what we here call a key point. In this matter we can distinguish two different strategies. The first dictates that the persuader, instead of arguing *all* the issues, as the strictly logical procedure would dictate, choose one or more as his key points and argue only on them. The persuader thus selects, shall we say, Issue A as the key point, and tries to argue it so compellingly that the audience forgets Issues B and C. Thus the persuader is using logic locally applied (merely to Issue A, the key point) to distract his audience from the demands of logic for complete proof. The second basic strategy dictates that the persuader select as the key point a matter that is *not* an issue and undertake to prove it. Here the persuader is using logic to distract from the logical demands of any real issue.

For an example of this second strategy, let us turn back to the argument between the husband and wife about moving to town (pp. 140–42). Suppose that the husband tries not to argue with his wife but to persuade her. To accomplish this, he might take as his key point the wife's love of music, arguing quite logically that her opportunities for hearing music would be much greater in town, for a symphony is being organized there, and so on. On this key point the husband may win the wife's assent to the move—though we know, from our previous analysis, that the availability of music is not really an issue.

We must remember, however, that certain occasions, by their very nature, permit no more than the illusion of logic; and in such instances this handling of logic may be legitimate. Let us examine the Gettysburg Address by Abraham Lincoln, which is justly admired as a noble utterance.

> Fourscore and seven years ago our fathers brought forth on this continent a new nation conceived in liberty and dedicated to the proposition that all men are created equal. Now we are engaged in a great civil war testing whether that nation, or any nation so conceived and so dedicated, can long endure. We are met on a great battlefield of that war. We have come to dedicate a portion of that field as a final resting-place for those who here gave their lives that that nation might live. It is altogether fitting and proper that we should do this. But, in a larger sense, we cannot dedicate, we cannot consecrate, we cannot hallow this ground. The brave men, living and dead, who struggled here have consecrated it far beyond our poor power to add or detract. The world will little note nor long remember what we say here, but it can never forget what they did here. It is for us the living rather to be dedicated here to the unfinished work which they who fought here have thus far so nobly advanced. It is rather for us to be here dedicated to the great task remaining before us—that from these honoured dead we take increased devotion to that cause for which they gave the last full measure of devotion—that this nation under God shall have a new birth of freedom, and that government of the people, by the people, for the people, shall not perish from the earth.

Matthew Arnold, one of the most important critics of the nineteenth century, as well as a fine poet, flung aside the newspaper report of this address after he got to the word *proposition*. He felt, presumably, that this hard, factual, almost technical word destroyed the eloquence appropriate to the occasion—the dedication of a cemetery on the field of a great battle. But was he right?

We maintain that Lincoln, not Arnold, was right. The word is appropriate and powerful, and for the very reason that Arnold found it offensive. No speech for such an occasion could undertake to argue the issues of the war, step by step. Lincoln could, in fact, only hint at his key point, for his purpose was simply to evoke a certain emotional attitude toward a particular desired end—the prosecution of the war. But the word *proposition* belongs to the world of argument, debate, and logic, and as such it smuggles into the occasion, as would a metaphor, the sense of rigor and precision associated with its origin. The word serves to say: "We have not time here to argue the whole meaning of the war, but I remind you that it has already been satisfactorily argued, and so we may now proceed to the present concern, our attitude as dictated by that meaning." The word serves to give the illusion of logic—more precisely, an "allusion" [7] to logic—as a basis for persuasion. This effect is continued in the next sentence by the word *testing,* which suggests that even the war itself may be taken metaphorically—at least—as a final stage in a logical process.

---

[7] In other words, it is assumed that the argument has already occurred, and all that is now required is a reference to it to establish a context, an "allusion."

I In the last set of Applications you wrote a section of a theme in persuasion, developing emotional appeals (p. 186). Now, for the same theme, develop a section of some 250 words, embodying the use of logic for persuasion.

II Look back over the last theme you wrote while studying Argument. Can you now see what issues might best be taken as key points in a theme of persuasion on the same topic? Take a key point that is *not* an issue and develop it in about 200 words.

Persuasion and Ethics

Does the mere ability to persuade entitle a man to the uninhibited use of the power that persuasion gives? This question, which is a fundamental one, appears as early as Plato's attack on the school of Sophists, in Athens, who were concerned with persuasion purely as a technique without reference to the ends to which it might be applied. The question is very much alive today. To take a few examples from among many possible ones: Has a politician running for office the right to inflame prejudice and passion on the matter of race? Has the manufacturer of cigarettes, which are presumably harmful, the right to persuade the public to smoke?

The particular question of ethics in persuasion turns on the general question of the relation of ends and means. Here we encounter two extreme views. The first, which we shall call the *technical,* holds that persuasion is merely a matter of technique. By this line of thought the power of persuasion is like, say, the power of nuclear fission: it can be used for good or ill, but is neutral in itself. Or it is like the power of a surgeon: he operates on flesh and bone laid before him without making any moral evaluation of the person whose flesh and bone are to be operated upon. The second view, which we shall call the *purposive,* holds that persuasion is directed toward ends and is therefore responsible for its ends.

In addition to the technical and the purposive views of the ethics of persuasion, we need to take into account another pair of perspectives: the *social* and the *personal.* What are the effects on society of different kinds of persuasion? And what kinds of persuasion are you, with your personal standards, willing to practice?

The social perspective

We must realize that the winning of assent has always had a fundamental role in the working of any society. Even the most tyrannical government has to gain some degree of assent, if merely from the palace guard. In modern democracies the base of necessary assent has been immeasurably broadened, and the achieving of assent is the essence of democratic government; it is also the essence of business. The crucial factors in today's world are the amount of control possible, the degree of the concentration of that control, and the responsibility of that control.

Within this century, there has been, as a result of technological development, and as a result of the concentration of financial control, a constant diminution of local and individual channels of expression and debate. Furthermore, public relations experts have tended to narrow the ground of thought and debate—that is, to fix on key points that have immediate impact and propaganda value rather than long-range significance. Moreover, the experts tend to reduce differences between persons and platforms, on the theory that in the clarification of issues more persuasive power is lost than gained. For example, various observers have noted that the opinions of candidates for office tend to get more alike as election day approaches. The world in which Abraham Lincoln and Stephen A. Douglas could seriously debate fundamental matters of the public interest has all but disappeared—or perhaps has already disappeared.

What is called the "image" of a man is more important than the man himself or what he stands for, in politics or in other activities. Raymond K. Price, one of the architects of President Nixon's election in 1968, is reported to have declared in the early stages of the campaign that rational arguments would "only be effective if we can get people to make the *emotional* leap . . ."

The report, written by a member of the campaign staff, continues:

> To do this, Price suggested attacking the "personal factors" rather than the "historical factors" which were the basis of the low opinion so many people had of Richard Nixon. "These tend to be more a gut reaction," he wrote, "unarticulated, nonanalytical, a product of the particular chemistry between the voter and the *image* of the candidate. *We have to be very clear on this point: that the response is to the image, not to the man . . .*"
> —JOE MC GINNISS: *The Selling of the President 1968.*[8]

The fundamental danger in the massive process of persuasion as we now know it, the danger that all criteria of thought and judgment will be eroded or perverted, is most clearly revealed in what is called saturation techniques, which depend on slogans rather than ideas, repetition rather than discussion, on hypnosis rather than awareness. This danger to thought and judgment is, of course, aggravated by the contempt for, or at least condescension toward, the public that characterizes at least a segment of the professional persuaders, an attitude fairly well indicated by the following remarks of the Whitaker of the famous public relations firm of Whitaker and Baxter:

> The average American, when you catch him after hours, as we must, doesn't want to be educated; he doesn't want to improve his mind; he doesn't want to work, consciously, at being a good citizen.

---

[8] From *The Selling of the President 1968,* by Joe McGinniss. Reprinted by permission of Trident Press. Copyright © 1969 by JoeMac, Inc. Reprinted by permission of the Sterling Lord Agency.

But there are two ways you can interest him in a campaign, and only two that we have ever found successful.

Most every American loves a *contest* . . . So *you can interest him if you put on a fight.* . . .

Then, too, most every American likes to be entertained. He likes the movies, he likes mysteries; he likes fireworks and parades. . . .

So if you can't fight, PUT ON A SHOW! . . .

—PATRICK O. MARSH: *Persuasive Speaking.*[9]

As Aldous Huxley has pointed out, in the early optimism engendered by general literacy and a free press, people were naive enough to believe that there were only two kinds of propaganda, the true and the false. They "did not foresee what in fact has happened, above all in our Western capitalist democracies—the development of a vast mass communication industry, concerned in the main neither with the true nor the false, but with the unreal, the more or less totally irrelevant." [10] And we may add another thing that was not foreseen: in the end, the contempt for, or condescension toward, the public affects the public's own view of itself; it becomes cynical toward its own opinions, more or less dimly realizing that those opinions may be a product of manipulation and are lacking in both intellectual and moral content.

The final contempt, and condescension, is to assume that it does not matter by what process assent is achieved if the assent is to a "good" thing—a good product, show, firm, candidate, or idea. This is a version of the notion referred to earlier that the end justifies the means, a notion that in most circles is not—at least, when baldly stated—regarded as respectable. When applied to persuasion the question becomes this: In what way and to what extent do the techniques devoted to achieving success debauch the capacity for judgment? When the persuadee is persuaded without reference to the grounds of assent, what Jacques Elluel, in *Propaganda: The Formation of Men's Attitudes,* calls the "elimination of individualizing factors" has occurred. That is, the person has ceased to be a person and has become a thing.

We cannot infer from the foregoing remarks that there ever was a time when rationality and high-mindedness generally reigned in human affairs, but today's expertly organized persuasion has raised doubts that the "examination of opinion," which Walter Lippmann, in *The Public Philosophy,* has called "one of the necessities of man," can survive without dangerous impairment. If there is a ground for optimism, it is that the disease may generate its own cure. The researches that arm the professional persuaders cannot be kept secret, and insofar as they become public knowledge they forewarn the public—unless, of course, the engendering of self-contempt in the public has passed the point of no return. And, too, education in general encourages—or is supposed to encourage—a critical attitude. That some

---

[9] Reprinted from p. 67 in *Persuasive Speaking* by Patrick O. Marsh (Harper & Row, 1967) by permission of Harper & Row, Publishers.

[10] "Propaganda in a Democratic Society," in *Brave New World Revisited* (New York, 1958).

change has been taking place, that there is an increase of awareness in the audience, is indicated by the increasing sophistication of advertising, chiefly in a strain of self-humor, a wink, as it were, at the audience that implies that "we both know this is a game we have to play."

But perhaps even advertising men can be victims of advertising, and politicians, of their own rhetoric. Then what?

The individual perspective

The question of persuasion in the social perspective is, of course, far more complicated than we have been able to suggest, but it is no less so in relation to the individual. He is torn between two roles. He is continually in the role of persuadee, exposed to the lure and benumbing of persuasion, to which he must bring what awareness and self-awareness he can muster. At the same time, to a greater or lesser degree, he plays the role of persuader. And both roles are complicated further by the fact that the ethical criteria applicable to one form of persuasion may not be, within certain limits, applicable to another. For instance, the illogic in much current advertising would not be ethically acceptable—or at least should not be—in a speech on a serious public issue.

What is acceptable to you? To you personally—not to a particular audience or in a particular form of persuasion? You are alone, then, with the question—and with yourself.

A note on rhetoric and persuasion

If the arts of rhetoric can be put to destructive uses when practiced by unscrupulous men, one may well ask: Should they be taught at all?

But clearly nothing is to be accomplished by trying to suppress the knowledge of rhetoric—as if it were a black art like witchcraft. The only remedy is for as many people as possible to learn something about how words work so that they will be armored against unscrupulous attacks on their minds and on their pocketbooks. The best defense against being overpowered by the rabble-rouser or bilked by the unethical advertiser is to become thoroughly aware of the power of words and to learn to distinguish legitimate appeals from illegitimate ones. Indeed, one function of the textbook that you are now reading is to help you become less vulnerable to the come-on of the demagogue and the manipulator of opinion.

■ APPLICATIONS

I Look up one of the following famous pieces of persuasion. Analyze the speech to determine how the speaker has achieved his ends. Does he use identification, appeal to emotion? What is his use of logic? Is his persuasion ethical?

1 Mark Antony's funeral oration from Shakespeare's *Julius Caesar*
2 Patrick Henry, speech in Richmond to Virginia Convention of Delegates to the Continental Congress (March 23, 1775)
3 William Faulkner, Nobel Prize acceptance speech (December 10, 1950)
4 Martin Luther King, "I Have a Dream" speech
5 John F. Kennedy, Inaugural Address

II You are now to write a theme in persuasion of some 700 words or more. If you like, you may use the material you have worked up for the previous Applications. In this theme you should try to use what you consider ethical methods of persuasion. Having written it, you are to take the same subject and write another version using whatever unethical appeals and devices may suggest themselves for the subject.

CHAPTER **8**

Description

Description, as we shall understand the word here, is the kind of discourse concerned with the impression that the world makes on our senses. It presents the qualities of objects, persons, conditions, and actions. It aims to suggest to the imagination the thing as it comes immediately to an observer. We call this kind of description *suggestive* to distinguish it from technical description, which is really a form of exposition. We have already discussed (pp. 96–99) the difference between technical description and suggestive description, but let us return to it, with new and more elaborate examples.

TECHNICAL:

The West Indies stand in a warm sea, and the trade winds, warmed and moistened by this sea, blow across all of them. These are the two great primary geographic facts about this group of islands whose area is but little larger than that of Great Britain.

These trade winds, always warm, but nevertheless refreshing sea breezes, blow mostly from the east or northeast. Thus one side of every island is windward, and the other side is leeward. The third great geographical fact about these islands is that most of them are mountainous, giving to the windward sides much more rain than the leeward sides receive. This makes great differences in climate within short distances, a thing quite unknown in the eastern half of the United States, where our slowly whirling cyclonic winds blow in quick succession from all directions upon every spot of territory. Thus both sides of the Appalachian Mountains are nearly alike in their rainfall, forest growth, and productive possibilities. On the contrary, the West Indian mountains have different worlds on their different slopes. The eastern or windward side, cloud-bathed and eternally showered upon, is damp and dripping. There are jungles with velvety green ferns, and forests with huge trees. The rainbow is a prominent feature of the tropic landscape. On the windward side one receives a striking impression of lush vegetation. On the leeward side of the very same ridge and only a few miles distant there is another kind of world, the world of scanty rainfall, with all its devastating consequences to vegetation. A fourth great geographic fact is the division of these islands into two great arcs, an outer arc of limestone and an inner arc of volcanic islands. The limestone areas are low. The volcanic areas are from moderately high to very high. Some islands have both the limestone and the volcanic features.

—J. RUSSELL SMITH and M. OGDEN PHILLIPS: *North America.*

SUGGESTIVE:

Take five-and-twenty heaps of cinders dumped here and there in an outside city lot; imagine some of them magnified into mountains, and the vacant lot the sea; and you will have a fit idea of the general aspect of the Encantadas, or Enchanted Isles. A group rather of extinct volcanoes than of isles; looking much as the world at large might, after a penal conflagration. . . .

It is to be doubted whether any spot on earth can, in desolation, furnish a parallel to this group. Abandoned cemeteries of long ago, old cities by piecemeal tumbling to their ruin, these are melancholy enough; but like all else which has once been associated with humanity they still awaken in us some thought of sympathy, however sad. Hence, even the Dead Sea, along with whatever other emotions it may at times inspire, does not fail to touch in the pilgrim some of his less unpleasurable feelings. . . .

In many places the coast is rock-bound, or more properly, clinker-bound; tumbled masses of blackish or greenish stuff like the dross of an iron furnace, forming dark clefts and caves here and there, into which a ceaseless sea pours a fury of foam; overhanging them with a swirl of grey, haggard mist, amidst which sail screaming flights of unearthly birds heightening the dismal din. However calm the sea without, there is no rest for these swells and those rocks, they lash and are lashed, even when the outer ocean is most at peace with itself. On the oppressive, clouded days such as are peculiar to this part of the watery Equator, the dark vitrified masses, many of which raise themselves among white whirlpools and breakers in detached and perilous places off the shore, present a most Plutonian sight. In no world but a fallen one could such lands exist.

—HERMAN MELVILLE: "The Encantadas,
or Enchanted Isles," *The Piazza Tales.*

The first of these passages, from a geography of North America, lists four "great geographic" facts and then indicates their influence on climate, vegetation, and appearance of the landscape. Occasionally there are feeble attempts to make the reader see the islands, as in the phrases "cloud-bathed" and "velvety green ferns," but the tendency is to give generalized information. For instance, concerning the rainbow, instead of giving us images that would stir our imaginations, the writers simply say, "The rainbow is a prominent feature of the tropic landscape." Or, instead of picturing for us the arid slopes of the leeward side of the mountains, the writers simply offer the phrase "all its devastating consequences to vegetation." Here the purpose of description is to present information; the chief structural features of the islands are identified, so that we may understand various other facts about the islands.

The second passage, like the first, is the description of a group of tropic islands. But Melville, the author, is not concerned with giving us a list of the great geographic facts and their consequences. His description naturally involves some of these facts, but the passage is not organized about an enumeration of them. It is organized in such a way as to return the reader continually to the sense of loneliness, ruin, and desolation that characterizes the islands. He wants to give the reader an impression of the islands, a feeling for them, rather than a systematic analysis of their characteristics.

The passage begins with the comparison of heaps of cinders in a dumping ground, associating the islands with the used-up, the finished, the dreary. The first paragraph ends with the phrase "penal conflagration," which implies ideas not merely of ruin and waste but also of sin and punishment—sin and punishment on a universal scale. The next paragraph is based on the ideas of the unhuman desolation, the blankness of the islands. In the last paragraph the image of the wasteland of cinders appears again in the phrases "clinker-bound" and "like the dross of an iron furnace," and again that of punishment, as suggested by the constant tumult of the sea, in the phrase "lash and are lashed." The idea of punishment and suffering becomes explicit in the last sentence, "In no world but a fallen one could such lands exist."

In other words, the whole passage is based on two things: the image of the cinder heap and the idea of sin and punishment, which combine to give the notion of a world after the Judgment, the final desolation. And it is this notion that provides the organizing principle for the description. It is the key to the interpretation that Melville gives to his facts.

Description: Scientist and Artist

In our study of exposition, we say (p. 96) that technical description is concerned with providing information *about* things, and we distinguish it from suggestive description, which is concerned with the direct presentation *of* things. These two kinds of description correspond, we may say, to the two kinds of motives that may underlie our use of description.

We may think of this distinction as the fundamental distinction between the motive of the scientist and the motive of the artist. The scientist appeals to our interest *about* the world and to our interest in explanations *of* the world. He is concerned with the general laws of nature. But the artist (of any kind—painter, poet, novelist, musician, and so on) appeals to our interest in the direct experience *of* the world. He is concerned with particulars as they strike him—particular experiences, particular objects. This is not to say that the artist may not also be concerned with generalizations—generalizations, for example, about human behavior. But the artist tends to approach even generalizations through the presentation of particulars. The novelist, for example, embodies his generalizations about human conduct in a particular story about a particular man.

This distinction between the two kinds of motives means that we find technical description characteristically in scientific writing and suggestive description characteristically in the work of literary artists—poets or essayists or fiction writers. For instance, the geographers describing the West Indies in our first example are writing as scientists. They want to give *information about* the climate, vegetation, and so on, of the islands. Melville, describing his islands, is writing as an artist; he wants to give us the direct *impression of* the place and to indicate to us how we might feel if we saw it.

We are not to assume that we find technical description only in scientific works and suggestive description only in artistic works. Technical description may occur in a letter, an essay, a guidebook, a history, an advertisement—wherever and whenever the impulse appears to give information about an object. By the same token, suggestive description may occur in any piece of writing at any point where the impulse for immediacy and vividness comes into play. Sometimes, both types appear in the same piece of writing.

■ APPLICATIONS

I At the end of this chapter (pp. 220–23), there is a group of examples of description. Read them carefully. Do you find any examples of technical description? In examples that are prevailingly suggestive, do you find any elements that might appear in technical description?

II Turn back to the chapter on Exposition and read the realtor's advertisement of a house and the corresponding piece of suggestive description of the house in the letter (p. 97). Also, glance again at the section on comparison and contrast in which we discussed how a thing may be regarded as belonging to different areas of interest—how, for example, a field may be regarded by a farmer, an infantry officer, and a painter (p. 57). Here, clearly, the farmer and infantry officer, if they had to write descriptions, would give us technical description. But the painter would be concerned with the appearance of the field, with the kind of description that might appear in a familiar letter or in a short story if the field were the setting of an episode.

Now select some object, such as the house, or some spot, such as the field, and write one paragraph—say 150 words—of technical description about it, in whatever area of interest you prefer. Then write a paragraph of suggestive description about the same thing.

Suggestive Description and the Senses

Suggestive description tells what impression the world makes on our senses. An apple is red, tweed is rough, lilies are fragrant. But these are crude and general bits of description and do not make us vividly aware of apple, tweed, or lily. A good writer would not be satisfied with this kind of description. He would want to make sharper discriminations. But to do so, he would have to cultivate his powers of observation. Even when writing of an imagined object rather than a real one before his eyes, he would have to call on his store of impressions drawn from real life. Observation gives us our sense of the world, and a person who wishes to become a good writer should make a real effort to train his powers of observation.

Powers of observation, however, are not useful to a writer who is not trained to put his perceptions into words. Discriminations among perceptions must be embodied in discriminations among words. Each sense absorbs an infinite variety of data, and each sense demands that we struggle toward a vocabulary of subtlety and precision. One way to train yourself is to focus attention, even for days at a time, on trying to discriminate among the data that one sense offers. Try to find the word for a particular sound, a particular color, a particular odor. Such an exercise will not only sharpen your sense of the relation of impression to word but will also train you in a basic method of description, the method of making one sense dominant in developing a general effect.

For example, here are three descriptive passages, each primarily concerned with impressions from a single sense. Note the discriminations made in each passage and the language used to record the observation.

> To tell when the scythe is sharp enough this is the rule. First the stone clangs and grinds against the iron harshly; then it rings musically to one note; then, at last, it purrs as though the iron and stone were exactly suited. When you hear this, your scythe is sharp enough; and I, when I heard it that June dawn, with everything quite silent except the birds, let down the scythe and bent myself to mow.
>
> —HILAIRE BELLOC: "The Mowing of a Field," *Hills and the Sea.*

> The thing I chiefly remember about my grandfather's barn is the way it smelled. I reckon this is because when I was there I was often lying with my eyes closed, on the hay in the loft, with only the smell coming to me, or I was down in my little workshop and so preoccupied that I was only aware of the smells. Up in the loft, when I lay there on a rainy day, all I had to do was close my eyes, and there was the impression of a hayfield on a hot summer day, one of the days when I had had such a good time, the kind of dry, sweet smell you get from the hay. When I was down in my workshop, there was the smell like ammonia from the stalls on one side, a clear, sharp sort of smell that makes your nose tingle. There was also the smell of good leather and saddle soap from the tackroom.　　　　—From a theme.

> When I think of hills, I think of the upward strength I tread upon. When water is the object of my thought, I feel the cool shock of the plunge and the quick yielding of the waves that crisp and curl and ripple about my body. The pleasing changes of rough and smooth, pliant and rigid, curved and straight in the bark and branches of a tree give the truth to my hand. The immovable rock, with its juts and warped surfaces, bends beneath my fingers into all manner of grooves and hollows. The bulge of a watermelon and the puffed-up rotundities of squashes that sprout, bud, and ripen in that

strange garden planted somewhere behind my finger tips are the ludicrous in my tactual memory and imagination.

—HELEN KELLER: *The World I Live In.*

In the first of these passages the sense of hearing is dominant; in the second, the sense of smell; in the third, the sense of touch. But in this third passage, which comes from a remarkable book written by a woman blind and deaf almost from birth, we also find temperature and pressure and strain: the coolness of water and the "upward strength" of the hill.

Thus far we have been speaking as though description depended on sorting out single words that are neatly matched to varieties of sense impressions. Within limits this is true. We hear the loud noise, and if we are to record the noise in a piece of description, the "loud noise" must become the crash, the bang, the thud, the boom, the bong, the clang, the howl, the wail, the scream—or whatever word most accurately presents the sound heard.

But often there is no word right for the occasion. Then we instinctively ask: "What was the sound *like?*"

Like the dry, echoless, air-cushioned report of a heavy board falling absolutely flat on cement? Like the cottony sound of a shotgun fired in distant woods, in fog? Like the anguished shriek of a saw in a sawmill when it strikes the pine knot? Like the dying suck and inhalation of the last greasy water going out of a sink? What was the sound *like?* We have to find some way to re-create the sound in the imagination of the reader.

So here we see in descriptive writing the natural tendency toward metaphor. For the vivid, for the specific, for the concrete—for all the things that it must present, description strains toward metaphor. Even in our brief examples above, the interfusion of observation and language occurs only in metaphor: the sound of the shotgun is "cottony," and the saw utters an "anguished shriek."

Massiveness of perception

Ordinarily, we do not depend on one sense exclusively to give us our feeling of the world, and in description we aim for the same massiveness we find in experience. If we say, "The apple is red," we are not giving a very good description of the apple, certainly nothing like our immediate impression of it. The apple is not only red; it is slick-looking and juicy-looking and fragrant. Our response to the apple is massive, involving several sense impressions, blending them into the impression of "appleness." Sometimes a single word may condense a whole series of qualities. If we say, "The ice is glassy," we evoke, with the word *glassy,* the slickness, the hardness, the transparency, and the brightness of glass.

■ APPLICATIONS

I   1   Among the examples at the end of the chapter do you find any that are, for the most part, based on one sense?

2 Do you find any instances of the attempt to give the massiveness of impression that we have been talking about?

3 Locate uses of metaphorical language. In each case, try to specify what purpose is served by the use.

II For use in the chapters on Description and Narration (description and narration are closely intertwined), you should keep a little notebook of observations. First work with each sense individually, trying to make all the discriminations possible. In this process try to enlarge your vocabulary of single words, but also try to think in metaphors. (At this point look at Chapter 12, Metaphor.) Then move on from such exercises to record observations and impressions of people, places, and events. Jot down your ideas quickly while they are fresh in your mind, but later try to revise them for greater effectiveness. At times specified by your instructor, turn in the notebook for his comment.

III After you have made entries in your notebook concentrating on individual senses, you should write a long paragraph of description focused on one sense. The paragraphs above will provide models, and your notebook should be a little mine of suggestions.

Description and the Other Kinds of Discourse

Not infrequently we encounter pieces of technical description in isolation—an article for a specialist or a technician of some kind—and we often find technical description as an extended part of long works of exposition and argument, or even in narration. But, aside from a limited number of works—for instance, certain essays and books of travel—we ordinarily find suggestive description subordinated to some other mode of discourse.

Does this mean that description is, therefore, a kind of discourse that we may dismiss lightly? No, for though it rarely stands alone and is often brief, the effect may be great. The vivid stroke, small in itself and seemingly unimportant, may give the touch of reality, the stimulus to the imagination.

Here is a piece of narrative that has been stripped of all its descriptive elements:

> The other waved the cigar, the other hand, in Horace's face. Horace shook it and freed his hand. "I thought I recognized you when you got on at Oxford," Snopes said, "but I—May I set down?" he said, already shoving at Horace's knee with his leg. He flung the overcoat on the seat and sat down as the train stopped. "Yes, sir, I'm always glad to see any of the boys, any time. . . ." He leaned across Horace and peered out the window at a station. " 'Course you ain't in my county no longer, but what I say a man's friends is his friends, whichever way they vote. Because a friend is a friend, and whether he can do anything for me or not. . . ." He leaned back, the cigar in his fingers.

The passage in its original form follows, with the descriptive elements italicized. Note how they give the sense of reality, of the immediately observable world, to what otherwise would be a bare synopsis of events.

> The other waved the cigar, the other hand, *palm-up, the third finger discolored faintly at the base of a huge ring,* in Horace's face. Horace shook it and freed his hand. "I thought I recognized you when you got on at Oxford," Snopes said, "but I—May I set down?" he said, already shoving at Horace's knee with his leg. He flung the overcoat—*a shoddy blue garment with a greasy velvet collar*—on the seat and sat down as the train stopped. "Yes, sir, I'm always glad to see any of the boys, any time. . . ." He leaned across Horace and peered out the window at a *small dingy station with its cryptic bulletin board chalked over, an express truck bearing a wire chicken coop containing two forlorn fowls, at three or four men in overalls gone restfully against the wall, chewing.* " 'Course you ain't in my county no longer, but what I say a man's friends is his friends, whichever way they vote. Because a friend is a friend, and whether he can do anything for me or not. . . ." He leaned back, the *unlighted* cigar in his fingers.
>
> —WILLIAM FAULKNER: *Sanctuary.*

Here, in a student theme, is an example of an almost completely bare narrative:

GETTING ENGAGED

It had been such a lovely day. There was bright sun and the ocean as still as the ocean ever gets. Joseph had taken me out in his little putt-putt to the island to fish and have a picnic. We fished from the boat, and then came ashore to eat lunch. We ate, then got in the shade of the rocks and sort of dozed off. At least, I did. I woke up with a start. Joseph had called me, I guess. It was easy to tell why. Off yonder, beyond where the sun was still shining, you could see the clouds piling up high.

It fascinated you to watch it. I couldn't take my eyes off it, and then I took a look at Joseph. He was looking at the clouds, too. It was a funny expression, sort of rapt and awe-struck, you might say. And suddenly he seemed so much younger than I had thought of him. It was like a little boy's face, with eyes wide while he looked at the clouds.

He came out of his trance. "Gosh," he said, "gosh, did you ever!" He suddenly went toward the boat, fast as a basketball player catching the ball and turning toward the basket for a shot. (Joseph is a wonderful basketball player.) "Grab the stuff, girlie, and come on!" he said.

I got in, and he shoved off and climbed over the side. He began to pull the lanyard to start the motor. He was nervous, not under control. Then the lanyard broke. I looked into his face and knew what had happened. We were in trouble.

Then he grinned. He looked somewhat scared, but he grinned. "Girlie," he said, "I got you into it, and that sticks me with getting you out."

Then he stopped grinning. He picked up the oars and put them in the oarlocks, not in a hurry. His face was different from what I had ever seen it to be. It looked like man's face now, and I knew the way he would look at forty or forty-five, or a thousand. I thought that that was a face I wouldn't mind looking at for a long time.

To make a long story short, we did manage to get in, but it was a tough trip. That evening I got engaged.

Here is the same theme as revised after discussion with the instructor. Some of the changes are, it is obvious, to improve paragraph and sentence structure, but by and large, the revision has been directed toward making the description of the scene and the actions more vivid.

GETTING ENGAGED

It had been such a lovely day, perfectly lovely, with bright sun and the ocean as still as the ocean ever gets, a slow swell like somebody breathing in an easy sleep, and instead of waves a lazy rippling now and then that made you think of a cat waking up and stretching in the sunshine, and then dozing off again. Joseph had taken me out in his little putt-putt to the island to fish and have a picnic. After we had fished and come ashore to eat our lunch, we lay in the shade of the rocks and sort of dozed off. At least, I did. I woke up with a start. Joseph had called me. It was easy to tell why.

Off yonder, beyond the glitter of the water where the sun still struck, you could see the clouds piling up like a cliff, black and slate-colored, streaked with purple. I said like a cliff, but it was like a cliff that somehow, momentarily, grew taller while you stared at it, looking awfully solid but somehow swelling and coiling upward at the same time, as though there were an interior force collecting itself for effort.

It fascinated you to watch it. I couldn't take my eyes off it, and then I sneaked a look at Joseph. He was staring at it, too. He had a funny expression, sort of rapt and awe-struck. And suddenly he looked so much younger than I had thought of him. It was a little boy's face, round and tanned, with eyes so wide suddenly that, against the tan of his face, the whites seemed to leap out at you. There was a smudge of oil on his left cheek, and some white sand stuck untidily in the oil against the brown skin. It was like the face of a little boy you wanted to tell, "Go and wash your face, you're a sight!"

But I didn't have time to say anything, for all at once he jerked out of his trance.

"Gosh," he said, "gosh, did you ever!" He suddenly swung toward the boat, fast as a basketball forward snagging the ball and swinging toward the basket for a shot. (Joseph is a wonderful basketball player.) "Grab the stuff, girlie, and come on!" he yelled.

I grabbed it, and in a numb blur of motion, I fell into the boat, and he shoved off and piled over the side, already reaching for the lanyard of the motor. Then, angrily, he was jerking the lanyard. It was a nervous motion, not steady and controlled, with the right pause, like a count, between tries. The lanyard snapped.

There was Joseph looking blankly down at the piece of cord hanging from his hand, his jaw loose and stupid. Then he looked at me, appealingly, as though I could do something about it. One look at his face, and I knew that we were in bad trouble. I felt sick, just looking at him.

Then he grinned. He grinned twistedly, with the lips tightening and a little white showing splotchily at the corners of the mouth, even under the tan. But it was a grin. "Girlie," he said, "Old Joe got you into this, and I reckon he will have to get you out." All at once, like the edge of a knife blade coming down, the grin was cut off. He grabbed the oars, fast all right, but he set them competently into the oarlocks, without any jiggling, and the first stroke was slow and steady. Lots of power but no hurry, as though he were on the crew following the count, and the blades came out clean from the water. We felt the oily lift and heave as the first swell took us, but the stroke didn't change.

Then I saw his face.

His face was different from what I had ever seen before. And all at once I knew it was a man's face, and I knew the way he would look when he was forty years old, or forty-five, or a thousand. I thought that that was a face I wouldn't mind looking at for a long time.

To make a long story short, we did manage to get in, but it was a tough trip. That evening we got engaged.

■ APPLICATION

Make a detailed study of the revision of the theme above. Perhaps the best way would be to underscore all the changes in the revised version, and then, item by item, to try to read the mind of the author who made the revisions. What, in each instance, is at stake?

The Dominant Impression

Even when description is used to support some other general intention, as in fiction, history, or reportage, it sometimes appears in a more or less extended form, with its own structure and development. We turn now to a study of the principles of that structure and development. And let us emphasize that we must have some grasp of them in order to make effective use of description even in its more incidental and supportive uses.

Often when we are trying to tell a friend how to recognize somebody, we say something like this: "Just watch for that nose; it's the only nose like it in the state. Just think of W. C. Fields and his nose, and you won't miss Jack Purden." Or: "No, Susie isn't good-looking, not if you look close. But you never look close, for she has those wonderful blue eyes. That's all you notice. They're so big and expressive."

When we speak this way, we are illustrating an important principle of description: the principle of the *dominant impression*. Jack Purden's big, bulbous nose (probably with grog blossoms, too) and Susie's wonderful, expressive eyes are dominant features. We recognize the individual by the dominant impression he makes. But the same thing may be true of a place or of anything else. Here, for example, is a paragraph from a student autobiography.

I was born and went to school in Cheyenne, Wyoming, but I never cared much about the town. What Easterners think romantic about it was just ordinary to me. What I cared about was the place we had for summers, not terribly far from Shoshone Falls. It is a valley with a river, and the valley and river suddenly widen out there with some alfalfa fields and trees and our place. But the big thing, the thing you always are conscious of, is the cliff on the west side. They call it Drum Mountain, because it looks like a drum, round-shaped, squat, and flat on top, an unusual shape for a mountain in that region. The first thing you look at in the morning is the sunlight hitting it and making the black rock glitter. It glitters then like it had fool's gold in it (iron pyrites, that is), but of course it hasn't. If it doesn't glitter, you think it won't be much of a day today, and the fishing will be rotten. Toward the middle of the afternoon, you suddenly know that the shadow of Old Drum is coming across everything. It makes a night down in the valley long before night comes, and it is peculiar to see bright sky off yonder, high up, when it is already getting dark in the valley. When there is going to be a full moon, the whole family will wait up to see when the moonlight first hits Drum Mountain. Then you go to bed, and I bet in some way Old Drum is always with you even when you are sound asleep.

Drum Mountain dominates the paragraph, provides the main impression, the unifying idea, even as it dominates the valley where the student spends his summers.

A prominent thing catches the eye. But sometimes the mere prominence of an object is not what is important, is not what catches our interest. Some mood or feeling provoked by the object, even though we find it hard to pin down to a particular detail, may strike us more strongly than any single physical feature, however prominent. So when we describe something, we may be concerned not so much with making it merely recognizable, with indicating salient features, as with indicating how we feel about it, how we interpret it. Of course, since we are using description, we must present the object, but the dominant impression that we strive to give may be a feeling provoked by the object—the mood, the atmosphere. We will select those elements in the object that contribute to the dominant impression.

We have seen how Melville, in describing the Encantadas, keeps emphasizing the ruined and tormented aspects of the islands, the aspects that point to his basic interpretation of the scene. True, the actual physical impression of the islands is strongly rendered. They are "clinker-bound," are like "the dross of an iron furnace." There are dark clefts and caves overhung by "a swirl of grey, haggard mist, amidst which sail screaming flights of unearthly birds." But this objective description constantly emphasizes Melville's own interpretation of the island as an image of ruin and punishment, as when, in the quotation above, he calls the birds "unearthly," and as when, in the last sentence of the piece, he winds up with an explicit statement, "In no world but a fallen one could such lands exist."

We do not need to be as explicit as Melville, however, to convey very strongly a dominant mood for a thing described. Look at the following description by Dickens of a country estate in England:

The waters are out in Lincolnshire. An arch of the bridge in the park has been sapped and sopped away. The adjacent low-lying ground, for half a mile in breadth, is a stagnant river, with melancholy trees for islands in it, and a surface punctured all over, all day long, with falling rain. My Lady Dedlock's "place" has been extremely dreary. The weather, for many a day and night, has been so wet that the trees seem wet through, and the soft loppings and prunings of the woodsman's axe can make no crack or crackle as they fall. The deer, looking soaked, leave quagmires where they pass. The shot of a rifle loses its sharpness in the moist air, and its smoke moves in a tardy little cloud towards the green rise, coppice-topped, that makes a background for the falling rain. The view from my Lady Dedlock's own windows is alternately a lead-coloured view, and a view in Indian ink. The vases on the stone terrace in the foreground catch the rain all day; and the heavy drops fall, drip, drip, drip, upon the broad flagged pavement, called, from old time, the Ghost's Walk, all night. On Sundays, the little church in the park is mouldy; the oaken pulpit breaks out into a cold sweat; and there is a general smell and taste as of the ancient Dedlocks in their graves. —CHARLES DICKENS: *Bleak House.*

All the details are selected to reinforce the impression of dampness, depression, and gloom. The river is "stagnant," the blows of the axe make only "soft loppings," the report of the rifle "loses its sharpness in the moist air," the church is "mouldy," and the pulpit "breaks out into a cold sweat." Note how the phrase "breaks out into a cold sweat," though applied quite literally to the damp wood of the pulpit, actually serves to remind us of a situation that would make a human being do the same thing and leads us up to the "general taste and smell as of the ancient Dedlocks in their graves."

Items that might contradict the impression that Dickens wants dominant are left out. For example, if Dickens had presented the roaring fires on the hearths of the Dedlock mansion and the steaming roasts and puddings, he would have distracted from the impression he wished to make. The Dedlock family undoubtedly would have had roaring fires and steaming roasts, but that is beside the point.

Dickens, as we have seen, depends primarily on the piling up of details supporting the main impression. Only twice does he use a word that is explicitly interpretive: *melancholy* (once) and *dreary* (once).

Atmosphere and feeling

In the passage above, Dickens has created what we call an atmosphere— the mood, the temper, the general feeling associated with the thing described. He gives us an impression of gloom and dampness and decay.

We know, however, even as we use these words to define the atmosphere of this piece of description, that the labels we put on the passage are too vague and loose to define the effect that it gives. Our defining words do not really define the atmosphere; they merely give a crude indication, a not very dependable hint, of the effect that we find in the actual description.

Our inability to define atmosphere in general terms indicates the importance of the way the author himself goes about presenting it to us. He knows that he cannot create the desired atmosphere simply by using loose, general words. Therefore, he undertakes to give such concrete details, such aspects of his object, as will stir our imaginations not only to grasp the appearance of the object (or the sound, the color, and so forth) but to adopt a certain feeling toward the object. And here, again, the language of metaphor is of prime importance. Notice how the last sentence of the passage from Dickens brings to focus the feeling of the whole, and how that sentence is dominated by the metaphor of the pulpit breaking "into a cold sweat."

We have said earlier that suggestive description aims *not to tell* us about its object, but *to give* us the object. It also can be said that it aims *not to tell* us what feelings to have about the object and what attitudes to take toward it, but *to create* those feelings and attitudes within us. Vividness and immediacy, not only in regard to the physical qualities of the object but in regard to the feelings and attitudes involved, are what the writer desires.

■ APPLICATIONS

I From the examples of description at the end of this chapter (pp. 220–23), select two that give a dominant impression by emphasizing some prominent feature of the thing described. Then select two that seem successful in creating a dominant impression of mood. In this second pair of examples, underscore the details that contribute to the dominant atmosphere. Do you find any contradictory details? Try to explain the effect of any examples of metaphor that you think help create the atmosphere.

II Think of some place that impresses you as having a definite atmosphere. In your notebook make an informal list of the items belonging to the place that contribute to this dominant impression. Make another list of items that seem contradictory. Now make a list of comparisons that might be used to support the dominant mood. In the future, as you encounter or remember some interesting subject, do the same thing.

Selection

In discussing the dominant impression, we made a distinction between features of an object that are impressive in themselves and features that are important because they contribute to the mood or atmosphere. We might say, then, that details in description are important for either vividness or significance. The power of observation, as we have said, is essential, but we cannot merely accumulate details. We must choose the telling ones. Description works by *selection,* and when we are reading description, we should get the habit of asking ourselves, over and over again, "Why did he select this detail?" Or, "Why that one?" Or, "Why does this detail stir my imagination, and why does that one fail to do so?"

With these questions in mind, let us look at two examples.

Here is the description of a town as approached from the sea. The most obvious quality of what is emphasized, the blinding brilliance of light, strikes the observer at the first moment.

> But when at last we anchored in the outer harbor, off the white town hung between the blazing sky and its reflections in the mirage which swept and rolled over the wide lagoon, then the heat of Arabia came out like a drawn sword and struck us speechless. It was midday; and the noon sun in the East, like moonlight, put to sleep the colors. There were only lights and shadows, the white houses and black gaps of streets; in front, the pallid lustre of the haze shimmering upon the inner harbors; behind, the dazzle of league after league of featureless sand, running up to an edge of low hills, faintly suggested in the far away mist of heat.
> —T. E. LAWRENCE: *Seven Pillars of Wisdom.*[1]

Vividness, however, may be gained by indicating some detail that might escape ordinary observation. In such a case, it is the precision and subtlety of the description that makes the thing being described come alive for us. John Burroughs, the naturalist, in a passage on the art of observation, gives a list of details that would escape most observers but that sharply evoke a series of scenes and moments:

> His [the naturalist's] senses are so delicate that in his evening walk he feels the warm and cool streaks in the air, his nose detects the most fugitive odors, his ears the most furtive sounds. As he stands musing in the April twilight, he hears that fine, elusive stir and rustle made by the angleworms reaching out from their holes for leaves and grasses; he hears the whistling wings of the woodcock as it goes swiftly by him in the dusk; he hears the call of the killdee come down out of the March sky; he hears far above him in the early morning the squeaking cackle of the arriving blackbirds pushing north; he hears the soft, prolonged, lulling call of the little owl in the cedars in the early spring twilight; he hears at night the roar of the distant waterfall, and the rumble of the train miles across country when the air is "hollow"; before a storm he notes how distant objects stand out and are brought near on those brilliant days that we call "weather-breeders." When the mercury is at zero or lower, he notes how the passing trains hiss and simmer as if the rails or wheels were red-hot.
> —JOHN BURROUGHS: *Leaf and Tendril.*

The rustling of the angleworms gives a vivid sense of the stillness, more vivid than any number of the usual and easily observable details. Or take the "squeaking cackle" of the blackbirds; it is the absolutely right phrase to describe the sound, and because of the accuracy of the observation, our imagination fills the sky with the flock of birds passing over. Or think how striking is the "hiss and simmer" of the train on the rails!

---

[1] From *Seven Pillars of Wisdom* by T. E. Lawrence. Copyright 1926, 1935 by Doubleday & Company, Inc. Reprinted by permission of the publisher.

■ APPLICATION

Return to the examples at the end of the chapter and select details that strike you as effective. Try to distinguish those that seem to be chosen primarily for vividness from those that seem chosen for significance. To do this, you will, of course, have to know what the dominant impression of each example is.

Caricature

The word *caricature* comes from the Italian word *caricatura*, which means a satirical picture; but the derivation of the Italian word is from a word meaning "to load," and so the satirical effect in caricature is associated with the idea of overloading, that is, with exaggeration. Caricature, then, comes from the forcing, the exaggeration, of the basic principle of good description—the principle of the dominant impression. We see this most obviously in the work of many cartoonists: the strong chin of the luckless politician becomes as big as a shovel; the strong nose becomes a bulbous potato. But the same principle is an old resource of literature. Here is a famous example from Dickens, who delighted in the method:

> Mr. Chadband is a large yellow man, with a fat smile, and a general appearance of having a good deal of train oil in his system. Mrs. Chadband is a stern, severe-looking, silent woman. Mr. Chadband moves softly and cumbrously, not unlike a bear who has been taught to walk upright. He is very much embarrassed about the arms, as if they were inconvenient to him, and he wanted to grovel; is very much in a perspiration about the head; and never speaks without first putting up his great hand, as delivering a token to his hearers that he is going to edify them.
>
> —CHARLES DICKENS: *Bleak House.*

Here the impression of oiliness and fattiness dominates the picture, first in a quite literal sense, but the literal oiliness becomes an interpretation of the character of Chadband; the smile is "fat," and his general manner is unctuous too, like that of a hypocritical preacher.

■ APPLICATIONS

I   From the examples at the end of the chapter pick out one or more instances of caricature. Do the physical details suggest an interpretation of character?

II   Write a theme of some 400 words using the method of caricature. The following titles may offer an idea:

> The Banker Who Is Every Inch a Banker
> The Man Who Never Got Over Being a Major in the Marine Corps
> The Perfect Professor
> The Campus Big Shot
> The Campus Revolutionary

The Novelist (or Poet) To Be
Miss Grimes, of the Third Grade

Look into the sketches in your notebook for suggestions.

Choice of words [2]

The inexperienced writer tends to make adjectives bear the burden in description. Such a writer forgets that suggestion is often better than enumeration and that the mere listing of qualities is not the best method of evoking an image in the reader's mind. Let us look at the following portrait:

> The woman's face was fat and shapeless, so fat that it looked very soft, flabby, grayish, and unhealthy. The features were blurred because her face was fat. But her small, black, glistening eyes had a quick inquisitive motion as they moved from one face to another while the visitors stated their errand.

In that description the writer has piled up the adjectives, trying to specify each of the qualities of the woman's face and eyes. The result is a rather confused impression. Let us now take the passage as William Faulkner originally wrote it (before we tampered with it):

> Her eyes, lost in the fatty ridges of her face, looked like two small pieces of coal pressed into a lump of dough as they moved from one face to another while the visitors stated their errand.
> —WILLIAM FAULKNER: "A Rose for Emily."

Here the writer has managed to dispense with most of the adjectives, for the word *dough* implies *soft, flabby, grayish, shapeless, blurred,* and (when associated with flesh) *unhealthy,* and the word *coal* implies *black* and *glistening.* The use of a comparison will frequently enable the writer to dispense with adjectives. But when the writer does use adjectives, he should be sure that each adjective really adds something essential to the description. Rather than give the list of adjectives above, one could simply say that the face was "fat and doughy."

The discussion above really returns us to the question of selection. But here we are talking about diction—the selection of words rather than details. Although adjectives are an essential part of every writer's equipment, one can frequently get greater vividness by using nouns, adverbs, verbs, and verbals. For instance, note the descriptive force of the italicized nouns in the following examples:

> They crept up the hill in the twilight and entered the cottage. It was built of *mud-walls,* the surface of which had been washed by many rains into *channels* and *depressions* that left none of the original flat *face* visible: while here and there in the thatch above a rafter showed like a *bone* protruding through the *skin.*   —THOMAS HARDY: "The Withered Arm."

---

[2] See Chapter 11, Diction.

And a wind blew there, tossing the withered tops of last year's grasses, and *mists* ran with the wind, and ragged *shadows* with the *mists,* and *mare's-tails* of clear *moonlight* among the *shadows,* so that now the boles of birches on the forest's edge beyond the fences were but opal *blurs* and now cut *alabaster.*

—WILBUR DANIEL STEELE: "How Beautiful with Shoes."

We can see that in these passages the nouns are of two kinds. First, there are those that simply point to some parts of the thing described, such as *channels, depressions, mists, shadows, moonlight.* Second, there are those that involve comparisons, such as *alabaster, bone,* and *skin.*

When we turn to adverbs, we find that this part of speech sometimes enables a writer to get an effect with great economy by fusing the quality of a thing with its action. When Dickens writes, in describing Chadband, that he "moves softly and cumbrously, not unlike a bear who has been taught to walk upright," the adverbs *softly* and *cumbrously* give a much more vivid and immediate effect than would be possible if we broke up the description in the following fashion: "Mr. Chadband is soft, heavy, and awkward-looking. When he walks his motion is not unlike that of a bear that has been taught to walk upright." But adverbs, like other parts of speech, are subject to misuse. Vague, overworked "intensifiers" like *very, so,* and *really* often actually weaken the effect of a passage.

In the use of verbs, the same concentration of effect is possible; for frequently the right verb can imply something about the nature of the thing or person performing an action as well as about the nature of the action. In the following passage, which describes a herd of wild horses corralled in a barn lot, note how the variety and accuracy of the italicized verbs and verbals give the impression of furious, aimless motion and define the atmosphere of violence of the scene:

"Come on, grab a holt," the Texan said. Eck grasped the wire also. The horses *laid* back against it, the pink faces *tossing* above the *backsurging* mass. "Pull him up, pull him up," the Texan said sharply. "They couldn't get up here in the wagon even if they wanted to." The wagon moved gradually backward until the head of the first horse was *snubbed* up to the tail-gate. The Texan took a turn of wire quickly about one of the wagon stakes. "Keep the slack out of it," he said. He *vanished* and *reappeared,* almost in the same second, with a pair of heavy wire-cutters. "Hold them like that," he said, and *leaped.* He *vanished,* broad hat, *flapping* vest, wire-cutters and all, into a kaleidoscopic maelstrom of long teeth and wild eyes and *slashing* feet, from which presently the horses began to burst, one by one like partridges *flushing,* each wearing a necklace of barbed wire. The first one crossed the lot at top speed, on a straight line. It *galloped* into the fence without any diminution whatever. The wire *gave, recovered,* and *slammed* the horse to earth where it lay for a moment, *glaring,* its legs still *galloping* in air. It scrambled up without having ceased to gallop and crossed the lot and *galloped* into the opposite fence and was *slammed* again to earth. The others were now freed. They *whipped* and *whirled* about the lot like dizzy fish in a bowl. It had seemed like a big lot until now, but now the very idea that all that fury and motion should be transpiring inside any one fence was something to be repudiated with contempt like a mirror trick.   —WILLIAM FAULKNER: *The Hamlet.*

We see from these examples that the choice of words for descriptive effect can be extremely complicated; and it is especially important to realize that the interaction of the parts of speech, this interpenetration of function, is not merely to give variety but is related to the very nature of perception. When the author looked at the horses surging in the lot, he perceived the scene totally. He did not see a horse, then add color to it, and then add motion, and then add a description of the motion. He perceived everything at once. This interaction and interpenetration of which we speak in reference to the use of language is simply a way of rendering the unity—what we have earlier called the massiveness—of perception (p. 201). This rendering conforms to the nature of the experience, to its vividness and immediacy.

■ APPLICATIONS

I   Write a brief description (250 words) of some action to illustrate the unity of perception.

II   In the passage by Cormac McCarthy (p. 222) at the end of this chapter, locate some adjectives, nouns, adverbs, and verbs that you think are used with strong descriptive effect. In each case try to explain what makes the word effective. How would you characterize the atmosphere of the passage?

Texture and Pattern in Description

Thus far in this chapter we have been concerned with the observation of details, the relation of such details to a dominant impression of the thing described, and the choice of words in giving a description. We may call the combination of these three things the *texture* of description.

Insofar as the details of description relate to the dominant impression, they have some principle of order, and in the last analysis the relation of details to the dominant impression is the most important single consideration. But we must also think of the way details are grouped in relation to the structure of the thing described—whatever that thing is, a landscape, an object, a human face. We cannot simply list details at random, even when they do contribute to a dominant impression. There must be a *pattern*.

Pattern and point of view

If one observes a person, an object, or a scene, one notes that each has its proper unity—in a flash we recognize a friend, a tree, a familiar room, a meadow with woods beyond. But if, when we set out to describe one of these things, we give a mere catalogue of unrelated details, a mere enumeration of this, that, and the other, the sense of vital unity is gone.

The reason is clear. When we look at something, even though our attention is focused on some one aspect, we are constantly aware of the totality; it is all there before us at one time. In description, however, the details are presented to us one after another; instead of the simultaneous presentation that we find in actuality, we now have presentation in sequence. Since simultaneous presentation is impossible in description, if the writer is to give the details a proper unity, he must provide some pattern into which the reader can fit them.

When we are dealing with visual description, which is by far the most common kind, it helps to give an impression of unity if we think of whatever is being described as seen by an observer. We need not specify the observer literally in the description; we may merely imply such a presence by the way we present the details. We simply ask how, under such-and-such conditions and from such-and-such a location, an observer would see the details.

FIXED OBSERVER

The most obvious and simple pattern is to assume an observer at some fixed point from which he views the whole scene or object and then reads off the details from left to right, from foreground to background, from bottom to top, or in some such way. In other words, we simply take the details as they come in the object itself, starting from some arbitrary point. Here is an example from a theme:

> When I went home from college for Christmas, I got in on the night train, and as soon as the excitement wore off, I went straight upstairs to bed in my old room, where I had been ever since my baby days. I was so sleepy I didn't see a thing. I just tumbled in. But I woke up early. I couldn't hear a sound in the house, and so I lay there idly just looking around. Suddenly I felt as though this were the first time I had ever been in that room, it was so strange.
>
> Way at the left of my range of vision was the closet, with the door open, the way I must have left it the night before. Inside I could see my summer dresses hanging up in covers, all neat as a pin, and my shoes on racks. I remembered how untidy I had left things and thought that my mother must have done that for me. Next was my dressing table, almost bare, for I had taken a lot of things with me to college, but what was there was in order, laid out to the quarter of an inch on the glass top. Around the mirror were still stuck some invitations and things, keepsakes from my last year in high school.
>
> Then I looked out the window, and I could see the blue patch of sky, no clouds at all, and the snow on the steep, jumbled-up roofs of the Madison place, which is very Victorian, with sharp roofs and little turrets, with lightning rods and weathervanes. I wondered about Jack Madison, for on the wall just to the right of the window was the Harvard pennant he had given me last summer because he was going to be a freshman at Harvard. I thought now that he was probably ashamed of that, as kid stuff.

Beyond the pennant was my high school picture, the ordinary kind, with the boys looking awful stiff and trying to be grown-up, and the girls all cocking their heads trying to look glamorous like movie stars. I sort of smiled, looking at them, they were so kid-looking and unsophisticated, you might say. Then, all at once I thought that I was in the picture, too, and the silliest one of the lot. I blushed to think how silly. Then suddenly I felt sad. It was as though I had died; that was why everything was so tidy in the room, and I was somebody else who happened to be sleeping in a strange room where somebody else used to live and had died.

The girl who wrote this theme has a general idea, of course. She is now grown-up and away at college, and she wants to tell how she feels when she comes back home for the first time. This idea provides the dominant impression she is trying to give: the sense of strangeness and, also, the awareness of a kind of loss. But what we are concerned with at the moment is not the impression she wants to convey, but the way the details that produce the impression are put into order. The order she uses is almost the simplest possible: as she lies on her pillow her glance moves from left to right, and she simply lists the things she sees.

MOVING OBSERVER

The piece of description above has been given from a fixed point—the girl's pillow when she wakes up. But often we find it useful to think of a moving observer—either a specified observer or one not specified, merely assumed. In the following example a person (the author) is climbing up a gorge in Arabia, over a pass, and down the other side. He reports things simply as he comes to them.

Our path took us between the Sakhara and the Sukhur by a narrow gorge with sandy floor and steep bare walls. Its head was rough. We had to scramble up shelves of coarse-faced stone, and along a great fault in the hill-side between two tilted red reefs of hard rock. The summit of the pass was a knife-edge, and from it we went down an encumbered gap, half-blocked by one fallen boulder which had been hammered over with the tribal marks of all the generations of men who had used this road. Afterwards there opened tree-grown spaces, collecting grounds in winter for the sheets of rain which poured off the glazed sides of the Sukhur. There were granite outcrops here and there, and a fine silver sand underfoot in the still damp water-channels. The drainage was towards Heiran.

—T. E. LAWRENCE: *Seven Pillars of Wisdom.*[3]

In the excerpt above, the observer is specified. But the same method, of course, may be used with an implied observer in motion, as in this theme:

The approach to ——— is anything but attractive, and it is made worse by the contrast with the nice hilly country the road has just passed through, where there are lots of woods and streams. The first thing one sees on the approach is a paper mill, where they convert the pulp. It is a big, sprawly,

---

[3] From *Seven Pillars of Wisdom,* by T. E. Lawrence. Copyright 1926, 1935 by Doubleday & Company, Inc. Reprinted by permission of the publisher.

disorderly looking mass of buildings, two of them very high. They are drab colored. The smell is awful, and what they do to Techifaloo River is a caution, for the waste goes in there.

After the paper plant come the real slums of the town. They are mostly shacks, but farther on are quite a few very nice houses, with good lawns and flowerbeds. This is where the skilled workers live. Next comes the new hospital, a really fine brick structure.

The warehouse section begins not far beyond the hospital, for here is where the railroads from the east cross the Techifaloo. . . .

There is some incidental comment and opinion here, along with the description, but the description itself is patterned by the eye of an unspecified observer assumed to be entering the town by the highway.

NO OBSERVER SPECIFIED OR IMPLIED:
IMPRESSIONISTIC METHOD AND GENERALIZED DESCRIPTION

In the following description of the main street of a small Midwestern town, no observer is specified. The details are pointed out, one after another, not even put in complete sentences, merely listed, jotted down as they appear. (This loose method, the use of jottings as a style of presentation, is called *impressionistic*.) The whole effect is as though a movie camera has simply swung over the street, picking up a detail here, a detail there.

From a second-story window the sign, "W. P. Kennicott, Phys. & Surgeon," gilt on black sand.

A small wooden motion-picture theater called "The Rosebud Movie Palace." Lithographs announcing a film called, "Fatty in Love."

Howland & Gould's Grocery. In the display window, black, overripe bananas and lettuce on which a cat was sleeping. Shelves lined with red crepe paper which was now faded and torn and concentrically spotted. Flat against the wall of the second story the signs of the lodges—the Knights of Pythias, the Maccabees, the Woodmen, the Masons.

Dahl & Oleson's Meat Market—a reek of blood.

—SINCLAIR LEWIS: *Main Street.*

The pure impressionistic method, the use of jottings as a style of presentation, seems easy, and therefore tempting—not only are we free of the problem of the order of presentation of detail; we don't have to bother with sentence structure or even with paragraph structure. But the very easiness is a danger. It is easy to be tedious, to accumulate too many details, to lose all sense of structure and of a dominant impression. To be effective in this method we have to be very careful that the details are telling, are sharp, and we must not pile up so many details that the sense of a whole is lost.

Pattern by interest

Thus far, except when dealing with the impressionistic method, we have been talking of unifying a description by assuming an observer who sees the details of the object in some physical order—say from left to right, or as he comes to them while moving. But let us assume an observer who is less passive, who brings some strong interest to the things described. This interest then gives us the unity for describing the object. Here is a soldier inspecting a bridge he is about to dynamite. The structure of the bridge and the location of the enemy defenses give focus to the description.

> The late afternoon sun that still came over the brown shoulder of the mountain showed the bridge dark against the steep emptiness of the gorge. It was a steel bridge of a single span and there was a sentry box at each end. It was wide enough for two motor cars to pass and it spanned, in solid-flung metal grace, a deep gorge at the bottom of which, far below, a brook leaped in white water through rocks and boulders down to the main stream of the pass.
>
> The sun was in Robert Jordan's eyes and the bridge showed only in outline. Then the sun lessened and was gone and looking up through the trees at the brown, rounded height that it had gone behind, he saw, now that he no longer looked into the glare, that the mountain slope was a delicate new green and that there were patches of old snow under the crest.
>
> Then he was looking at the bridge again in the sudden short trueness of the little light that would be left, and studying its construction. The problem of its demolition was not difficult. As he watched he took out a notebook from his breast pocket and made several quick line sketches. As he made the drawings he did not figure the charges. He would do that later. Now he was noting the points where the explosive should be placed in order to cut the support of the span and drop a section of it back into the gorge. It could be done unhurriedly, scientifically and correctly with a half dozen charges laid and braced to explode simultaneously; or it could be done roughly with two big ones. They would need to be very big ones, on opposite sides and should go at the same time.
>
> —ERNEST HEMINGWAY: *For Whom the Bell Tolls*.[4]

● CAUTION

Remember that, sometimes, the mood itself may serve as the device for unifying a description, as for instance in Dickens's description of the Dedlock estate.

Frame image

So far we have been concerned with unifying description by reference to an observer, specified or unspecified, but the use of an observer is not the only possibility. For instance, a writer may compare the rather complicated object he is describing with something simpler and more easily visualized. This simpler object is then imagined as providing a kind of frame image into which we can fit the details of the original thing to be

---

[4] Reprinted with the permission of Charles Scribner's Sons from *For Whom the Bell Tolls* (Copyright 1940 Ernest Hemingway; renewal copyright © 1968 Mary Hemingway). Reprinted by permission of Jonathan Cape Ltd. and the Executors of the Ernest Hemingway Estate.

described. Here is the image of an arm used to give unity to an impression of Cape Cod:

> Cape Cod is the bared and bended arm of Massachusetts; the shoulder is Buzzard's Bay; the elbow, or crazy-bone, at Cape Mallebarre; the wrist at Truro; and the sand fist at Provincetown,—behind which the state stands on her guard, with her back to the Green Mountains, and her feet planted on the floor of the ocean, like an athlete protecting her Bay,—boxing with northeast storms, and, ever and anon, heaving up her Atlantic adversary from the lap of earth,—ready to thrust forward her other fist, which keeps guard while upon her breast at Cape Ann.
>
> —HENRY DAVID THOREAU: *Cape Cod.*

Mixed patterns

We have been trying to distinguish several ways of unifying description and have given examples of relatively simple and unmixed methods. But the methods can be mixed, and sometimes the most effective description does combine the methods, as in this passage:

> About four in the morning, as the captain and Herrick sat together on the rail, there arose from the midst of the night, in front of them, the voice of the breakers. Each sprang to his feet and stared and listened. The sound was continuous, like the passing of a train; no rise or fall could be distinguished; minute by minute the ocean heaved with an equal potency against the invisible isle; and as time passed, and Herrick waited in vain for any vicissitude in the volume of that roaring, a sense of the eternal weighed upon his mind. To the expert eye, the isle itself was to be inferred from a certain string of blots along the starry heaven. And the schooner was laid to and anxiously observed till daylight.
>
> There was little or no morning bank. A brightening came in the east; then a wash of some ineffable, faint, nameless hue between crimson and silver; and then coals of fire. These glimmered awhile on the sealine, and seemed to brighten and darken and spread out; and still the night and the stars reigned undisturbed. It was as though a spark should catch and glow and creep along the foot of some heavy and almost incombustible wall-hanging, and the room itself be scarcely menaced. Yet a little after, and the whole east glowed with gold and scarlet, and the hollow of heaven was filled with the daylight.
>
> The isle—the undiscovered, the scarce believed in—now lay before them and close aboard; and Herrick thought that never in his dreams had he beheld anything more strange and delicate. The beach was excellently white, the continuous barrier of trees inimitably green; the land perhaps ten feet high, the trees thirty more. Every here and there, as the schooner coasted northward, the wood was intermitted; and he could see clear over the inconsiderable strip of land (as a man looks over a wall) to the lagoon within; and clear over that, again, to where the far side of the atoll prolonged its pencilling of trees against the morning sky. He tortured himself to find analogies. The isle was like the rim of a great vessel sunken in the waters; it was like the embankment of an annular railway grown upon with wood. So slender it seemed amidst the outrageous breakers, so frail

and pretty, he would scarce have wondered to see it sink and disappear without a sound, and the waves close smoothly over its descent.

—ROBERT LOUIS STEVENSON: *The Ebb Tide.*

In this passage we have a location and an observer specified. At one time, in the course of the description (the view across the atoll), we find the method of simple spatial ordering used, the method of the fixed point of view. At another time, the principle of sequence comes into play, the method of the moving point of view. In fact, it comes into play in two different ways. First, we have the principle of sequence in time, in the coming of dawn, and then we have it in space, as the schooner coasts northward along the island. But we also find the frame image used to give us a clearer notion of the island: Herrick, the observer, "tortured himself to find analogies," and to describe the atoll we find the frame images of the "rim of a great vessel sunken in the waters" and of the "embankment of an annular railway grown upon with wood." We may note that there is an organization in terms of climax, for only at the end of the passage as given here do we get the full statement of the frame image and of the basic mood, Herrick's response to the fragile and dreamlike beauty of the island, which is the dominant impression.

■ APPLICATIONS

I   At the end of this chapter there are a number of descriptive passages. List the different types of patterns that are illustrated in them.

II   Here are three exercises in description:

1   You are now sitting in a room. Look at your extreme left, then turn your eyes slowly from left to right. What do you see? Describe what you see, nothing more, nothing less, in order, in perhaps 150 to 200 words. What impression, what mood if any, seems dominant as you read your paragraph? What mood or impression strikes you as you look about you again? With this in mind, revise what you have written.

2   Think of your home town, the block you live on, or some familiar spot. Imagine that you are approaching it. What do you see, item by item, and in what order? What feelings and ideas suggest themselves as you imagine approaching the scene? Write a paragraph or two of description, with the objects and your feelings in mind.

3   You have some special interest. You hunt, you fish, you play baseball, you collect postage stamps, you watch birds, you watch people. Think of some scene or occasion that appealed to your special interest. Then write a description of that, using your interest as the device for giving the scene unity.

III   This exercise comes later, perhaps a day or a week. You now have your grade on the work requested above. Read over what you have written, and at the same time try to remember your imagined subject and your feelings about your subject. Do the words now before you give you an impression of that subject and of your feelings about it? Be honest with yourself. If you are dissatisfied with what you have written, how would you now improve it?

Selections

On the following pages are a number of examples of description. These have already been referred to in Applications in this chapter, and your instructor may frame new problems for investigation. For review, however, the following suggestions may be helpful:

1 Locate instances of appeals to different senses. What words, phrases, and comparisons make such appeals?
2 Find instances of several types of patterns.
3 Are there any instances of caricature?
4 In instances in which description is used to suggest a character, an atmosphere, or a state of feeling, try to state in your own words what the character, atmosphere, or state of feeling is. What details contribute to your impression?
5 Locate a number of comparisons. Which are used for vividness? Which are used for interpretive significance? Are there any that seem too strained to be effective? Are there any that seem stale?

A   A knot of country boys, gabbling at one another like starlings, shrilled a cheer as we came rattling over a stone bridge beneath which a stream shallowly washed its bank of osiers.

　　　　　　　　　　—WALTER DE LA MARE: *Memoirs of a Midget.*

B   Without being robust, her health was perfect, her needlework exquisite, her temper equable and calm; she loved and was loved by her girlfriends, she read romantic verses and select novels; above all, she danced. That was the greatest pleasure in life for her; not for the sake of her partners— those were surely only round dances, and the partners didn't count; what counted was the joy of motion, the sense of treading lightly, in perfect time, a sylph in spotless muslin, enriched with a ribbon or flower, playing discreetly with her fan, and sailing through the air with feet that seemed scarcely to touch the ground.

　　　　　　　　　　—GEORGE SANTAYANA: *Persons and Places.*

C   Leaning over the parapet, he enjoyed, once more, the strangely intimate companionship of the sea. He glanced down into the water, whose uneven floor was diapered with long weedy patches, fragments of fallen rock, and brighter patches of sand; he inhaled the pungent odor of sea wrack and listened to the breathing of the waves. They lapped softly against the rounded boulders which strewed the shore like a flock of nodding Behemoths. He remembered his visits at daybreak to the beach—those unspoken confidences with the sunlit element to whose friendly caresses he had abandoned his body. How calm it was, too, in this evening light. Near at hand, somewhere, lay a sounding cave; it sang a melody of moist content. Shadows lengthened; fishing boats, moving outward for the night-work, steered darkly across the luminous river at his feet. Those jewel-like morning tints of blue and green had faded from the water; the southern cliff-scenery, projections of it, caught a fiery glare. Bastions of flame. . . .

The air seemed to have become unusually cool and bracing.
—NORMAN DOUGLAS: *South Wind.*

D He was a Mr. Cornelius Vanslyperken, a tall, meagre-looking personage, with very narrow shoulders and very small head. Perfectly straight up and down, protruding in no part, he reminded you of some tall parish pump, with a great knob at its top. His face was gaunt, cheeks hollow, nose and chin showing an affection for each other, and evidently lamenting the gulf between them which prevented their meeting. Both appear to have fretted themselves to the utmost degree of tenuity from disappointment in love; as for the nose, it had a pearly round tear hanging at its tip, as if it wept.
—FREDERICK MARRYAT: *The Dog Fiend.*

E But I eat. I gradually lose all knowledge of particulars as I eat. I am becoming weighed down with food. These delicious mouthfuls of roast duck, fitly piled with vegetables, following each other in exquisite rotation of warmth, weight, sweet and bitter, past my palate, down my gullet, into my stomach, have established my body. I feel quiet, gravity, control. All is solid now. Instinctively my palate now requires and anticipates sweetness and lightness, something sugared and evanescent; and cool wine, fitting glove-like over those finer nerves that seem to tremble from the roof of my mouth and make it spread (as I drink) into a domed cavern, green with vine leaves, musk-scented, purple with grapes. Now I can look steadily into the mill-race that foams beneath. By what particular name are we to call it? Let Rhoda speak, whose face I see reflected mistily in the looking-glass opposite; Rhoda whom I interrupted when she rocked her petals in a brown basin, asking for the pocket-knife that Bernard had stolen. Love is not a whirl-pool to her. She is not giddy when she looks down. She looks far away over our heads, beyond India. —VIRGINIA WOOLF: *The Waves.*

F The nether sky opens and Europe is disclosed as a prone and emaciated figure, the Alps shaping like a backbone, and the branching mountain-chains like ribs, the peninsular plateau of Spain forming a head. Broad and lengthy lowlands stretch from the north of France across Russia like a grey-green garment hemmed by the Ural mountains and the glistening Arctic Ocean. —THOMAS HARDY: *The Dynasts.*

G I studied M. de Charlus. The tuft of his grey hair, the eye, the brow of which was raised by his monocle to emit a smile, the red flowers in his buttonhole formed, so to speak, the three mobile apices of a convulsive and striking triangle. —MARCEL PROUST: *The Guermantes Way.*

H In search of a place proper for this, I found a little plain on the side of a rising hill, whose front towards this little plain was steep as a house-side, so that nothing could come down upon me from the top; on the side of this rock there was a hollow place, worn a little way in, like the entrance or door of a cave; but there was not really any cave, or way into the rock at all.

On the flat of the green, just before this hollow place, I resolved to pitch my tent. This plain was not above an hundred yards broad, and about twice as long, and lay like a green before my door, and at the end of it descended irregularly every way down into the low grounds by the seaside. It was on the NNW. side of the hill, so that I was sheltered from the heat every day, till it came to a W. and by S. sun, or thereabouts, which in those countries is near the setting. —DANIEL DEFOE: *Robinson Crusoe.*

The drover waved his staff and scrabbled away over the rocks like a thin gnome. Holme sat for a while and then rose and followed along the ridge toward the gap where the hogs were crossing.

The gap was narrow and when he got to it he could see the hogs welled up in a clamorous and screeching flume that fanned again on the far side in a high meadow skirting the bluff of the river. They were wheeling faster and wider out along the sheer rim of the bluff in an arc of dusty uproar and he could hear the drovers below him calling and he could see the dead gray serpentine of the river below that. Hogs were pouring through the gap and building against the ones in the meadow until these began to buckle at the edges. Holme saw two of them pitch screaming in stiff-legged pirouettes a hundred feet into the river. He moved down the slope toward the bluff and the road that went along it. Drovers were racing brokenly across the milling hogs with staves aloft, stumbling and falling among them, making for the outer perimeter to head them from the cliff. This swept a new wave of panic among the hogs like wind through grass until a whole echelon of them careening up the outer flank forsook the land and faired into space with torn cries. Now the entire herd had begun to wheel wider and faster along the bluff and the outermost ranks swung centrifugally over the escarpment row on row wailing and squealing and above this the howls and curses of the drovers that now upreared in the moil of flesh they tended and swept with dust had begun to assume satanic looks with their staves and wild eyes as if they were no true swineherds but disciples of darkness got among these charges to herd them to their doom.

Holme rushed to higher ground like one threatened with flood and perched upon a rock there to view the course of things. The hogs were in full stampede. One of the drovers passed curiously erect as though braced with a stick and rotating slowly with his arms outstretched in the manner of a dancing sleeper. Hogs were beginning to wash up on the rock, their hoofs clicking and rasping and with harsh snorts. Holme recoiled to the rock's crown and watched them. The drover who had spoken to him swept past with bowed back and hands aloft, a limp and ragged scarecrow flailing briefly in that rabid frieze so that Holme saw tilted upon him for just a moment out of the dust and pandemonium two walled eyes beyond hope and a dead mouth beyond prayer, borne on like some old gospel recreant seized sevenfold in the flood of his own nether invocations or grotesque hero bobbing harried and unwilling on the shoulders of a mob stricken in their iniquity to the very shape of evil until he passed over the rim of the bluff and dropped in his great retinue of hogs from sight.

Holme blinked and shook his head. The hogs boiled past squealing and plunging and the chalky red smoke of their passage hung over the river and stained the sky with something of sunset. They had begun to veer from the bluff and to swing in a long arc upriver. The drovers all had sought shelter among the trees and Holme could see a pair of them watching the herd pass with looks of indolent speculation, leaning upon their staves and nodding in mute agreement as if there were some old injustice being righted in this spectacle of headlong bedlam.

When the last of the hogs had gone in a rapidly trebling thunder and the ochreous dust had drifted from the torn ground and there was nothing but quaking silence about him Holme climbed gingerly from his rock. Some drovers were coming from the trees and three pink shoats labored up over the rim of the hill with whimpering sounds not unlike kittens and bobbed past and upriver over the gently smoking land like creatures in a dream.

—CORMAC MC CARTHY: *Outer Dark.*[5]

[5] From *Outer Dark* by Cormac McCarthy. Copyright © 1968 by Cormac McCarthy. Reprinted by permission of Random House, Inc.

CHAPTER **9**

Narration

Narration is the kind of discourse concerned with action, with events in time, with life in motion. It answers the question "What happened?" It tells a story. As we use the word here, a story is a sequence of events—historically true or false—so presented that the imagination is stimulated. This is not a full account of narration, but it is enough to start with.[1]

The kind of narration we are concerned with here is to be sharply distinguished from expository narration, which characteristically appeals to the understanding (pp. 102–05). Let us, for an extreme contrast, set the directions for gluing felt to wood, which we have earlier given as an example of expository narration (p. 103), against a fairy tale, say Hans Christian Andersen's "The Tinder Box." After reading this piece of expository narration, anyone will understand how to glue felt to wood: he can really go ahead and do it. If we read the fairy tale we learn what happened to the little soldier, how he met the witch, and how, by a series of marvelous adventures, he married the king's daughter and possessed the kingdom; but it certainly cannot be said that we have come to "understand" how to get possession of a kingdom. We cannot even see how the success of the little soldier has any logic. He didn't succeed because he was intelligent, industrious, or honest, or because he embodied any virtue whatsoever. Success merely "happened" to him—wonderfully, marvelously, and that was that. Nor, to follow this thought, can it be said that the tale is directed to making us "understand" that life often seems illogical, and that success may come by accident—as we know it may. No, the tale makes the child (or the adult, who

---

[1] We ordinarily think of storytelling as the special province of fiction. But fiction is only one kind of narration. There is, for example, history or sports reporting. Here we are concerned with narration in general—as a mode of discourse—though later we shall touch on some of the special problems of fiction.

always retains something of the child deep in him) live imaginatively in the world of wonder and marvel, where success comes with the effortlessness of a dream. In fact, the tale is a kind of dream, in which we escape from the hard logic of the world into the realm of unthwarted desire.

Intention

The contrast between these two examples—the directions for gluing felt to wood and the fairy tale—is, as we have said, extreme. In actual practice we rarely find the distinction so clear-cut. Let us look at another piece of narration, from a book about wolves:

> One factor concerning the organization of the family [of wolves] mystified me very much at first. During my early visit to the den I had seen *three* adult wolves; and during the first few days of observing the den I had again glimpsed the odd wolf several times. He posed a major conundrum, for while I could accept the idea of a contented domestic group consisting of mated male and female and a bevy of pups, I had not yet progressed far enough into the wolf world to be able to explain, or to accept, the apparent existence of an eternal triangle.
>
> Whoever the third wolf was, he was definitely a character. He was smaller than George, not so lithe and vigorous, and with a gray overcast to his otherwise white coat. He became "Uncle Albert" to me after the first time I saw him with the pups.
>
> The sixth morning of my vigil had dawned bright and sunny, and Angeline and the pups took advantage of the good weather. Hardly was the sun risen (at three A.M.) when they all left the den and adjourned to a nearby sandy knoll. Here the pups worked over their mother with an enthusiasm that would certainly have driven any human female into hysterics. They were hungry; but they were also full to the ears with hellery. Two of them did their best to chew off Angeline's tail, worrying it and fighting over it until I thought I could actually see her fur fly like spindrift; while the other two did what they could to remove her ears.
>
> Angeline stood it with noble stoicism for about an hour and then, sadly disheveled, she attempted to protect herself by sitting on her tail and tucking her mauled head down between her legs. This was a fruitless effort. The pups went for her feet, one to each paw, and I was treated to the spectacle of the demon killer of the wilds trying desperately to cover her paws, her tail, and her head at one and the same instant.
>
> Eventually she gave it up. Harassed beyond endurance she leaped away from her brood and raced to the top of a high and sandy ridge behind the den. The four pups rolled cheerfully off in pursuit, but before they could reach her she gave vent to a most peculiar cry.
>
> The whole question of wolf communication was to intrigue me more and more as time went on, but on this occasion I was still laboring under the delusion that complex communications among animals other than man did not exist. I could make nothing definite of Angeline's high-pitched and

yearning whine-cum-howl. I did, however, detect a plaintive quality in it which made my sympathies go out to her.

I was not alone. Within seconds of her *cri-de-coeur,* and before the mob of pups could reach her, a savior appeared.

It was the third wolf. He had been sleeping in a bed hollowed in the sand at the southern end of the esker where it dipped down to disappear beneath the waters of the bay. I had not known he was there until I saw his head come up. He jumped to his feet, shook himself, and trotted straight toward the den—intercepting the pups as they prepared to scale the last slope to reach their mother.

I watched, fascinated, as he used his shoulder to bowl the leading pup over on its back and send it skidding down to the lower slope toward the den. Having broken the charge, he then nipped another pup lightly on its fat behind; then he shepherded the lot of them back to what I later came to recognize as the playground area.

I hesitate to put human words into a wolf's mouth, but the effect of what followed was crystal clear. "If it's a workout you kids want," he might have said, "then I'm your wolf!"

And so he was. For the next hour he played with the pups with as much energy as if he were still one himself. The games were varied, but many of them were quite recognizable. Tag was the steady, and Albert was always "it." Leaping, rolling and weaving amongst the pups, he never left the area of the nursery knoll, while at the same time leading the youngsters such a chase that they eventually gave up.

Albert looked them over for a moment and then, after a quick glance toward the crest where Angeline was now lying in a state of peaceful relaxation, he flung himself in among the tired pups, sprawled on his back, and invited mayhem. They were game. One by one they roused and went into battle. They were really roused this time, and no holds were barred— by them, at any rate.

Some of them tried to choke the life out of Albert, although their small teeth, sharp as they were, could never have penetrated his heavy ruff. One of them, in an excess of infantile sadism, turned its back on him and pawed a shower of sand into his face. The others took to leaping as high into the air as their bowed little legs would propel them; coming down with a satisfying thump on Albert's vulnerable belly. In between jumps they tried to chew the life out of whatever vulnerable parts came to tooth.

I began to wonder how much he could stand. Evidently he could stand a lot, for not until the pups were totally exhausted and had collapsed into complete somnolence did he get to his feet, careful not to step on the small, sprawled forms, and disengage himself. Even then he did not return to the comfort of his own bed (which he had undoubtedly earned after a night of hard hunting) but settled himself instead on the edge of the nursery knoll, where he began wolf-napping, taking a quick look at the pups every few minutes to make sure they were still safely near at hand.

His true relationship to the rest of the family was still uncertain; but as far as I was concerned he had become, and would remain, "good old Uncle Albert."   —FARLEY MOWAT: *Never Cry Wolf.*[2]

---

[2] From *Never Cry Wolf* by Farley Mowat, by permission of Little, Brown and Co. and Little, Brown and Co. (Canada) Limited, Toronto. Copyright © 1963 by Farley Mowat.

This account is the work of a scientist, a biologist employed by the Canadian government to make a study of *canis lupus* to determine whether the creature should be exterminated. The overall intention of the biologist is, then, expository, or perhaps argumentative. The first paragraph is basically expository: Mowat wants us to understand the structure of the family of *canis lupus*, the type of family organization characteristic of the species. But we can sharply distinguish this intention, and that of the whole book, from the fact that this account, considered in itself, is a rounded piece of narrative appealing to the imagination, a charming and humorous little tale.

In the following anecdotes we see even more sharply this distinction between the nonnarrative frame (exposition) and the narrative illustration.

> Undergraduate life at Cambridge [Massachusetts] has not lacked for bitter passages, which compel notice from any anatomist of society. On the one hand there has long been a snobbery moulded of New England pride and juvenile cruelty which is probably more savage than any known to Fifth Avenue and Newport. Its favorite illustration is the time-worn tale of the lonely lad who to feign that he had *one* friend used to go out as dusk fell over the yard and call beneath his own windows, "Oh, Reinhardt!" And on the other it has moments of mad, terrible loyalty—exampled by the episode which is still recalled, awesomely without names, over the coffee and liqueurs when Harvard men meet in Beacon Street or in the South Seas. It is the true story of a Harvard senior at a party in Brookline, who suddenly enraged by a jocular remark made concerning the girl whom he later married, publicly slapped the face of his best friend—and then in an access of remorse walked to an open fire and held his offending hand in the flame until it shrivelled away to the wrist.
>
> —DIXON WECTER: *The Saga of American Society.*[3]

Each of these two anecdotes serves perfectly as the illustration of a general idea (pp. 62–67). But each is, in itself, a well-organized little narrative. We can readily see how each might be the germ of a fully developed short story.

Interest and method

We have seen that a piece of narrative may be found in a context that has an overall nonnarrative intention. But let us take a case in which precisely the same materials may be treated with different methods, one being exposition, the other narration.

> George Barton, a poor boy about twelve years old, was forced to sell the mastiff, which he had reared from a puppy and was much attached to, for two reasons. First, having lost his job, he could no longer buy proper food for a dog of such size. Second, after it had frightened a child in the neighborhood, he was afraid that someone would poison it.

---

[3] Reprinted with the permission of Charles Scribner's Sons from *The Saga of American Society* by Dixon Wecter. Copyright 1937 Charles Scribner's Sons; renewal copyright © 1965 Elizabeth Farrar Wecter.

This paragraph involves an action, the fact that the boy sells the dog, but its primary concern is with the causes of the action rather than with the immediate presentation of the action in time. Let us rewrite the passage:

> George Barton owned a mastiff, which he had reared from a puppy. He loved it very much. But he lost his job and could no longer buy proper food for it. Then the dog frightened a little child in the neighborhood, who was eating a piece of bread. George was afraid that someone would poison the dog. So he sold it.

Here, as before, the causes of the action are given, but now the emphasis is different, and they are absorbed into the movement of the action itself. When we wrote in the first version that George sold the dog for two reasons, we violated the whole nature of narrative—the movement in time—because we made the causes of the action, not the action itself, the primary interest. The first piece of writing is primarily expository; it explains why the boy sold the dog. The second is primarily narrative; it tells us what happened.

Narration and absorbed forms of discourse

Just as narration can be a part of a larger piece of writing that is a different mode of discourse, so narration can absorb other modes to its dominant intention. To take a simple instance, a novel involving a bank robbery might well include expository narration in presenting the method used by the robbers. The same novel, in giving the psychological background of a robber, might also tell how childhood circumstances had warped his character, and this would be an example of causal analysis. When writing about the black sedan careening down the dark street, the author would, no doubt, use some descriptive touches. And after the gang had made its getaway, the members might well fall into an argument, or one robber, in a fit of conscience, thinking of his dear, gray-haired old mother, might argue with himself as to whether he should give himself up.

● CAUTION

To discriminate and tag the various forms of discourse involved in a piece of narration, as we have just done with the hypothetical story of the bank robbery, is not, in itself, an end, but is merely a way to understand more clearly the relation of other forms of discourse to the narrative intention. Remember:

1 Subordinate intentions must fulfill their own functions.
2 Subordinate intentions must be significantly related to the main function.

Furthermore, the end effect of a piece of narration involving subsidiary intentions should be one of easy absorption and not of jagged differences.

Summary

Narration gives us a moving picture, objects in motion, life in its flow, the transformation of life from one moment to the next. It does not *tell about* a story. It *tells* a story.

It aims to give immediacy, a sense of the event before our eyes, involving us, our interest, and perhaps our sympathy. Description, too, aims to give immediacy, but its purpose is to give the quality of an action, not the movement of the action itself.

Action is what narration presents.

Action and Sequence

Action is motion, and narration gives us this motion in time. But mere sequence does not constitute an action.

Suppose we should read:

> President Wilson presented his war message to Congress on April 6, 1917. War was declared. Thus the United States embarked on its first great adventure in world affairs. On April 8, 1917, just two days later, Albert Mayfield was born in Marysville, Illinois. He was a healthy baby and grew rapidly. By the time of the Armistice he weighed 22 pounds. On December 12, 1918, the troopship *Mason,* returning to New York from Cherbourg, struck a floating mine off Ireland and sank. Two hundred and sixteen men were lost.

Several events are chronologically recounted in this passage, but as they are presented to us, nothing holds those events together. They have no significant relation to one another. Merely a sequence in time, they do not constitute an action. But suppose we rewrite the passage:

> President Wilson presented his war message to Congress on April 6, 1917. War was declared. Thus the United States embarked on its first great adventure in world affairs. On April 8, 1917, just two days later, Albert Mayfield was born in Marysville, Illinois. Scarcely before the ink had dried on the headlines of the extra of the Marysville *Courier* announcing the declaration of war, Albert embarked on his own great adventure in world affairs. He was a healthy baby and grew rapidly. By the time of the Armistice he weighed 22 pounds. On December 12, 1918, the troopship *Mason,* returning to New York from Cherbourg, struck a floating mine off Ireland and sank. Two hundred and sixteen men were lost. Among those men was Sidney Mayfield, a captain of artillery, a quiet, unobtrusive, middle-aged insurance salesman, who left a widow and an infant son. That son was Albert Mayfield. So Albert grew up into a world that the war—a war he could not remember—had defined. It had defined the little world of his home, the silent, bitter woman who was his mother, the poverty and the cheerless discipline, and it had defined the big world outside.

Now we are moving toward an action. The random events are given some relationship to one another. We have unity and meaning. We may want to go on and find out more about Albert and about the long-range effects of the war on his life, but what we have is, as far as it goes, an action in itself as well as part of a bigger action, the story of Albert's life.

We have said that an action must have unity of meaning. This implies that one thing leads to another or that both things belong to a body of related events, all bearing on the point of the action. For instance, in the paragraph about Albert Mayfield, the declaration of war by the United States did not directly cause the floating mine to be in a particular spot off Ireland, but both events belong in the body of events contributing to the formation of Albert's character.

An action is, to sum up, a structure.

We shall speak of the structure of action under the categories of *time*, *logic*, and *meaning*.

Time

An action takes place in time. The movement of an event is from one point in time to another. But narration gives us a *unit* of time, not a mere fragment of time. A unit is a thing that is complete in itself. It may be part of a larger thing, and it may contain smaller parts, which themselves are units, but in itself it can be thought of as complete. A unit of time is that length of time in which a process fulfills itself.

We must now emphasize, not the mere fact of movement in time, but the movement from a beginning to an end. We begin a story at the moment when something is ripe to happen, when one condition prevails but is unstable, and end it when something has finished happening, when a new condition prevails and is, for the moment at least, stable. In between the beginning and the end are all the moments that mark the stages of change, that is to say, the process of the event.

We move, as it were, from A to Z, A the beginning, Z the end; and every item in between has a necessary order in time. We can make a little chart to indicate this natural sequence in time:

NATURAL ORDER IN TIME	A B C D E F G H I — etc. — U V W X Y Z

But we recall narratives that do not begin with the first moment when something was ripe to happen, that is, with our A. For instance, a narrative *may* begin with a man in the very midst of his problems, say on the battlefield, in a moment of marital crisis, or at a time when he hears that he has lost his fortune, and then it may cut back to his previous history and experience to explain how he came to be in such a situation. Such a narrative does not move in an orderly fashion from A to Z. It may begin, instead, with G, H, and I and then cut back to A, B, and C. But we must distinguish here between two things: how the narrator treated the sequence in time and how the sequence existed in time. The narrator may have given us G, H, and I first in order to catch our interest. He may have thought that A, B, and C would not be interesting to us until we knew what they were to lead to. But when he does finally cut back to A, B, and C, we become aware of the full sequence in time and set it up in our imaginations, thus, A, B, C, . . . G, H, I, ... In other words, we must distinguish between the *way* (G, H, I—A, B, C, . . .) in which the narrator presents an action to us and the *action* (A, B, C, D, E, F, G, . . .) which he presents.

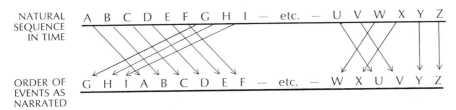

This is a distinction that we easily grasp, for we have long been acquainted with it in all sorts of narration, from conversation, newspaper stories, novels, and so on. But it is an important distinction, because when we talk about *action,* as we use the word here, we are referring to the events in the *natural order* in time and not in the *narrative order* unless the two orders happen to coincide, as they often do.

To repeat: an author confronts the *natural order* in the action that he is going to relate. In his narrative, he may keep it. But he may, for any number of different reasons, change the natural order—to build suspense, to develop a character, to make an interpretation.

Logic and causality

We have said that an action is not a mere sequence of events. It is a sequence in which "one thing leads to another." This is the very essence of narration, and here, as several times before, we are dealing with the notion of causality.

But what causes what? If "one thing leads to another," what is the "thing" that leads or is led to? We say that one event leads to another, and so it does. But in most narratives that hold our interest we are dealing with human beings in the process of living, and so matters of human motive and human character are involved. It is obvious that motive or character leads to an event. Jim embezzles from the bank where he works because he cannot bear to see his aged grandmother lose the old home place. Jack kills Mr. Tracy because Mr. Tracy filed the complaint that led to his arrest and conviction. Jim's motive and Jack's motive can be stated precisely. But motive blends back into character. A person is capable of having a particular motive only if it is consonant with his character. Jim's motive would not be comprehensible to Jack, nor Jack's motive to Jim. The point is, however, that action in life, or in narrative, is significant and interesting only insofar as it represents human agency.

We know, too, that events lead to character and motive. One of the most common ideas is that the individual's character is, to a considerable degree, molded by accidents of birth, social background, education, and all the other factors that we lump together as environment. This idea is necessarily important when we consider the logic of narrative. For a simple example, look back at the passage on the birth of Albert Mayfield (p. 229). The death of his father, when the troopship *Mason* is sunk by a floating mine, condemns the infant to poverty, bad education, and the bitterness of the woman who is his mother. His character, and in turn particular motives developed from that character, are to be understood as "caused" by the loss of the troopship, ironically after the war was over. There are, of course, an infinite number of other illustrations. Almost all fiction is concerned with the causes of human behavior, as are history and biography. Pick up any biography of George Washington, and the frontier will be discussed as an element in the molding of his character.

This concern with the *why* of things is at the very center of narration. If the writer of narrative is concerned with *what* happens and *how* it happens—with rendering the immediate texture of events, and their vividness, even as they come into being—he must be equally concerned with the *why*. He may give a certain immediacy and vividness merely by rendering the *what* and the *how*, but he cannot give a sense of life if he omits the *why*. No matter how immediately and vividly an event may be presented, it does not long hold our attention if we do not sense that it adds up to something, that it has some meaning. One of our deepest concerns is to find, or to create, some pattern in our own living. The question of *why* is intertwined with all our feeling for life.

Narrative does not *necessarily* undertake to deal with the *why* in general terms. It characteristically aims to embody the *why* in the *what* and *how*, to give a sense of the depth and massiveness of experience. But the logic of the *why* is, always, the dynamic of narrative. *What brings on what?*

DIVISIONS OF ACTION

In narration, logic manifests itself as structure as well as causality. We feel action as an unbroken flow through time. But we can think of action in terms of a series of stages, divisions in time, each having its own function in a structure. For action is a structure as well as a flow. Aristotle, more than two thousand years ago, divided the action of tragedy into the beginning, middle, and end; and though that division seems too obvious to be worth a comment, it has profound consequences for the discussion of any kind of action. For when we move from the notion of action as a mere flow in time to action as composed of significant stages in a structure, we are moving toward the notion of meaning as embodied in action. We are discussing the structure, the pattern, of an action, and a structure implies meaningful order, not arbitrary arrangement.

Beginning   An action does not spring from nothing. It arises from a situation. The situation, however, must be an unstable one, ready to lead to change and containing in it the seeds of future developments. Take, for example, Shakespeare's *Romeo and Juliet,* which offers an excellent example of a beginning. There is the feud between the houses of Capulet and Montague; bloodshed and violence are imminent; Romeo is an idealistic young man anxious to fall truly in love. We are given enough information to account for future events.

The beginning, the presentation of the situation, enables us to understand the subsequent narrative. Therefore, that part of the narrative—the beginning—is often given the name of *exposition.* But we must keep this special sense of this word distinct from the more general sense in which it applies to one of the modes of discourse.

Though the exposition of a narrative seems to be merely preliminary, it is not to be regarded as a kind of mere make-ready, a necessary evil to be passed over, a body of dull information. There is a great art to managing exposition, to trapping the reader's interest. The exposition need not consist of explanatory or descriptive material in isolation or a colorless summary of the situation from which the action stems. Instead, the exposition may appear as an episode, a fragment of action, interesting in itself. If we think back on the opening scene of *Romeo and Juliet,* we remember that in it we see a street fight. We are not *told about* the feud between the rival houses of Capulet and Montague, we actually see it in operation. Not all kinds of exposition can take a direct form, but in general it can be said that whenever possible exposition should be dramatically presented, that is, directly presented.

Middle The middle is the main body of the action. It is a series of stages in the process. It involves the points of mounting tension, or increasing *complication,* developing from the original situation. *Romeo and Juliet* will again illustrate. In spite of the hostility of their two families, Romeo and Juliet meet, pledge their love to each other, and are secretly married by Friar Laurence. But the action receives a most important complication when Romeo kills Juliet's kinsman and is banished from the city; and further complication still when Juliet's father decides to force her into marriage with the young nobleman, Paris. In this crisis of tension, Friar Laurence sees only one way out: Juliet must take the potion that will put her into a deathlike sleep. She will then be placed in the tomb—from which Romeo will rescue her. Juliet's resolution to take the risk might be regarded by many readers as the climax of the play; that is, the point of greatest intensity or greatest suspense. The climax is the focal point, the turning point of the narrative.

End The end of an action is not simply the point at which the action stops. It is, rather, the point at which the forces implicit in the situation have worked themselves out. Whether it is the gag line of a joke or Juliet and Romeo dead in their tomb, the principle is the same. The end of an action may be the physical victory of one set of forces over another, or it may be the reconciliation of forces or the fusion of previously opposing forces to create a new force. As a matter of fact, the end of an action may simply be a new awareness on the part of a person involved, directly or indirectly, in the action. We know that often we can look back on an experience and recognize the point at which an attitude we held was changed by it.

When we come to writing a narrative, we regard the end as the point where the action achieves its full meaning. It is the point at which the reader is willing to say, "Oh, yes, I see what it is all about." It is the point where the structure as well as the meaning is fulfilled. To put it another way, it is the point where we most fully sense that structure and meaning are aspects of the same thing: they are the thing itself.

The technical name for the end of a narrative is *denouement.* The word means an "untying." With the denouement, the complications are finally untangled and resolved. In *Romeo and Juliet,* for example, the lovers consummate in death their ill-starred love, and their families remorsefully give up the enmity that has destroyed their children.

PATTERN AND PROPORTION

The relation of the parts of a narrative to one another raises the question of proportion. In one way this term is misleading, for it implies a mere mechanical ratio in the size of the parts. Actually, we cannot look at the question in that way. We cannot say, for instance, that the complication should be three times longer than the exposition or five times longer than the denouement.

We need to ask, rather, whether the parts are adequate to the needs of the special narrative we are dealing with. What would be a satisfactory proportion for one narrative might be quite unsatisfactory for another. In any given instance, does the exposition give all the information necessary to establish the situation for the reader? Is it burdened with information that is unnecessary and distracting? Does the complication clearly present the essential stages of the development of the action? Does it confuse the reader by presenting material that does not bear on the development of the action? Does the denouement give the reader enough information to make the point of the narrative clear? Does it blur the point by putting in irrelevant material or by so extending relevant material that a clear focus is lost?

EXAMPLES OF NARRATIVE PATTERN

Let us look at two examples of narrative with the idea of indicating the structure, or pattern, of each. The first is the account of how Robinson Crusoe, who fancied himself absolutely alone on his desert island, found a footprint:

> It happened one day about noon, going towards my boat, I was exceedingly surprised with the print of a man's naked foot on the shore, which was very plain to be seen in the sand. I stood like one thunderstruck, or as if I had seen an apparition: I listened, I looked around me, but I could hear nothing, nor see anything. I went up to a rising ground, to look farther; I went up the shore and down the shore, but it was all one; I could see no other impression but that one. I went to it again to see if there were any more, and to observe if it might not be my fancy; but there was no room

for that, for there was exactly the print of a foot, toes, heel, and every part of a foot; how it came thither I knew not, nor could I in the least imagine; but, after innumerable fluttering thoughts, like a man perfectly confused and out of myself, I came home to my fortification, not feeling, as we say, the ground I went on, but terrified to the last degree; looking behind me at every two or three steps, mistaking every bush and tree, and fancying every stump at a distance to be a man. Nor is it possible to describe how many various shapes my affrighted imagination represented things to me in, how many wild ideas were found every moment in my fancy, and what strange unaccountable whimsies came into my thoughts by the way.

—DANIEL DEFOE: *Robinson Crusoe.*

Though a piece of narrative could scarcely be simpler than this, we see that it follows the basic pattern. The situation is given, as are the time and place. The complication follows on the discovery of the print—the first reaction, the looking about and listening, the going to higher ground for a wider view, the returning to verify the existence of the print. Then come the flight and the terror consequent upon the discovery. And it is this terror, changing the whole aspect of the familiar landscape, that constitutes the denouement. Crusoe's life cannot be the same again. This fact is not specified, but it is strongly implied.

Here is a more fully developed narrative, the story of Andrew Jackson's most famous duel, the duel with Charles Dickinson, who had made some remarks reflecting on the character of Rachel, Andrew Jackson's wife.

EXPOSITION:

On Thursday, May 29, 1806, Andrew Jackson rose at five o'clock, and after breakfast told Rachel that he would be gone for a couple of days and meanwhile he might have some trouble with Mr. Dickinson. Rachel probably knew what the trouble would be and she did not ask. Rachel had had her private channels of information concerning the Sevier affray. At six-thirty Jackson joined Overton at Nashville. Overton had the pistols. With three others they departed for the Kentucky line.

Mr. Dickinson and eight companions were already on the road. "Goodby, darling," he told his young wife. "I shall be sure to be home tomorrow evening." This confidence was not altogether assumed. He was a snap shot. At the word of command and firing apparently without aim, he could put four balls in a mark twenty-four feet away, each ball touching another. The persistent tradition in the countryside, that to worry Jackson he left several such examples of his marksmanship along the road, is unconfirmed by any member of the Dickinson or Jackson parties. But the story that he had offered on the streets of Nashville to wager he could kill Jackson at the first fire was vouchsafed by John Overton, the brother of Jackson's second, a few days after the duel.

Jackson said he was glad that "the other side" had started so early. It was a guarantee against further delay. Jackson had chafed over the seven days that had elapsed since the acceptance of the challenge. At their first interview, Overton and Dr. Hanson Catlett, Mr. Dickinson's second, had agreed that the meeting should be on Friday, May thirtieth, near Harrison's Mills on Red River, just beyond the Kentucky boundary. Jackson protested at once. He did not wish to ride forty miles to preserve the fiction of a delicate regard for Tennessee's unenforceable statute against dueling. He did not wish to wait a week for something that could be done in a few hours. Dickinson's excuse was that he desired to borrow a pair of pistols. Overton offered the choice of Jackson's pistols, pledging Jackson to the use of the other. These were the weapons that had been employed by Coffee and McNairy.

As they rode Jackson talked a great deal, scrupulously avoiding the subject that burdened every mind. Really, however, there was nothing more to be profitably said on that head. General Overton was a Revolutionary soldier of long acquaintance with the Code. With his principal he had canvassed every possible aspect of the issue forthcoming. "Distance . . . twenty-four feet; the parties to stand facing each other, with their pistols down perpendicularly. When they are READY, the single word FIRE! to be given; at which they are to fire as soon as they please. Should either fire before the word is given we [the seconds] pledge ourselves to shoot him down instantly." Jackson was neither a quick shot, nor an especially good one for the western country. He had decided not to compete with Dickinson for the first fire. He expected to be hit, perhaps badly. But he counted on the resources of his will to sustain him until he could aim deliberately and shoot to kill, if it were the last act of his life.

COMPLICATION:

On the first leg of the ride they traversed the old Kentucky road, the route by which, fifteen years before, Andrew Jackson had carried Rachel Robards from her husband's home, the present journey being a part of the long sequel to the other. Jackson rambled on in a shrill voice. Thomas Jefferson was "the best Republican in theory and the worst in practice" he had ever seen. And he lacked courage. How long were we to support the affronts of England—impressment of seamen, cuffing about of our ocean commerce? Perhaps as long as Mr. Jefferson stayed in office. Well, that would be two years, and certainly his successor should be a stouter man. "We must fight England again. In the last war I was not old enough to be any account." He prayed that the next might come "before I get too old to fight."

General Overton asked how old Jackson reckoned he would have to be for that. In England's case about a hundred, Jackson said.

He spoke of Burr. A year ago, this day, Jackson had borne him from the banquet at Nashville to the Hermitage. He recalled their first meeting in 1797 when both were in Congress. Jackson also met General Hamilton that winter. "Personally, no gentleman could help liking Hamilton. But his political views were all English." At heart a monarchist. "Why, did he not urge Washington to take a crown!"

Burr also had his failings. He had made a mistake, observed Jackson, with admirable detachment, a political mistake, when he fought Hamilton. And about his Western projects the General was none too sanguine. Burr relied overmuch on what others told him. Besides, there was Jefferson to be reckoned with. "Burr is as far from a fool as I ever saw, and yet he is as easily fooled as any man I ever knew."

The day was warm, and a little after ten o'clock the party stopped for refreshment. Jackson took a mint julep, ate lightly and rested until mid-afternoon. The party reached Miller's Tavern in Kentucky about eight o'clock. After a supper of fried chicken, waffles, sweet potatoes and coffee, Jackson repaired to the porch to chat with the inn's company. No one guessed his errand. At ten o'clock he knocked the ashes from his pipe and went to bed. Asleep in ten minutes, he had to be roused at five in the morning.

The parties met on the bank of the Red River at a break in a poplar woods. Doctor Catlett won the toss for choice of position, but as the sun had not come through the trees this signified nothing. The giving of the word fell to Overton. Jackson's pistols were to be used after all, Dickinson taking his pick. The nine-inch barrels were charged with ounce balls of seventy caliber. The ground was paced off, the principals took their places. Jackson wore a dark-blue frock coat and trousers of the same material; Mr. Dickinson a shorter coat of blue, and gray trousers.

"Gentlemen, are you ready?" called General Overton.

"Ready," said Dickinson quickly.

"Yes, sir," said Jackson.

"Fere!" cried Overton in the Old-Country accent.

DENOUEMENT:

Dickinson fired almost instantly. A fleck of dust rose from Jackson's coat and his left hand clutched his chest. For an instant he thought himself dying, but fighting for self-command, slowly he raised his pistol.

Dickinson recoiled a step horror-stricken. "My God! Have I missed him?"

Overton presented his pistol. "Back to the mark, sir!"

Dickinson folded his arms. Jackson's spare form straightened. He aimed. There was a hollow "clock" as the hammer stopped at half-cock. He drew it back, sighted again and fired. Dickinson swayed to the ground.

As they reached the horses Overton noticed that his friend's left boot was filled with blood. "Oh, I believe that he pinked me," said Jackson quickly, "but I don't want those people to know," indicating the group that bent over Dickinson. Jackson's surgeon found that Dickinson's aim had been perfectly true, but he had judged the position of Jackson's heart by the set of his coat, and Jackson wore his coats loosely on account of the excessive slenderness of his figure. "But I should have hit him," he exclaimed, "if he had shot me through the brain."

—MARQUIS JAMES: *The Life of Andrew Jackson.*[4]

The event narrated above is historically true. It had causes running back before the episode of the duel (Dickinson had insulted Jackson's wife) and was to have consequences long after the duel. But the writer is not immediately concerned with causes or effects. He is concerned with rendering the episode itself, the duel, and through the duel, something of the character of Jackson. We can see that in doing so he naturally gives his account in three sections—the exposition, the complication, and the denouement.

The exposition describes the attitudes of the two duelists as they make ready and gives the terms of the duel. The complication seems to have a good deal of material off the point—Jackson's long conversation about

---

[4] From *The Life of Andrew Jackson,* copyright 1933, 1937, 1938 by Marquis James, reprinted by permission of the publishers, The Bobbs-Merrill Company, Inc.

politics—but even this apparent digression is related to the point the author wishes to make in his narrative: Jackson's cool certainty. Then the complication gives the details as the opponents face each other and Dickinson fires. The denouement falls into two related parts, Jackson's self-command when hit and his shooting of Dickinson, and his remark after the event.

Marquis James is using narrative to make a point in much the same way that narrative is used as illustration in, say, the account of the wolf family by Farley Mowat (pp. 225–26). This kind of point—James's wish to exhibit the iron will of Jackson—is somewhat different from the kind of point we characteristically find in fiction. This is a distinction we shall come to later. For the moment, what should be emphasized is that though James is using narrative for the purpose of illustration, he works within the basic structure: that is, narrative fulfills itself as narrative.

■ APPLICATIONS

I Read the theme "Getting Engaged" (pp. 204–05). Indicate the general divisions in it. In the middle, how many stages of complication can you distinguish? Does the denouement have more than one element? What point, what meaning, do we find in the denouement?

II You are now to begin work toward writing a narrative. Cast around for your subject, real or imaginary. Here the notebook you began to keep for description and narration should be of great help as a source of suggestions for narratives and for bits of description to flesh out narratives. But you should not follow the notebook slavishly. Look there for starting points rather than for passages that may be transferred as a block.

Once you have settled on a subject, real or imaginary, you should make a set of informal notes, perhaps in your notebook. Follow almost at random whatever ideas and impressions begin to assemble themselves about your subject. This process, by the way, may take several days. Some of your best ideas may come while you are brushing your teeth or walking down the street. Keep the notebook handy. Be alert to trap any fleeting notion. You cannot tell where it may lead. It may even lead you to an entirely new subject, one more exciting than what you have chosen.

When you have assembled your material and begun to feel at home with the subject, ask yourself if your narrative has, first, a point, and then, a structure. Organize your notes into a sentence outline. Is the point clear? Is the structure clear? If not, rethink your material. Perhaps you have tried to draw into your plan irrelevant material simply because it was interesting in itself. This would blur the point and confuse the structure. Or perhaps your material is not adequate for your needs. Again, the trouble may not lie in the material but in your organizing of it. Test each division. Does the beginning really serve as an exposition? Does the middle offer complications that, stage by stage, move toward a climax? Does the end really "untie" the complications and bring the narrative to a significant fulfillment?

When you have satisfied yourself as best you can, lay the outline aside. But continue to think about it. Take out the notebook for a little while every day and read over your work. You should have more and better thoughts before you begin to write. Let the narrative grow in your imagination.

Meaning in narrative

AN EXAMPLE

We shall now trace the development of a narrative from the simple germ situation to the end. The purpose here is not, however, to study further the divisions of narrative. Rather, it is to probe into the process by which narrative achieves meaning—that is, the third aspect of the structure of action.

Let us repeat the paragraph about George Barton and his dog, which we have at the beginning of this chapter:

> George Barton owned a mastiff, which he had reared from a puppy. He loved it very much. But he lost his job and could no longer buy proper food for it. Then the dog frightened a little in the neighborhood, who was eating a piece of bread. George was now afraid that someone would poison it. So he sold it.

This is a very poor, dull, and incomplete piece of narration. For one thing, it can scarcely be said to *present* an event at all. It gives us little sense of the immediacy of the event. It is so bare of detail that the imagination of the reader finds little to work on. For another thing, we do not know what it means. It has no point.

Let us rewrite it to try to answer the first objection:

> George Barton was a nondescript little boy, scarcely to be distinguished from the other boys living in Duck Alley. He had a pasty face, not remarkable in any way, eyes not blue and not brown but some vague hazel color, and a tangle of neutral-colored hair. His clothes were the drab, cast-off things worn by all the children of Duck Alley, that grimy street, scarcely a street at all but a dirt track, which ran between the bayou and a scattering of shanties. His life there was cheerless enough, with a feeble, querulous father, a mother who had long since resigned herself to her misery, and a sullen older brother, with a mean laugh and a hard set of knuckles, who tormented George for amusement when he was not off prowling with his cronies. But this home did not distinguish George from the other children of Duck Alley. It was like many of the others. What distinguished George was his dog.
>
> One day two years back—it was the summer when he was ten—George had found the dog. It was a puppy then, a scrawny, starving creature with absurd paws, sniffing feebly in the garbage dump at the end of Duck Alley. No one could have guessed then that it would grow into a sleek, powerful animal, as big as a pony.
>
> George brought it home and defended it against the protests and jeers and random kicks of the family. "I'll feed him," he asserted. "He won't never eat a bite I don't make the money to pay for." And he was as good

as his word. There was no job too hard for him, for he could look forward to evening when he would squat by the old goods box that served as a kennel and watch Jibby gnaw at the hunk of meat he had bought.

Suppose we begin the narrative in that way. We have added several elements to the bare synopsis given before. We know now why the dog is so important to the boy. There is no direct statement on this point, but we see that he lives an isolated and loveless life and that the dog satisfies a craving in his nature for companionship and affection. We also see that now George has a reason for his efforts, a center for his life. In other words, we can imaginatively grasp his state of mind. The reason for George's attachment to the dog, as we have just stated it, is given as explanation, as exposition, but in the narrative itself this expository element is absorbed into situation and action. Similarly, the little bits of description are woven into the narrative to help us visualize the scene and George himself.

What should be emphasized here is that the narrative is concerned to make us sense the fullness of the process, to make us see, hear, feel, and understand the event as a unit. Description alone might make us see or hear some aspect of the event. Exposition might make us understand its meaning, its causes, or its results. But narrative, when it is fully effective, makes us aware directly of the event as happening. The sharp detail is the life of narrative.

To return to our little narrative: suppose we should carry on our suggested revision to the moment when George sells his dog. Would there be anything still lacking to make the narrative fully satisfactory? Perhaps there would be. Perhaps the meaning of the action would not be very clear. Let us pick up the narrative at a point after George has lost his job and the dog has frightened the child and see how it can be developed.

> George sold the dog to John Simpson, a boy who lived in one of the big brick houses on the hill back of town. John Simpson's father was rich. John could feed Jibby. John could take care of him. No one would poison Jibby up at John Simpson's house, behind the high iron fence. George comforted himself with these thoughts.
>
> Sometimes, however, these thoughts did not comfort him enough, and he felt the old loneliness and emptiness that he had felt before Jibby came. But he was getting to be a big boy now, big and tough, and he put those feelings out of his mind as well as he could. He did not work regularly now, but hung around with the Duck Alley gang in the railroad yards. He almost forgot Jibby.
>
> One day on the main street of town he met John Simpson and the dog, such a big, powerful, sleek dog now that he scarcely recognized him. He went up to the dog. "Hi, Jibby! Hi, boy!" he said and began to pull the dog's ears and scratch his head as he had done three years before, in the evening, back by the goods box, after Jibby had bolted his supper. The dog nuzzled him and licked his hands. George looked up at the other boy and exclaimed, "Jeez, look at him. Look at him, will ya. Ain't he smart? He remembers me!"
>
> John Simpson stood there for a moment and did not utter a word. Then he said, "Take your hands off that dog. He belongs to me."

George stepped back.

"Come here, Blaze," John Simpson ordered, and the dog went to him. He fondled the dog's head, and the dog licked his hands.

George stood on the pavement and watched John Simpson and the dog disappear down the street.

Neither looked back.

This goes beyond the sale of the dog to add another element of meaning to the narrative. If we stop with the sale of the dog, we have an example of narration, but the reader no doubt is somewhat confused about the exact meaning of the event presented. Perhaps the reader feels sorry for the boy. Perhaps he is aware that poverty is the cause of the boy's loss of the dog. Those reactions may be taken as meanings of the piece of narration, but these meanings are not brought to focus. The reader may not be sure exactly what is intended. He is certain to feel that the narrative is rather fragmentary. With the addition of the section dealing with the meeting of George and John Simpson, the reader, however, is somewhat more certain that the narrative does have a direction, is moving toward a meaning. In fact, the contrast between John Simpson, who owns the dog, and George, who merely loves it, is in itself significant—though the significance is rather too general to be fully satisfying as an end.

We sense that more is at stake than is offered in the mere fact of the contrast. When the dog licks John Simpson's hands, just as he had licked George's, we realize that the act was for George a kind of betrayal. But a hardheaded reader may find this rather sentimental; he may ask, "What did George expect the dog to do? Is he just standing there enjoying his self-pity?"

Let us suppose that, aware of this sort of criticism, we continue:

George continued to stand there, filled with rage, which was not new for him, but with something else that was new, a peculiar, disorienting sickness in his heart. Then he discovered that the rage was, all at once, as much against himself as it was against John Simpson or the dog—or even against the world. The rage was against himself for being weak enough to have that strange feeling of weakness and loss.

"A dog," he said out loud, standing there looking down the street, which was now empty. "Nothing but a God-durn dog." Then, "Anybody give him a hunk of meat, and he'll slobber all over him."

He let the spit gather slowly in his mouth, then, very deliberately, he spat on the spot where the dog had come and fawned on him. He set his foot on the spit and smeared it with a quick movement of disgust. He walked away, not looking back.

We have, now, another stage. George has gone beyond his old feeling. Jibby is now just another "God-durn dog," ready to slobber on anybody who has a hunk of meat. But this realization is, again, vague. We want a sharper focus. And so we try once more:

The next day George hunted for a job. He found one at the lumberyard where he had worked before, when Jibby was a puppy. He worked as steadily now as he had worked in the old days when he looked forward to getting home to feed the dog and squat by him in the dusk, or, if it were winter, in the dark. But he was through with that sort of thing now.

If now he worked with a grim and driving energy, it was because he had learned one lesson. It was a lesson he was never to forget. He had learned that even love was one of the things you cannot get unless you have the money to pay for it.

These paragraphs give us a positive conclusion. They give the effect of the event on George, not merely the first reaction of resentment or hurt feelings, but the effect that prevails over a long period of time. Neither the reader nor the writer may agree that what George learns is the truth—that money is the basis of everything, even of such things as love and loyalty and kindness—but what George learns is the "truth" for him, the rule by which he will conduct his life for a time to come.

The important thing to understand here is that a point is made. For our present purposes the question is not whether the point is universally true. It is whether the point is psychologically credible. That is, whether, given the sequence of events, George may come to feel it as true. If we accept this, we can accept the narrative as complete. George has reached a significant point in his life, a point at which he recognizes a difference in his feelings about himself and the world he lives in.

The narrative is not complete merely because a summarizing statement has been made by the writer. Certainly, the summarizing statement by itself would not make the narrative complete if what it says did not grow convincingly out of the events. Many narratives, in fact, imply rather than state their meaning. The crucial question is always this: Does the meaning, given the persons involved and the full context, really develop from the events?

We have just said that the narrative is complete. This, however, does not mean that George will never change his mind about the meaning of the experience he has had. The narrative might well be part of a long story or novel that showed how for thirty years George conducted his life by the hard, materialistic "truth" he had learned and then found, even in the moment of his practical success, when he had grown rich and powerful, that his "truth" was really a profound mistake and that he had to learn a new truth. But the particular action given here is, in its own terms, complete.

INTERPRETATION

The meaning of this action is what George takes it to be. Meaning, in the sense we are talking about, is never mathematically absolute. It is what some particular person takes it to be. The meaning is an interpretation.

But what of the author's interpretation? He wrote the narrative, didn't he? This question raises another important matter. We must always distinguish between meaning for a person, real or imaginary, in a narrative, and what we take to be the author's interpretation. Let us suppose that the author of this unwritten novel about George Barton did not accept the hard materialistic "truth" that George had arrived at. The point of his novel— the final interpretation proposed by the author—might be that anybody can live by that "truth." So the novel might go on to show that this philosophy brought George Barton, in the end, to ruin; or that he came to realize his error in some other way. The point is, of course, that the attitude of a character and that of the author do not necessarily coincide. The attitude of the author must be sought in the overall meaning of a work.[5]

● CAUTION

Remember that a feeling is also an interpretation. This is true of an interpretation made by a character in a narrative, by the author, or by the reader. For the moment, however, we are primarily concerned with the question of the author's interpretation as embodied in a work; we are concerned with the "feeling" a work may convey to the reader.

If a work of narration brings you to a new attitude—or merely to a new feeling—that is an interpretation. If the episode of the wolves (pp. 225–26) makes you change your feeling about wolves, that is an interpretation. When the novel *Uncle Tom's Cabin,* by Harriet Beecher Stowe, changed the feeling of many readers toward slavery, that was an interpretation. In fact, in almost all good narrative there is the element of the awakening and modifying of feeling, even when the author seems to use the narrative merely for purposes of exposition. For instance, look back at the anecdote of the lonely Harvard student (p. 227).

■ APPLICATIONS

I Try to state the meaning—or meanings—of the following selection. Try to define what feelings are appealed to by it. It will be useful to know that it is an excerpt from the autobiography of a young black who grew up in the slums of Harlem. His mother and father had come from the rural South and could never accept the values of their new environment. Pimp is the younger brother of the author; he has already entered a life of crime but is trying to free himself from it.

> The real reason I wanted to be in Harlem was to spend more time with Pimp. But I couldn't. There just wasn't enough time. I couldn't take him to live with me. He was still too young. I couldn't have him hang out with me. I couldn't go back home. I'd just see him sometimes and talk to him.
>
> He got in trouble once with some kids, something childish like snatching a pocketbook. It didn't seem too important at the time. I was a little bothered about it, and I spoke to him. He said they'd just done it for kicks. I was trying real hard to keep a check on him from a distance. I knew what he was doing.

---

[5] Let us pursue the question of interpretation a little further: the interpretation by a character is part of the content of the work; it may or may not coincide with the meaning of the work, which is the author's interpretation. But there is also the interpretation arrived at by the reader, which may or may not coincide with that of the author. The author intends to convince the reader of his view of things—of the experiences related in his work and of life in general, but he may fail. Thus, the reader's interpretation must also be considered in making any assessment of a work.

He had started shooting craps, but this was nothing, really. All the young boys shot craps and gambled. This was what they were supposed to do. But Mama was worried about it. I suppose she and Dad were getting kind of old. She used to tell me, "Oh, that boy, he stays out real late." It seemed as though they were trying to throw their burden of parenthood on me, and I kind of resented that, but I cared about Pimp. I wanted to do something for him.

The only trouble was that I had set such a high standard for him, such a bad example, it was hard as hell to erase. People knew him as my brother. The boys his age expected him to follow in my footsteps. He was my brother, and I had done so much, I had become a legend in the neighborhood. They expected him to live up to it.

I used to try to talk to him. I'd say, "Look, Pimp, what do you want to do, man?" I tried to get him interested in things. He used to like to play ball and stuff like that, but he wasn't interested in anything outside of the neighborhood. He wasn't interested in getting away. He couldn't see life as anything different. At fourteen, he was still reading comic books. He wasn't interested in anything except being hip.

I was real scared about this, but I knew that I couldn't do anything. He was doing a whole lot of shit that he wasn't telling me about. I remember one time I asked him, just to find out if he had started smoking yet, if he wanted some pot. He said, "No, man, I don't want any, and if I wanted some, I'd have it. I know where to get it." I was kind of hurt, but I knew that this was something that had to come. He would've known, and I suppose he should've known. When I was his age, even younger, I knew.

I couldn't feel mad about it, but I felt kind of hurt. I wanted to say, "Look, Pimp, what's happenin', man? Why aren't we as tight as we were before?" He still admired me, but something had happened. It was as though we had lost a contact, a closeness, that we once had, and I couldn't tell him things and get him to listen any more the way he used to do. I felt that if I couldn't control him, nobody could, and he'd be lost out there in the streets, going too fast, thinking he was hip enough to make it all by himself.

I'd take him to a movie or something like that. I'd take him downtown to the Village, and we'd hang out for a day, but I noticed something was missing. We didn't talk about all the really intimate things that we used to talk about. He wouldn't share his secrets with me any more, and this scared me, because I didn't know how far he'd gone. I wanted to say, "Pimp, what happened to the day that you and I used to walk through the streets with our arms around each other's shoulder? We used to sleep with our arms around each other, and you used to cry to follow me when I went out of the house." I wanted to say it, but it didn't make sense, because I knew that day had gone.

—Claude Brown: *Manchild in the Promised Land.*[6]

II You are now to write the theme for which you have been preparing notes. But first, ask yourself if, in the light of what you have studied since you began to make your notes, you are still satisfied with your idea and your outline. If not, start over. Remember that you are to write a fully rounded narrative—of some 600 to 700 words or more if you wish.

---
[6] Reprinted with permission of The Macmillan Company from *Manchild in the Promised Land* by Claude Brown. Copyright © Claude Brown, 1965. Reprinted by permission of Jonathan Cape Ltd.

If you are not satisfied with what you have done, perhaps you may find a suggestion for a subject in this list:

My First Love	Why Girls Leave Home
My First Hate	Hot Rod
The First Animal I Ever Shot	Why I Hung onto the Job

Don't be afraid of writing a funny theme.

How Interest Determines Action

The narrative by Marquis James (pp. 235–37) is a self-contained and tidy example of narrative structure. It is drawn from fact, from historical records. This circumstance raises a question: Did the facts come to James in this tidy structure? Can we expect the world to offer us action so conveniently ready for packaging?

Sometimes the world of fact does offer us an action in nearly perfect form, but this is rare. The world is enormously complex and experience enormously fluid, and there is constant interfusion of events. In connection with the narrative of Jackson's duel, we have already mentioned the long and complicated history leading to it. Jackson's marriage had provoked slanderous accusations of bigamy against Rachel, and these had been entwined with the rancorous political struggles of Jackson's career; the duel with Dickinson sprang, in fact, from a remark he had made about Rachel.

In the full-length biography of Jackson from which this episode is excerpted, the author, Marquis James, gives an elaborate treatment of this background; but when he gets to the duel itself, he focuses on what the action demonstrates about Jackson's character. James is not writing a tract against dueling. He is not concerned with the pathos of the death of a promising young man. He is not trying to evoke our sympathy for the young Mrs. Dickinson. All of these considerations may be implicit in the situation. (A little after our excerpt, in fact, James tells how Mrs. Jackson exclaimed, "Oh, God have pity on the poor wife—pity on the babe in her womb!") But the main intention never wavers—to exhibit in action the iron will of Jackson.

Since James has based his structure on this intention, we can lift his account out of its context and find it complete and unified as an action. An interest has determined an action.

Selection

We have already seen how important the principle of selection is for description (pp. 208–09), and that same principle is what we have been considering in our discussion of how interest determines an action.

Even in a narrative dealing with fact the author may heighten the interest by leaving out merely casual material. In treating the episode of Jackson's duel, Marquis James may know that after his opponent was hit

Jackson actually said more than is given here. The author, however, presents just those remarks that contribute to our awareness of Jackson's character. In dealing with matters of fact, a writer does not want to distort the truth by omissions, but neither does he want to lose the significance of the action by obscuring it behind a screen of mere facts. Certainly, the narrator is concerned with facts, but primarily with significant facts. When he is dealing with imaginary events, the writer has a freer hand and a greater responsibility; for now he cannot rely on the interest that mere fact as fact can sometimes evoke in the reader. With the imaginary narrative a detail can never pay its way simply because it is interesting in itself. It must be relevant.

Relevance

The kind of relevance we have been discussing concerns the main interest, the meaning, the point of the action. Let us call this the "relevance of theme." But there is another sort of relevance that makes its own demands—demands sometimes contradictory to those of theme. These demands spring from the fact that narrative, to be effective, must be, in large part, an immediate presentation of events. Therefore, there must be selection in terms of vividness—the detail, the small gesture, the trivial word that can stir the imagination. And the details that, strictly speaking, are descriptive may be absorbed into the narrative effect. For instance, the cut and color of Jackson's and Dickinson's clothes, the kind of woods by which the meeting took place, and the Irish accent of General Overton when he gave the command to fire contribute to the impression of reality. Marquis James is much concerned to give an immediate presentation. These are examples of what we may call the "relevance of immediacy." They make us see the event—and seeing is believing. (See Chapter 8, Description, and Chapter 11, Diction.)

● CAUTION

The effectiveness of a narrative often depends on skillful interweaving of details dictated by relevance of theme with those dictated by relevance of immediacy.

Consider the function of each detail you use.

Be sure that the details are not offered in solid blocks—one block of one kind and one of another. Weave details into a unified texture, with the action and with each other, so that the reader, without stopping for analysis, may feel the significance of the narrative as it progresses. The narrative, in other words, must have unity of impact.

■ APPLICATION

Make a criticism of your last theme on the basis of relevance of detail. Revise it where you think desirable.

Point of View

We have used the term *point of view* in connection with description (pp. 213–16) to indicate the physical relation of a spectator to the thing observed. In connection with narration, the phrase has a somewhat different meaning, a meaning that implies some of the more important problems of narration. In narration, point of view involves a person who bears some relation to the action, either as observer or participant, and whose intelligence serves the reader as a kind of guide to the action. Point of view, then, concerns two questions:

1 Who is the narrator?
2 What is his relation to the action?

In general, there are two possible points of view, the first person and the third person. When we read, "That summer when we were staying at Bayport, I had the most astonishing experience of my life," we know that we are dealing with the first-person point of view. When we read, "When Jake Millen, at the age of sixty, surveyed the wreck of his career, he knew that only one course was left open to him," we know that we are dealing with a third-person point of view. That is, in the first example, an "I," real or fictitious, is telling us about an experience in which he himself was involved; in the second example, an author, writing impersonally, is telling us about an experience in which another person was involved.

There are, however, certain shadings and variations possible within these two broad general divisions of point of view. In actual practice, such shadings and variations may be of the greatest complication and subtlety, and it must be held in mind that any attempt to schematize them can only be crudely indicated.

What are the variations possible within the first person? The distinctions here are to be made on the basis of the relation of the first-person narrator to the action that he narrates. Two extreme positions can be taken. First, the narrator may tell of an action in which he is the main, or at least an important, participant. That is, he tells his "own story." We are all familiar with this type of treatment. Most autobiographies are of this kind. Occasionally, we encounter a piece of informal history using this method; for example, T. E. Lawrence's *Seven Pillars of Wisdom.* Many short stories and novels create an imaginary "I" who is the main character of the story and who tells the story; for example, Daniel Defoe's *Robinson Crusoe* and Ernest Hemingway's *A Farewell to Arms.*

At the other extreme, the narrator, either real or imaginary, recounts an action of which he is merely an observer. This, also, is a familiar type of treatment. Memoirs tend to take this form, for frequently the writer of memoirs has not played a conspicuous role in affairs but has been in a position to observe important events. Theodore Sorensen, in *Kennedy,* and Arthur Schlesinger, Jr., in *A Thousand Days,* have both given accounts of President John F. Kennedy's administration. The same type of treatment occurs, naturally, in fiction. Poe's "The Fall of the House of Usher" is a notable instance, and Ring Lardner's story "Haircut" is another.

Thus we may have the two types of the first-person point of view: *narrator–main character* and *narrator-observer*. But in between these two extremes many variations are possible, narratives in which the narrator participates directly in the action and has something at stake in its outcome but is not the main character. We may call this the method of *narrator-involved observer*.

A set of pictures may be helpful:

CIRCLE OF ACTION

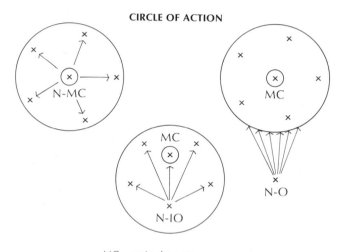

MC main character
N-MC narrator–main character
N-IO narrator–involved observer
N-O narrator–observer
X other characters

(Observe that these are variants of the first person. The "narrator" in each instance is the teller of the tale as an "I.")

But what of the variations possible within the third-person point of view?

In this point of view the narrative is given by an author writing impersonally, that is, as a kind of disembodied intelligence before whom the events are played out. What is the relation of this impersonal author, this disembodied intelligence, to the action? In the first place, he does not participate in the action; he is merely an observer. The question then becomes this: "How much of the action does the author observe?" And here, as in dealing with the first-person point of view, we can define two extreme positions.

One extreme we may call the *panoramic*—or *omniscient*—point of view. In this method the author may report any aspect or all aspects of an action and may go into the head of any or all of the characters involved in the action. His eye, as it were, sweeps the entire field, and he reports whatever is interesting or relevant. In an imaginary narrative there is no necessary limit to what may be seen or reported according to this method; the most private acts and the most secret thoughts or sensations of any or all of the characters may be reported, for the author is the creator of the whole. But when a writer is using this method in presenting a nonimaginative narrative, say a piece of history, he is, of course, limited by what facts or plausible deductions are available to him. He cannot be as thoroughgoing in applying the method as the writer of an imaginary narrative, though within the limits of the facts available to him he may do so. Many pieces of historical and biographical writing use this method, and, of course, it is common in fiction. For instance, it appears in the following scene from Thackeray's novel *Vanity Fair,* presenting the city of Brussels when the false news comes that Napoleon has won the Battle of Quatre Bras, an engagement just before Waterloo:

> Crowds rushed to the Namur gate, from which direction the noise proceeded, and many rode along the level *chaussée,* to be in advance of any intelligence from the army. Each man asked his neighbor for news; and even great English lords and ladies condescended to speak to persons whom they did not know. The friends of the French went abroad, wild with excitement, and prophesying the triumph of their Emperor. The merchants closed their shops, and came out to swell the general chorus of alarm and clamor. Women rushed to the churches, and crowded the chapels, and knelt and prayed on the flags and steps. The dull sound of cannon went on rolling, rolling. Presently carriages with travellers began to leave the town, galloping away by the Ghent barrier. The prophecies of the French partisans began to pass for facts. "He has cut the army in two," it was said. "He is marching straight on Brussels. He will overpower the English, and be here tonight." "He will overpower the English," shrieked Isidor to his master, "and will be here tonight." The man bounded in and out from the lodgings to the street, always returning with some fresh particulars of disaster. Jos's face grew paler and paler. Alarm began to take entire possession of the stout civilian. All the champagne he drank brought no courage to him. Before sunset he was worked up to such a pitch of nervousness as gratified his friend Isidor to behold, who now counted upon the spoils of the owner of the laced coat.
>
> The women were away all this time. After hearing the firing for a moment, the stout Major's wife bethought her of her friend in the next chamber, and ran in to watch, and if possible to console, Amelia. The idea that she had that helpless and gentle creature to protect, gave additional strength to the natural courage of the honest Irishwoman. She passed five hours by her friend's side, sometimes in remonstrance, sometimes talking cheerfully, oftener in silence, and terrified mental supplication.
>
> —WILLIAM MAKEPEACE THACKERAY: *Vanity Fair.*

At the other extreme from the panoramic point of view we find what we may call the point of view of *sharp focus.* The author does not sweep the entire field of the action, but keeps his, and the reader's, attention focused on one character and on that character's relation to the action; he does, however, "know all" about the character on whom he has chosen to focus his interest. Accordingly, the parts of the action not directly participated in by the selected character are not reported by the author. To use a figure of speech, the character may be regarded as a kind of prism through which the action is refracted. Here is an example of this method:

> He was hungry, for, except for some biscuits which he had asked two grudging curates to bring him, he had eaten nothing since breakfast-time. He sat down at an uncovered wooden table opposite two work-girls and a mechanic. A slatternly girl waited on him.
> "How much is a plate of peas?" he asked.
> "Three halfpence, sir," said the girl.
> "Bring me a plate of peas," he said, "and a bottle of ginger beer."
> He spoke roughly in order to belie his air of gentility, for his entry had been followed by a pause of talk. His face was heated. To appear natural he pushed his cap back on his head and planted his elbows on the table. The mechanic and the two work-girls examined him point by point before resuming their conversation in a subdued voice. The girl brought him a plate of grocer's hot peas, seasoned with pepper and vinegar, a fork and his ginger beer. He ate his food greedily and found it so good that he made a note of the shop mentally. When he had eaten all the peas he sipped his ginger beer and sat for some time thinking of Corley's adventure. In his imagination he beheld the pair of lovers walking along some dark road; he heard Corley's voice in deep energetic gallantries, and saw again the leer of the young woman's mouth. This vision made him feel keenly his own poverty of purse and spirit. He was tired of knocking about, of pulling the devil by the tail, of shifts and intrigues. He would be thirty-one in November. Would he never get a good job? Would he never have a home of his own? He thought how pleasant it would be to have a warm fire to sit by and a good dinner to sit down to. He had walked the streets long enough with friends and with girls. He knew what those friends were worth: he knew the girls too. Experience had embittered his heart against the world. But all hope had not left him. He felt better after having eaten than he had felt before, less weary of his life, less vanquished in spirit. He might yet be able to settle down in some snug corner and live happily if he could only come across some good simple-minded girl with a little of the ready. —JAMES JOYCE: "Two Gallants," Dubliners.[7]

Between the extremes of the panoramic point of view and the point of view of sharp focus there are, of course, all sorts of gradations and mixtures of the two methods. The choice of one of the methods or the mixing of the two is not a matter to be settled arbitrarily, for the method should reflect a special interest involved in the narrative. For instance, the panoramic point of view is well suited to the rendering of some large and complicated action —a battle, a mob scene, the burning of a city—in which the interest lies in the sweep of events. The point of view of sharp focus is suited to a narrative in which the interest is primarily in the psychology of a single char-

---

[7] From *Dubliners* by James Joyce. Originally published by B. W. Huebsch, Inc., in 1916. Copyright © 1967 by the Estate of James Joyce. All rights reserved. Reprinted by permission of The Viking Press, Inc. Reprinted by permission of Jonathan Cape Ltd., the Executors of the James Joyce Estate, and The Society of Authors as the literary representative of the estate of James Joyce.

acter. A narrative may well involve both such interests, and then the writer may mix his methods according to the needs of the moment.

But the use of the panoramic point of view is not restricted to action that covers a physically broad field, such as a battle. Take, for example, this section from a student theme:

> The family sat around, waiting for Jack to come home. He was the youngest, and they were all partial to him. And now he was the first ever to be picked up by the police, and the family didn't even know what it was about. They had to sit there and wait for news.
>
> Waiting had never been easy for the father. He paced around, picking up a newspaper, glancing at it as though nothing had happened, then throwing it down. He chewed his underlip, the way he did when something was building up inside him. *He kept telling himself not to blow up, but misery was welling up in him till he felt sick.* He was a man built for action, and waiting was not his dish.
>
> The mother sat in the rocking chair. She pretended to sew, but all the time her mind was on Jack. She was a religious woman, sincere and without any exhibitionism, and if her lips were moving now, she was praying. *But her prayer consisted only of the name of her son, "Jack, Jack," over and over again.* She finally said to her husband, "John, why don't you sit down? You're wearing out the carpet." It was an old joke between them.
>
> Susie, the daughter of the family, came in about nine, wearing her usual air of self-satisfied virtue. When they told her what had happened, that look of self-satisfied virtue became even more obvious, and she got out a few dramatic sobs, saying, "Poor Jackie, poor Jackie, I've always cautioned him about that car." Then she began to rearrange flowers, humming to herself the gayest little tune as she passed close to her brother Bill. *She felt great and full of energy, as if she were going to a party.*
>
> "You're damned pleased about it, aren't you?" he demanded, in his savage way, and she flounced out of the room. But she came back in a minute and wanted to know if she couldn't get a glass of milk and some cake for "poor Father."
>
> "For God's sake," Bill said, in disgust, and rose from his chair.
>
> "Don't swear, son," the mother said.
>
> "It's enough to make you swear," he said. "When she comes in with that saintly look and wants to do somebody a favor, you know she is getting ready to pull a fast one."
>
> He was right.

Here the event is rendered in the third person, as it would appear to a mere observer. The scene is restricted, but it is treated with a sweeping, panoramic view; that is, we seem to stand back from the scene while the family is waiting. We see them all, one after another, as if a movie camera were slowly sweeping the room, catching each person in some significant gesture or word. But notice that we do have certain intimate glimpses of the minds and feelings of several characters (the passages set in italics in the text). If these passages were omitted, the panorama would be purely objective, not omniscient.

I   What point of view is used in the following selections?

    1   The student theme, "Getting Engaged" (pp. 204–05)
    2   The excerpt by Cormac McCarthy (pp. 222–23)

II You are now to do your final theme of this chapter. You may make it either a piece of reportage or a short story. It should not be shorter than 750 words.

If you make it reportage, you are required to use some incident that you have actually witnessed. If you want to do something in this form and think nothing in your recent experience satisfactory as a subject, go out and cover an event that you think might prove fruitful. In writing your report use as fully as possible the material you have studied up to this point, again with reference to your notebook.

If you decide to try your hand at fiction, it might be a good idea to reread several stories that you have found interesting in the past. In rereading them, try to define as clearly as possible the meaning the story has for you. Then decide how the author has conveyed his meaning. What methods has he used? Does his practice sharpen for you the principles that you have been studying? And again refer to your notebook.

Now write.

PART THREE

SPECIAL PROBLEMS
OF DISCOURSE

CHAPTER 10

The Paragraph and
the Sentence

Thus far in this book we have been talking about the writing of whole themes. We have considered how one might go about describing the process of training a dog (p. 51); or how one might outline to another person the steps to be followed in gluing a piece of felt to wood (p. 103). Such problems demand extended solutions and require writing several hundred words. We have been thinking in terms of whole compositions and only incidentally in terms of paragraphs and sentences.

But the process of writing is, of course, a double one: though the writer must constantly keep in mind the developing shape of the composition as a whole, nevertheless, he proceeds by writing individual sentences and paragraphs. The process of revision also requires attention to particular paragraphs and sentences.

In any case, the student is not encountering the problems of paragraph construction for the first time. In his precollege work he has studied the paragraph and the sentence as rhetorical structures—and the sentence as a grammatical structure as well. Many high schools stress the writing of paragraphs. The student who has had sound training of this sort may well regard what follows as simply an intensive review.

The Paragraph as a Convenience to the Reader

The paragraph, since it is a unit of thought, has a certain structure, and like the larger composition of which it is part, it is bound to embody (or fail to embody) the principles of unity, coherence, and emphasis.

When the writer divides his composition into paragraphs, he is indicating to his reader that each of the subdivisions so marked off constitutes a unit of thought. The writer thus undertakes to make his thought structure visible upon the page itself. To do so is surely a courtesy to the reader, and since communication between writer and reader is difficult enough at best, the writer who wants his reader to understand him will make his best use of this device.[1]

Obviously, paragraphing can be of no help to the reader if the paragraphs so set off are not really meaningful segments of the writer's thought. If they pretend to be units of thought but are in fact simply formless blobs arbitrarily divided from each other, they can only mislead the reader. *For a paragraph undertakes to discuss one topic or one aspect of a topic.*

How long should a paragraph be? Common sense dictates that the ordinary paragraph will neither be reduced to a single sentence nor include a hundred sentences. To turn every sentence into a paragraph would be as bad as having no paragraphs at all; and very long paragraphs would tell the reader almost as little as a series of one-sentence paragraphs. In neither case would the writer have provided a means for readily distinguishing the stages of his developing discourse.

Yet this is not to say that an *occasional* very short paragraph may not tell the reader a great deal, for the very shortness of the paragraph—if the brevity is justified—gives special emphasis. Turn back to pages 204–05 and read the theme "Getting Engaged." At the climax of the action, when Joseph puts himself in command of the situation, the author presents a single sentence as a separate paragraph:

> Then I saw his face.

In the following paragraph, the author explains the meaning of that sentence—the maturity revealed by Joseph in the moment of crisis, which leads to the couple's becoming engaged. By setting off the sentence as a separate paragraph, the author stresses and dramatizes her point.

A single sentence or even a single word, then, may sometimes warrant being treated as a paragraph. Conversely, in some special circumstances, an abnormally long paragraph may sometimes be justified. The young writer, however, will do well to avoid either of these extremes, and particularly he will do well to avoid very long paragraphs. Long paragraphs, as thoughtful reconsideration may reveal, are often nothing more than large blobs of words, not organized, or if organized, needing to be marked off into two or three shorter paragraphs.

---

[1] A special convention with reference to the paragraph needs to be noted. When there is direct quotation of a conversation, the change of speakers is normally indicated by a new paragraph. Thus:

"How much is a plate of peas?" he asked.
"Three halfpence, sir," said the girl.
"Bring me a plate of peas," he said, "and a bottle of ginger beer." (See p. 250.)

The Structure of the Paragraph

A well-conceived and well-constructed paragraph is a unit, and often this unity is indicated by a key sentence—what is called the *topic sentence*. The topic sentence states the central thought, which the rest of the paragraph develops. We can think of the topic sentence as a kind of backbone, a spine, which supports the body of the paragraph and around which the rest of the structure is formed. Here is an example:

> *The reader of a novel—by which I mean the critical reader—is himself a novelist; he is the maker of a book which may or may not please his taste when it is finished, but of a book for which he must take his own share of the responsibility.* The author does his part, but he cannot transfer his book like a bubble into the brain of the critic; he cannot make sure that the critic will possess his work. The reader must therefore become, for his part, a novelist, never permitting himself to suppose that the creation of the book is solely the affair of the author. The difference between them is immense, of course, and so much so that a critic is always inclined to extend and intensify it. The opposition that he conceives between the creative and the critical task is a very real one; but in modestly belittling his own side of the business he is apt to forget an essential portion of it. The writer of the novel works in a manner that would be utterly impossible to the critic, no doubt, and with a liberty and with a range that would disconcert him entirely. But in one quarter their work coincides; both of them make the novel.　　—PERCY LUBBOCK: *The Craft of Fiction.*

In this paragraph the first sentence (which we have italicized) is the topic sentence. There are obvious advantages in presenting at the very beginning of the paragraph a brief statement of the thought that the paragraph is to develop. But the topic sentence need not open the paragraph. Consider the following example:

> The artistic temperament is a disease that afflicts amateurs. It is a disease which arises from men not having sufficient power of expression to utter and get rid of the element of art in their being. It is healthful to every sane man to utter the art within him; it is essential to every sane man to get rid of the art within him at all costs. Artists of a large and wholesome vitality get rid of their art easily, as they breathe easily, or perspire easily. But in artists of less force, the thing becomes a pressure, and produces a definite pain, which is called the artistic temperament. Thus, very great artists are able to be ordinary men—men like Shakespeare or Browning. There are many real tragedies of the artistic temperament, tragedies of vanity or violence or fear. *But the great tragedy of the artistic temperament is that it cannot produce any art.*
> —G. K. CHESTERTON: "On the Wit of Whistler," *Heretics.*

The final sentence of this paragraph (italicized) makes a generalized statement about the point developed in the paragraph as a whole. Thus in this instance, the topic sentence serves as a kind of summary. Though a topic sentence frequently occurs at the beginning or at the end of a paragraph, it may in fact occur at any point within the paragraph.

I The following paragraphs contain topic sentences. Point them out.

A   "The Rebuilding of London" proceeds ruthlessly apace. The humble old houses that dare not scrape the sky are being duly punished for their timidity. Down they come; and in their place are shot up new tenements, quick and high as rockets. And the little old streets, so narrow and exclusive, so shy and crooked—we are making an example of them, too. We lose our way in them, do we?—we whose time is money. Our omnibuses can't trundle through them, can't they? Very well, then. Down with them! We have no use for them. This is the age of "noble arteries."

—Max Beerbohm: *Yet Again.*

B   It is odd that American men are so frequently presented in European caricatures of the type, in fiction, plays, and films, as being extremely ill-mannered, loud, rough customers. Such Americans exist, of course, just as sneering Englishmen, bullying Teutons, insolent Latins also exist. But it has always seemed to me that American manners in general tend to err on the side of formality and solemnity. They are rather like those of elderly English dons and clergymen. The ordinary English are much more casual. We do not take enough trouble, for example, with our introductions. Terrified of appearing pompous, we hastily mumble names or hastily accept a mumble of names, so that our introductions do not serve their purpose, and often, not knowing to whom we are talking, we saunter into the most dreadful traps. The deliberate ceremony that most Americans make of introductions protects them from these dangers and errors.   —J. B. Priestley: *Midnight on the Desert.*

II Look back at the student theme "Training a Dog" (p. 51). How many of its eight paragraphs may be said to contain topic sentences?

III Construct paragraphs that will incorporate as topic sentences three of the following:

1   Students should have a part in the promotion of university professors and in granting permanent tenure.
2   Television is bringing about the death of the imagination.
3   The medium is indeed the message.
4   The prime problem of civilization today is overpopulation.
5   The prime problem of civilization today is the hydrogen bomb.
6   Set a thief to catch a thief.

Though every true paragraph is a unit, not every paragraph includes a topic sentence. Sometimes the idea or emotion or aspect of experience with which the paragraph is principally concerned need not be summed up in such fashion. Consider the following paragraph from G. M. Trevelyan's *History of England:*

As Drake entered Plymouth Sound after nearly three years' absence from Europe, his first question to some passing fishermen was whether the Queen were alive and well. Yes, in spite of all her enemies, she was still alive, and well enough to come next year and knight him on board his ship at Deptford. It was the most important knighthood ever conferred by an English sovereign, for it was a direct challenge to Spain and an appeal to the people of England to look to the sea for their strength. In view of this deed, disapproved by her faithful Cecil, who shall say Elizabeth could never act boldly? Her bold decisions are few and can be numbered, but each of them began an epoch.[2]

Few readers would contend that this paragraph is not unified, but there is no clear topic sentence. One might try to make a case for the third sentence, but then one might make an equally good case for the fourth sentence, or even the fifth. Narrative prose (such as this is) and descriptive prose abound in paragraphs without topic sentences. The student might, for example, look at the paragraphs quoted on pages 200–01 (from *The World I Live In*); pages 207 and 210 (from *Bleak House*); page 209 (from *Seven Pillars of Wisdom*); page 216 (from *Main Street*).

Methods of Paragraph Organization

Whether or not the writer makes use of a topic sentence, he faces, nevertheless, the problem of organizing his paragraphs. What are some of the typical structural principles that can be employed? Not surprisingly, they turn out to be, by and large, the same as those that govern the composition as a whole. In the chapter on Exposition, we described various methods of organization, such as classification, comparison and contrast, illustration, and definition. These are methods that may be used to shape the smaller as well as the larger units of composition.

By illustration

On page 63 we offered a single paragraph of T. H. Huxley's "The Herring" as an instance of organization by illustration. Though we printed the whole of the selection from *The Saga of Billy the Kid* (pp. 64–66) to show this same principle of organization at work, inspection will make it clear that the opening paragraph itself manifests organization by illustration.

By comparison and contrast

Comparison and contrast, a method often used for building up the whole essay, may also serve to shape an individual paragraph. See the paragraph quoted from John Corbin's *An American at Oxford* (p. 59).

---

[2] From *History of England* by G. M. Trevelyan. Reprinted by permission of Longmans Group Ltd.

By syllogistic pattern

We remarked in Chapter 3 (p. 29) that the "order of logic" was one of the four general modes for achieving coherence and that in "exposition and argument, the order is always that of logic." But in some paragraphs this logical arrangement becomes very strict, sometimes approaching that of a formal syllogism. (See pp. 154–57.) Here is an example:

> A really great pitcher must have control. Charles Ramsey had wonderful speed and a curve that broke as sharply as any that I have ever seen. He dazzled opposing batters with his fastball or made them break their backs reaching for pitches that broke sharply away from the plate. Charles had nearly everything—he even fielded his position brilliantly—but he lacked control. Even on his best days his control was less than certain. Shrewd batters learned this, and waited him out, frequently successfully, for a base on balls. On his worst days he simply couldn't find the plate. A pitcher without control cannot win close games. For this reason I do not consider Ramsey a great pitcher.

Analysis shows that we have here a *major premise* ("A really great pitcher must have control"), a *minor premise* ("Charles Ramsey lacks control"), and a *conclusion* ("Therefore Charles Ramsey is not a great pitcher"). This method of organization is, however, rare, and in general the more complex methods of organization discussed in the chapters on Exposition and Argument, such as functional analysis or causal analysis, do not occur in single paragraphs, for paragraphs are relatively short and their structures necessarily simple.

By sequence in time

To tell what happened first and then what happened next constitutes the most primitive of all the ways of organizing prose. Though it can be as simple as a child's narrative, it can also be put to uses as sophisticated as those in a Henry James novel. It is an indispensable mode of expressing our experience as human beings, for we live in a world of time and are constantly involved in actions and processes. We construct paragraphs in terms of time sequence, then, not only when we attempt fiction but also when we describe a process like that of training a dog (see p. 51) or gluing felt to wood (see p. 103).

By arrangement of objects in space

Some of the simplest and most natural ways of organizing a paragraph are found in descriptive prose in the various schemes by which visible objects may be ordered. (The student might at this point review what has been said earlier in "Texture and Pattern in Description," pp. 213–19.)

Consider a paragraph from Joseph Conrad's story "The Secret Sharer":

On my right hand there were lines of fishing-stakes resembling a mysterious system of half-submerged bamboo fences, incomprehensible in its division of the domain of tropical fish, and crazy of aspect as if abandoned for ever by some nomad tribe of fishermen now gone to the other end of the ocean; for there was no sign of human habitation as far as the eye could reach. To the left a group of barren islets, suggesting ruins of stone walls, towers, and blockhouses, had its foundations set in a blue sea that itself looked solid, so still and stable did it lie below my feet; even the track of light from the westering sun shone smoothly, without that animated glitter which tells of an imperceptible ripple. And when I turned my head to take a parting glance at the tug which had just left us anchored outside the bar, I saw the straight line of the flat shore joined to the stable sea, edge to edge, with a perfect and unusual closeness, in one levelled floor half brown, half blue under the enormous dome of the sky.

Here we have a fixed observer. He tells us what he sees on his right hand, then on his left, and finally, turning his head, what he sees behind him. (There is even an implied look upward: "the . . . dome of the sky.") The order of composition is simple and even mechanical, though the writing itself is not mechanical. Note, for example, the sense of finality and completeness given by the last sentence. The observer's survey comes to rest in "the straight line" of shore and sea "under the enormous dome of the sky." The paragraph thus rounds out and completes its chosen topic. It is thoroughly unified, though it does *not* contain a topic sentence.

We may also have a paragraph describing a scene through the eyes of an observer who is shifting his position. The paragraph from T. E. Lawrence's *Seven Pillars of Wisdom* (p. 215) furnishes an illustration of this. Or a scene may be described in terms of an image that provokes a frame of reference. Thoreau, for example, describes Cape Cod through the image of a human arm (see p. 218).

By mood or dominant interest

Various other ways in which descriptions of a scene may be organized have been discussed in Chapter 8. The description may be keyed to some sense, hearing or touch or sight; dominated by a special mood; focused upon a particular detail; and so on. All these methods of describing a scene apply to descriptive *paragraphs* as well as to the larger units of description. In fact, the examples that we used in Chapter 8 to illustrate methods of presenting description turn out to be, almost without exception, distinct paragraphs. The student can learn from them, therefore, a great deal about paragraph development.

■ APPLICATION

The paragraphs referred to below exemplify some of the following structures: (a) illustration, (b) comparison and contrast, (c) causal analysis, (d) frame image, and (e) description organized by a dominant impression. Which method of organization is exemplified in each of the following paragraphs?

1 Paragraph 2 of the quotation from Smith and Phillips (p. 196)
2 Paragraph 3 of the passage by Melville (p. 197)
3 Paragraph F (p. 221)
4 Paragraph by Wecter (p. 227)

Unity and Coherence in the Paragraph

Unity implies coherence. As we have pointed out (pp. 27–28), the various elements in a unified piece of writing must cohere—that is, they must have a meaningful relation to each other. Yet though unity implies coherence, the inexperienced writer may discover that unity does not guarantee it. Even though he may have carved out a paragraph that is related to *one* idea and does *one* job within the composition, the parts of that paragraph may not actually hang together.

Consider what happens to the coherence of the paragraph quoted from Chesterton on page 257 when we rearrange it to read as follows:

> Artists of a large and wholesome vitality get rid of their art easily, as they breathe easily, or perspire easily. It is healthful to every sane man to utter the art within him; it is essential to every sane man to get rid of the art within him at all costs. The artistic temperament is a disease that afflicts amateurs. It is a disease which arises from men not having sufficient power of expression to utter and get rid of the element of art in their being. Thus, very great artists are able to be ordinary men—men like Shakespeare or Browning. But in artists of less force, the thing becomes a pressure, and produces a definite pain, which is called the artistic temperament. There are many real tragedies of the artistic temperament, tragedies of vanity or violence or fear. But the great tragedy of the artistic temperament is that it cannot produce any art.

The paragraph as rearranged is "about" one general topic, the nature of the artistic temperament. But a careful comparison of the rearranged paragraph with the original will illustrate how much blurring of thought occurs when we do not think out the relation of sentence to sentence within the paragraph. (It is only fair to observe that an author often achieves much of the finer articulation of part with part only with revision. See Chapter 15.)

■ APPLICATION

The sentences in the paragraph that follows have been hashed.

1 Attempt to restore what you take to be the original order.
2 List the words in these sentences that helped you most in restoring the original order.

The most elaborate filing systems of library catalogues are arranged by author, subject, and sometimes date of publication, with cross references between these files. The human brain, with one million times as many cells, is unique not only for its ability to store vast amounts of information in a small storage space and for requiring vanishing amounts of operating power, but also for the speed and ease with which any remembered item can be produced. The human file of ideas, however, classifies each idea in an infinite variety of ways; the word "red" can be connected with "green" or "hot" or "blush" or "Skelton" or "Communist" or "blood" or "herring," to mention only a few. Computers can refer to their memories only in a systematic fashion, well planned and explained beforehand, and cannot create new cross indexing for themselves.

Emphasis in the Paragraph

In Chapter 3 we have discussed unity, coherence, and emphasis at some length. In this chapter we have applied the first two terms to the special problems of paragraph organization. It remains to say something about emphasis as it relates to the paragraph. In general, emphasis is a function of coherence; that is, only when we have made our thought truly coherent can we expect that it will express a proper scale of emphasis. (The rewriting of Chesterton's paragraph, for example, destroys the emphasis as well as the coherence of his thought.)

In a paragraph, the beginning and the end are the places of greatest emphasis. It is no accident that topic sentences—obvious devices for emphasis—tend to occur at the beginning or the end of the paragraph.

Yet topic sentences are not necessarily required for emphasis any more than they are required for unity (p. 258). Look again at the paragraph from Conrad's "The Secret Sharer" (p. 261). Conrad has found a way to bring his hero's panoramic vision of sea and sky to a definite point of reference and the paragraph to a satisfying conclusion.

Clearly this handling of emphasis is not at all a matter of set formula or of the application of a mechanical rule. Moreover, one quickly realizes that it is not determined merely by structural considerations. The content is also highly important. For example, how much of the emphasis in the paragraph quoted on page 221 from Frederick Marryat depends upon the fact that the author has found a startling image with which to complete his portrait of Cornelius Vanslyperken?

● CAUTION

The writer who raises certain expectations in a topic sentence at the beginning of a paragraph must fullfill them as the paragraph is developed. Suppose he writes: "George is cowardly and cruel." If the paragraph then devotes itself to George's cowardice and gives no attention to his cruelty, it is lopsided in emphasis—unless, of course, the author means to deal with George's cruel nature in a subsequent paragraph or paragraphs. In that case, he might do well to state the fact of George's having cowardly and cruel traits—either as necessarily related to each other or as a rather startling paradox—in a short paragraph devoted to that issue and then subsequently devote a paragraph or more to each of George's two salient traits.

Summary

A review of these schemes for paragraph development serves to reinforce a point made earlier. There is no formula by which either the length or the structure of a paragraph may be determined. The student must use his best judgment, his common sense, and his taste. Unless he is very sure of his ground, he will tend to employ paragraphs of medium length and to use the more conventional paragraph structures. But in following these common-sense rules, he must not conceive of paragraphs as mechanical units of even length and of homogeneous make-up. He should feel free, on occasion, to formulate paragraphs of "felt unity," relying upon his own impression of the "rightness" of the structure. For the student must never forget that the paragraph is a part—a meaningful part—of a larger structure and therefore cannot be formulated mechanically any more than can the larger structure of which it is a part.

■ APPLICATION

Comment on coherence and emphasis in the following paragraphs. What structural principles are to be found in each? If you judge that the paragraph has no real structure, say so and indicate why.

1 The second of the three paragraphs from Leo Tolstoy's *War and Peace* quoted on p. 107.
2 The paragraph from James Joyce's *A Portrait of the Artist as a Young Man* quoted on p. 331.
3 The paragraph from John Burroughs' *Leaf and Tendril* quoted on p. 209.

Linking Paragraph with Paragraph

By transitional words and phrases

Since paragraphs are parts of a whole work, elements in an ordered sequence, it is important that they be properly linked together. Even when the chain of development embodied in the series of paragraphs has been thought out carefully, the reader will still be grateful for signposts to direct him. The judicious use of transitional words and phrases, such as *therefore, consequently, hence, thus, accordingly, on the contrary, however, nevertheless, furthermore, finally, in the same way,* and *moreover,* constitutes one way of helping the reader. The writer may also make use of the coordinate conjunctions *for, and, but, or,* and *nor* as signs of connection between paragraphs. Since, however, we ordinarily use these conjunctions to join the parts of a sentence, or to join sentence with sentence, we employ them less frequently to tie a paragraph to a preceding paragraph.

In carrying on an argument it is particularly important that these "controls," as we have called them, should be used accurately and responsibly. In this connection the student might reread pages 28–30.

● CAUTION

If we do provide the reader with transitional words as signposts, obviously we must use them accurately. We must not begin a paragraph by writing "In the same way" unless what follows *is* "in the same way"; we must not write "Consequently" unless what follows is in fact a consequence of the preceding paragraph.

By the repetition of key words and phrases

The repetition of a key word or phrase is a useful device for linking paragraphs, especially if we wish to avoid the formality of style suggested by the employment of transitional words and the abruptness occasioned by the use of *and, but,* or *or.* To illustrate: T. H. Huxley in his famous essay on "The Method of Scientific Investigation" effects the transition between his eighth and ninth paragraphs in the following manner (we have italicized the key words here and in the examples that follow):

> You mean to say exactly what you know; but in reality you are giving expression to what is, in all essential particulars, an hypothesis. You do not know it at all; it is nothing but an hypothesis rapidly framed in your own mind. And it is an *hypothesis* founded on a long train of *inductions* and *deductions.*
>
> What are those *inductions* and *deductions,* and how have you got at this *hypothesis?* You have observed in the first place. . . .

The exact word or phrase, of course, need not be repeated if the idea is carried over. Here is Huxley's transition from paragraph five to six:

> He sees that the experiment has been tried under all sorts of conditions, as to time, place, and people, with the same result; and he says with you, therefore, that the law you have laid down must be a good one, and he must believe it.
>
> In science we *do the same thing.* . . .

A variant of the key-word device for linking paragraphs is the use of synonyms. As an illustration, consider the following passage.

> *Mary* walked slowly along the street, pondering the character of her interview. It had been more difficult than she had supposed it would be.

Mr. Jones had almost glared at her—or so it seemed to her at the time—as he inquired about her speed in typing and her experience in handling business forms. True, he had not said in so many words that she would not be hired. But he had certainly not been very encouraging, nor had he been very mannerly in his questioning.

The girl was nearly on the point of tears, but she . . .

■ APPLICATION

Here is a sequence of two paragraphs and the beginning of a third from Dorothy Sayers' *The Mind of the Maker*. What devices does Miss Sayers use to link these paragraphs? Underscore any transitional words and phrases, key terms that are repeated, or synonyms.

> It is for this reason that I have prefixed to this brief study of the creative mind an introductory chapter in which I have tried to make clear the difference between fact and opinion, and between the so-called "laws" based on fact and opinion respectively.
>
> In the creeds of Christendom, we are confronted with a set of documents which purport to be, not expressions of opinion but statements of fact. Some of these statements are historical, and with these the present book is not concerned. Others are theological—which means that they claim to be statements of fact about the nature of God and the universe; and with a limited number of these I propose to deal.
>
> The selected statements are those which aim at defining the nature of God, conceived in His capacity as Creator. They were originally . . .

By the use of demonstrative pronouns

Another device for linking paragraphs is the use of the demonstrative (pointing) pronouns: *this (these), that (those);* but such a method must be used with care. The writer is sometimes tempted to a vague use of the demonstrative pronouns. He assumes that the context will make plain the idea or object to which they refer. But often the reference is not clear, and instead of a tight and neat coupling of the two paragraphs, we have only the vague and clumsy suggestion of a tie. For example, consider the following passage in which the author has been describing an experiment to determine whether bees can distinguish colors. He first puts out a red card and a blue card. He baits the blue card with syrup. After the bees have discovered the syrup and continue to return to the blue card, he puts out fresh blue and red cards; but this time he puts no syrup on the blue card. The author then writes:

> After we have arranged these new cards, we have not long to wait. Very soon bees arrive again, and it can be seen that they fly straight on to the blue card; none go to the red card.
>
> —H. MUNRO FOX: "The Colors That Animals Can See," *The Personality of Animals.*

A young writer might be tempted to begin his next paragraph with: "This seems to indicate two things. The first is . . ." But what the author actually wrote was: "This behavior of the bees seems to indicate two things. . . ."

A little reflection will indicate that his judgment was sound. He intends to state clearly a process of proof. In this context, *this* would be a pronoun with a very large antecedent. The author has, therefore, wisely employed *this* as a demonstrative adjective modifying a specific noun, *behavior*.

● CAUTION

The fault of indefinite antecedent is so common in student themes that the student ought to check each composition he writes in order to make sure that any *this* or *that* standing at the beginning of a paragraph or at the beginning of a sentence refers unmistakably to some specific person, thing, or action.

Paragraphs of specialized function

Since paragraphs are parts of a larger structure of meaning, individual paragraphs will often have specialized functions. Thus, the opening paragraph (or paragraphs) must introduce the whole essay;[3] the final paragraph (or paragraphs) must bring the essay to a suitable conclusion. Within the essay itself, individual paragraphs may have specific jobs to do: one paragraph states a particular argument, another provides an illustration, a third makes a transition between two sections of the essay, and so on.

As we have said earlier, the make-up of any particular paragraph is determined by the part the paragraph plays in the whole composition. Thus, there is only a limited and provisional value in studying it in isolation. The overriding consideration will rarely be the neatness or the force of the paragraph viewed in isolation; it will be rather what the paragraph contributes to the composition as a whole.

■ APPLICATION

Reread G. Lowes Dickinson's "Red-bloods and Mollycoddles" (pp. 60–62). Point out the topic sentence in each paragraph, if any. Is each paragraph coherent and emphatic? Explain. Point out transitional devices used to link the paragraphs.

Rhetoric and Grammar of the Sentence

A sentence is primarily a grammatical construction, and since it is, we may usefully say a brief word here about the relation of grammar to rhetoric.

---

[3] On pages 16–22 we have discussed a series of typical introductory paragraphs.

The grammar of a language is a systematic account of how that language functions to provide intelligible discourse.[4] But rhetoric also is concerned with intelligible discourse and the choice and arrangement of words in such discourse. What is the distinction between grammar and rhetoric? Perhaps it can be put most clearly by using an analogy with the game of football. The rules that govern the play of football may be called the grammar of the game. Thus, a forward pass caught beyond the sideline does not count; if a team in possession of the ball does not gain ten yards in four downs, the ball goes over to the other team; a touchdown is worth six points; a field goal, three; and so forth. These rules are conventional and conceivably can be changed; indeed, occasionally they are changed.[5]

In order to play the game of football, one must observe the rules; but a mere keeping of the rules would not ensure that the team necessarily played well or that it won any games. The rhetoric of football, then, would be a knowledge of strategy and maneuver that leads to effective play and a winning game. To play the game correctly would not *necessarily* be to play it effectively, though effective play would have to conform to the rules of the game.

What has just been said, however, does not mean that there is a sharp division between grammar and rhetoric. In fact, there is a large area of overlap. For example, if someone writes: "Laughing through her tears, we heard the hysterical girl try to tell her story," we say (grammatically speaking) that "Laughing through her tears" constitutes a *dangling participle* and is thus an error in grammar (see p. 274); but the sentence is also rhetorically defective, for the statement is garbled and even ludicrous. We are not, of course, really confused about what the writer is trying to say; but we do smile at his bungling: to hear him tell it, *we* were the ones laughing while the girl wept.

The fixed word order of the normal sentence

An important practical application of rhetorical principles to the individual sentence has to do with the arrangement of elements within the sentence. For, as we shall see, the expressiveness of English depends heavily on the order in which the various elements of the sentence succeed each other.

When the Anglo-Saxons came into the island of Britain in the fifth century, they spoke a rather highly inflected language. By Chaucer's time, however, many of the original inflections had been lost, and by the end of the Middle Ages, English had relatively few inflections. Instead of relying

---

[4] Grammar has to do with such matters as the inflection of words and their syntactic arrangement. In his preparation for college, the student has presumably acquired a working knowledge of English grammar. The student's possession of such knowledge is assumed by the authors of this textbook, for their primary concern here is not with grammar but with rhetoric.

[5] Since grammar is based ultimately on usage, and since usage changes, the rules of grammar are subject to change too, though the changes tend to be very gradual.

primarily on inflections for indicating grammatical relations, modern English makes use of the *position* that words occupy in the sentence pattern. Indeed, the change of position can result in a radical change in meaning. Thus, "The boy hit the ball" means something very different from "The ball hit the boy." [6] The shift of position here produces a direct reversal of meaning. Though other rearrangements of normal word order alter the meaning less drastically, they do change it, and if we value the clarity and force of our writing, we shall want to be able to manipulate the arrangement of sentence elements so as to achieve a precise shading of meaning.

The normal order of the English sentence [7] may be diagrammed as follows:

SUBJECT	+	VERB	+	INNER COMPLEMENT (IF ANY)	+	OUTER COMPLEMENT (IF ANY)
John		stood				
He		is				John
He		is				tall
John		gave				a book
John		gave		me		a book

The verb *stood* does not require anything to complete its meaning and here takes no *complement*. The verb *is* acts here as a linking verb and has its meaning completed by *John,* a predicate moninative. In the third sentence the linking verb has its meaning completed by *tall,* a predicate adjective. In the fourth sentence, *book* (which indicates what John gave and is the outer complement) is a direct object. In the fifth sentence we have, in addition to the outer complement (direct object), an inner complement (indirect object, the word that indicates to whom John gave the book).

---

[6] We still have considerable inflection in our pronouns. Thus, in spite of the word order, "Him I hit" means that I delivered the blow and "Me he hit" means that I received it. Yet so strong is our sense of the normal word order (which requires us to say "I hit him" and "He hit me") that though there is no possibility of mistaking their meaning, "Him I hit" and "Me he hit" sound to us intolerably archaic and pretentiously "literary." Thus, "Me he hit" is *grammatically* correct but in most contexts it would be *rhetorically* inept.

[7] One can easily demonstrate how powerfully embedded in our consciousness is this normal word order. We may not know precisely what the word *meniscus* means, but if we read a sentence saying "The meniscus was clearly visible," we know at once that it must be the name of something that is capable of being seen. We may be hazy about the meaning of *fibrillate,* but if we read "The patient's heart began to fibrillate," we know that *fibrillate* is a verb and describes some action performed by the heart or some condition in which the heart became involved.

The power of normal English sentence structure to convey syntactic relations can be even more forcibly illustrated by constructing a sentence out of what are frankly nonsense words. For example, suppose we write: "The snory womped the ogly glomp." Meaningless as this "sentence" is, it does convey *syntactic* relationships. We know, for example, that "snory," preceded as it is by the article *the,* must be a noun, the name of something, and that this snory, whatever it is, did something (in the past, since *-ed* is a sign of the past tense of the verb) to a "glomp," whatever *that* is. We know also that "ogly" describes the glomp; that is, that ogly is an adjective. So strongly ingrained is the sense of normal English structure that even an English speaker who had never studied formal grammar would know all this simply from the position that these words take in relation to each other.

Use of the Passive Voice   Although it is a sound rule for the writer to use normal English word order unless there is a compelling reason to do otherwise, such reasons do exist. There are occasions on which one very properly varies the order. Suppose, for example, that we want to stress *what* it was that John gave. By using a passive construction, we can move into emphatic position at the beginning of the sentence what is normally an outer complement, *book,* and so put lighter stress on John (normally the subject) or even leave John out of account altogether. Thus we can write: "A book was given by John" or perhaps simply "A book was given." [8]

Expletive Constructions   Another device for emphasizing a particular word (whether the normal complement or the normal subject) is the so-called expletive construction, in which we begin the sentence with "It is" or "There is." Thus, we can write: "It was a book that John gave" (or simply "It was a book"). But we can also write, throwing stress on the normal subject: "It was John who gave the book."

To take an example: Alexander Smith, in an essay entitled "A Lark's Flight," writes:

> It is taken for granted that the spectators of public executions—the artizans and country people who take up their stations overnight as close to the barriers as possible, and the wealthier classes who occupy hired windows and employ opera-glasses—are merely drawn together by a morbid relish for horrible sights.

Normal word order would call for something like this:

> Everyone takes for granted that a morbid relish for a horrible sight draws together the spectators of public executions—the artizans, etc.

The normal word order, as a matter of fact, gives us a reasonably effective sentence. Why, then, did the author, almost instinctively, one supposes, use the expletive construction (with the passive) in this sentence? Because here the normal subject requires no emphasis. The normal subject is everybody and anybody. What is important here is not *who* takes it for granted but *what is taken for granted:* the character of the spectators.

● CAUTION

Be on your guard against drifting into expletive or into passive constructions. Obviously we achieve no emphasis if, out of sheer thoughtlessness, we begin a good half of our sentences with "It is" or "There is" or if we use passive constructions indiscriminately, sometimes for no better reason than that we are too lazy or vague to think who or what the true subject is. All emphasis or haphazard emphasis is no emphasis.

---

[8] Imagine that someone says "John gave her a book," but so mumbles his words that his companion has to ask: "Did you say John gave a book or a box?" Here there is no question as to who the giver was. What is in question is the gift; and so the first speaker says: "A book was given." Or, since in such conversation "was given" would be understood, the first speaker simply says "A book."

I Examine the following paragraph in which Helen Keller, blind and deaf from early childhood, tells of how she learned her first word:

> There was a well-house, covered with honeysuckle, and attracted by the smell of the honeysuckle we took a walk down the path to it. There was someone who was drawing water there and my hand was placed under the spout by my teacher. So there was a cool stream gushing over my hand and the word *water* was spelled out into the other hand by my teacher, first slowly and then rapidly. I stood still, because my whole attention was fixed upon the motions of her fingers. Suddenly there was a misty consciousness that came over me as of something forgotten—there was a thrill of returning thought; and somehow the mystery of language was revealed to me. The wonderful cool something that was flowing over my hand was the thing that was meant by "w-a-t-e-r." My soul was awakened by the living words; it was given light, hope, joy, and it was set free! There were barriers still, it is true, but these were barriers that could in time be swept away.

Compare this garbled rewriting with the version that Helen Keller actually wrote (p. 5). The original version contains one instance of expletive and three of passive construction. Can you say why they are justified, if you think that they are, and why those that we have introduced into the garbled rewriting are not?

II Convert the following sentences to normal word order; that is, reestablish the pattern of *subject, verb, inner and outer complements,* and, where necessary, eliminate *expletive* and *passive* constructions.

1 Icebergs, he could see wherever he looked.
2 The arrival of five cruisers and twenty destroyers was reported.
3 The great bear was surrounded by a horde of yapping, excited dogs.
4 When I was five years old, I was given my first book by my grandmother.
5 It was a book that was my first present.

THE POSITION OF ADJECTIVAL MODIFIERS

We have been considering the normal order of subject, verb, and the complements. But modifiers also have their normal positions in the order of the sentence. Adjectival modifiers are relatively fixed in position. Individual adjectives come immediately before the substantive that they modify. Consequently, variations from this normal position constitute a means of emphasizing the modifier. Ordinarily we write "three houses" or "three lakes" or "three soldiers." But when Kipling came to choose a title for one of his books, he called it *Soldiers Three.* By departing from the normal order he emphasized, as he wanted to do, the word *three.* Normally, we would write "a great queen," but we refer to a certain Russian empress as Catherine the Great. The adjective *great* is placed in an emphatic position because it serves to distinguish her from the other Catherines. We usually speak of a "beautiful house," but John Bunyan in his *Pilgrim's Progress* has Christian come upon an edifice which is called "The House Beautiful."

Variations of the normal position of the adjective, like other emphatic devices, are to be used sparingly and with discretion. But so used, the variations can sometimes be quite effective:

An automobile, *shabby and mud-splashed,* rounded the corner.
A small face, *dirty,* appeared at the window.

Though single-word adjectives normally come before the word that they modify, phrases and clauses that function as adjectives come *after* the word they modify. Thus:

The man *to see* is Jim. (infinitive used as an adjective)
The house *in the country* was charming. (prepositional phrase used as an adjective)
The house *that I saw* was of red brick. (relative clause used as an adjective)
The house *I saw* was of red brick. (relative clause, not headed by a relative pronoun, used as an adjective)

Though the position of single adjectives raises few problems for the writer, the position of adjectival *phrases* does; for they almost seem to invite careless positioning, and when carelessly placed, they can sometimes cause confusion. For example, a newspaper published the following advertisement:

Bird cage and parrot offered by refined young lady, having green feathers and a yellow beak.

"Having green feathers and a yellow beak" is a participial phrase that obviously is meant to modify *parrot,* not *young lady.* Accordingly, the phrase ought to be shifted to a position immediately after the word *parrot.*

■ APPLICATION

In the following sentences, some of the adjectival modifiers are awkwardly placed. Rearrange the modifiers and, where necessary, rewrite the sentences to improve clarity and effectiveness.

1 A man in the army that I served with gave me this book.
2 It was the man I knew whom I now saw.
3 The lady whom I knew from Boston has not returned.
4   Boy is missing in first pair of long pants.   —The Detroit *Free Press.*
5   Rex Parsons laid an egg on our table that had been previously laid on the nest by a little white Leghorn hen that was 3 inches in length and 6½ inches in circumference the smallest way.   —The Farmington *Franklin Journal.*

THE POSITION OF ADVERBIAL MODIFIERS

Adverbs that modify adjectives or other adverbs normally are placed immediately in front of the adjective or the adverb that they modify. Thus, we write: "The screen was *intensely* white" or "The horse ran *very* swiftly." But adverbs that modify *verbs,* and all adverbial phrases and clauses, are rather freely movable. Clumsy and inept placing of these can obscure thought and even plunge the whole sentence into absurdity. Consider the following advertisement for a television show:

> Joan Fontaine plays a European countess who returns to her home town in Ohio and charms a young married man tonight at 9 on G.E. Theater.

Surely the writer intended to say:

> On G.E. Theater at 9 tonight, Joan Fontaine plays a European countess who returns to her home town in Ohio and charms a young married man.

When we remember that adverbial modifiers tell us *when,* or *where,* or *how,* or *why* some action took place and that subordinate clauses, such as those beginning with *since, although, because, if, in order that,* and so forth, have an adverbial function, it becomes easier to understand why adverbial modifiers can take so many positions in the sentence. The writer who can place them skillfully has found an important means for making fine shadings and discriminations of his thought.[9] Conversely, the writer who makes a clumsy disposition of his adverbial modifiers often obscures his thought.

Here are three ways of saying the same thing—or do these sentences say *quite* the same thing?

> At ten o'clock, when I heard the news, I felt a pang though I had assured myself that I would be prepared for it.

> Though I had assured myself that I would be prepared for it, when, at ten o'clock, I heard the news, I felt a pang.

> I felt a pang when I heard the news at ten o'clock, though I had assured myself that I would be prepared for it.

Which arrangement of the modifiers do you prefer? Which seems most natural? Which most clumsy?

■ APPLICATIONS

I   Max Beerbohm describes his first sight of the poet Algernon Swinburne. Which of the following versions would you guess to be the one that he actually wrote?

A   Sparse and straggling though the grey hair was that fringed the immense pale dome of his head, and venerably haloed though he was for me by his greatness, there was yet about him something—boyish? girlish? childish, rather; something of a beautifully well-bred child.

---

[9] To put the matter in terms of unity-coherence-emphasis: proper attention to the disposition of the movable modifiers constitutes one of the most effective means of achieving coherence and proper emphasis within the sentence.

B   Though the grey hair that fringed the immense pale dome of his head was sparse and straggling, and though for me he was venerably haloed by his greatness, there was yet about him something—boyish? girlish? childish, rather; something of a beautifully well-bred child.

II   Grammar demands that adjectival phrases modify some substantive but not that adverbial phrases do so. When a confused writer treats an adjectival phrase as if it were an adverbial phrase and leaves it unattached to any substantive, he produces what is called a "dangling" modifier. The following sentences contain dangling modifiers. Remove them (a) by rewriting the sentence so that the modifier is provided with a substantive to modify or (b) by converting the dangling modifier into a subordinate clause. For example, the following sentence contains a dangling modifier: "Singing merrily, our music put the whole company into a jolly mood." We can correct it to read: (a) "Singing merrily, we put the whole company into a jolly mood." Or (b) "As we sang merrily, we put the whole company into a jolly mood." Revise the following sentences so as to eliminate the dangling modifiers.

1   Hurrying and out of breath, scurrying up the depot stairs, the 9:01 for Grand Central swept past us.
2   The afternoon drowsed on to an end, sipping lemonade and listening to records.
3   Hanging on for dear life, the car careened to the edge of the road.
4   Thinking as hard as we could, the answer still could not be found.
5   Turning the corner, the gigantic skeleton of New York's newest and the world's highest building comes into view.   —The New York *Herald Tribune.*

III   In the following sentences, the modifiers that are printed in italics have been shifted out of the order in which they were originally written. Try to restore what you believe to be the proper order.

1   Though the Greek scientist Eratosthenes had, *with only a small error,* calculated the distance of the sun from the earth and the earth's circumference at the equator, this theory of a global world was received by men of common sense *with polite scorn.*
2   In myriad private hotel rooms of myriad hotels the Alumni Weekly Lunch is, *today,* being celebrated, *as every day.*
3   *Because their maxims would not have expressed their hearts,* they would not have been perfect moralists *then,* even if their theory had been correct (which I think it was, *though not in statement,* in intention).
4   There can be no miracles *unless there exists something else which we may call the supernatural, in addition to Nature.*

Some special patterns of sentence structure

PARALLELISM

We have thus far examined the structure of the sentence with reference to one principle: the arrangement of its basic constituents (subject, predicate, and complements) and the arrangement of the various kinds of modifiers. But other principles may determine the make-up of a sentence. One of these is parallelism. Parallelism is a method of adjusting grammatical pattern to rhetorical pattern. In its simplest terms, parallelism means that *sentence elements of like grammatical order or function should be put in like constructions.*

The Balanced Sentence   The general idea that parallel construction may be used to emphasize parallel ideas seems simple enough, but in practice, an enormous variety of effects is thus made possible. Let us begin with some rather simple examples:

1   I like blondes; Bill likes brunettes. We both like red-heads.
2   Jack Sprat could eat no fat;
     His wife could eat no lean. . . .
3   Some books are to be tasted, others to be swallowed, and some few to be chewed and digested. . . .   —SIR FRANCIS BACON.

Here follow some more complicated instances:

1   As the hart panteth after the water brooks, so panteth my soul after Thee, O God.
2   He was sick of life, but he was afraid of death; and he shuddered at every sight or sound which reminded him of the inevitable hour.
3   To examine such compositions singly cannot be required; they have doubtless brighter and darker parts; but when they are once found to be generally dull, all further labor may be spared; for to what use can the work be criticized that will not be read?

The parallel elements may be represented in the following scheme:

1   as   so
    hart   soul
    panteth   panteth (repetition)
    water brooks   Thee

2   sick   afraid
    life   death

3   singly   generally
    required   spared
    once found   all further
    be criticized   be read

Sentences like the foregoing, especially those that show a rather elaborate balancing of item against item, are called "balanced sentences."

Two of the most widely celebrated statements of the last few years take the form of balanced sentences.

Never ask what your country can do for you; ask rather what you can do for your country.   —PRESIDENT JOHN F. KENNEDY.

> That's one small step for a man; a giant leap for mankind.[10]
> > —NEIL ARMSTRONG, on first setting foot on the moon.

Here is a statement by a famous seventeenth-century prose writer:

> If we begin with certainties, we shall end in doubts; but if we begin with doubts, and are patient in them, we shall end in certainties.
> > —SIR FRANCIS BACON.

Note that in Bacon's sentence, the arrangement of key terms is as follows: certainties-doubts, doubts-certainties. In the older rhetoric this pattern was called *chiasmus* (that is, a "criss-cross" like the Greek letter chi, *X*). The rather fancy term doesn't matter, but the device does, for it has its usefulness in heightening emphasis by reversing the arrangement of the key terms. Consider these rather simple examples:

> Love's fire heats water, water cools not love.—SHAKESPEARE, Sonnet 154.

> He [Christ] saved others; himself he cannot save.—ST. MATTHEW 27:42.

Note that in the criss-cross pattern, the paired terms need not be identical. In the first example we get fire-love, heats-cools, and water-water; in the second, he-he, saved-save, and others-himself. What is essential to the criss-cross is that the wording of the second clause should reverse that of the first.

■ APPLICATION

Using the scheme employed with reference to the three passages on page 275, indicate the parallel elements in the passages quoted above.

More elaborate uses of parallelism   Parallel constructions can, of course, be combined with other rhetorical devices. In the example that follows (from Edmund Burke's speech "On Conciliation with America") the antitheses (e.g., "Ægypt and Arabia and Curdistan" as against "Thrace," or "in his centre" as against "in all his borders") are used primarily to enforce a dominant comparison: "the circulation of power" is likened to the circulation of the blood—most powerful at the *heart* of the empire rather than at its extremities.

> In large bodies the circulation of power must be less vigorous at the extremities. Nature has said it. The Turk cannot govern Ægypt and Arabia and Curdistan as he governs Thrace; nor has he the same dominion in Crimea and Algiers which he has in Brusa and Smyrna. Despotism itself is obliged to truck and huckster. The Sultan gets such obedience as he can. He governs with a loose rein, that he may govern at all; and the whole

---

[10] In the newspapers (including the *New York Times*) this statement was first printed as "That's one small step for man; a giant leap for mankind." Can you see why "for *a* man" improves the "balance" of the sentence? (In terms of sense and "balance" is there something to be said for "a giant leap" instead of "one giant leap"?)

of the force and vigour of his authority in his centre is derived from a prudent relaxation in all his borders.

The following rather elaborate example (from G. K. Chesterton's *Heretics*) uses parallel structure to enforce contrasts—the contrast between the earth-shaking accomplishments of the scientist and his gentle and harmless demeanor, and between the awesome consequence of his acts and the guilelessness of his motives. (Chesterton writes of the splitting of a grain of *sand* [by the chemist?], for at the time of his writing the physicist had not yet split the *atom:* subsequent events have given more rather than less consequence to what he then had to say.)

> Men find it extremely difficult to believe that a man who is obviously uprooting mountains and dividing seas, tearing down temples and stretching out hands to the stars, is really a quiet old gentleman who only asks to be allowed to indulge his harmless old hobby and follow his harmless old nose. When a man splits a grain of sand and the universe is turned upside down in consequence, it is difficult to realize that to the man who did it, the splitting of the grain is the great affair, and the capsizing of the cosmos quite a small one. It is hard to enter into the feelings of a man who regards a new heaven and a new earth in the light of a by-product. But undoubtedly it was to this almost eerie innocence of the intellect that the great men of the great scientific period, which now appears to be closing, owed their enormous power and triumph. If they had brought the heavens down like a house of cards, their plea was not even that they had done it on principle; their quite unanswerable plea was that they had done it by accident.

G. Lowes Dickinson in his essay "Red-bloods and Mollycoddles" makes considerable use of balanced sentences. (See pp. 60–62.)

● CAUTION

The balanced sentence, like every other deviation from the normal pattern, is emphatic (see p. 275 above) and therefore should be used sparingly. All emphasis is no emphasis: a succession of balanced sentences might first impress the reader as artificially shrill but finally would be merely monotonous.

■ APPLICATION

In the passages quoted above from Burke and Chesterton indicate the parallel elements, pointing out which element "balances" which.

Violations of Parallelism   The very richness of the English language tempts us to violate parallelism. We have, for example, two noun forms of the verb, the infinitive (*to swim*) and the gerund (*swimming*). Consequently, the careless writer may blunder into a sentence like this: *"To swim* and *hunting* are my favorite sports." But here the distinction between infinitive and gerund awkwardly distracts the reader from what is really a coordinate relation. He ought to write: *"Swimming* and *hunting* are my favorite sports." Or: "I like best *to swim* and *to hunt."*

It is, however, our great variety of movable modifiers that most tempts us to violate parallelism. We may carelessly write: "Being lazy by nature and because I am clumsy, I have never liked tennis." A more vigorous sentence would read: "Being lazy by nature and also clumsy, I have never liked tennis." Or, "Because I am clumsy and am naturally lazy, I have never liked tennis." Violations of parallelism such as these easily creep into first drafts—even into the first drafts of a good writer. Careful rewriting is the obvious remedy.

COORDINATION AND SUBORDINATION

It is possible to regard coordination as an aspect of parallelism, and it may be convenient to do so here. In preceding pages we have been considering the rhetorical effectiveness of putting elements of like grammatical function into like constructions and the confusion that often results from our failure to do so. But we must also take care not to treat as parallel any elements that are not really parallel; that is, we must not treat as coordinate sentence elements that are not coordinate. The less important elements must be made subordinate to the more important.

Someone was ill and he stayed at home. If he writes: "I stayed at home; I was ill," he has merely juxtaposed the two ideas. He has not defined the relationship of one statement to the other. It is possible to define that relationship in various ways:

> Because I was ill, I stayed at home.
> While I was staying home, I was ill.
> Although I stayed at home, I was ill.
> Feeling ill, I stayed at home.
> I stayed at home, quite ill.

The precise form of subordination that is used will, of course, depend upon the writer's specific meaning.

Simple uncritical writing, such as that done by a child, tends to present a succession of coordinate units: "Then the bear got hungry. He came out of his den. He remembered the honey tree. And he started walking toward the honey tree." The mature writer indicates the relation of his statements, one to another, by subordination. Thus he writes: "The hungry bear came out of his den, and remembering the honey tree, started walking toward it." The amount of subordination will naturally depend upon a number of things: the circumstances to be discussed or told about, the nature of the audience whom the writer means to address, and the writer's own temperament. A novelist like Henry James is famous for the intricate patterns of subordination that he employs. The following is an example:

> The two ladies who, in advance of the Swiss season, had been warned that their design was unconsidered, that the passes would not be clear,

nor the air mild, nor the inns open—the two ladies who, characteristically, had braved a good deal of possibly interested remonstrance were finding themselves, as their adventure turned out, wonderfully sustained.

—HENRY JAMES: *The Wings of the Dove.*

Contrast with the James passage Ernest Hemingway's characteristic pattern of light subordination:

Before daylight it started to drizzle. The wind was down or we were protected by mountains that bounded the curve the lake had made. When I knew daylight was coming I settled down and rowed hard. I did not know where we were and I wanted to get into the Swiss part of the lake. When it was beginning to be daylight we were quite close to the shore. I could see the rocky shore and the trees.

—ERNEST HEMINGWAY: *A Farewell to Arms.*[11]

Subordination as a Means for Interpretation The writer who, instead of simply leaving relationships to be inferred by the reader, points them up, obviously makes the reader's task easier. He not only gives facts but supplies an interpretation of the facts: the pattern of subordination constitutes an interpretation. If, however, the writer does assume this burden of interpretation, he must be sure that his use of subordination correctly expresses the relation of idea to idea. Unless he does so, he may end up by writing sentences like this: "My head was feeling heavy when I took an aspirin." Such a sentence confuses the reader with a subordination that inverts the real relationship. Rather than do that, the writer might have done better simply to write: "My head was feeling heavy; I took an aspirin." (The proper subordination, of course, is obvious: "Because my head was feeling heavy, I took an aspirin." Or "When my head began to feel heavy, I took an aspirin.")

Here is a further example of improper subordination:

The workman snored loudly and he had a red face.

Alter to:

The workman, who had a red face, snored loudly.

Or to:

The red-faced workman snored loudly.

Though subordination is important as a means for tightening up a naïve and oversimple style, the student ought not to be browbeaten into constant subordination. In certain contexts a good writer might actually prefer:

The workman snored loudly. He had a red face.

This way of saying it has the merit of bringing into sharp focus the detail

---

[11] Reprinted with the permission of Charles Scribner's Sons from *A Farewell to Arms* by Ernest Hemingway. Copyright 1929 Charles Scribner's Sons; renewal copyright © 1957 Ernest Hemingway. Reprinted by permission of the Executors of the Ernest Hemingway Estate and Jonathan Cape Ltd.

of the red face. It might even suggest a leisurely observer, looking on with some amusement. For instances of some other effects secured by a simple and uncomplicated style, the student might look at page 217.

Summary We may sum up this topic as follows: grammatical subordination must conform to the rhetorical sense; it must not mislead by inverting it. On the positive side, subordination is an important means for securing economy. Careful subordination tends to give the sense of a thoughtful observer who has sifted his ideas and arranged them with precision.

LOOSE SENTENCES AND PERIODIC SENTENCES

Sentence structure can be viewed in still another way. We can distinguish between those sentences in which the sense is held up almost until the end (periodic sentences) and those in which it is not held up (loose sentences). Holding up the sense creates suspense: we do not know how the sentence is "coming out" until we have reached, or nearly reached, the end of it. Here is an example:

> It was partly at such junctures as these and partly at quite different ones that with the turn my matters had now taken, my predicament, as I have called it, grew most sensible. —HENRY JAMES.

If we convert the sentence to loose structure (that is, to normal English word order), we get something like this:

> With the turn my matters had now taken, my predicament, as I have called it, grew most sensible, partly at such junctures as these and partly at quite different ones.

The loose sentence is the normal sentence in English; the structure of the periodic sentence is abnormal. As we have noted above, deviation from the norm always tends to be emphatic. The periodic sentence, in skillful hands, is powerfully emphatic. By inversion, by use of the "It was" construction, or by interposition of movable modifiers between subject and predicate, the sentence and its primary statement are made to end together. But like all deviations from the norm, the periodic sentence—and the balanced sentence—are somewhat artificial and should not be overused.

Sentence length and sentence variation

How long should a sentence be? It may be as short as one word. "Go!" is a perfectly good sentence; it has a predicate with subject implied. On the other hand, a sentence may be forty or fifty words long. In fact, by tacking together elements with *and*'s and *but*'s, we can construct sentences of indefinite length. These are the possible extremes. But with the sentence, as with the paragraph, common sense and taste set reasonable limits. A succession of very short sentences tends to be monotonous. Extremely long sentences tend to bog the reader down in a quagmire of words.

This is not, of course, to say that the writer should not feel free to use a one-word sentence whenever he needs it or a succession of short sentences to gain special effects. According to the same reasoning, he ought to feel free to use very long sentences in order to gain special effects. The following sentence from Lytton Strachey's *Queen Victoria* will illustrate:

> Perhaps her fading mind called up once more the shadows of the past to float before it, and retraced, for the last time, the vanished visions of that long history—passing back and back, through the cloud of years, to older and ever older memories—to the spring woods at Osborne, so full of primroses for Lord Beaconsfield—to Lord Palmerston's queer clothes and high demeanour, and Albert's face under the green lamp, and Albert's first stag at Balmoral, and Albert in his blue and silver uniform, and the Baron coming in through a doorway, and Lord M. dreaming at Windsor with the rooks cawing in the elm-trees, and the Archbishop of Canterbury on his knees in the dawn, and the old King's turkey-cock ejaculations, and Uncle Leopold's soft voice at Claremont, and Lehzen with the globes, and her mother's feathers sweeping down towards her, and a great old repeater-watch of her father's in its tortoise-shell case, and a yellow rug, and some friendly flounces of sprigged muslin, and the trees and the grass at Kensington. —LYTTON STRACHEY: *Queen Victoria.*

Strachey is imagining what may have passed through the old Queen's dying mind as she slipped from consciousness. He imagines the succession of memories as going backward in time, from those of adult life to those of youth, and on back to the memories of childhood. The loosely linked series of clauses that constitute the sentence can be justified on two counts: the memories are presented as those of a dying mind, and, as the memories go backward in time, they become those of a child. Dramatically considered, the jumping from scene to scene (as suggested by the dashes) and the loose tacking on of additional scenes (by *and*'s) make sense. This long sentence, which closes Strachey's book with what amounts to a recapitulation of Victoria's life, is thus used to gain a special effect.

The normal limitations and requirements of the human mind dictate how much can be taken in satisfactorily "at one bite." Unless the writer is striving for some special effect, he ought to regard with suspicion very short and—most of all—very long sentences.

VARIETY IN SENTENCE LENGTH

The human mind requires variety: sentences should not all be monotonously of the same length. Let us consider a particular case. Look back at the paragraph from Virginia Woolf quoted on page 221. These thirteen sentences range in length from three words to fifty-two. The fourth sentence is quite long; the seventh sentence, very long. But three short sentences lead up to the fourth sentence, and two short sentences separate the fourth and seventh sentences.

VARIETY IN SENTENCE PATTERNS

Sentences that repeat a pattern become monotonous. Here is an example:

I was twenty that April and I made the glen my book. I idled over it. I watched the rhododendron snow its petals on the dark pools that spun them round in a swirl of brown foam and beached them on a tiny coast glittering with mica and fool's gold. I got it by heart, however, the dripping rocks, the ferny grottos, the eternal freshness, the sense of loam, of deep sweet decay, of a chain of life continuous and rich with the ages. I gathered there the walking fern that walks across its little forest world by striking root with its long tips, tip to root and root to tip walking away from the localities that knew it once. I was aware that the walking fern has its oriental counterpart. I knew also that Shortia, the flower that was lost for a century after Michaux found it *"dans les hautes montagnes de Carolinie,"* has its next of kin upon the mountains of Japan. I sometimes met mountain people hunting for ginseng for the Chinese market; long ago the Chinese all but exterminated that herbalistic panacea of theirs, and now they turn for it to the only other source, the Appalachians.

The "I was—I idled—I gathered" formula is relieved somewhat by the long descriptive phrases and relative clauses. Even so, it is irritatingly monotonous. Here is the original passage:

The glen was my book, that April I was twenty. I idled over it, watching the rhododendron snow its petals on the dark pools that spun them round in a swirl of brown foam and beached them on a tiny coast glittering with mica and fool's gold. But I got it by heart, the dripping rocks, the ferny grottos, the eternal freshness, the sense of loam, of deep sweet decay, of a chain of life continuous and rich with the ages. The walking fern I gathered there, that walks across its little forest world by striking root with its long tips, tip to root and root to tip walking away from the localities that knew it once, has its oriental counterpart; of that I was aware. And I knew that Shortia, the flower that was lost for a century after Michaux found it, *"dans les hautes montagnes de Carolinie,"* has its next of kin upon the mountains of Japan. Sometimes I met mountain people hunting for ginseng for the Chinese market; long ago the Chinese all but exterminated that herbalistic panacea of theirs, and now they turn for it to the only other source, the Appalachians.

—DONALD CULROSS PEATTIE: *Flowering Earth.*[12]

There are many ways in which to vary sentence structure. Nearly everything said earlier in this chapter can be brought to bear on this problem. We can invert the normal pattern or rearrange the pattern to throw emphasis on what is normally the subject or complement; we can subordinate severely or rather lightly. Most of all, we can dispose the modifiers, particularly the movable modifiers, so as to vary the pattern almost indefinitely.

The effort to secure variety should never, of course, become the overriding consideration. A sentence should take the structure best adapted to its special job. The writer will usually find that he is thoroughly occupied in discharging this obligation. Moreover, it is well to remind ourselves here once again of the claims of the whole composition. We never write a "col-

---

[12] From *Flowering Earth* by Donald Culross Peattie. Reprinted by permission of Noel R. Peattie and his agent, James Brown Associates, Inc. Copyright © by Donald Culross Peattie.

lection of sentences"; we write an essay, a theme, a total composition. The good sentence honors the claims exerted upon it by the total composition. And in our writing, and especially in our *rewriting*, we need to see that we have avoided monotony of sentence length or of sentence structure.

■ APPLICATIONS

I Try to determine which of the following sentences are periodic in structure and which are loose. Rewrite the periodic sentences into loose sentences, and the loose into periodic. Pick out the balanced sentences, if any.

1   The power, and the restriction on it, though quite distinguishable when they do not approach each other, may yet, like the intervening colors between white and black, approach so nearly as to perplex the understanding, as colors perplex the vision in marking the distinction between them.
                                                            —John Marshall.

2   Peace cannot be secured without armies; and armies must be supported at the expense of the people. It is for your sake, not for our own, that we guard the barrier of the Rhine against the ferocious Germans, who have so often attempted, and who will always desire, to exchange the solitude of their woods and morasses for the wealth and fertility of Gaul.   —Edward Gibbon.

3   The night, the earth under her, seemed to swell and recede together with a limitless, unhurried, benign breathing.   —Katherine Anne Porter.

4   And it is precisely because of this utterly unsettled and uncertain condition of philosophy at present that I regard any practical application of it to religion and conduct as exceedingly dangerous.   —Charles S. Pierce.

5   If we begin with certainties, we shall end in doubts; but if we begin with doubts, and are patient in them, we shall end in certainties.
                                                            —Sir Francis Bacon.

6   If he be my enemy, let him triumph; if he be my friend, as I have given him no personal occasion to be otherwise, he will be glad of my repentance. It becomes me not to draw my pen in the defense of a bad cause, when I have so often drawn it for a good one.   —John Dryden.

II The following paragraphs are taken from *Time*. *Time* style has long been celebrated for its inversions of, and its drastic departures from, normal sentence order. The motive, presumably, is a desire for condensation and emphasis. Rewrite these paragraphs so as to restore normal sentence order. Can you justify the departures from normal order? Is emphasis intelligently used? Or does too much emphasis result in no emphasis?

An abandoned lime quarry at Makapangsgat, Transvaal, yielded two bones last year to Dart's diggers: part of an occiput (the back part of the skull) and a lower jaw, from a pygmy moppet who had died while still getting his second teeth. Near by were many baboon skulls, bashed in from above or behind with a club which had a ridged head (the distal end of the humerus).

Most startling was Dart's evidence, from a number of charred bones, that the little man had learned to use fire. He lived in the early Ice Age, from 300,000 to 500,000 years before Peking Man, hitherto the earliest known user of fire. In honor of both his fire-bringing record and his prophetic skills, the new little man was named *Australopithecus prometheus*.[13]

III The passage from *Time* quoted above dates from the 1950's. Some people think that they have observed of late a return to more normal word order in *Time*. Do the following paragraphs (from the July 25, 1969, issue) seem to you to bear this out?

> The ghostly, white-clad figure slowly descended the ladder. Having reached the bottom rung, he lowered himself into the bowl-shaped footpad of *Eagle*, the spindly lunar module of Apollo 11. Then he extended his left foot, cautiously, tentatively, as if testing water in a pool—and, in fact, testing a wholly new environment for man. That groping foot, encased in a heavy multi-layered boot (size 9½B), would remain indelible in the minds of millions who watched it on TV, and a symbol of man's determination to step—and forever keep stepping—toward the unknown.
>
> With a cautious, almost shuffling gait, the astronaut began moving about in the harsh light of the lunar morning. "The surface is fine and powdery, it adheres in fine layers, like powdered charcoal, to the soles and sides of my foot," he said. "I can see the footprints of my boots and the treads in the fine, sandy particles." Minutes later, Armstrong was joined by Edwin Aldrin. Then, gaining confidence with every step, the two jumped and loped across the barren landscape for 2 hrs. 14 min., while the TV camera they had set up some 50 ft. from *Eagle* transmitted their movements with remarkable clarity to enthralled audiences on earth, a quarter of a million miles away. Sometimes moving in surrealistic slow motion, sometimes bounding around in the weak lunar gravity like exuberant kangaroos, they set up experiments and scooped up rocks, snapped pictures and probed the soil, apparently enjoying every moment of their stay in the moon's alien environment.[14]

If you feel that there is a distinct difference, try to rewrite the preceding paragraphs in the earlier *Time* style; if not, then rewrite these paragraphs in a more conventional style of normal word order.

[13] Reprinted by permission; Copyright Time Inc.
[14] From *Time* magazine, July 25, 1969. Reprinted by permission; Copyright Time Inc. 1969.

CHAPTER **11**

Diction

Good diction is the result of the choice of the right words. Accurate, effective expression obviously requires the right words, the words that will represent—not nearly, not approximately, but exactly—what we want to say. This is a simple rule; but to apply it is far from simple. The good writer must choose the right words, yes; but how does he know which are the right words?

Diction would be no problem if there existed for each object and each idea just one word to denote specifically that object or idea—if there were one name and one name only for each separate thing. But language is not like that. Most words are not strictly denotative; that is, they do not merely point to a specific object. Some words in English, it is true, particularly scientific words, do represent the only name we have for a specific object or substance. *Lemming,* for example, is the only name we have for a certain mouselike rodent; *purine* is the only name of a compound, the chemical formula of which is $C_5H_4N_4$. The language of science ideally is a language of pure denotation. But this constitutes a special case, and its problems are different from those of more ordinary language.

Actually, instead of one word and only one word for each thing, the writer often finds several words competing for his attention, all of them denoting more or less the same thing. Moreover, even those words that explicitly refer to the same thing may have different associations—different shades of meaning.

For example, *brightness, radiance, effulgence,* and *brilliance* may be said to have the same general denotation, but there is a considerable difference in what they connote, or suggest. *Radiance* implies beams radiating from a source, as the words *brilliance* or *brightness* do not. *Brilliance,* on the other hand, suggests an intensity of light that *effulgence* and *brightness* do not. Again, *brightness* is a more homely, everyday word than are *radiance, brilliance,* and *effulgence.* These are only a few suggested contrasts among the connotations of these words, all of which describe a quality of light.

Varying connotations in words of the same denotation may also be illustrated from the names of common objects. To most people, *firefly* seems more dignified than *lightning bug; taper,* than *candle.* The relative dignity of *bucket* and *pail* is not so easily settled. But for many modern Americans *bucket* is more likely to seem the ordinary word, with associations of everyday activity; whereas *pail* will seem a little more old-fashioned and endowed with more "poetic" suggestions. It connotes for some readers a bygone era of pretty milkmaids in an idyllic setting. But *bucket,* too, may have sentimental associations, someone will exclaim, remembering the song entitled "The Old Oaken Bucket." For words change in meaning from period to period, and their associated meanings change, as a rule, much more rapidly than do their primary meanings.

Words, then, are not static, changeless counters but are affected intimately, especially on the level of connotation, by the changing, developing, restless life of the men who use them.

As Justice Oliver Wendell Holmes said: "A word is not a crystal, transparent and unchanging, it is the skin of a living thought and may vary greatly in color and content according to the circumstances and time in which it is said."[1] Some words wear out and lose their force. Some words go downhill and lose respectability. Other words rise in the scale and acquire respectability. In 1710, Jonathan Swift, the author of *Gulliver's Travels,* poked fun at some of the clipped and slang forms of English that were coming into vogue in his day. Some of these words—for example, *mob* (a clipped form of *mobile*) and *banter* (origin unknown)—have since acquired respectability and now perform useful functions in our language. But other words upon which Swift cast scorn, such as *pozz* (for *possible*), *plenipo* (from *plenipotentiary,* "big shot" in modern slang), and *phiz* (from *physiognomy,* that is, *face*), have disappeared, as Swift hoped they would. One can observe a similar process at work in our own day. Some of the slang of fifty years ago—indeed, some of ten years ago—may now seem oddly quaint.

■ APPLICATION

Do you know, or can you figure out, the origin of the instances of current slang that follow?

the fuzz	groovy	drip	cop out
dig	uptight	turn on	rap

---

[1] Decision, *Town versus Eisner.*

The process of growth and decay in language is so strong that many words in the course of generations have shifted not only their associations but their primary meanings as well; some have even reversed their original meanings.[2]

The fact that what was once merely a secondary meaning may sometimes oust the old primary meaning and become the new primary meaning tells us something about the power of secondary meanings and associated meanings. If we want to write effectively, we have to take the associations of a word into account. We have to control not one but two dimensions of our language—that is, not only the prime meaning but the cluster of sub-meanings surrounding it. Thus, in a romantic tale (or perhaps for ironic or humorous effect) one might appropriately use the word *steed* because of its special associations. But in most contexts, one would call a horse a *horse*. Yet there are still other contexts in which the writer might choose a word with negative associations. If the animal in question was particularly ill-favored or was obviously the worse for wear, he might call it a *plug* or a *nag*. If the man were especially disgusted with it—he had placed a big bet on the horse and it had come in eighth—he might even refer to it as *crowbait*.

Two Distinctions: General and Specific; Abstract and Concrete

We call a word "general" when it refers to a group or a class; "specific," when it refers to a member of that class. *Tree* is a general word, but *oak, elm, poplar* are specific. We must remember, however, that the terms *general* and *specific* are relative, not absolute, in their reference. *Coat,* for example, is more specific than *garment,* for a coat is a kind of garment. But *coat* is itself more general than *hunting jacket,* for a hunting jacket is a kind of coat. So with our trees above. *Oak* is more specific than *tree* but more general than *black oak* or *water oak* or *post oak.*

The specific word tends to give color and tang, tends to appeal to the imagination. Suppose we write: "He saw a ship on the horizon." What can our reader's imagination do with that? It can put some sort of floating object, large, manmade, and designed for transportation, on the imagined horizon. But what is the shape of the object? Will there be a smudge of smoke or the glint of white sail? The word *ship* is a general word and, therefore, cannot give a vivid image in that split second in which the reader's eye rests upon the sentence. Suppose we substitute *liner, schooner, brig, tanker, junk,* or some other specific word. Then there is something for the imagination to seize on. There is no blur on the horizon; there is a shape.

But suppose, one may object, that we write *brig* and that the reader

---

[2] Later in this chapter we shall have occasion to return to the history of words when we discuss the use of the dictionary. (See also pp. 293–95.)

does not know what sailing-rig such a craft carries. Does he then have a shape on the horizon? Most readers would get the glint of sail and not the smudge of smoke, for their information might go that far. Yet the mere fact of the use of the specific word gives some sort of nudge to the imagination, gives some sense of knowingness, makes the reader kid himself a bit. If we use the word *brig,* even the reader totally ignorant of nautical matters, as most of us are, feels, just for the moment, a little like an old salt.

There is another distinction that is important in our choice of words. It has to do with concreteness and abstraction. *Peach, pear, quince, apple,* and *apricot* are *concrete* words. The word *peach* implies certain qualities: a certain shape, a certain color, a certain kind of sweetness. But *peach* implies these qualities as "grown together," as we should actually find them embodied in a peach. (The Latin word from which *concrete* derives means literally "grown together.") We can, of course, *abstract* (this word literally means "take away") these qualities from the actual peach and refer to them in isolation: *sweetness, fuzziness, softness.* Isolating these qualities, we get a set of *abstract* words. *Sweetness* isolates a quality common to peaches, and common, of course, to many other things; *sweetness* is thought of as an idea in its own right.

Words that refer to ideas, qualities, and characteristics *as such* are usually abstract. Words that name classes of objects and classes of actions are usually general. Words that refer to particular objects and particular actions are usually both concrete and specific. These are, on the whole, our most vivid words; they reflect immediately the world of things known to our senses. This comment is not meant to imply that concrete and specific words are somehow "better" than abstract and general words. For some purposes they are indeed better, but for others, not. The world of ideas and concepts requires its terms just as urgently as does the world of particular things.

■ APPLICATIONS

I Arrange the sentences in the following groups in ascending order of specificity, putting the sentence with the most general word first and the one with the most specific word last. (Your concern in Groups A and C will be with nouns and noun phrases; in B, with verbs.)

A 1 She wore an Yves Saint Laurent evening gown.
   2 A rather shapeless garment enveloped her.
   3 She put on a neat print dress.

B 1 The old crone put herself in motion.
   2 The child skipped along the path.
   3 The youth walked briskly forward.

C 1 She bought a large head of Boston lettuce.
   2 I saw that we needed greens of some sort for salad.
   3 I am not fond of lettuce.

II In the following paragraph William Faulkner describes a woman in her sixties, who lives in a shabby-genteel house on what was years ago the best street of a small Southern town. She lives alone, quite cut off from society, and she is a known eccentric. We have omitted a good many words from Faulkner's description. How would you fill the blanks? Use your imagination: try to make your reader see this woman. (Whether or not you manage to reconstruct Faulkner's precise description is not the main concern here.)

[The parlor] was furnished in heavy, leather-covered furniture. When the Negro opened the blinds of one window, [the callers] could see that the leather was _____, and when they sat down, a faint _____ rose _____ about their thighs, _____ with _____ motes in the _____ sun-ray. On a _____ gilt easel before the fireplace stood a _____ portrait of Miss _____'s _____.

They rose when she entered. [She was] a _____ woman in _____, with a _____ gold chain _____ to her waist and _____ into her belt, leaning on an ebony cane with a _____ gold head. Her skeleton was _____ and _____; perhaps that was why what would have been merely _____ in another was obesity in her. She looked _____, like a body long submerged in _____ water, and of that _____ hue. Her eyes, lost in the fatty ridges of her face . . .[3]

The student may derive some useful hints by looking back at another section of this passage quoted on page 211.

III Assume that, in an account of a motor trip through one of the New England states, you have written the following paragraphs:

> We stopped the car beside the stone wall near the gate that had led to the farmhouse door. The house was gray and unpainted. It must have been unlived in for years. Some of the windows were broken. The roof was in disrepair.
>
> The house was set in what had been a thriving apple orchard, and now on this October day, the old trees were worth looking at. A majority of them were filled with fruit. The sun was shining, and the sight was very pretty, even though some of the trees were rotted. A lot of them had vines growing up their trunks, and Jim said it was poison ivy.

Rewrite this passage so as to make the reader see the scene. Your revision will certainly call for changes in diction, but do not hesitate to make more extensive changes.

The misuse of abstract and general words

Writing that is woolly with abstractions is usually ineffective and may not even make much sense to the reader. For example:

[3] From "A Rose for Emily" from *Collected Stories of William Faulkner* by William Faulkner. Reprinted by permission of Random House, Inc. Reprinted by permission of Curtis Brown Ltd. Copyright 1930 and renewed 1958 by William Faulkner.

> Quite significantly, the emphasis is being placed upon vocational intelligence, which is based upon adequate occupational information for all pupils in secondary schools. . . . This emphasis upon vocational guidance for the purpose of making young people intelligent concerning the world of occupations and the requirements for entering occupations need not conflict seriously with other views of guidance that take into account everything pertaining to the education of the pupil.

There are a number of things wrong with this flabby statement, among them, the large number of abstract words. The author might have written:

> High schools today insist that the student learn enough about jobs to choose his own job wisely. The student needs to learn what various jobs pay, what training they require, and what kinds of people find them interesting. He can learn these things while he is learning the other things that schools are supposed to teach. Both kinds of learning are preparations for life, and one need not interfere with the other.

The rewritten version still makes use of general and abstract words (*training, preparation,* and so on); but some of the cloudiest of the abstractions (*vocational intelligence, occupational information*) have been removed, and the rewritten version is not only simpler but has more force.

● CAUTION

Abstract-general diction is not necessarily to be avoided. The student is not to conclude that concrete and specific words are somehow "better" than abstract and general words. Sometimes we need to name qualities and classes. If, for example, we lacked the word *sympathy,* how would we say something so simple as "A child needs sympathy"? We can make an attempt: "A child does not like frowns. Cold looks scare him. He flinches from harsh words," and so forth. But trying to convey the notion of sympathy in this way is as awkward as trying to pick up a pin with a gloved hand.

We do need abstract terms and we need general terms. For example, compare "He lived in a house of medium size" with "His home did not have the suburban air of a bungalow, and it certainly had nothing of the rustic style of a lodge. It was much smaller than a mansion, but somewhat larger than a cottage." *Mansion, cottage, bungalow,* and *lodge* (not to mention *cabin, hut, villa,* and *chateau*) are *overspecific* for the writer's purpose here; he needs the simple, general term *house.*[4]

In choosing words, the overriding consideration, of course, will always be the particular effect that the writer wishes to obtain. Description

---

[4] The clumsy expressions into which we are sometimes forced by overspecific terms are well illustrated from the English personal pronouns, which for some purposes are overspecific. It would, for example, be very convenient if our language possessed a pronoun that could mean either "he" or "she" (and have neutral terms for "his" or "her," "his" or "hers," "him" or "her"). Since we don't have such a pronoun, we have to write "Someone has left his or her pen" or "Someone has left his pen," with the understanding that "his" in this context can also mean "her."

and narration, for example, thrive on the concrete and the specific. Note the number of concrete and specific terms in the following passage:

> He knew the inchoate sharp excitement of hot dandelions in young Spring grass at noon; the smell of cellars, cobwebs, and built-on secret earth; in July, of watermelons bedded in sweet hay, inside a farmer's covered wagon; of cantaloupe and crated peaches; and the scent of orange rind, bitter-sweet, before a fire of coals.
> —THOMAS WOLFE: *Look Homeward, Angel.*[5]

Exposition and argument, on the other hand, by their very nature, call for a diction in which general and abstract words are often important.

> Marx's interpretation of the past is explicit and realistic; his forecast of the future seems to me vague and idealistic. I have called it utopian, but you object to that word. I do not insist on it. I will even surrender the word "idealistic." But the point is this. Marx finds that in the past the effective force that has determined social change is the economic class conflict. He points out that this economic class conflict is working to undermine our capitalistic society. Very well. If then I project this explanation of social changes into the future, what does it tell me? It seems to tell me that there will be in the future what there has been in the past—an endless economic class conflict, and endless replacement of one dominant class by another, an endless transformation of institutions and ideas in accordance with the changes effected by the class conflict.
> —CARL BECKER: "The Marxian Philosophy of History,"
> *Everyman His Own Historian: Essays on History and Politics.*

Language Growth by Extension of Meaning

We have said that a word has not only a primary meaning but also implied meanings. The implied meanings are obviously less definite than the primary meaning, and therefore less stable and more amenable to change. In scientific language the specific meanings are rigidly stabilized, and the hazy and shifting implied meanings are, insofar as possible, eliminated. In a colorful and racy use of everyday language, just the reverse is the case. The implied meanings are rich and important. We are often tempted to use a word, not *literally* (that is, adhering strictly to the specific meaning), but *figuratively,* stressing the associations of the word. It is through such a process that words have shifted their meanings in the past; but this process of extension of meaning is constantly at work even in our own time. Let us consider an illustration of the process.

---

[5] Reprinted with the permission of Charles Scribner's Sons from *Look Homeward, Angel,* page 401, by Thomas Wolfe. Copyright 1929 Charles Scribner's Sons; renewal copyright © 1957 Edward C. Aswell, C.T.A. and/or Fred W. Wolfe. Reprinted with permission of William Heinemann Ltd.

The casual view of language sees each word as fastened neatly and tightly to a certain specific object: *weasel* means a certain kind of small, furry mammal of slender body, which moves furtively, preys on birds, rats, and rabbits, sucking their blood, and occasionally also sucking eggs; *cooking* means the preparation of food by exposing it to heat; *spade* means an instrument for digging in the earth. But words are not actually so neatly fastened to the objects for which they stand. Even when we are determined to speak forthrightly and "call a spade a spade," we rarely do so. It is against the nature of language that we should be able to do so.

For example, Bob, who is determined to call a spade a spade, says: "Well, Joe has weaseled out on us again. Yesterday when I told him the Collins deal was finally cooking, he pretended he had never heard of it and said he wouldn't buy a pig in a poke." But obviously one is not calling a spade a *spade* when he attributes to another human being the actions of a weasel, describes the preparation of a business deal as a piece of cookery, and makes the agreement to be signed the purchase of a pig enclosed in a bag.

Weasel and *cooking*—not to mention the pig—are not being used literally here; their meanings have been extended through analogy. In the case of *cooking* the extension of meaning is very easy to grasp: one sort of preparation—cooking—is extended to mean another and more general sort of preparation. *Weaseling* is more difficult. There may be some implication of "weasel words," that is, words that have had the substance sucked out of them, like eggs sucked by a weasel; but the more probable analogy here is that between Joe's wriggling out of his promise and the weasel's bodily movements as it glides through apparently impossibly small apertures.

The situation we have just considered is thoroughly typical. Many common words have been extended from their original meanings in just this fashion. We speak of the *eye* of a needle, the *mouth* of a river, the *legs* of a chair, the *foot* of a bed. The hole in the end of a needle might have been given a special name; instead, men called it an *eye* because of its fancied likeness to the human eye. So, too, with examples such as these: a *keen* mind, a *bright* disposition, a *sunny* smile, a *black* look. Someone saw an analogy between the way in which a keen blade cut through wood and the way in which a good mind cut into the problem with which it was concerned. The smile obviously does not really shed sunlight, but it may seem to affect one as sunlight does, and in a way quite the opposite of a black look.

But the point to be made here does not concern the basis for the analogy, whether of physical resemblance (the *jaws* of a vise), similarity of function (the *key* to a puzzle), similarity of effect (a *shining* example), or anything else. The point to be made is, rather, that people normally use words in this way, extending, stretching, twisting their meanings, so that they apply to other objects or actions or situations than those to which they originally applied. This is the metaphorical process, about which we shall have more to say in the next chapter. The essence of metaphor inheres in this transfer of meaning, in the application of a word that literally means one thing to something else. (See Chapter 12.)

Development of complex words out of simple words

Thus far we have taken our illustrations from common words. But less common words and learned words will illustrate the same process of extension of meaning. Indeed, most of our words that express complex ideas and relationships have been built up out of simpler words. For example, we say, "His generosity caused him to overlook my fault." *Overlook* here means to "disregard or ignore indulgently." But *overlook* is obviously made up of the simple words *look* and *over*. To look over an object may imply something more cursory than a minute inspection of it; for example, one *looks over* an assignment. *Overlook*, then, in the sense of "disregard" is an extension and specialization of one of the implied meanings of *look over*. We have said "one of the meanings," for *look over* obviously implies other possible meanings. Consider the nearly parallel expression "to see over." From it we get the word *oversee*. This word normally means today *to direct, to supervise*—something quite different from "overlook." *Supervise* is built out of the same concepts as *oversee*, for *super* in Latin means "over," and *-vise* comes from the Latin verb *videre* (past participle *visus*), which means "to see." Thus we hope that an alert supervisor will not overlook matters that he ought to take note of. A bishop, by the way, is literally an *overseer*. For *bishop* comes originally from two Greek words: *epi*, which means "over," and *skopein*, which means "to look." Thus, such diverse words as *overlook, oversee, overseer, supervise*, and *bishop* represent particular extensions of much the same primitive literal meaning.

The dictionary: a record of meanings

The etymology (that is, the derivation and history) of a word is not only highly interesting but also useful. The full mastery of a particular word frequently entails knowing its root meaning. By learning that meaning, we acquire a firm grasp on its various later meanings, for we can see them as extended and specialized meanings that have grown out of the original meaning.

Here, for example, is the entry in the *Standard College Dictionary* for the word *litter:*[6]

> **lit·ter** (lit′ər) *n.* **1.** Waste materials, scraps, or carelessly dropped objects strewn about; clutter. **2.** Untidy or chaotic condition; mess. **3.** The young brought forth at one birth by any mammal normally having several offspring at one time. **4.** A stretcher used for carrying sick or wounded persons. **5.** A vehicle consisting of a couch carried between shafts by men or beasts of burden. **6.** Straw, hay, etc., spread in animal pens, or over plants as protection. **7.** The uppermost layer of a forest floor, consisting of slightly decomposed leaves, twigs, etc. — **Syn.** See FLOCK. — *v.t.* **1.** To make untidy or unsightly by strewing or carelessly discarding trash, etc. **2.** To drop or scatter carelessly. **3.** To provide with litter, as for bedding, covering, etc. **4.** To give birth to (pups, kittens, whelps, etc.) — *v.i.* **5.** To give birth to a litter of young. **6.** To drop or scatter refuse, especially in public places. [< OF *litiere* < Med.L *lectaria* < L *lectus* bed]

---

[6] By permission from *Funk & Wagnalls Standard*® *College Dictionary*, copyright 1968 by Funk & Wagnalls, A Division of Reader's Digest Books, Inc.

The word is first listed as a noun (*n.*). Seven meanings of the noun are given. But the word is also a transitive verb (*v.t.*), for which four meanings are given. For *litter* as an intransitive verb (*v.i.*), two meanings are given. The word comes from an Old French word (OF *litiere*), which was derived from Medieval Latin *lectaria* (MED. L *lectaria*) and goes back ultimately to the Latin word for bed (L *lectus* bed). Synonyms (words of nearly the same meaning) for *litter* will be found under *flock* (**Syn.** See FLOCK.).

Let us consider the various meanings given for *litter*. At first glance there seems little to connect meaning 2, "Untidy or chaotic condition," with meaning 3, "The young brought forth at one birth," and even less with meaning 4, "A stretcher used for carrying sick or wounded persons." But once we grasp the fact that *litter* comes originally from a Latin word meaning "bed," it is fairly easy to see how its various apparently unconnected meanings developed. Meanings 4 and 5 obviously refer to special sorts of portable beds; and meaning 6 ("Straw, hay, etc., spread in animal pens") and meaning 3 of *litter* as a verb ("To provide with litter, as for bedding, covering, etc.") also derive (note the idea of *bedding*) from the original Latin root. Primitive human beds did not differ too much from animal beds, for they consisted of straw or rushes heaped together. Such being the case, it is easy to see how any scattering of straw or hay might come to be called a *litter,* and the process of strewing it, a process of *littering*. Meanings 1 and 2 of *litter* as a noun and 1 and 2 of *litter* as a verb are obvious further extensions of the root idea of bed, but in these meanings the emphasis has been shifted from the purpose of making a bed to an aimless and untidy strewing about.

Meanings 3 of the noun and 4 and 5 of the verb derive from the original meaning "bed" by another chain of development. The mother animal frequently makes a sort of rude bed in which she lies to give birth, and by association the rude bed (*litter*) comes to be used for what is found in the bed, the young animals themselves.

Let us consider another example, this time from *Webster's New Collegiate Dictionary*. Here is the dictionary entry for the common word *sad:*[7]

> sad \ˈsad\ *adj* sad·der; sad·dest [ME, fr. OE *sæd* sated; akin to OHG *sat* sated, L *satis* enough] **1 a :** affected with or expressive of grief or unhappiness **:** DOWNCAST **b** (1) **:** causing or associated with grief or unhappiness **:** DEPRESSING ⟨∼ news⟩ (2) **:** DISMAYING, DEPLORABLE **c :** INFERIOR **2 :** of a dull somber color **:** DRAB — **sad·ly** *adv*

The word is an adjective (*adj*). The forms for the comparative and superlative degrees are given; then comes the derivation: *sad* occurs in Middle English (ME), but comes from the Old English *sæd*, meaning "sated" (fr. OE *sæd* sated). Sad is related to Old High German *sat*, meaning "sated" (OHG *sat* sated) and to Latin *satis*, meaning "enough" (L *satis* enough). The dictionary lists two principal meanings of the word, the first having to do with the emotion of grief or unhappiness; the second, with color.

Meaning 1 is subdivided into three submeanings: 1a, 1b, and 1c. Under submeaning 1b two sub-submeanings are distinguished, (1) and (2). This dictionary prints in small capitals what it calls "synonymous cross-references." For example, under b(1), DEPRESSING, as in "depressing news" < ~ news >. The synonymous words are called cross-references to indicate to the student that they may be looked up in the dictionary on their own account. Finally, the dictionary notes the form of the adverb derived from *sad* (sad-ly *adv*).

Even so brief a notice as the foregoing hints at a history of developing meanings. Inspection of a larger dictionary, such as *Webster's New International Dictionary* or the *Oxford English Dictionary* (also known as *A New English Dictionary*), with its fuller information as to the derivation of the word and its finer discrimination of meanings (including the various earlier meanings), enables us to make out a detailed history of the meanings of the word.

As we have seen, the German and Latin cognates of *sad* indicate that the basic root from which all meanings are descended must have meant something like "sated with food." Now, a man who has had a big dinner is torpid and heavy, not lively or restless, and so *sad* came to carry the suggestion of "calm," "stable," "earnest." Shakespeare frequently uses it to mean the opposite of "trifling" or "frivolous." But a person who seems thus sober and serious *may* be so because he is grieved or melancholy, and the word thereby gradually took on its modern meaning of "mournful" or "grieved." But we must not end this account without mentioning other lines of development. The sense of "torpid" or "heavy" was extended from animate beings, which can eat to repletion, to inanimate things, which cannot—to bread, for example, that fails to rise, or to a heavy laundry iron (sad-iron). *Webster's New Collegiate Dictionary,* in its definition of *sad-iron,* tells us that the word is made up of *sad* (in the sense of "compact" or "heavy") plus *iron.*

Meaning 2 ("of a dull somber color") represents still another extension of *sad* in the sense of "stable" or "sober." It means the kind of color that a sobersides (as opposed to a gay and sprightly person) would wear: that is, dull, sober colors.

Has the process of extension now ceased? Hardly. In the phrase "sad sack" (U.S. Army slang) a related meaning of *sad* gained wide temporary currency just after World War II, but most speakers now have returned to *sorry* (rather than *sad*) to express the meaning of "inferior" (note 1c above with its synonymous cross-reference INFERIOR) or "worthless": we say "a sorry team," "a sorry outfit," "a sorry job."

■ APPLICATIONS

I Look up in the *Oxford English Dictionary* or *Webster's International* the origins of the following words:

nostril	enthusiasm	fast (adj.)
aristocracy	urbane	egregious
plutocracy	Bible	sympathetic
complicate	fine (adj.)	malaria
thrilling	infant	starboard

Does knowledge of its origin clarify the meaning of any of these words? Does it help you understand the relationship between current discrepant meanings (that is, "This *fine* print hurts my eyes" and "He was a big, *fine,* upstanding man")? Does knowledge of the origin of the word help account for such uses as "legal *infant*" and "the Book" (as applied to the Bible)?

II With the help of the dictionary discriminate as carefully as you can among the words in the following groups:

1 sulky, petulant, peevish, sullen, morose, crabbed, surly
2 skeptic, infidel, atheist, freethinker, agnostic
3 reasonable, just, moderate, equitable, fair-minded, judicial
4 rebellion, revolt, insurrection, revolution
5 belief, faith, persuasion, conviction, assurance, reliance
6 sneak, skulk, slink
7 trick, fool, hoodwink, bamboozle, deceive, beguile, delude, cheat, mislead

Does a knowledge of the origin of the word throw light upon the special connotations of any of these words?

The Company a Word Keeps:
Informal (Colloquial) and Formal

Earlier, in discussing the implied meanings of words, we touched briefly upon the way in which these meanings may determine the appropriateness of a word for a particular context (pp. 285–87). The word *steed,* we saw, would be proper for some contexts, *nag* for others, and *horse* for still others. But the problem of appropriateness is important and deserves fuller treatment.

In the first place, there is what may be called the dignity and social standing of the word. Like human beings, a word tends to be known by the company it keeps. Words like *caboodle* and *gumption* are good colloquial words and perfectly appropriate to the informal give-and-take of conversation. But they would be out of place in a dignified and formal utterance. For example, a speech welcoming a great public figure in which he was complimented on his "statesmanlike gumption" would be absurd. To take another example, many of us use the slang term *guy,* and though, like much slang, it has lost what pungency it may once have had, its rather flippant breeziness is not inappropriate in some contexts. But it would be foolish to welcome our elder statesman by complimenting him on being a "wise and venerable guy." It is only fair to say that the shoe can pinch the other foot. Certain literary and rather highfalutin terms, in a *colloquial* context, sound just as absurd. We do not praise a friend for his "dexterity" or for his "erudition," not, at least, when we meet him on the street or chat with him across the table.

The fact that words are known by the company they keep does not, however, justify snobbishness in diction. Pretentiousness is, in the end, probably in even worse taste than blurting out a slang term on a formal occasion. Words must be used with tact and common sense. But the comments made above do point to certain areas of usage of which most of us are already more or less aware.

The various kinds of diction (and their necessary overlappings) are conveniently represented in the following diagram: [8]

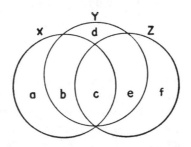

The three circles X, Y, Z, represent the three sets of language habits indicated above.
   X—formal literary English, the words, the expressions, and the structures one finds in serious books.
   Y—colloquial English, the words, expressions, and the structures of the informal but polite conversation of cultivated people.
   Z—illiterate English, the words, the expressions, and the structures of the language of the uneducated.
   b, c, and e represent the overlappings of the three types of English.
   c—that which is common to all three: formal literary English, colloquial English, and illiterate English.
   b—that which is common to both formal literary English and colloquial English.
   e—that which is common to both colloquial English and illiterate English.
   a, d, and f represent those portions of each type of English that are peculiar to that particular set of language habits.

Modern slang, for example, falls into segment *e*—and possibly *d*. It would be properly available for colloquial and informal writing. (But segments *d* and *e,* of course, include more than slang: they include colloquial terms of all kinds that do not occur in formal literary English.) Segment *a* includes the terms that occur only in formal literary English, but the overlap of formal literary English with colloquial and illiterate English is large— so large that most of the words used in writing of the most formal style are to be found in writings at the other extreme of style.

It would be misleading, therefore, to suggest that there is a mechanical rule for selecting the diction that one uses in an informal essay, or in a formal treatise, or to express the dialogue of "low characters" in a novel. The degrees of height and lowness of style and shadings of formality and informality are so many—and vary so much even within one work—that we cannot hope to find our appropriate diction segregated for us in one compartment. But our chart should make plain that in this matter of levels of diction, the dictionary can be of real help. It marks, as such, colloquial words, slang, technical words, and so on. Yet recourse to the dictionary is not a substitute for developing a feeling for language. The dictionary can help, but wide reading and practice in writing can help even more.

● CAUTION

Avoid both pretentiousness and inappropriate slanginess.

■ APPLICATION

Rewrite the following sentences, removing (a) any stilted diction and (b) any slang or illiterate diction. In general try to make the diction fit an informal standard. (In setting up this exercise, we are not forgetting that the absurdities in such instances as these may be intentional; writers often use disparities of this sort for humorous effect.)

1 We approached Emporium City from Route 60, driving like a bat out of hell.
2 Miss Warner was a young creature of patrician elegance and of disdainful hauteur but really pretty dumb.
3 It sure was picturesque! Titanic vistas solicited our view. It was all mighty grand.
4   I am the true nonpareil. All others are but tawdry copycats.
                                          —From a fan-dancer's advertisement.

How Associations Control Meanings

Thus far we have seen how associated meanings determine what may be called the social tone of a word. But we must go on to consider the very important way in which these meanings actually determine, though sometimes subtly, the effect of the word, that is, the way in which they actually determine meaning. In our time especially, propaganda and advertising have made this whole matter very important. So also has much of the polemical writing of our day. Benjamin DeMott in an essay entitled "The Age of Overkill" points out that a feature of our time is the use of an almost hysterical rhetoric. Instead of a biting epithet calculated to strike down an enemy, the writer fires a rhetorical atomic bomb with blast enough to destroy whole institutions, classes, and races. Thus, we read that "The family is the American fascism"; that "The white race is the cancer of history"; and that "We can learn more from any jail than we can from any university," and so forth. We live in an age of inflamed rhetoric. Far from using precise and exact terms, the writers of our "scientific" and rational society often exaggerate, overstate, and caricature.

Another manifestation of the exaggerated rhetoric of our age is the tendency to play up the emotional impact of a word at the expense of accurate reference. The associations that surround a word may actually become more important than its primary meaning. Not long ago, the verb *involved* became very fashionable with people who wished to indicate a sensitive response to social conditions. Taking advantage of the favorable associations that had gathered around the word, an advertising copywriter argued that since South America was "a very involved continent," visitors to South America ought to get there by means of "a very involved airline." If any reader had been tempted to ask with what or in what either the continent or the airline was involved, it is doubtful that an answer would have been forthcoming. Evidently *involved* had become such a favorable term that the writer felt it was sufficient recommendation merely to say someone or something was "involved." Like virtue, involvement was its own reward and its own excuse for being. (It is amusing to note that only a few years previously *involved* had quite other associations: if it was whispered that a woman had been "involved," the implication was that she was mixed up in a scandalous affair; or if a man was said to be "involved," the reference was generally taken to be to a shady financial deal.)

Yet, whether used responsibly or simply abused, the connotations of a word are important, and the writer who hopes to be effective must take them into account. A group of words that point to more or less the same thing may range in their associations from highly favorable to highly unfavorable. For example, we may call an agriculturist a "farmer," a "planter," a "tiller of the soil," or, in more exalted fashion, "the partner of Mother Nature;" but we can also refer to him as a "peasant," a "rube," a "hayseed," or a "hick." Many of our words do more than merely *name* something. They imply a judgment about its value as well. They make a favorable or an unfavorable evaluation. Consider, for example, these roughly synonymous terms:

Favorable	*Neutral*	*Unfavorable*
secret agent	informant	stool pigeon
cherub	child	brat
self-control	discipline	regimentation

■ APPLICATIONS

I Can you fill the blanks in the table below with appropriate "synonymous" terms (more than one if you like)?

Favorable	Neutral	Unfavorable
	policeman	
		political boss
	status quo	
	publicity agent	

II For the following words, try to find synonyms of differing or even opposite associations:

rebellion	reformer	dictator
tycoon	conventional	liberal
discrimination	diplomacy	theoretical

The power of association is also illustrated by our recourse to euphemisms. Certain words, even necessary words, which refer to unpleasant things, are avoided in favor of softening expressions or indirect references. In many contexts *bastard* is felt to be too brutal; so *illegitimate* is substituted for it. Even a word like *died* may be shunned in favor of *deceased* or *passed away* or *went to his reward*. Undertakers have taken to calling themselves *morticians,* and butchers in some parts of the country prefer to be known as *meat-cutters*. Whatever one may think of the substitutions, they at least testify to the power of past associations and the desire of men to avoid words with unpleasant or disparaging associations.

The power of association is illustrated positively in our tendency to disparage human beings by associating them with unpleasant animals or insects. Thus, we express contempt by calling a man a *rat*, a *louse*, or a *worm;* a certain admiration for his cleverness, by calling him a *fox;* hatred (and perhaps fear), by calling him a *snake*. In general, the animal creation is a rich source of expressions of attitude toward other human beings, particularly of hostile or contemptuous attitudes. But we may use associations drawn from all sorts of areas: "He is a tower of strength"; "He is as hard as flint"; "She is as neat as a pin." In the next chapter (see pp. 312–13), we shall discuss in detail the uses of figurative language of this sort.

Here follows the account of an incident as it might be reported by a relatively impartial writer:

> Democratic (or Republican) Senator Briggs expressed surprise at being met by reporters. He told them that he had no comment to make on the "Whitlow deal." He said that he had not known that Whitlow was in the employ of General Aircraft and observed that the suggestion that he had received favors from Whitlow was an attempt to discredit him.

How might a hostile reporter describe the incident? He would perhaps give an account something like this:

> Senator Briggs, Democratic (or Republican) wheelhorse, was obviously startled to find himself confronted by newspapermen. He stubbornly refused to comment on what he called the "Whitlow deal" and professed not to have known that Whitlow was a lobbyist. The Senator complained that he was being smeared.

The second account seems to be substantially the same as the first. The "facts" are not appreciably altered. But the emotional coloring and, with it, the intended effect on the reader have been sharply altered. The senator is now a "wheelhorse," with its suggestions of a hardened and (probably) calloused political conscience. Whitlow is a "lobbyist," and again suggestions of political corruption are insinuated. Moreover, the senator's actions and speech ("obviously startled," "stubbornly refused," "professed not to have known," and "complained") are made to suggest guilt.

The attitudes expressed in any piece of writing are extremely important and are, indeed, an integral part of its "meaning."

■ APPLICATIONS

I Alter the diction of the following passages in order to present (a) a more favorable view; (b) a less favorable view. (The sample sentence, with its optional terms, will illustrate the kind of alteration that the student is to make.)

The veteran (*still-youthful, aging*) movie star walked (*swept, minced*) into the strong (*brilliant, harsh*) light and paused for a moment to look at (*glance at, ogle*) the crowd.

A The old woman walked up to the counter and priced the scarf. She hesitated, seemed to think for a moment, and then opened her black purse, and extracted a five-dollar bill. She laid it on the counter and began to finger the bright piece of cloth.

B The mayor, a stocky man of middle age, stepped forward to the microphone with a sheaf of papers in his hand. He placed these on the lectern and cleared his throat. His face was serious as he began his speech.

C The two boys, fifteen and seventeen, were ill at ease when they appeared before Judge Baker, who regarded them impersonally from the bench. An atmosphere of tension prevailed in the courtroom as lawyers began shuffling their papers.

II In one of our more picturesque cities debate arose as to whether to build an expressway that would skirt the oldest part of the city. The following account appeared on the editorial page of a newspaper.

> The Metropolitan Area Committee last week urged construction of the proposed Riverfront Expressway at ground level. The organization's views on the long-simmering issue will be transmitted to John A. Volpe, secretary of transportation. The resolution had been proposed by the MAC executive committee, which had been convoked March 5 after the President's Advisory Council on Historic Preservation had announced it was recommending to Volpe that the expressway be relocated or, in the alternative, that it be constructed as a depressed roadway. MAC is a biracial, nonpartisan citizens action group consisting of more than 500 members from many fields. The ground

level concept has been under relentless attack from so-called preservationists who maintain that it would desecrate the French Quarter.

—The New Orleans *Times-Picayune*, March 16, 1969.

Judging by its editorial comment, would you say that this newspaper was for the ground-level expressway or against it?

III The following excerpt is taken from a novel. In the novel it appears as a note scrawled on the back cover of a copy of *Life* "around all four edges of the Winston ad." We learn that the author of the note is a brilliant, eccentric physician, much given to drinking and wenching. Where a choice of words is indicated, can you determine which word was actually used by the author? Or, if you feel that an author may not be infallible, which word would *you* choose in this context?

[J. F.] Kennedy. With all the
 campaign biographies,
 praise for him,   no one has said what
 hogwash,

he was. The reason he was a great
 man
 statesman   was that his
 politician
 ironic manner
 self-deprecation
 derisiveness

kept pace with his
 charm
 beauty   and his
 handsome face
 dedication to
 love of   country. He
 affection for

is the only
 public man
 politician   I have ever believed. This is because no man now
 statesman

is
 credible
 convincing   unless he
 believable
 is derisive.
 deprecates himself.   In him I saw the old
 is ironic.

eagle
 virtue
 beauty   of the United States of America. I
 integrity
 admired
 worshipped   him.
 loved

They, the _____ (unreadable: bourgeois? burghers? bastards?) wanted him dead. Very well, it will serve them right because now——

Worn-out Words and Clichés

We began this chapter by saying that the problem of diction is that of finding the right words, the words that will say exactly what the writer wants to say. But we have seen that exactness in language cannot be attained simply and mechanically, that words work on a number of levels in a number of different ways. Words are not static. They have a history; they have biographies; they even have, one is tempted to say, personalities. Most of all, since they are not changeless and inflexible, but to some extent plastic, changing their shape a little under the pressure of the context in which they occur, they offer a continual stimulus and challenge to the imagination of the writer.

Language, as we have seen, changes, develops, grows, and, by the same token, language wears out. We are not thinking, however, of the normal sloughing off of words that have died natural deaths and now either do not occur in a modern dictionary at all or, if they do occur, are marked *obsolete* (*shoon* for *shoes*) or *archaic* (*e'en* for *even*). We are thinking rather of words that have been thoughtlessly used in certain contexts so often that they have lost nearly all their force. We call these threadbare expressions "trite" or "hackneyed" or term them "stereotypes" and "clichés."

■ APPLICATION

Consult the dictionary for the etymology of *trite* and *hackneyed*. What do the terms mean precisely? Check also the origin (or literal meaning) of *stereotype* and *cliché*. Does a knowledge of the origin of these terms help you to understand why the qualities they name are to be avoided?

Common stereotypes, including slang

Clichés are produced by writers who do not think out what they want to say but find a worn groove in the language into which they let their thoughts slide. Books on rhetoric sometimes supply lists of threadbare expressions against which the student is warned: "the more the merrier," "last but not least," "to trip the light fantastic toe." Hackneyed phrases of this sort have probably by now become too literary, too old-fashioned, to offer much temptation to a modern student—even to a lazy one. But stereotyping continues, and much of the writing and conversation to which we are constantly exposed is a tissue of trite expressions. Society-page editors have their own brand of stereotypes: "social function," "gala affair," "making one's bow to society," and so forth. Howard Jacobs provides a neat list of political clichés in the following skit.

QUIZ KIDS DENOUNCE "BLOATED PLUTOCRATS"

With the mayoral race in the offing and since political spellbinders soon will be loose on the land, it behooves us to review the entrance exams for Professor Chick Hannery's School of Political Science. Let us mosey to the school with the Quiz Kids, Flotsam and Jetsam.

Says the professor: "Now I'm going to ask you some questions to determine your aptitude. First, if your opponent has been defeated in a previous election, how can you best capitalize on the fact?"

"We would always refer to him as discredited, or repudiated," replies Flotsam.

"What makes you think 'discredited' or 'repudiated' are synonymous with 'defeated'?" demands the professor.

"Because we are studying political science, not Webster's definitions," responds Jetsam.

"Very good," remarks the professor. "Now, what should any move of the opposition make our blood do?"

"Boil."

"And what should any move of our own faction give us a solemn sense of?"

"Pride."

"All right," says the professor, "now, how should you refer to our own faction?"

"An organization."

"And that of the opposition?"

"A gang, or a machine, or 'that crowd.' "

"And how would you describe the opposition when at least one of their candidates has completed the payments on his automobile?"

"Bloated plutocrats."

"Excellent. And what would you call a compromise between two different factions opposing you?"

"A sellout."

"And what about a compromise between your faction and one of the opposition?"

"An understanding."

"Good. And what body of water is the opposition always going to sell the people down?"

"The river."

"Perfect. Now suppose you are in office and want to get reelected, at what would you point the finger of pride?"

"The record."

"And if you were out of office and wanted to get in, at what would you point the finger of scorn?"

"The record."

"And what would you call one of your candidates with original ideas?"

"A man of vision."

"And one of the opposition who has original ideas?"

"A visionary."

"One last question. Who is supporting your side?"

"A sturdy coalition of decent, self-respecting citizens."

"And that of the opposition?"

"An unholy alliance of politicians and others of their ilk wishing to feed at the public trough."

"O.K.," says the professor. "You can report for elementary training next week and I'll put a cross by your names. On second thought you should be ready for the advanced course, so we'll make it a double cross."

—HOWARD JACOBS: The New Orleans *Times-Picayune,* April 27, 1969.[9]

---

[9] Reprinted from the New Orleans *Times-Picayune,* April 27, 1969, by permission of the New Orleans *Times-Picayune.*

To come still closer home, there is slang. Some slang expressions may once have been pungent and colorful. The sportswriter who first described the strike-out of a slugging batter by saying "he made three dents in the atmosphere" conveyed the scene sharply and humorously. When slang is thus "tailor-made" for the occasion, it may be bright and perceptive, though, if it is still fresh and vivid, one could question whether it ought to be viewed as "slang" at all. But, as most of us use it, slang is a worn and impoverished language, not bright and irreverent and lively, but stale and dead: "the party was a washout"; "I'm fed up"; "he crabbed a lot"; "he blew his top." The real sin committed here is not so much that of bringing slang's flippant associations into a serious context. We do not often commit this fault. The real sin in using slang consists in using a thin and inexpressive language—slang that has lost its edge.

Jargon: the degenerative disease of prose

We have to step up, however, to a somewhat more exalted plane to find the stereotypes that most damage modern prose and that are likely to do the student most harm. These stereotypes are such expressions as "along the lines of," "in the last analysis," "socioeconomic considerations," "the world of business affairs," "according to a usually reliable source." Such locutions puff out many an official document, many a political speech, and, it must be admitted, many a professor's lecture or article.

This wordy, murky style is sometimes called "officialese." Congressman Maury Maverick called it "gobbledygook," submitting as a horrible sample the following extract:

> Whereas, national defense requirements have created a shortage of corundum (as hereafter defined) for the combined needs of defense and private account, and the supply of corundum now is and will be insufficient for defense and essential civilian requirements, unless the supply of corundum is conserved and its use in certain products manufactured for civilian use is curtailed; and it is necessary in the public interest and to promote the defense of the United States, to conserve the supply and direct the distribution and use thereof. Now, therefore, it is hereby ordered that . . .

Here follows a paragraph of jargon with a more academic smack:

> This relationship would define certain linkages between the social and physical structure of the city. It would also provide a precise definition of the commonalities among several spatial distributions. By the same token, the correlation between the residential desirability scale and the continuum of socio-economic status would provide an estimate of the predictive value of aerial photographic data relative to the social ecology of the city.

Malcolm Cowley, who garnered the specimen of jargon just quoted, comments as follows:

Mr. Green has used 160 words—counting "socio-economic" as only one —to express an idea that a layman would have stated in thirty-three. As a matter of fact, he has used many more than 160 words, since the whole article is an elaboration of this one thesis. Whatever may be the virtues of the sociological style, or Socspeak, as George Orwell might have called it— it is not specifically designed to save ink and paper.

—"Sociological Habit Patterns in Linguistic Transmogrification,"
The Reporter, Sept. 20, 1956.

George Orwell himself has written on the subject of the sociological style:

Prose (nowadays) consists less and less of *words* chosen for the sake of their meaning, and more and more of *phrases* tacked together like the sections of a prefabricated henhouse. . . . There is a huge dump of wornout metaphors which have lost all evocative power and are merely used because they save people the trouble of inventing phrases for themselves. . . . Modern writing at its worst . . . consists in gumming together long strips of words which have already been set in order by someone else.

By using apt comparisons ("sections of a prefabricated henhouse," "dump of worn-out metaphors," "gumming together long strips of words") Orwell vividly makes the two points of his indictment: the jargon writer's careless and slovenly craftsmanship and the secondhand quality of his materials.

Orwell goes on to illustrate his point by suggesting how a modern writer of hand-me-down phrases would express the following passage from Ecclesiastes: "I returned, and saw under the sun, that the race is not to the swift, nor the battle to the strong, neither yet bread to the wise, nor yet riches to men of understanding, nor yet favor to men of skill; but time and chance happeneth to them all."

Such a writer, says Orwell, would probably turn it out like this: "Objective consideration of contemporary phenomena compels the conclusion that success or failure in competitive activities exhibits no tendency to be commensurate with innate capacity, but that a considerable element of the unpredictable must invariably be taken into account."

If good prose is designed to inform and persuade the reader, then jargon, which befogs the reader's comprehension, has no place in it. Jargon may also befog the writer himself—may deceive him into thinking that he has stated a forceful argument when he may in fact have done no more than present a few insights that, however interesting, do not make up an argument.

■ APPLICATION

Attempt to rewrite the following paragraph from Eric Hoffer's *The True Believer* to eliminate jargon and unclarity. If you feel no rewriting is required, be prepared to say why.

Offhand one would expect that the mere possession of power would automatically result in a cocky attitude toward the world and a receptivity to change. But it is not always so. The powerful can be as timid as the weak. What seems to count more than possession of instruments of power is faith in the future. Where power is not joined with faith in the future, it is used mainly to ward off the new and preserve the status quo. On the other hand, extravagant hope, even when not backed by actual power, is likely to generate a most reckless daring. For the hopeful can draw strength from the most ridiculous sources of power—a slogan, a word, a button. No faith is potent unless it is also faith in the future; unless it has a millennial component. So, too, an effective doctrine: as well as being a source of power, it must also claim to be a key to the book of the future.[10]

JARGON: SOME ANTIDOTES

Jargon, of course, involves more than stereotypes. Jargon is nearly always compounded of clusters of words that are general and abstract. Though there is no certain prescription against jargon, it is easy to state some practical antidotes.

1   Use words that are as specific and concrete as possible; that is, never use a word more general and indefinite than is called for. Hazy and indefinite expressions represent the easy way out for a writer who is too timid to commit himself or too lazy to think through what he wants to say.

2   Avoid stereotypes of all kinds—prefabricated phrasings that come easily to mind but that may not represent precisely your own ideas and emotions. But note this carefully: you should never avoid a word because it seems simple and common. If the sense calls for a simple, common word, it is generally best to repeat the word, if necessary, again and again. There is little to be said in favor of what is sometimes called elegant variation, that is, the substitution of some synonym in order to avoid repetition. Here is an example: "Mr. Jones was a powerful *financier*. As a *tycoon* he had a deep suspicion of socialism. He shared the feelings of his associates who were also *bankers*." The variations are irritating and can be confusing. Either recast the sentence or repeat *financier*.

You should, on the other hand, learn to be suspicious of *strings of words* —phrasings—that are common and therefore probably stereotyped. Though they are not to be prohibited, inspect them all carefully, especially in revising your work. If you really need to say "along the lines of" or "in consideration of" or "in the last analysis," do so. But make sure that what you are talking about really is *along the lines of* whatever it is you refer to or that the matter of *consideration* is uppermost or that the "analysis" you mention is really the ultimate one.

The rule of thumb would be: (1) never shy away from an individual word merely because it is frequently used, but (2) always be chary of frequently used *phrases*.

---

[10] From pp. 8–9 in *The True Believer* (Handbound Ed.) by Eric Hoffer. Copyright, 1951 by Eric Hoffer. Reprinted by permission of Harper & Row, Publishers.

3   Use live words, remembering that finite verbs are the most powerful words that we have. The following sentence is an instance of vagueness from the failure to use finite verbs.

> Keenly aware of the painstaking scholarship and of the high creative effort that over the centuries has accumulated the body of subject matter we call "English," a group of our ablest teachers conceive their role to be to transmit this product of human endeavor, this hard-won store of learning and of art, this rich portion of man's heritage of culture, to the oncoming generations. . . .

This sentence is packed with ideas, but the only finite verb in it (aside from *has accumulated* and *call,* in the two subordinate clauses) is the verb *conceive.* A participle, *aware,* is made to carry the weight of the first twenty-six words; and the whole latter part of the sentence hangs from two successive infinitives, "to be" and "to transmit." The sentence has so little stamina that it sprawls. It sprawls because the writer has starved it of finite verbs. The author might better have written:

> Our ablest teachers realize what effort has gone into the making of that body of subject matter we call "English." They know it is a precious thing, for it embodies the effort of painstaking scholars and of great poets and novelists. They want to transmit this heritage of culture to the oncoming generations.

Finite verbs are more powerful than strings of participles, gerunds, or infinitives. A specific verb is usually stronger than a more general verb qualified by modifiers. Compare "He walked along slowly" with "He strolled," "He sauntered," "He dawdled," "He lagged." Frequently, it is true, we need the qualifiers. But we ought not to forget the wealth of concreteness that the English language possesses in its great number of verbs that name specifically, and therefore powerfully, certain modes of action. In this general connection, see the chapter on Description (pp. 211–12).

4   Use as the staple of your discourse simple sentences in normal sentence order (see p. 269). An essay so written may be childishly simple, and it can become monotonous; but it will seldom collapse into the spineless flabbiness of jargon.

● CAUTION

Jargon cannot be dealt with summarily. It is our most pervasive kind of "bad" style, and, like style in general, it is the product of the interplay of many elements. We shall have to return to this topic in the chapters that follow, especially in the discussion of metaphor.

■ APPLICATIONS

I The following passages are badly infected with jargon. Try to determine what the author in each case means to say, and then put it into English for him. (You might apply the four antidotes to jargon described above.)

A The chemical age gives every highly technical nation a choice between self-sufficiency and trade on whatever barter or bargaining basis it desires, thus upsetting time-honored geographical alignments of monopolies of certain natural products and altering the whole concept of imperialism. This is an entirely new situation for agriculture. For centuries the threat of eventual scarcity of food and land hung over the world. Within a few decades the march of science has brought about a complete reversal. On the one hand the chemist and the technologist have made possible the production of greater and greater quantities of products on less and less land, resulting in enormous surpluses of acreage, crops, and labor. At the same time, ironically enough, the chemist is removing one product after another from the soil into the laboratory, throwing still more land out of cultivation and further reducing the amount of labor needed.

B The maintenance of democracy will, I believe, require not only a deflation of executive power and its restoration to popular control but a public vigilance greater than that heretofore manifest. Whether it is possible to expect private citizens to make the necessary sacrifices of time and effort to see to it that representative government is not frustrated, only time can tell. But if the electorate will not insist upon congressional control of public policy, executive government will come by default and the historical cycle through which other countries have passed may well be reflected here.

As a way of life our people heretofore valued the freedom and respect for the human personality which the Constitution was designed to insure. Even that has suffered inroads, necessarily because of legitimate legislative restraints but unnecessarily also because the protection of civil liberties lies for the most part with the local communities, and many elements of our population are becoming indifferent to the fundamental importance of civil liberties. Some people insist that economic well-being explains the luxury of democracy, and that hard times and insecurity promote the surrender of freedom. This only means that the effort to maintain democracy is now more difficult. It should not be allowed to go by default.

II The student will probably conclude that the writing in the following passage is quite effective. It is, on the whole, rather straightforward prose. The sentences are simple in structure. How much of the effectiveness of the passage depends upon the choice of diction? How many hackneyed or slang expressions does it contain, if any? Are any of these expressions justified? Why?

Dutchmen don't get excited over nothing. I was in an airliner over Holland, when the Dutch aboard started crowding each other at the windows: below us, green and shining, was a farm landscape that has only just recently come out of the sea. It is the first piece of a whole new province (a new state, we would say) that Holland is adding to itself: "Flevoland."

I went back later, by car, by boat, by Piper Cub, and looked into this land-making operation. It's the pride of the Dutch. It's what makes their eyes shine.

The main method is this: you build an earthen dam from shore out into the shallow sea and back to shore, so as to fence in part of the sea. Then you pump the water out. You wait a few years for the rains to wash the salt out of the soil. Then you start farming! Such a piece of land—saucer-shaped, lying below sea level, is called a "polder." It's a necessary word, and not translatable. Nobody has polders but the Dutch. They have been making them for five hundred years—small ones—and now, with big money and big machines, they make them big.

I drove out on a dyke that is fencing off one future piece of Flevoland. You drive on the top of the dyke, and you do sixty. We went out of sight of land, and still the road kept going. I thought: "This is big." You hold it against the American scale of things—Hoover Dam, TVA, Empire State Building—and it is still big. You hold it against the size of Holland—six Hollands wouldn't fill the State of Kansas—and it becomes colossal. It's as if we wanted to push the Gulf of Mexico back and build a second Texas. . . .

And this is what makes Holland Holland. Windmills, for instance: land below sea level doesn't drain. You have to keep pumping the rain out. The windmills do that—still do it, though most of the pumping now is electric, or diesel. And those wooden shoes? (You still see them quite a bit.) Why? Much of the soil is always wet, and wooden shoes are watertight and warm. You can't run in them—but then, a Dutchman is well organized; he starts early and has no need to run. Little boys who feel like running have a special Dutch boys' gesture: you take your shoes off and carry them both in your left hand, and run.   —J. Wolfgang Langewiesche: "The Dutch Hustle," *Harper's Magazine*, April, 1956.

CHAPTER **12**

Metaphor

In metaphor there is a transfer of meaning[1]—the Greek word from which metaphor is derived means "to transfer." A word that applies literally to one kind of object or idea is applied by analogy to another. Thus a ray of sunshine *cuts* the gloom (as if it were a knife); a ship *courses* the seas (its motion likened to that of a greyhound); a man *weasels* out of his promise (as a ferretlike animal wriggles through a small hole).[2]

In the preceding chapter we considered some of the simpler kinds of metaphor. Thus on page 292 we spoke of the *eye* of a needle, the *legs* of a chair, the *bed* of a river. As we have seen (pp. 291–95), language normally grows by a process of metaphorical extension; we extend old names to new objects. But when, in this process of extension, a metaphor is completely absorbed into the common language (as in the *bed* of a river), it loses its metaphorical force; it becomes a dead metaphor. Compare, for example, "the bed of a river" with "the dance of life." The first phrase carries no suggestion that the bed is a place of repose or that the river is sleepy! We use "the bed of a river" as a pure denotation from which the associated meanings that apply to *bed* in its usual senses are quite absent. But it is very

---

[1] Refer to the second paragraph of the Clark selection on pp. 89–90. Language normally develops through a series of such transfers.

[2] In this chapter we have used *metaphor* in the largest and most inclusive sense. We have not distinguished metaphor proper from *simile* (an *explicit* comparison, usually introduced by *like* or *as:* "she glided into the room *like a swan*," "he was as bald *as an egg*"), or *metonymy* (the use of a part to designate the whole: "he employed twenty *hands* on his farm"), or other such specializations of the metaphoric principle. Such classifications are, in our considered opinion, of little practical importance to the writer.

different with the phrase "the dance of life." This metaphor is still alive. (At least, when a certain writer, Havelock Ellis, used it as the title of one of his books, he must have hoped that it would seem alive.) Here the suggestions, the associations, are thoroughly relevant to Ellis's purpose. The suggestions (of something rhythmic, of patterned movement, even, perhaps, of gaiety and happiness) are meant to be associated with life.

The term *dead metaphor* can itself illuminate the problem now being considered. With "dead" metaphors, we can say *rigor mortis* has set in: they have no flexibility; they have stiffened into one meaning. Metaphors that are still alive prove that they are alive by their flexibility; and because they are still alive, they can be used to give color and life to a piece of writing. They are concrete and particular; they reflect the world of the senses. They can still excite the imagination.

In metaphors that are still recognizably such, there are, of course, varying degrees of life. The following examples are not very lively, but they do show that metaphor is a perfectly natural and important part of our normal speech: we say, for example, "John is a square"; "Jane is a doll"; "He ran out on the deal"; "That remark threw him for a loss." Such expressions are rather worn and faded. But their original metaphorical character is plain enough, and we still think of them, and use them, as metaphors. The list of expressions that are badly shopworn but are still recognizably metaphors could be extended almost indefinitely: "hot as the devil," "independent as a hog on ice," "lazy as a dog," "crazy as a bat," and so on.

■ APPLICATION

Draw up a list of a dozen dead (or nearly dead) metaphors.

The Importance of Metaphor in Everyday Language

Our preference for the concrete and the particular, as these examples show, is not only normal, it is deeply and stubbornly rooted in the human mind. Consider the following situation: It is a hot day. We can say, "It is hot" or "It is very hot," or, piling on the intensives, we can say, "It is abominably and excruciatingly hot." But most of us, afflicted with heat, will resort to a metaphor of some kind: "It's hot as hell," or more elaborately, "It's hot as the hinges of hell." Evidently metaphor is felt to add forcefulness, and evidently the forcefulness has some relation to sharpness of detail and concreteness of expression.

That is one point, then: in metaphor, force and sharpness of detail, especially of sensory detail, tend to go together. Indeed, we are usually attracted to metaphor in the first place because ordinary language seems worn and stale. A second point to be made is this: metaphor tends to accompany the expression of emotions and attitudes. If we want to give a precise account of the weather, all we need to say is that the temperature is 97.6 degrees Fahrenheit, the relative humidity is 92 percent, and the wind a bare two miles an hour from the southwest. But this cool statement of the facts doesn't begin to express our feelings of discomfort on a muggy afternoon in midsummer.

Let us consider another simple case. Suppose we feel a special kind of happiness and try to express our feelings. We can say, "I feel happy." Or we can try to find a word that more accurately pinpoints this special feeling: *merry, gay, ecstatic, cheerful, glad, jolly,* or *joyous.* There are many synonyms for *happy*, as the dictionary will quickly reveal, and they differ in their shades of meaning. For example, *jolly* suggests the heartiness and good humor that go with comfortable living; *ecstatic* suggests an elevating rapture; *gay* suggests sprightliness, a nimble lightheartedness. We shall do well to consult a dictionary to learn (or remind ourselves of) the wealth of resources at our disposal. Even so, we rarely find an adjective that exactly expresses our feelings. We tend to resort to metaphor. We say, "I'm happy as a June bug," or "I feel like a million dollars," or "I'm walking on air this morning," or "I feel like a colt in springtime." Writers of popular songs, for instance, are constantly trying to devise fresh comparisons in order to express the singer's delirious happiness (or maybe his desolating sadness).

If the feeling is very special or complex, we are usually *forced* to resort to metaphor. Here are the ways in which a writer of fiction expresses the special kind of happiness that one of his characters, a young soldier, experiences when the brilliant woman who has dazzled him shows him a small attention:

> She regarded him with her kindly glances, which made something glow and expand within his chest. It was a delicious feeling, even though it did cut one's breath short now and then. Ecstatically he drank in the sound of her tranquil, seductive talk full of innocent gaiety and of spiritual quietude. His passion appeared to him to flame up and envelop her in blue fiery tongues from head to foot and over her head, while her soul appeared in the center like a big white rose. . . .
> —JOSEPH CONRAD: "The Warrior's Soul," *Tales of Hearsay.*

The author tries to do justice to the intense emotion that the young soldier feels, and in doing so, he twice resorts to metaphor. The first is a rather simple and even conventional metaphor of a feeling of warmth within his chest—something that seems to "glow" and to "expand." The second attempts to interpret as well as present the quality of the emotion—the lady is encircled in flame, but the flames, though fierce ("blue fiery tongues"), do not injure her and may even be said to protect her. The white rose, which in his ecstatic vision stands for her soul, is not scorched or shriveled.

Choose metaphors that will describe *how you feel* in the following situations. Do not necessarily take the first metaphor that comes to mind; try to avoid worn-out metaphor; try to find a metaphor that describes as accurately as possible your own feelings.

1 On getting an A when you would have been happy to settle for the grade of C.
2 On getting well splashed by a passing car when on your way to an appointment.
3 On your first experience of stage fright.
4 On seeing a serious accident.
5 On first discovering that a close friend has betrayed your friendship.

Slang and metaphor

While we are discussing metaphor, it will be useful to consider once more slang and jargon, two abuses of language that we have already touched on in the preceding chapter (pp. 302–08). The general impulse to use slang springs from a perfectly respectable motive, our preference for the concrete and the particular. Most slang expressions originated as metaphors, and the misuse of slang cannot be dealt with apart from the more general problem of the use and the abuse of figurative language. For that reason, it doesn't do much good for the instructor to tell the student—or for the student to tell himself—to stop using slang. Most of us want to make our writing warm, colorful, and lively. To substitute abstract expression for such figurative language as we have would be the wrong thing to do.

The student ought not to discard his figurative language, but to improve it. He should try to eliminate all metaphors that are worn and trite, all comparisons that seem pretentious, and all analogies that are not valid or that jangle with the rest of the composition. On the positive side, the student ought to seek out fresh and accurate metaphors. The practical result of such procedures will be that most of the slang will be sloughed off, but sloughed off *because it proves to be poor and ineffective metaphor*, not because an abstract statement is "better."

The truth of the matter is that few writers are able to avoid the use of metaphor, even if they try to do so. But the writer should want his metaphors to be alive rather than dead, responsible and controlled rather than random and irresponsible.

Jargon and worn-out metaphor

So much for the relation of slang to metaphor. As for jargon, though it is a mishmash of trite expressions of every sort, a great number of these are dead or all-but-lifeless metaphors. One can illustrate by citing a passage from a recent popular book, which in a few years has sold far more than a million copies.

> Poets, novelists, and philosophers throughout the centuries have written their most somber and frightening lines when dealing with the menace of death. They grow bitter at the shears of fate which ruthlessly sever the thread of being. They draw vivid word portraits of the unbearable pain of separation, the unfairness of destiny which too frequently plunges its dagger into the pulsating bodies of lovers even as they drain the cup of ecstasy. Poets weep, and make us weep, at the fate of young lives cut short while senility stumbles meaninglessly along its blind highway. They rebel, and make us rebel, at the dark magic of the universe which in the twinkling of an eye can transform the breathing, laughing, creating artist, scientist, son, mother, wife, into a silent, unoccupied tenement of clay, a shroud of darkness, a crumbling clod of earth.
>
> —JOSHUA LOTH LIEBMAN: *Peace of Mind*.[3]

This passage is, indeed, to use Orwell's phrase on page 306, "a dump of worn-out metaphor." There is, for example, the reference to the shears of fate. The Greeks had a myth about the three Fates, sister goddesses, one of whom spun the thread of a man's life, one of whom measured it, and one of whom snipped it. An allusion to this well-known myth is appropriate in this context, but unless the writer can reinvigorate the story, perhaps he should play it down rather than up. As used here, the figure of the shears is at once perfunctory and yet elaborate and so shows all too clearly how worn it is.

A few lines later, after turning fate into "destiny," the writer does make an attempt at a vigorous and even violent image: destiny "plunges its dagger into the pulsating bodies of lovers." But to say that the lovers "drain the cup of ecstasy" is to drop back into old-fashioned grandiloquence. Modern lovers don't "drain" glasses of champagne when they toast each other, just as they don't "drain" cocktails at a cocktail party. "Cup of ecstasy" is itself a rather faded piece of the highfalutin style. When the writer has villainous destiny plunge its dagger into the bodies of these throbbing lovers as they toss off their cups of ecstasy, the reader finds it hard to take the expression seriously: it is not much more than a needlessly roundabout way of saying that destiny kills them at the height of their pleasure. (If the reader *does* take the expression seriously, he finds himself looking at an unbelievable and therefore unconsciously funny scene from an old-fashioned melodrama.)

The statement that "senility stumbles meaninglessly along its blind highway" may raise as a primary question: What does the metaphor—whether dead or alive—mean? Does the writer mean that the eyes of old age are too dim to see the highway? Thus, is the adjective *blind* applied to the highway as a kind of transferred epithet? Or is the highway literally blind (*cf.* blind alley) in that it proves to be a dead end? But if the writer's point is that the

---

[3] Reprinted from *Peace of Mind* by Joshua Loth Liebman by permission of Simon & Schuster, Inc. Reprinted by permission of William Heinemann Ltd.

highway of life leads only to death, isn't youth's course along the highway quite as meaningless as senility's? If both youth and age are headed for the dead end of death, there isn't much choice between stumbling or skipping one's way to it: it's a blind highway in either case.

Finally, we get another metaphor, or rather a cluster of them. The corpse is compared to "a silent, unoccupied tenement of clay." ("Tenement of clay" is, by the way, another piece of faded grandiloquence.) Not many of us today think of the body as a tenement (that is, a house) that has the soul for its occupant, and the writer has done nothing in this context to re-stress this idea. (Incidentally, a more careful writer would have stated that it was the *body* of the son, mother, wife, etc., that was transformed into an "unoccupied tenement of clay.")

Perhaps the writer's suspicion that all was not well with his tenement comparison prompted him to add, as an appositive phrase, "a shroud of darkness." But the new comparison brings up its own problems. Literally, the dead body is "shrouded" (dressed in burial clothes); yet to write "transform . . . the wife . . . into . . . a shroud of darkness" suggests that the body *itself* becomes a shroud enclosing "darkness." (In that case, the conversion of the body into a shroud may seem to be *too* lively—too bold a metaphor.) Or does "shroud of darkness" as used here mean no more than "shroud composed [made up] of darkness"? Perhaps the writer would have done well to scratch out both the tenement and the shroud figures and to retain only his third and least ambitious phrase: "a crumbling clod of earth." For the three comparisons do not really support each other, and they may even conflict with one another. What is the relation of the clod of earth to the shroud of darkness? And what is the relation of the shroud to the tenement? It would be hard to say, and this lack of precision is one of the characteristics of jargon: the writer has not come to terms with his own thought; he moves from one murky concept to another without articulating any clear relation between one item and the next. The moral would seem to be that even when one is writing about death, he should use metaphors that are alive.

■ APPLICATION

Rewrite the paragraph from *Peace of Mind* (p. 315). Give special attention to removing not only confused metaphors but other bits of jargon as well. Try first to make plain, simple sense of it. Then, if you feel you can, improve it by the use of appropriate metaphor.

Confused metaphor: further instances

The following passage is an excerpt from the advertisement of a savings-and-loan association:

The little squirrel, with a God-given instinct to prepare for tomorrow, stores away nuts and has plenty to eat . . . when winter comes.

Is he smarter than *you* are? Think about this.

Now, today, is the time to start "salting away" that nest egg you'll need sure as fate.

In this advertisement the writer has not been content to compare the savings that the human being puts away with the nut that the squirrel buries for winter food. He insists on finding two more analogies: salting away meat and leaving a nest egg.

Before modern refrigeration methods came into being, meat was laid down in salt to preserve it through the winter and other times of scarcity. The phrase *salt away* was then extended to all sorts of things that were to be reserved and preserved for future use. A "nest egg" was the egg left in the hen's nest so that she would continue to lay. Again, by analogy the term has been extended to other sorts of things that a person, in the hope of getting something more, delays gathering for present use. But the three metaphors, already trite, are here woefully mixed and jostle against one another. You don't *salt away a nest egg*. A human being ought not be asked to attempt what a squirrel has better sense than to try. Of course, we *know* what the copywriter means to say. But that is not the point. The point is the ineffectiveness of the way he chooses to say it.

Sportswriters quite often refer to football coaches' "taking their hair down" as a more vivid way of saying that they were willing to state their true opinions. In doing so, they choose a particularly unfortunate cliché. ("The coach leveled with me" or "He finally came clean" are clichés too, but at least they are not absurd.) For if we try to *visualize* the scene, we have an image of the coach removing his hairpins and letting down his tresses.[4] If we *don't* visualize the scene—if the metaphor is completely dead, stone cold—then there is not much point in using it anyway.

Advertising copywriters and journalists are not, however, the only writers who bungle their metaphors or who have the misfortune to have one of their "dead" metaphors unexpectedly come alive. Robert Graves, in *Reader Over My Shoulder,* quotes an amusing instance from a book by a distinguished Cambridge University professor of English literature. The professor argues that we ought to be willing to admit new words into the English language because by doing so "we infuse new blood into a tongue of which . . . our first pride should be that it is flexible, alive, capable of responding to new demands of man's untiring quest after knowledge and experience." By "tongue" he means, of course, "language." But the metaphor of blood transfusion is likely to wake up the dormant physical image in tongue, all the more so when the writer goes on to describe that tongue as "flexible" and "alive." (Even if this grotesque image doesn't arise in the reader's mind, the author's management of metaphor is still not very happy, for the image of performing a blood transfusion on a "language" is itself mildly grotesque.)

---

[4] The first sportswriter to use the expression may have meant to be funny. But if so, subsequent repetition has worn out the joke.

The following passages are taken from reputable books and magazines. Make a criticism of the use of metaphor in these passages. Where the metaphors seem garbled or inappropriate, rewrite the passage, substituting more appropriate metaphors.

1 As his fame was slowly ascending, partly because of this social skill of his, into more illustrious circles, so was it trickling down among the more numerous obscure.

2 . . . the writers [of our day] want to be against the *status quo,* but it can't be done. The *status quo* changes too quickly for them. And in changing it buys them off: it salves their wounds with money; it stuffs those cultural gaps with hard cash.

3 It's not the hurt the other fellow does you that keeps on rankling; it's the hurt you do yourself by your own remembering. That sticks in your skin and infects your mind. I guess that's the secret of all successful forgetting. Don't let it break through your insulation at the start. Don't let it make a deep and lasting brand on the sensitive recording plate of your consciousness.

4 A century and a half ago English poetry left those formal gardens brought to perfection by Dryden and Pope, where now their successors seemed able only to raise forced blooms and artificial flowers, and went out to the wilderness for a change of air, a transfusion of blood.

5 Therefore, when he championed his middle class, he instinctively set his face against everything that threatened to substitute quantity for quality— against the encroachments of commerce and the new imperialism which the progressively minded among both Whigs and Tories were imbibing from Chatham. And the caveat against the dangers lurking in materialistic panaceas is not without implications that carry beyond the time and the place.

The Function of Metaphor

Thus far we have stressed the abuses of figurative language. Aside from some references to metaphor as a means for making language more colorful and for expressing our emotional responses, we have said little about the positive function of metaphor. Yet if we are to understand why metaphor constitutes one of the great resources of the writer, we shall need to define much more clearly what its essential function is.

It is all the more important to do so in view of the conventional ways of stating the uses of metaphor, for they tend to be misleading. Thus, we often hear it said that the purpose of metaphor is to provide an illustration or to give an emotional heightening. But either of these explanations suggests that metaphor is a kind of "extra" that may be a useful or pleasant addition to a statement but that does not constitute an essential part of it. Certainly one practical use of metaphor is to provide a concrete illustration of a point that has been stated more abstractly. In the pages that follow we shall consider examples of such illustrations. But illustration is not its primary or essential use. Still less essential is the use of metaphor to provide a sort of rhetorical decoration—as if the metaphor were a silk ribbon tied around a box of candy.

Metaphors used for the sake of illustration are indeed "extras." They can be left off. Yet if we think of metaphor as something that can be left off, we shall never come to understand why the proper control of metaphor is essential to good writing.

Why strictly notational statement does not require metaphor

There is, to be sure, one very special kind of discourse in which metaphor is indeed inessential. If we wish to say "$2 + 2 = 4$" or that "the square of the hypotenuse of a right triangle is equal to the sum of the squares of the other two sides," we shall not require metaphor. Metaphor would in fact be in the way. Such statements as these, however, are very special; the terms used in them are (or aspire to be) pure denotations. Thus, as was implied in the preceding chapter (p. 285), if such terms have associations at all, the associations are irrelevant. For the "words" employed are not being used as words in the usual sense; whereas most words are capable of metaphorical extension, these "words" are not. They are, as scientific terms, frozen to one specific meaning, and the purest scientific statements are able to dispense with ordinary words altogether: thus $2 + 2 = 4$, or $H_2SO_4 + Fe \rightarrow FeSO_4 + H_2\uparrow$.

But important as such statements are, they represent a stringently specialized discourse. Most of the discourse that interests us as human beings and that we must use as writers goes far beyond abstract relationships of this kind. Most of our discourse has to do with the "full" world of our human experience, not with the colorless, soundless, abstract world of physics, say, or mathematics.

Metaphor as illustration

Yet though metaphor is not necessary to purely scientific statement, the scientific writer very often needs to go beyond such stringently limited discourse, and then for him too, metaphor, employed as illustration, may be highly useful. The following passage from Bertrand Russell's *The Scientific Outlook* will illustrate this point. The book is addressed to a general audience, and Russell is attempting to convince his reader that "what is actually experienced is much less than one would naturally suppose." He proceeds to analyze a typical experience for us—what happens scientifically when we "see" someone:

You may say, for example, that you see your friend, Mr. Jones, walking along the street: but this is to go far beyond what you have any right to say. You see a succession of coloured patches, traversing a stationary background. These patches, by means of a Pavlov conditioned reflex, bring into your mind the word "Jones," and so you say you see Jones; but other people, looking out of their windows from different angles, will see something different, owing to the laws of perspective: therefore, if they are all seeing Jones, there must be as many different Joneses as there are spectators, and if there is only one true Jones, the sight of him is not vouchsafed to anybody. If we assume for a moment the truth of the account which physics gives, we shall explain what you call "seeing Jones" in some such terms as the following. Little packets of light, called "light quanta," shoot out from the sun, and some of these reach a region where there are atoms of a certain kind, composing Jones's face, and hands, and clothes. These atoms do not themselves exist, but are merely a compendious way of alluding to possible occurrences. Some of the light quanta, when they reach Jones's atoms, upset their internal economy. This causes him to become sunburnt, and to manufacture vitamin D. Others are reflected, and of those that are reflected some enter your eye. They there cause a complicated disturbance of the rods and cones, which, in turn, send a current along the optic nerve. When this current reaches the brain, it produces an event. The event which it produces is that which you call "seeing Jones." As is evident from this account, the connection of "seeing Jones" with Jones is a remote, roundabout causal connection. Jones himself, meanwhile, remains wrapped in mystery. He may be thinking about his dinner, or about how his investments have gone to pieces, or about that umbrella he lost; these thoughts are Jones, but these are not what you see. . . .

—BERTRAND RUSSELL: *The Scientific Outlook.*

The passage may be regarded as an instance of exposition by use of illustration. (See pp. 62–63.) Notice that Russell has completed his analysis with the last statement of the passage; yet apparently he feels that the account may prove too technical and that his reader may fail to understand. Therefore, he adds a concluding illustration: "To say that you see Jones is no more correct than it would be, if a ball bounced off a wall in your garden and hit you, to say that the wall had hit you. Indeed, the two cases are closely analogous." Most readers will be grateful for the analogy. Most minds find abstractions so alien to them that they need a concrete statement such as this analogy provides. Even if the writer is able, as Bertrand Russell is able here, to state his analysis directly, the extra illustration—the concrete analogy drawn from daily experience—is helpful.

■ APPLICATIONS

I The authors of the following passages have supplied illustrative or summarizing comparisons to make clearer or more emphatic what they had to say. We have printed here the author's comparison along with two alternate comparisons. Can you pick out the author's own? Try to justify your choice.

A   These molecules move with very high speeds; in the ordinary air of an ordinary room, the average molecular speed is about 500 yards a second. This is roughly the speed of a rifle-bullet, and is rather more than the ordinary speed of sound. As we are familiar with this latter speed from everyday experience, it is easy to form some conception of molecular speeds in a gas. It is not a mere accident that molecular speeds are comparable with the speed of sound. Sound is a disturbance which one molecule passes on to another when it collides with it, rather like

1   an infection that one human being passes on to another.
2   relays of messengers passing a message on to one another, or Greek torchbearers handing on their lights.
3   a set of box-cars when the locomotive's engineer suddenly applies the brakes and each car passes on the jolt to the next.
        —Sir James Jeans: "Exploring the Atom," *The Universe Around Us*.[5]

B   An insect, therefore, is not afraid of gravity; it can fall without danger, and can cling to the ceiling with remarkably little trouble. It can go in for elegant fantastic forms of support like that of the daddy-long-legs. But there is a force which is as formidable to an insect as gravitation to a mammal. This is surface tension. A man coming out of a bath carries with him a film of water of about one-fiftieth of an inch in thickness. This weighs about a pound. A wet mouse has to carry about its own weight of water. A wet fly has to lift many times its own weight and, as everyone knows, a fly once wetted by water or any other liquid is in a very serious position indeed. An insect going for a drink is in as great danger as

1   a man leaning out over a precipice in search of food.
2   a New Yorker trying to cross 42nd Street at Madison Avenue.
3   a gazelle approaching a waterhole where lions may lie in wait.
        —J. B. S. Haldane: "On Being the Right Size," *Possible Worlds*.

II In the following passage the author has made much use of illustrative metaphor. Try to restate what is said in language as unmetaphorical as you can devise. Do not be surprised if you find that the rewritten version requires a good many more words than the original passage.

    We, then, the animals, consume those stores in our restless living. Serenely the plants amass them. They turn light's active energy to food, which is potential energy stored for their own benefit. . . .
    Animal life lives always in the red; the favorable balance is written on the other side of life's page, and it is written in chlorophyll. All else obeys the thermodynamic law that energy forever runs down hill, is lost and degraded. In economic language, this is the law of diminishing returns, and it is obeyed by the cooling stars as by man and all the animals. They float down its Lethe stream. Only chlorophyll fights up against the current. It is the stuff in life that rebels at death, that has never surrendered to entropy, final icy stagnation. It is the mere cobweb on which we are all suspended over the abyss.
        —Donald Culross Peattie: *Flowering Earth*.[6]

Metaphor as essential statement

In strict scientific statement, then, metaphor has no place, and in less strict scientific discussion it would seem to be auxiliary and optional. But in most of what we read—political speeches, articles on international affairs, letters to friends, expressions of opinion, fiction, poetry, drama, attempts to persuade and convince, essays in which we invite other people to share our experiences and evaluations of life—and in nearly everything that we write, metaphor is a primary device of expression. It is no mere decoration, no "extra." It often represents not only the most compact and vigorous way of saying a thing but also the only way in which the particular thing can be said at all. This last remark holds especially true when "the thing to be said" involves an interpretation or evaluation. Metaphor is indeed an indispensable instrument for interpreting experience.

Let us illustrate. In the sentence that follows, Helen Keller describes what tactile sensation means to a person who has always been blind and deaf: "The immovable rock, with its juts and warped surface, bends beneath my fingers into all manner of grooves and hollows." The rock, of course, does not literally bend; it is "immovable." But under her sensitive fingers, which do duty for eyes, the rock itself seems to respond dynamically to her touch. For what is being described is not the fumbling of an ordinary person who is blindfolded. We are, rather, being let into Helen Keller's "world," a world of exciting qualities that most of us do not know at all. Metaphor here is the only means by which it may be made known to us, since this world does not exist in our experience and cannot be pointed to; it can only be created for us. (The student should compare Helen Keller's account of touch, as given in fuller detail on pages 200–01, with Bertrand Russell's account of sight, page 320. They are radically different in purpose, and therefore in method.)

Consider what metaphor accomplishes in the two following passages.

> In rivers the water that you touch is the last of what has passed and the first of that which comes: so with time present.   —LEONARDO DA VINCI.

This figure may seem to be no more than mere illustration; yet there are other elements. What is being described is not an object but a metaphysical concept, the imaginary boundary—itself without duration—that divides time past from time future. Da Vinci finds the image he requires in the analogy of a moving stream: time present is like the moving water that cannot be caught and held for inspection but at the moment of touching us is already hurrying away. The analogy, in spite of its vividness, preserves in itself something of the mystery that it undertakes to reveal to us. It has "poetic" character—not in the sense that it is pretty or sentimental, but in the sense that it makes a profound revelation.

Thoreau also likens the passage of time to a moving stream and goes on to develop explicitly certain related metaphysical implications: eternity as a concept in our experience of time.

> Time is but the stream I go a-fishing in. I drink at it; but while I drink, I
> see the sandy bottom and detect how shallow it is. Its thin current slides
> away, but eternity remains. I would drink deeper; fish in the sky, whose
> bottom is pebbly with stars.   —HENRY DAVID THOREAU: *Walden.*

Time is impermanent, thin, "shallow," necessary for men (they must
drink of it) and providing them with pleasure and sport ("go a-fishing in");
but the speaker yearns for a deeper draft and more sublime sport than time
can provide.

■ APPLICATION

Has Thoreau used his metaphors responsibly? Is his figure strained? Badly
mixed? What is the relation of stream bed to sky? Pebbles to stars? How are all
the subsidiary metaphors related to each other? Can you fill in the gaps among
them? Through this complicated figure, what is Thoreau trying to "say"?

We must not, however, allow our choice of examples to make the process of using metaphor seem too complicated and "literary." Consider a
passage from a student theme, which was quoted in full on pages 204–05:

> Off yonder, beyond the glitter of the water where the sun still struck, you
> could see the clouds piling up like a cliff, black and slate-colored, streaked
> with purple. I said like a cliff, but it was like a cliff that somehow, momen-
> tarily grew taller while you stared at it, looking awfully solid but somehow
> swelling and coiling upward at the same time as though there were an in-
> terior force collecting itself for effort.

The comparison to a swelling and coiling cliff enables the reader to visualize
what the storm cloud looked like as it boiled up. But it does more; it goes
far to suggest the awe and fright that the storm cloud excited in the mind of
the girl who describes it.

The nature and function of metaphor can be further illustrated from
passages quoted in the earlier chapter on Description. It might be useful
for the student to go back and review some of the descriptive passages
quoted there. He may well be struck with the amount of metaphor in these
passages and also with the *amount of work* that the metaphors actually do.
For a starter, the student might reread the description of the Arabian town
on page 209 where the heat is "like a drawn sword," or the account of
Mr. Chadband on page 210, a man who "moves softly and cumbrously,
not unlike a bear who has been taught to walk upright."

A few paragraphs above we cited a passage written by Helen Keller in
which she gives an account of her sense of touch. We must admit that the
world of Helen Keller's experience is a special world that can be conveyed
to us only through suggestion and analogy. Yet, a little reflection will show
us that the world of experience belonging to each of us is far more special
than we may think, for our world is to a great extent determined by our

values, moods, and emotional biases. The world as seen by the girl watching the storm cloud is special in this sense, and so too is that of Henry Thoreau. If we are to communicate our experience with any accuracy, figurative language is frequently the only way by which we can do so. By means of metaphor we grasp not only the experience as an entity but its "meaning," its value, to us as well.

■ APPLICATION

In the following passage, the author is describing the changes that have oc-curred in a small town as "progress" takes over.

> Apartment houses—regular flat buildings, with elevator service and all that—shoved their aggressive stone and brick faces up to the pavement line of a street where before old white houses with green shutters and fluted porch pillars had snuggled back among hackberries and maples like a row of broody old hens under a hedge. The churches had caught the spirit too; there were new churches to replace the old ones. Only that stronghold of the ultra con-servatives, the Independent Presbyterian, stood fast on its original site, and even the Independent Presbyterian had felt the quickening finger of progress. Under its gray pillared front were set ornate stone steps, like new false teeth in the mouth of a stern old maid, and the new stained glass memorial windows at either side were as paste earrings for her ancient virginal ears. The spinster had traded her blue stockings for doctrinal half hose of a livelier pattern, and these were the outward symbols of the change.
> —Irvin Cobb: "Black and White," *Back Home.*

Is the comparison of the "ornate stone steps" to "new false teeth" an effective figure? Is it merely visual? Or does it do something more? Does it tell us anything about the members of the Independent Presbyterian Church? Their taste? Their attitude toward progress? Their attitude toward religion? Notice that the comparison of the church to an old maid develops into an ex-tended analogy. Is the extension of the figure successful? Write a brief account describing what this figure accomplishes (or fails to accomplish).

What Makes a "Good" Metaphor?

In judging the value of a metaphor, the physical similarity of the items com-pared is easily overestimated. In many finely effective comparisons the degree of physical similarity is not very great. Of course, there must be some element of resemblance. But a good comparison is not necessarily one in which there is close resemblance, since "illustration," as we have seen, is not the primary purpose of metaphor.

The element of similarity in metaphor

To realize this last point, let us consider one of the tritest comparisons of all: "Her eyes were like stars." Far from seeming strained or overingenious, the comparison will seem to most of us entirely too simple and easy. Yet even in this well-worn analogy the objects compared are really very dissimilar. Certainly the human eyeball and the flaming mass of elements that make up the stars have very little in common. If this examination, which compares the two objects as scientifically considered, seems somewhat unfair, we can go on to point out that the eyes, even those of a lovely woman, do not much resemble the glinting points of light that are the stars as we see them. The truth of the matter is that what supports this oldest and most hackneyed of comparisons is not the physical resemblances so much as the associations: the associations of stars with brilliance, with the high and celestial. It is these associations that make the stars seem "like" the glances of the eyes of someone loved.

Thus every comparison has a very important subjective element in it; its proper task is to interpret, to evaluate—not to insist upon physical analogies. Its proper function is, as we have said, to define attitude.

Let us consider a celebrated comic comparison from English literature. In his satire "Hudibras," Samuel Butler describes the rosy sky of dawn:

> . . . like a lobster, boyl'd, the morn
> From black to red began to turn.

We think of this as an absurd comparison, and so it is—appropriately so—for "Hudibras" is a humorous poem, and Butler is casting good-humored scorn upon his hero. Yet it is worth asking why the comparison strikes us as absurd. We are likely to say that it is absurd because the dawn does not in the least resemble a boiled lobster. But the colors to be seen in the shell of a boiled lobster may very closely resemble the exact shade of red to be seen on some mornings. The absurdity does not come from any lack of physical resemblance; it comes from the absurd contrast of the small with the large, the commonplace and homely with the beautiful and grand, the grotesque creature in the steaming pot with the wide, fresh expanse of the dawn sky. Butler has, for humorous effect, deliberately played these elements against each other.

The element of contrast in metaphor

Though we commonly call metaphors (and related figurative expressions) "comparisons," it is plain that we might just as accurately call them "contrasts." For the elements of dissimilarity between the terms of a metaphor may be of quite as much importance as the elements of likeness. One can go further still: in an effective metaphor there must be *some degree of contrast*. If we say "the river roared like a flood" or "the dog raged like a wild beast," we feel that the metaphor is weak or nonexistent. A river is already too much like a flood, and a dog, though a tame beast, too nearly resembles a wild beast. If, on the other hand, we say "the fire roared like a flood" or "the fire raged like a wild beast," we begin to feel some metaphoric force. Even though these are rather poor metaphors, fire and flood or fire and beast are sufficiently dissimilar for us to feel that a degree of metaphorical transfer occurs; in these expressions one discerns the "new namings" that constitute metaphor.

We are usually taught to reject what are rather awkwardly called "far-fetched" comparisons. (The term is awkward because it suggests that the terms of a good comparison are close together, though we have seen that even "eyes" and "stars" are not really very close.) But if comparisons must not be too "far-fetched," neither must they be too "nearly fetched." They have to be fetched some distance if we are to have a recognizable metaphor at all.

The criteria for good metaphor

Because figurative language is such an essential part of effective discourse, it is, as we have seen, easier to indicate what is wrong with a metaphor than what is right with it. Indeed, a brief description of the value of an apt metaphor amounts to little more than the remark that it is properly expressive and plays its due part in the total context. (If we want to say more, and say it in some detail, we shall probably find ourselves discussing the relation of the metaphor to the whole context.) There is no handy list of short rules for determining a good metaphor.

In view of these limiting considerations, perhaps our best procedure is to examine in some detail a variety of metaphors that seem appropriate and successful, plus one or two problem cases that may stimulate us to think further about what makes an acceptable metaphor.

Here is Robert Lowell's picture of the "bleak Revere Street dining room" in which he sat through family Sunday dinners, "absorbing cold and anxiety from the table."

> Here, table, highboy, chairs, and screen—mahogany, cherry, teak—looked nervous and disproportioned. They seemed to wince, touch elbows, shift from foot to foot. High above the highboy, our gold National Eagle stooped forward, plastery and doddering. The Sheffield silver-plate urns, more precious than solid sterling, peeled; the bodies of the heraldic mermaids on the Mason-Myers crest blushed a metallic copper tan. In the harsh New England light, the bronze sphinxes supporting our sideboard looked as though manufactured in Grand Rapids. All too clearly no one had worried about synchronizing the grandfather clock's minutes, days, and months with its mellow old Dutch seascape-painted discs for showing the phases of the moon. The stricken, but still striking gong made sounds like steam banging through pipes. Colonel Myers' monumental Tibetan screen had been impiously shortened to fit it for a low Yankee ceiling. And

now, rough and gawky, like some Hindu water buffalo killed in mid-rush but still alive with mad momentum, the screen hulked over us . . . and hid the pantry sink. —ROBERT LOWELL: *Life Studies.*[7]

In this highly personal account, the very furnishings and decorations behave like human beings: they "look nervous"; they "wince, touch elbows, shift from foot to foot"; they "blush." In short, they reflect all the anxieties of the boy who used to look at them and who now, much later, is describing them. These anthropomorphic metaphors also make vivid the sense of clutter arising from crowding too many heterogeneous pieces into one room. Lowell's climactic figure illustrates this "disproportioned" quality of the décor. (He has said that the furnishings "looked nervous" *and* "disproportioned.") The most imposing piece, the Tibetan screen, has been cut down to fit the "low Yankee ceiling." Now, "like some Hindu water buffalo killed in mid-rush but still alive with mad momentum," it "hulked over us." The comparison does a number of things at once: it gives a dramatic instance of the "disproportioned" quality; it presents the screen as an exotic trophy, captured and maimed though still alive; and it suggests the vague menace that seems to emanate from it.

Metaphor, then, plays an important part in suggesting to the reader the special character and atmosphere of this particular room. Lowell is obviously interested in giving more than a mere factual description of the pieces of furniture and the various *objets d'art.* He presents a *state of mind*—no mere arrangement of domestic possessions.

The example of metaphor, from Lowell, is elaborate and complicated, but a brief, condensed figure can also be thoroughly effective. The hero in one of Reynolds Price's novels clasps the hand of a friend of his mother's. He tells us that it was like touching "a hot little plush unused pincushion." The metaphor is vivid and evocative. It suggests a plump little woman with smooth skin. For some of us it will also suggest the kind of woman who dotes on plush pincushions and has around the house unused, spare ones, never stuck by a pin. (We find out as we read the novel that the character is sixtyish, voluble, kindly, lives alone in her little house, and spends most of her time watching television programs.)

Here is another brief comparison from a piece of fiction. We read in one of Faulkner's early novels that when, toward evening, one of the characters opened the street door, "twilight ran in like a quiet violet dog. . . ." The image of the violet dog is incongruous. True, the general idea does make a kind of sense: dogs do sometimes wait quietly outside a familiar door in the hope that someone will open it and give them the chance to slip in. The twilight in this old city is waiting too, and when the door is opened, it seems to rush quietly into the room. Yet the comparison will probably strike the

[7] Reprinted with the permission of Farrar, Straus & Giroux, Inc., from *Life Studies* by Robert Lowell, copyright © 1956, 1958, 1959 by Robert Lowell. Reprinted by permission of Faber and Faber Ltd.

average reader as "contrived," and not quite worth the effort that has been expended in working it up.[8]

Another metaphor in the same novel, however, will probably win the reader's acceptance. Faulkner describes September as "a month of languorous days as regretful as woodsmoke." Is woodsmoke regretful? That will depend on the reader's own experience and on his own past associations. But the comparison at least makes a strong invitation to the reader's imagination to associate the bluish haze of a September day with the blue of woodsmoke, and the woodsmoke itself with the pensive, even sad, coming of the fall and the ebbing of the year.

As the last two examples probably suggest, metaphor is the particular instrument of poetry. But, as we have seen, it is by no means confined to poetry and, in fact, it is one of the most important resources for the prose writer. It is the best means by which to intimate a mood, to imply the shading of an attitude, and, most of all, to stimulate and involve the imagination of his readers.

Metaphor: the importance of the context

Effective metaphor suits the context in which it occurs. Moreover, an effective metaphor pays its own way—that is, justifies itself by making a real contribution to the writer's total expression. As we have remarked, the violet-dog metaphor may ask more of the reader's attention than it contributes to the meaning of the work. Not every fresh and piquant metaphor is good: contrariwise, not every tame and familiar metaphor is poor. What counts is the "work," in the given context, that each figure performs.

Here is an example. Eudora Welty, in an essay entitled "How I Write," tells us that the inspiration for a story is like "a pull on the line . . . the outside signal that has startled or moved the creative mind to complicity and brought the story to active being. . . ."

Her figure obviously derives from fishing, probably not fly-fishing, but old-fashioned fishing with a baited hook. The tug on the line means that the fisherman has a bite. The metaphor is not new, but the implied analogy is a thoroughly just one. The story lies hidden in the depths of the mind just as the fish lies concealed in the pool. The tug on the line signals no more than a possibility, which may not be fulfilled. In any case, both the fisherman and the fiction writer must exercise skill and have luck in the bargain, if either fish or story is to be landed. One must not jerk the line too quickly and scare the fish away. One has to set the hook and, if the fish is a big fellow,

---

[8] Why isn't this comparison worth the effort? Why should it be labeled "contrived"? These are proper questions, and the student has a right to decide them for himself. But in that case he must look at the context in which the image occurs (*Mosquitoes,* pp. 13–14) and ask himself such questions as these: How does Faulkner lead up to the image? Is it appropriate to Mr. Talliafero (the character in the novel past whom the violet dog runs)? What does the image tell us about Talliafero? What does it accomplish? In terms of setting the atmosphere and mood? The student's final judgment will be in part a subjective one; but so is ours. There is no set formula for deciding the success of a metaphor.

play him carefully before the fish (or story) can be pulled up into the light, seen for what he is, and drawn up safely onto the bank.

Miss Welty merely alludes in passing to this rather complex analogy.[9] But that is, for her purposes, all that she needs to do. The perceptive reader will get the point, probably without any conscious working out of the terms. If he wants to work them out, or if he needs to do so, there is nothing to deter him: the analogy has been honestly used and it supports fully Miss Welty's argument. Why should its familiarity debar it from her use? She hasn't pretended that it was a novel analogy, as her rather glancing reference to it makes plain.

This last example provides an opportunity to stress one more time the supreme importance of the context. Metaphors are related to a total context and contribute to it or fail to do so. They accord with it or they strike a dissonance. Good metaphors contribute their strength to, and draw their ultimate justification from, the whole body of the discourse. They are not isolated sugarplums that have been thrust into the pudding by the writer in the hope that the alert reader will from time to time put in his thumb and triumphantly bring them out with a flourish to prove the writer's ingenuity and his own skill in finding them. They are rather an integral part of a total meaningful discourse or dramatic rendering of an experience.

■ APPLICATIONS

I   The following metaphors may seem to be primarily *illustrative,* that is, the metaphor makes something plain by comparing it with a simpler or more familiar thing. But are they *merely* illustrative? Are any of the metaphors used to *state* a meaning as well as to *illustrate* a meaning? Test them on this point by trying to restate precisely "the thing said" in nonmetaphorical language.

A   On each side of the [bee's] abdomen are four little wax-pockets situated in the joints of the hard-surfaced body; and here the supply of wax may be seen issuing, the flat, light-colored wax appearing somewhat like a letter which a man has tucked up under his waistcoat.
   —Charles D. Stewart: "The Bee's Knees."

B   Intellectual assimilation takes time. The mind is not to be enriched as a coal barge is loaded. Whatever is precious in a cargo is taken carefully on board and carefully placed. Whatever is delicate and fine must be received delicately, and its place in the mind thoughtfully assigned.
   —Arlo Bates: "Reading on the Run," *Talks on the Study of Literature.*

C   Bed is the perfect laboratory—just the right degree of withdrawal from the world, yet with the comforts at hand, and errands delegated to someone else. The toast crumbs, accumulating among the sheets, set up the irritation inside the shell and start the pearl growing.
   —E. B. White: "Peavy, Book and Guitar."

---

[9] One does not have to make a *conscious* elaboration of the pull-on-the-line figure in order to feel it as effective. Moreover, the pull on the line may just possibly suggest to some readers not a hooked fish but the pull of a full bucket in the well or the pull exerted by a fellow mountain-climber on the safety rope.

II Do the authors of the following passages avoid drifting into jargon? In this connection, observe carefully their use of dead metaphor and confused metaphor.

A   Despite the precept that man cannot pull himself up by his bootstraps, psychology shows us that we can make consistent and gratifying gains in the direction of love, warmth, and tolerance.

—Joshua Loth Liebman: *Peace of Mind.*

What is the writer trying to say? That the precept is wrong since it is possible for a man to lift himself toward *love,* merely by using his own resources? Or that to move oneself in the direction of love is not a matter of lifting oneself up by his bootstraps? Or what does he mean? Try to determine what he is trying to say and frame a sentence (with proper metaphors, if possible) that will express his thought.

B   Even with the most virtuous *at the levers,* how can control be exercised for the good of all when there are so many voices emerging from different conditions, inheriting different traditions, committed to different ideals, and demanding different solutions? Every man wants to realize the opportunities of human knowledge, but each is inclined to believe that all will benefit if knowledge is *mobilized* in the service of his ideals and his traditions. Though their own powers are universal, men's values are local and *mired in the mud of history.* Power is too often *untamed by* responsibility to the world.

Few want to *turn back the clock of science and technology.* Most approve the trend toward an integration of the world so that its resources, its experience, its knowledge will be available to everyone, but they do not want to *turn their backs* entirely on the customs, the morals, the language, the institutions which they have inherited from their ancestors. . . . [*Italics ours.*]

—Quincy Wright: "The Universities and the World Order,"

A.A.U.P. Bulletin.

Consider the italicized phrases. Are the metaphors that Wright uses doing any constructive "work"? Or do they obscure the thought?

III Do any of the following metaphors seem far-fetched and extravagant? Do any seem tame and flat? What principle, if any, seems to determine the matter of acceptability?

Are any of the passages ineffective because the metaphors are "mixed"? Is it possible to shift rapidly from one metaphor to another without producing confusion? Are we never to mix metaphor? What principle, if any, seems to determine this matter?

A   The chickens he raised were all white meat down through the drumsticks, the cows were tended like children, and the big ram he called Goliath had horns with a curl like a morning-glory vine and could butt through an iron door. But Dan'l wasn't one of your gentleman farmers; he knew all the ways of the land, and he'd be up by candlelight to see that the chores got done. A man with the mouth of a mastiff, a brow like a mountain and eyes like burning anthracite—that was Dan'l Webster in his prime.

—Stephen Vincent Benét: *The Devil and Daniel Webster.*

B   [From a novel: a young man thinks bitterly of modern-day misuses of the word *love*.]

> So much the worse for prosperous America, sick with the failure built into its own dream (that men are equal, can be equally good); barnacled already, past scraping, with deceit; sinking slowly from the sheer weight of hot air but savagely swelling, a wallowing balloon.
>
> —Reynolds Price: *Love and Work*.

C   We must be vigilantly on our guard to protect our sacred institutions against the boring from within of subversive elements, those blood-thirsty termites who like to fish in troubled waters.   —From a commencement address.

IV   What is the analogical basis for each of the following metaphors? Do you think that the element of likeness is adequate? What is the function of each of these metaphors? What, in other words, does the metaphor accomplish?

A   The furnished room received its latest guest with a first glow of pseudo-hospitality, a hectic, haggard, perfunctory welcome like the specious smile of a demirep.   —O. Henry: "The Furnished Room," *Strictly Business*.

B   [A young man looks at a picture of his mother.]

> . . . her large head tipped back, bright eyes on the flashbulb, mouth wide to laugh or to launch a small joke with a fresh-painted dinghy any moment now, to sweeten the day.   —Reynolds Price: *Love and Work*.

C   [An old woman is dying.]

> Her bones felt loose, and floated around in her skin, and Doctor Harry floated like a balloon around the foot of the bed. He floated and pulled down his waistcoat and swung his glasses on a cord.
>
> —Katherine Anne Porter: "The Jilting of Granny Weatherall."

D   [Stephen Dedalus has an experience that commits him to be an artist.]

> A girl stood before him in midstream: alone and still, gazing out to sea. She seemed like one whom magic had changed into the likeness of a strange and beautiful seabird. Her long slender bare legs were delicate as a crane's and pure save where an emerald trail of seaweed had fashioned itself as a sign upon the flesh. Her thighs, fuller and softhued as ivory, were bared almost to the hips where the white fringes of her drawers were like feathering of soft white down. Her slate-blue skirts were kilted boldly about her waist and dovetailed behind her. Her bosom was a bird's, soft and slight, slight and soft as the breast of some dark-plumaged dove. But her long fair hair was girlish: and girlish, and touched with the wonder of mortal beauty, her face.
>
> —James Joyce: *A Portrait of the Artist as a Young Man*.[10]

---

[10] From *A Portrait of the Artist as a Young Man* by James Joyce. Copyright 1916 by B. W. Huebsch, renewed 1944 by Nora Joyce. Copyright © 1964 by the Estate of James Joyce. All rights reserved. Reprinted by permission of The Viking Press, Inc. Reprinted by permission of Jonathan Cape Ltd., the Executors of the James Joyce Estate, and The Society of Authors as the literary representative of the Estate of James Joyce.

CHAPTER 13

Tone and Other Aspects of Style

Tone as the Expression of Attitude

Every piece of discourse implies a particular situation. A politician is attempting to convince a hostile audience; a mother is attempting to coax a child into doing something that the child dislikes; a legislator who can assume agreements on ends is trying to persuade his colleagues that certain procedures constitute the best means by which to secure these ends. (Even technical treatises, which attempt no persuasion, do imply a special situation; the writer assumes that he is writing for people whose interest in the truth is so absorbing that rhetorical persuasions would be unnecessary and even positively irritating.)

Just as every discourse implies a situation in which the writer is related to his audience, so every discourse also implies a certain tone. This term *tone* is based frankly on a metaphor. We all know how important in speech the tone of voice may be in indicating the precise meaning of the words. For instance, the words *very well* uttered in a certain tone of voice imply enthusiastic agreement, but spoken in another tone of voice they indicate nothing more than surly compliance. The "tone" of a piece of writing, in the same way, may show the writer's attitude, and in so doing may heavily qualify the literal meaning of the words.

The importance of tone is easily illustrated by the misunderstandings that personal letters so often provoke. In conversation, even a rather clumsy and inadequate knowledge of language can be so supplemented by the actual tone of the voice that little serious misunderstanding will occur. But when such a speaker writes a letter—where, of course, the "tone of voice" cannot be actually heard but has to be implied by the words themselves—all sorts of misunderstandings can, and frequently do, occur. The practiced writer, however, is able even in this medium to control what we have called the "tone."

Although we have rarely used the word, we have been dealing with the problem of tone throughout this book. For example, when in the chapter on Persuasion (pp. 178–80) we talked about the occasion of an argument and the right way to present it, we were concerned with the problem of tone. In the chapter on Diction (pp. 298–301) we touched upon the problem of tone when we discussed the associations of words and the way in which certain words are colored by our attitude—the word *cop,* as used to refer to a police officer, and *rube,* as used to refer to a farmer. Again, we saw in the chapter on Metaphor (p. 312) the ways in which comparisons—"He's a square," "She's a doll," "He's a nut"—express our attitudes. All such devices represent means for controlling tone. But tone is more than these devices; it is a pervasive quality that characterizes the whole composition, and it is a matter so important in its own right that it deserves special discussion.

The importance of tone

In most of our writing an important part of what we are trying to "communicate" is our own attitude. This is certainly true of poetry and fiction, but it is also true of most essays, sermons, orations, and letters. It is true too of much of what we are inclined to regard as pure exposition. For even in expository writing the author is rarely content to give us mere facts, or mere propositions. He feels that to do this is to be painfully and technically "dry."

Farley Mowat's narrative about the wolf family (pp. 225–26) will provide an example. As we pointed out on page 227, Mr. Mowat is a biologist, who was employed by the Canadian government to make a study of the wolf. His narrative comes from a book, *Never Cry Wolf,* which was a result of that study. Thus, his overall intention is to present his observations. Yet sticking to scientific observation does not require Mowat either to hold his reader at arm's length or to leave out his personal delight in the behavior of the wolves. His narrative is like that of a friend retelling an amusing experience. The tone may be described as one of friendly and relaxed informality.

What attitude does Mowat adopt toward his reader? How does he envisage his reader? Clearly, he does not expect him to be a professional zoologist. He aims at a general, nonprofessional reader who does not require special rhetorical accommodation as a fellow scientist might. Yet though Mowat does not expect his reader to have technical knowledge, he does obviously assume that the reader is generally well informed about the world that scientists and laymen alike share. If he knows nothing about the behavior of wolves, he does know something about the behavior of dogs and other domesticated animals. He has intelligence and common sense. He can follow a clearly stated argument, though with unfamiliar material he will benefit from concrete illustrations.

Attitude toward subject

There are, of course, subjects that scarcely permit informality of tone, even when being presented to intimates. To take an extreme case, here is a quotation from a sermon by the great seventeenth-century poet and preacher John Donne:

> Make haste to have these spiritual graces; to desire them is to begin to have them: But make not too much haste in the way. Do not think thy self purer than thou art because thou seest another do some such sins as thou hast forborne.
>
> Beloved, at last, when Christ Jesus comes with his scales, thou shalt not be weighed with that man, but every man shall be weighed with God: *Be pure as your Father in heaven is pure,* is the weight that must try us all; and then, the purest of us all that trusts to his own purity must hear that fearful *Mene Tekel Upharsin,* Thou art weighed, thou art found too light. . . .

Donne addresses his congregation intimately and directly. He even calls them "beloved," but no matter how close a relation the preacher assumes to exist, the urgency of the subject forbids informality. He uses simple and realistic language, that is true; but the seriousness of the subject pervades his language.

One is apt to think of death as a subject that always requires seriousness of tone. Banter about a mother's grief for the loss of her son or jesting at the plight of a man condemned to death would indicate that the jester was silly or callous. Yet this is not to say that humor and wit are incompatible with the presentation of even so serious a subject as death. A standard joke is that which tells how a condemned man, being led out to the gallows in the cold dawn, asks for a handkerchief to put around his neck to keep from catching cold. When Mercutio, in Shakespeare's *Romeo and Juliet,* makes a joke about his death wound and says that it is "not so deep as a well, nor so wide as a church door; but 'tis enough, 'twill serve," we are not offended. The condemned man and Mercutio are making light of their own distress. This is a very different matter from someone's making fun of another's agony. Moreover, Mercutio's ability to joke at his own plight has something gallant about it. It works as a kind of understatement, under-cutting the expected note of seriousness.

Levity about serious subjects, then, is acceptable when somehow the writer recognizes his own share, directly or merely by sympathy, in some human situation, and through humor rises above it. For example, jokes, and humor in general, about sex and death are universal; but these are subjects for humor only because they are of universal importance and concern us all. Because we have, with reference to these subjects, enormously compli-cated attitudes, a well-calculated, humorous thrust can sometimes resolve the emotional complication, strike through to a simple attitude, and provide a sudden sense of release in laughter.

Yet we must remember that humor on a serious subject always requires tact and discrimination. It may help us understand the need for tact if we will think of our "writing situation" as analogous to a social situation. (See pp. 18–22.) What kind of reader are we addressing? What can we assume about him? Is he a person who can respond to the humor, or is he a person who will be shocked by it? Sometimes, of course, the writer wants to shock. But then he should ask himself whether he wants to shock just to show off, or whether the shock is to make a point, to bring some new awareness to the reader. And always we can recognize that there are certain situations in which levity can only be offensive and, worse, silly. To take a most extreme instance, it is hard to imagine a person who would show levity in discussing the Passion of Christ. Blasphemy would be, in a sense, comprehensible, for, in a backhand way, blasphemy always recognizes the seriousness of the thing blasphemed. It is like an inverted prayer, we might say. But levity would be incomprehensible.

■ APPLICATION

Student unrest is a serious issue. It is certainly so for university administrators and faculties and of course for most students. Important principles are at stake and passions have run high. Here is the way in which Art Buchwald treats the student revolt in his newspaper column for February 27, 1969.

SON OFF TO CAMPUS WARS; PARENTS SOB

"You'd better get over to the Diamonds' right away," my wife said when I came home the other night.

"What's the trouble?"

"I don't know, but they sounded terribly upset."

I dashed over to the Diamond house and found Larry and Janet in the living room looking as if the world had fallen apart.

"What is it?" I asked.

"Billy got his draft notice," Janet said.

"He's been drafted?"

"It's worse," Larry said. "He's just been accepted for college."

"That couldn't be so bad."

"He's been accepted at the University of Wisconsin," Janet cried.

I didn't know what to say.

Larry shook his head. "You work all your life for your children and then one day, out of the blue, they grab them and that's it."

"But even if they accepted him, he doesn't have to go," I said.

"You don't understand," Janet said. "He wants to go. He said he can't sit at home doing nothing when so many college kids are sacrificing so much on the campuses."

Larry said, "He wants to be where the action is."

"Billy always had a sense of duty," I said.

"I tried to talk him into going into the Army instead," Larry told me. "But he said, 'Dad, I would be shirking my responsibilities. That's the coward's way out. I have to go where my friends are fighting.'"

Janet sobbed, "I told him to go into the Army for four years and then perhaps the fighting on the campuses would be over. But he said, 'Mother, I could never face my children if they asked me some day what I did during the war on campus and I had to tell them I was in the Army while it was going on.'"

"You have to be proud of him," I said.

"What do you mean, proud?" Larry said. "It's foolhardy. He doesn't know what he's getting into. All he sees is the glamor of it. The blue jeans and the dirty sweater and the beard. But I told him there's more to going to college than that. College is a dirty, miserable business, and it isn't just bands playing and flags waving and girls kissing you in the dormitories."

Janet nodded her head sadly. "I guess he saw too many TV programs about college riots and it went to his head."

Larry said, "Even as a little boy he always had his heart set on college. He used to stage sit-ins in the kitchen, and he picketed our bedroom at night, and once he locked his grandfather in the bathroom because his grandfather wouldn't grant him amnesty for using a naughty word.

"I thought it was a stage all kids go through, so I didn't take it seriously. If I had known he was truly thinking of going to college, I certainly wouldn't have encouraged it."

I tried to cheer my friends up. "Maybe he'll be all right. Don't forget, not everybody who goes to college gets arrested. If he comes out of it without a criminal record, it could be a very broadening experience. Why, some kids even get an education from college."

Janet was really crying. "You're just saying that to buck us up. You really don't believe it, do you?"

I looked at the distraught couple. "I have friends at the University of Wisconsin," I told them. "Perhaps I could use my influence to get Billy into night school. Then, at least, he'll be safe." [1]

What is the tone of this short narrative? Does Buchwald take a frivolous attitude toward what is really a matter of grave concern? Does this bit of fantasy strike you as funny or as reprehensible? If you do find it funny, why? Might it seem funny even to an activist student? Why might such a student see the humor in it? What has Buchwald done to ensure that the reader takes it "in the right way"?

So much for possible treatments of an essentially serious issue. For a light subject a light treatment is obviously appropriate. We do not want deadpan solemnity—unless, of course, that solemnity is indeed part of the joke. To look ahead (p. 339), observe the mock-serious, almost mock-heroic, elements in the passage from "Farewell, My Lovely," Lee Strout White's essay on the Model T Ford.

---

[1] "Son Off to Campus Wars; Parents Sob" by Art Buchwald, *Washington Post*, February 27, 1969. Reprinted by permission of Art Buchwald.

Thus far we have concerned ourselves with two extremes: seriousness and levity. Needless to say, there are hundreds of shadings between these extremes. The possible variations of tone are almost infinite.

Attitude toward the audience

Up to this point, we have, for the most part, emphasized tone as indicating the writer's attitude toward his subject, or the attitude that the subject might demand from the writer. But the writer's attitude toward the audience is equally important. It is so important that one can scarcely talk about the attitude toward the subject without drifting over into a discussion of the audience.

Let us suppose that we are writing in support of (or maybe attacking) our country's present policy toward Red China. The subject itself would, of course, allow certain different kinds of tone. We know that there is no merely mechanical equation between subject and tone. But the subject is a serious one, and though humor and satire might enter, flippancy could not. The demands of the subject would, however, be only one consideration in our attempt to find a proper tone. Our presentation of the topic to a friendly audience, one that tended to agree with the basic policy that we were advancing and that merely wanted further clarification, would scarcely be adequate for a hostile audience. We might want to persuade the hostile audience and lead them bit by bit to agreement. We might want to find the common ground (pp. 123–26) and try to show that once they recognize it they will have to follow, step by logical step, to the policy we advocate. We might want to shock the audience into an awareness of the necessity of that policy. We might, in fact, try any number of approaches, and each approach, or combination of approaches, would imply a different tone. And each possible tone would, of course, be different from the tone appropriate to mere explanation that we might use with a friendly audience.

Considerations of friendliness and hostility are, however, not the only ones that determine the writer's attitude toward his audience. The knowledge that a special audience possesses and their interests and concerns are also determining factors. It will make a difference if our essay about our China policy is to appear in a technical journal edited for specialists in political science; or in *Fortune* magazine edited for prosperous businessmen; or on a newspaper editorial page; or in *Harper's Magazine*. It will make a difference if we read a paper on the subject before a college forum, or a California audience with its keen awareness of the Orient, or a midwestern chamber of commerce dinner. The same tone would not necessarily serve for all.

The advertising page will furnish another example of the way in which a writer's attitude toward his audience determines tone. Advertising puts a special premium on catching and holding the interest of the reader. The advertising copywriter who did not understand some of the elementary principles of the control of tone would soon be on his way to the nearest government unemployment relief office.

I Here are the leads into three advertisements in a recent issue of *The New Yorker:*

A   In Palm Beach, the important people will live at The Sun and Surf. . . .

B   Norman Hilton isn't everywhere. Just at the stores that are accustomed to catering to the clothing needs of a select clientele. . . .

C   Sophisticated people like the simplest things. Like the table shown [below], for instance. (Or is it a desk?) It's just a basic rectangle of steel and rosewood. Simple. . . .

What is the basis of the appeal made in each of these advertisements? What attitude toward the reader is implied by this appeal?

II   Tom Cat. A man's cologne for a tiger state of mind. A prestige collection of manly lotions. . . .

Does this advertisement flatter the reader? Promise anything? Capitalize on his sense of inadequacy? Try to state the attitude taken toward the reader.

III   Select five advertisements from current magazines and state the primary basis of the appeal made to the reader. What attitude is taken toward the reader? What statements or devices in the advertisement suggest this attitude?

IV   Reread the student theme "Teachers I Have Known" (pp. 75–76) and imagine that you are writing it for a teacher who you think probably knows something about his subject but who is quite dull in the classroom. Perhaps you might turn in this draft to him as it stands. Perhaps it will not hurt his feelings, or the hurt may actually be good for him. But with him in mind, could you render this theme more persuasive? Try rewriting some sections of it, particularly paragraphs 3 and 4, to see whether you can improve the tone as directed toward the special reader we have described.

Tone as a Qualification of Meaning

We began our discussion of tone with special emphasis on tone as a reflection of the author's attitude—his specification as to how we are to "take" what he is saying. But it should be apparent by now that tone also represents a qualification of meaning—a shaping of what is to be said. Indeed, a little reflection will show that full meaning is rarely conveyed by merely literal statement. In order to understand a letter we find that we must "read between the lines," and we usually discover that if we are to understand fully a conversation with a friend it helps to take into account his tone of voice and facial expression. Tone as a guide to meaning is particularly important in essays that deal with evaluations and judgments.

For example, consider the importance of the tone in the following passage describing the old Model T Ford:

> I see by the new Sears Roebuck catalogue that it is still possible to buy an axle for a 1909 Model T Ford, but I am not deceived. The great days have faded, the end is in sight. Only one page in the current catalogue is devoted to parts and accessories for the Model T; yet everyone remembers springtimes when the Ford gadget section was larger than men's clothing, almost as large as household furnishings. The last Model T was built in 1927, and the car is fading from what scholars call the American scene—which is an understatement, because to a few million people who grew up with it, the Old Ford practically *was* the American scene.
>
> It was the miracle God had wrought. And it was patently the sort of thing that could only happen once. Mechanically uncanny, it was like nothing that had ever come to the world before. Flourishing industries rose and fell with it. As a vehicle, it was hard-working, commonplace, heroic; and it often seemed to transmit those qualities to the persons who rode in it. My own generation identifies it with Youth, with its gaudy, irretrievable excitements; before it fades into the mist, I would like to pay it the tribute of the sigh that is not a sob, and set down random entries in a shape somewhat less cumbersome than a Sears Roebuck catalogue.
>
> The Model T was distinguished from all other makes of cars by the fact that its transmission was of a type known as planetary—which was half metaphysics, half sheer friction. Engineers accepted the word "planetary" in its epicyclic sense, but I was always conscious that it also means "wandering," "erratic." Because of the peculiar nature of this planetary element, there was always, in Model T, a certain dull rapport between engine and wheels, and even when the car was in a state known as neutral, it trembled with a deep imperative and tended to inch forward. There was never a moment when the bands were not faintly egging the machine on. In this respect it was like a horse, rolling the bit on its tongue, and country people brought to it the same technique they used with draft animals.
>
> —LEE STROUT WHITE: "Farewell, My Lovely." [2]

To enjoy the passage just quoted one must be aware that the author laments the passing of the Model T with mock seriousness. The game that the author plays is to invest with literary allusions and sentimental clichés a piece of machinery that seems to belong to a nonliterary and nonsentimental world. Suppose we remove the tone of mock lament and simply state the facts literally and directly. Here is what we might have:

> The new Sears Roebuck catalogue indicates that one may still purchase an axle for a 1909 Model T Ford. But this possibility, though interesting, does not mean that the Model T Ford is any longer an important factor in American transportation. The section of the catalogue devoted to Ford parts, once larger than that devoted to men's clothing, has now shrunk to a single page. No Model T's have been built since 1927, and this model is rapidly disappearing from the American highway.

[2] "From "Farewell, My Lovely," by Lee Strout White, *The New Yorker,* May 16, 1936. This is part of the essay which originally appeared in *The New Yorker.* Reprinted by permission. Copr. © 1936, 1964 The New Yorker Magazine, Inc.

The rewriting, by altering the tone, destroys the humor. It does something more. It destroys a good deal of what the passage "says." For the real content of the passage is the presentation of a certain complex attitude toward some aspects of American life. The author's real concern is with American social history, and he presents that history, not clinically and "sociologically," but affectionately and a little whimsically. The tone, then, is a most important element in "what" the author is saying.

Lest the importance of tone in "Farewell, My Lovely" be thought a special case, consider the importance of tone in the following definition of a weed:

> What is a weed? I have heard it said that there are sixty definitions. For me, a weed is a plant out of place. Or, less tolerantly, call it a foreign aggressor, which is a thing not so mild as a mere escape from cultivation, a visitor that sows itself innocently in a garden bed where you would not choose to plant it. Most weeds have natal countries, whence they have sortied. So Japanese honeysuckle, English plantain, Russian thistle came from lands we recognize, but others, like gypsies, have lost all record of their geographic origin. Some of them turn up in all countries, and are listed in no flora as natives. Some knock about the seaports of the world, springing up wherever ballast used to be dumped from the old sailing ships. Others prefer cities; they have lost contact with sweet soil, and lead a guttersnipe existence. A little group occurs only where wool waste is dumped, others are dooryard and pavement weeds, seeming to thrive the more as they are trod by the feet of man's generations. Some prized in an age of simpler tastes have become garden *déclassés* and street urchins; thus it comes about that the pleasant but plebeian scent of Bouncing Bet, that somewhat blowsy pink of old English gardens, is now one of the characteristic odors of American sidewalk ends, where the pavement peters out and shacks and junked cars begin.
>
> —DONALD CULROSS PEATTIE: *Flowering Earth.*[3]

We could describe a weed as follows:

> A weed may be defined as a plant that, though growing in cultivated ground, is economically useless and is a detriment to the crop being cultivated. Yet, it must be conceded that this definition is somewhat subjective, for a plant considered useless by one person might be counted useful by another, and a plant ordinarily cultivated for its own sake might be regarded as a nuisance when found in a field planted to some other crop. But there is general agreement on most of the plants that we call weeds. Some examples would be dog fennel, dock, mullein, and ragweed.

This paragraph may be thought to give substantially the same definition as that given in the paragraph by Peattie. But it is relatively toneless. The author is not visualizing any particular audience, and he does not seem to have a particular attitude toward his subject. As a consequence, this paragraph is quite without personality.

---

[3] From *Flowering Earth* by Donald Culross Peattie. Reprinted by permission of Noel R. Peattie and his agent, James Brown Associates, Inc. Copyright © 1939 by Donald Culross Peattie.

Notice how much of the writer's personality comes through in the original passage. Peattie is obviously familiar with the various "flora" and knows which plants are listed in them and which are not. But his discussion is not intended to be a technical description; rather it is a more desultory and amiable account of weeds. Peattie is a man of perception, with keen senses ("the pleasant but plebeian scent of Bouncing Bet," "the characteristic odors of American sidewalk ends"). He evidently has a sense of humor. He is aware of current politics ("foreign aggressor"). He has a sense of history.

In short, in this passage we get the play of an informed and sensitive mind—a mind that special knowledge has not made stuffy—and of a personality that savors, with evident enjoyment, the varied and amusing world. In this connection notice how a central metaphor that treats the weed as a human being who has broken bounds runs through the whole passage, and how this metaphor is varied through the passage to express the varying aspects of weeds in general and of certain weeds in particular. One weed may be like a "foreign aggressor" to be resisted; another, like an immigrant or colonist from another land; still another, like a gypsy whose original homeland is lost in obscurity. Some weeds, like groups of immigrants, remain near the seaports where they made their first entry. Other weeds have migrated from country to city. They have moved in from the provinces and have become citified and now lead a "guttersnipe" existence. Still other weeds are like human beings who have come down in the world and, having lost pride of class and dignity, are now happily and frowsily plebeian. The general comparison of the weed to the human migrant is flexible enough to provide quite specific illustrations of the various kinds of weeds. The metaphor not only renders the abstract definition concrete, but it suggests Peattie's own attitude toward weeds and, in fact, the world in general—an attitude of genial and good-humored amusement.

Notice, too, how the diction unobtrusively but powerfully supports the variations of the basic metaphor. "Foreign aggressor" is pointed up by the use of the word "sortied." (The word *sortie* means a sally of troops, a military raid.) "Guttersnipe existence" sharpens the hint given by "others prefer cities." "Plebeian" and "somewhat blowsy" support and extend the suggestions made by *"déclassés."*

The diction, of course, does something more. Though Peattie is willing to use a technical term like *flora,* most of his words are specific and concrete. Moreover, he does not hesitate to use colloquial expressions like "knock about" and "peters out." Peattie is not at all like the fabled scholar who knew all the pedantic terms but could not address a dog in his own dialect. He accommodates his diction to the wholesome vulgarity of his subject.

The preceding discussion of Peattie's paragraph may seem overelaborate, but it is usually difficult to define a particular tone without using many more words than the author himself used to achieve it. There is, moreover, a justification for the attention that we have given to this one paragraph. We have wanted to illustrate the fact that a particular tone depends upon various factors—diction and metaphor as well as the larger principles of composition. Tone, indeed, represents a kind of final integration of all the elements that go into a piece of writing. Writing that is toneless or confused in tone is usually bad writing.

■ APPLICATIONS

I Art Buchwald ends a protest against a proposal to ground airline stewardesses at the age of thirty-two with the following paragraphs:

> Younger stewardesses also have a tendency to upset the passengers. Many times I've witnessed wives becoming furious at their husbands because the husbands were watching a pretty young thing in uniform strut down the aisle. I've also seen grown men upset trays of food, just because some young hostess leaned over to adjust their safety belts. But nothing happens with the older, more mature hostesses. They have the air of a professional nurse about them. Your eyes don't have to stray from your magazine every time they walk by. You can keep your thoughts on where you're going and what you're going to do.
>
> And one more thing. Older hostesses know how to cook better. Have you ever compared a meal prepared on board a plane by a twenty-one-year-old hostess with one prepared by a thirty-two-year-old hostess?
>
> There is just no comparison.
>
> There are many of us flying today who are not interested in looking at a young, pretty, sexy girl in uniform. We believe in chic older women in their thirties.
>
> I sincerely hope American Airlines reconsiders its policy almost as much as I hope my wife reads this.[4]

How would you describe the tone? What are some of the ways in which Buchwald lets you know that his "protest" is very much tongue-in-cheek?

II For what audience is the following paragraph written? Has the audience been visualized by the writer? Could it be said that the writing is "toneless"? If so, is its tonelessness a defect or a virtue?

> Before intelligent criteria can be developed for the selection of superimposed leaders, the organization, through its professional staff, must first clearly define the objectives of its group program and establish qualifications for group leadership. Second, these objectives must be made clear to the leaders. In group work terminology the concept *socialization* appears as the central objective, but in the experience of the writer little effort has been made to define this concept so as to be understandable to the leader.
>
> —From a magazine of social research.

---

[4] Reprinted by permission of The World Publishing Co. from *I Chose Capitol Punishment* by Art Buchwald. Copyright © 1962, 1963 by Art Buchwald. Reprinted by permission of Art Buchwald.

Literal statement and ironical statement

Irony always involves a discrepancy between what is said literally and what the statement actually means. On the surface the ironical statement says one thing, but it means something rather different. In a lighthearted, laughingly ironical statement, the literal meaning may be only partially qualified; in a bitter and obvious irony (such as sarcasm), the literal meaning may be completely reversed. An example of rather lighthearted and affectionate irony occurs in the discussion of the Model T Ford by Lee Strout White above. The little car is treated in almost mock-heroic style ("It was the miracle God had wrought. . . . it was patently the sort of thing that could only happen once. . . . before it fades into the mist, I would like to pay it the tribute of the sigh that is not a sob. . . ."). The informal essay frequently makes use of some form of gentle irony such as this.

A sample of ordinary sarcasm might be represented by a student's outburst at his roommate: "A fine friend you turn out to be, borrowing my car and taking my girl on a date." The literal meaning that proclaims the roommate to be a fine young man is just the opposite of what his irate friend means to say about him.

Between the more delicate ironical qualifications and the sarcastic reversal there are a thousand shadings possible, and it may seem a pity that we do not have specific terms by which to describe them. Yet, on second thought, our lack of such terms may be no real handicap. We can develop these qualifications of meaning without in the least needing to give them a label. Having a glossary of terms is not important; what is important is to be aware of the fact of ironical qualification.

The following passage is from a review of Gertrude Stein's account of her own life in a book entitled *Everybody's Autobiography*. The review was written by Katherine Anne Porter, the short-story writer and novelist.

> Still earlier she was a plump solemn little girl abundantly upholstered in good clothes, who spent her allowance on the works of Shelley, Thackeray, and George Eliot in fancy bindings, for she loved reading and *Clarissa Harlowe* was once her favorite novel. These early passions exhausted her; in later life she swam in the relaxing bath of detective and murder mysteries, because she liked somebody being dead in a story, and of them all Dashiell Hammett killed them off most to her taste. Her first experience of the real death of somebody had taught her that it could be pleasant for her, too. "One morning we could not wake our father." This was in East Oakland, California. "Leo climbed in by the window and called out that he was dead in his bed and he was." It seems to have been the first thing he ever did of which his children, all five of them, approved. Miss Stein declared plainly they none of them liked him at all: "As I say, fathers are depressing but our family had one," she confessed, and conveys the notion that he was a bore of the nagging, petty sort, the kind that worries himself and others into the grave.
>
> Considering her tepid, sluggish nature, really sluggish like something eating its way through a leaf, Miss Stein could grow quite animated on the

subject of her early family life, and some of her stories are as pretty and innocent as lizards running over tombstones on a hot day in Maryland.

—KATHERINE ANNE PORTER: *The Days Before.*

In this passage there is, to be sure, a certain amount of perfectly direct commentary. But what gives the passage its biting power is the calm assumption by the author that what she is describing in Miss Stein's conduct is somehow perfectly characteristic of her. The tone of detached, clinical commentary sets up an ironic contrast with the material that is actually under discussion and so becomes powerfully expressive. (Incidentally, is "sluggish" a pun? If you judge that it is intended to be one, do you think it is justified here?)

● CAUTION

The effectiveness of writing in which the tone is skillfully controlled by a master of style may so impress a young writer that he will try to exercise the same kind of subtlety. And well he may, in aspiration at least, for skillful management of tone is an ideal toward which he should strive. But a successful manipulation of tone does not come easy, and in his early efforts at more subtle tonal effects the novice may blunder into awkwardness or into an irony that seems too contrived and "cute." He must be cautious about going beyond his own resources at the beginning. Even so, it will not hurt for him to begin to experiment with indirection and the oblique approach. Besides, he is no stranger to irony as a mode. He has been using it in conversation all his life. Slang and college repartee, for example, are full of irony and sarcasm.

■ APPLICATIONS

I The following paragraph occurs in Thackeray's novel *Vanity Fair:*

> Being an invalid, Joseph Sedley contented himself with a bottle of claret, besides his Madeira at dinner, and he managed a couple of plates full of strawberries and cream, and twenty-four little rout cakes, that were lying neglected in a plate near him, and certainly (for novelists have the privilege of knowing everything), he thought a great deal about the girl upstairs. "A nice, gay, merry young creature," thought he to himself. "How she looked at me when I picked up her handkerchief at dinner! She dropped it twice. Who's that singing in the drawing-room? Gad! shall I go up and see?"

What is Sedley's attitude toward himself? Toward food? Toward girls? Has Thackeray, by pretending to take Sedley's invalidism seriously, given us an insight into what kind of young man he is?

II The scene described below is a British club in India, some decades ago. The orchestra has just played "God Save the King." What is the author's attitude toward his fellow countrymen? The passage is obviously ironic, but what is the precise shading of irony? Is the author indignant? Mocking? Bitter? Or what?

Meanwhile the performance ended, and the amateur orchestra played the National Anthem. Conversation and billiards stopped, faces stiffened. It was the Anthem of the Army of Occupation. It reminded every member of the club that he or she was British and in exile. It produced a little sentiment and a useful accession of will-power. The meager tune, the curt series of demands on Jehovah, fused into a prayer unknown in England, and though they perceived neither Royalty nor Deity they did perceive something, they were strengthened to resist another day. They poured out, offering one another drinks. —E. M. Forster: *A Passage to India.*

What does Forster mean by the "series of demands on Jehovah"? (Are you familiar with the words of "God Save the King"?)

III In Application IV (p. 338), you were asked to rewrite sections of the student theme "Teachers I Have Known" (pp. 75–76), in order to make the theme more persuasive. Now let us consider the possibility of making the tone ironical. As it now stands, the theme shows traces of irony. For example, the student asks: "Did they become teachers because they were really interested in their subject and in young people, or did they just drift into the profession through indifference or necessity?" But in general, the judgments are given directly and explicitly. Would there be any advantage in presenting the judgment against such teachers indirectly and ironically? Try rewriting this theme, making use of an ironical approach. Pretend, for example, that you are praising all teachers; or try to give a deadpan account of the teachers' faults as if you did not realize that they were faults.

Overstatement and understatement

We have been occupied with the distinction between a literal and a nonliteral (including an ironic) use of words. But it is also useful to consider the problem of tone in the light of another distinction, that between overstatement and understatement. Overstatement, as the term implies, is redundancy: one says more than he needs to say. The term connotes gushiness —a straining after effects. In Bret Harte's story "The Outcasts of Poker Flat," a gambler and two prostitutes rise to heroism as they try to shelter and protect an innocent girl who has fallen into their company when they are overtaken by a severe snowstorm in the mountains. The gambler and the older prostitute starve themselves in order to provide more food for the young woman. In the last two paragraphs of the story, which follow, Harte describes the last days of the innocent girl and the younger prostitute.

> The wind lulled as if it feared to waken them. Feathery drifts of snow, shaken from the long pine boughs, flew like white-winged birds, and settled about them as they slept. The moon through the rifted clouds looked down upon what had been the camp. But all human stain, all trace of earthly travail, was hidden beneath the spotless mantle mercifully flung from above.
>
> They slept all day that day and the next, nor did they waken when voices and footsteps broke the silence of the camp. And when pitying

fingers brushed the snow from their wan faces, you could scarcely have told from the equal peace that dwelt upon them which was she that had sinned.

Here the author, in his eagerness to describe the pathos of the scene and the redemption of the fallen woman, is not content to let the scene speaks for itself. The wind lulls the two women; the moon looks down upon them; a "spotless mantle" is "mercifully flung from above." The pseudo-poetic language, the suggestion that nature mercifully hides "all human stain," the general absence of restraint and reserve—all indicate that the tone here is one of *sentimentality;* that is, emotion in excess of the occasion.

What was Bret Harte's own attitude? One has to conclude that either he himself was "soft" (that is, that he was taken in by his own attempt to "work up" an effect), or else he was cynically trying to seduce his reader into an emotional response that is not justified by the dramatic occasion that he provided. Whatever Harte's attitude, most sensitive readers will feel that the tone is sentimental. Sentimentality usually betrays itself by a straining to work up the reader's feelings. In a sense, of course, any appeal to our emotions represents an attempt to "work up" an effect. But it is one thing to do this legitimately by presenting a scene with imaginative power, and it is quite a different thing to try to bully or trick the reader into the desired emotional response. Readers may disagree on whether a particular response has been sought legitimately or illegitimately, but the principle involved is crucial. Otherwise any writer, however tawdry or mawkish, could demand our response simply by making a direct assault on our feelings.

The student may feel that in the kind of writing that he does there is little danger of his falling into sentimentality; and it is quite true that the particular temptations to which Bret Harte yielded are not likely to entrap him. But student themes present their own opportunities for overwriting. The theme in which a student tries to describe his grandfather and his mother (pp. 58–59) will illustrate. A few phrases like "the dearest Mom in all the world" would alter the effect much for the worse. The student's affection for his mother emerges quite clearly, but he lets us infer it from the way in which he writes about her. (The student themes quoted earlier in this text are in general admirably free from gush.)

We must not, however, associate overwriting merely with the softer emotions of love and pity. It can show itself in a strained attempt at humor or a hectic gaiety or a pretentious heartiness. Advertising copy will provide obvious instances (see pp. 338 and 348).

■ APPLICATION

The following is a paragraph from a late Victorian novel. A little boy who has brought a ray of sunshine into his wicked uncle's life has been asked by the dying man to watch beside his bedside.

When the first faint streaks of early morning entered slowly at the half-curtained window, and chased away the shadows of the night, they fell upon a strange sight in the great silent room! An old man with motionless and pallid features, lying with his head turned a little to the light, and his hands crossed upon his breast,—the pitiful remnant of a worn-out and bootless life; and near him, in the deep arm-chair, a beautiful sleeping child, with bright hair falling loosely about his neck, and rosy rounded cheeks, and warm, moist dimples,—a soft, living, breathing creature, in the full flush of health and youth; the very symbol of life, as it lay there side by side with Death!
—Marguerite Bouvet: *A Little House in Pimlico.*

Count the adjectives in this passage. Why are so many used? Could it be that the author is straining for an emotional effect not really warranted by the occasion? What other evidences of sentimentality are present?

THE VIRTUES OF UNDERSTATEMENT

Overstatement usually suggests a writer's lack of confidence in himself or in his reader. He is afraid to let his account speak for itself. Understatement, by contrast, assumes that the reader is sufficiently sensitive to make the proper response. Consequently, in skillful hands, understatement can become a powerful device for securing certain effects.

The rhetorical device of understatement is one that the student will constantly be using in his own work. It has already appeared in some of the student themes that we have read in earlier sections of this book. (See pp. 37, 58, and 239.) For example, in the student theme "Getting Engaged" (p. 204), the basic technique is that of understatement. The writer's fear at the coming of the storm and her excitement at the dangerous trip from the island to the mainland are merely implied. The writer has preferred to "understate" both of them. She has chosen to convey her own emotions about the former by giving us a detailed description of the storm cloud and then a detailed description of Joseph's face as he watches it. About her excitement at the perils of the trip home, she writes merely this:

> To make a long story short, we did manage to get in, but it was a tough trip. That evening we got engaged.

The engagement is the climax of the events of the day. Therefore, the writer has quite properly insisted upon putting it into sharp focus. But the mere announcement of the engagement is all that we need to know, for obviously it was the experience of real danger shared that made the young people realize that they wanted to spend the rest of their lives together.

The foregoing remarks should not leave the student with the feeling that he ought not to write as vividly as he can about exciting experiences. But first things should come first, and underplaying certain aspects of a composition may be a necessary way of putting certain other aspects into proper focus. Understatement is, among other things, a means of bringing about a proper proportioning of the various elements of the composition.

The problem of tone, then, is most important. There are obviously too many shadings of tone for us to be able to set down elaborate rules for achieving the proper tone. But it is possible to set down a few "don'ts" that have very general application.

1 WRITING DOWN One must not "write down" to his audience. The sense of oversimple statement and painfully careful explanation can disgust the reader as quickly as any offense of which the writer is capable. Prose that is properly suited to an audience of eight-year-olds would prove completely tiresome or, on the other hand, unintentionally funny, to a mature audience. Take into account your reader's lack of special knowledge of your subject, but never underestimate your reader's intelligence. Don't explain your jokes.

2 FALSE ENTHUSIASM The reader is also likely to resent any hint of artificial breeziness and false camaraderie. Modern advertising leads the way in perpetuating this fault. Bug-eyed young matrons oo-la-la-ing over the purchase of sheets or toothbrushes and the synthetic joviality of supersalesmen fill advertisements. The student obviously wishes to gain a kind of liveliness and warmth in his style, but an artificial concoction of informality and sprightliness can be more depressing than a rather painful dryness.

3 SENTIMENTALITY This third fault is hardly likely to appear in most simple expository writing, but as we have seen in earlier chapters, there is very little writing that is "simply expository." Sentimentality may show itself as pure gushiness or as a kind of hair-trigger emotional sensitiveness. But whatever form it takes, sentimentality always involves an implied demand on the part of the writer for a greater emotional response than the situation warrants; and it implies, on the part of the sentimental reader, a willingness to respond emotionally when the response is not actually justified.

Rhythm and Clarity of Meaning

Earlier in this chapter (p. 332) we pointed out that the term *tone* itself is derived from the speaking voice. We said that the tone of one's voice frequently qualifies the literal meaning of what is being said—sometimes can even reverse it—and that in general the tone of voice constantly indicates how the hearer is to "take" the meaning of the statement. Prose rhythm, too, is closely related to the living voice and, as we shall see, like the voice itself can make important qualifications of meaning. The pauses we make and the stresses we place upon particular words affect meaning.

In committing his thoughts to writing a man deprives himself of the resources of gesture, facial expression, tone of voice, natural pause, and emphasis—all of which are part of actual conversation. Yet, as we have remarked in connection with the discussion of tone (p. 332), this deprivation need not be crippling. Nor need it be so with reference to rhythm. By a sound choice and arrangement of the words that he sets down, the writer may achieve an expressive management of this important element. But before we get to the subject of rhythm, let us look at some examples of what the living voice can achieve in the way of emphasis. Consider the following simple sentence: "Are you going to town?" If we stress the word *are,* the sentence becomes an emphatic question; and if we stress it heavily, it may even suggest surprise. But if we stress *you,* the question then centers on whether it is *you* who are going rather than someone else. If we stress *town,* we get a third variation; the question now has to do with the destination.

Thus the rhythmic inflection of a sentence, with its lighter or heavier stresses on particular words, is a very important way in which we express our meanings. When we put the sentence on paper, we can, of course, indicate some of this stress by underlining the words to be emphasized. But mere underlining is a relatively crude substitute for the living voice, and it is the mark of a clumsy writer to have to rely upon constant underlining. The writer, by his control of the rhythms of his sentences, should be able to suggest where the proper emphases are to fall. Rhythm also suggests pauses in the sentences. Punctuation (as we learn from grammar school onward) is another device for signaling pauses, but punctuation is effective only when it follows the natural pauses coincident with rhythm and emphasis. Punctuation that denies, and even contradicts, the natural units of thought—the natural pauses—is badly done even when it is "grammatically" correct.

Like tone, rhythm is the result of the interplay of various elements. On page 282 we suggested some of the ways in which Donald Peattie varied his sentence patterns to avoid monotony and thus achieved—though we did not there use the term—a more varied rhythm. (We might compare this passage with another paragraph by the same author on page 340. There we pointed out Peattie's management of diction and metaphor to establish a particular tone.) Because both tone and rhythm involve the simultaneous control of diverse elements, there is no neat set of rules which will guarantee an appropriate tone or a harmonious rhythm. In fact, tone and rhythm come close—each in its own way—to embodying the very spirit of the work in question. Rhythm in particular resists complete analysis, though a reader with any fineness of discrimination can readily sense it.

Nevertheless, control of rhythm, difficult though it may be to achieve by mere rule, is very important for clarity of meaning. This fact is illustrated by the muddled and monotonous rhythms of technological jargon. Look back at Maury Maverick's example of gobbledygook and at the example of academic jargon on page 305. Prose of this sort is, for a variety of reasons, difficult to read. It is fuzzy, abstract, and dull. It lacks flavor. But it lacks clarity as well; for there are no natural emphases, no obvious points of primary stress, and often no natural pauses.

The student may feel that any conscious attempt to achieve a particular rhythm—let alone that of heightened prose—is simply out of his range. The student may well be right. In any case, we have full sympathy for any shrinking from the artificial and the mannered. Our concern in *Modern Rhetoric* is practical: we assume that most readers of this text want to form a simple natural style—not a highfalutin style.

Yet a concern for rhythm is in one important aspect thoroughly practical. As we have already remarked, a too monotonous rhythm or a limping rhythm signals that something is amiss with the structure of one's prose. The student should test his composition by reading it aloud, and as he reads it, listen for the jangling discord or the halting rhythm that signals something in the sentence is awry.

This test of reading aloud is particularly useful in the proper disposition of modifiers, adverbial phrases, and the like. (See pp. 271–74.) The student may find that reading his composition aloud and "listening" to it may be the most practical way of detecting sentence elements that have not been placed in their best order. The following sentence will illustrate:

> Oriental luxury goods—jade, silk, gold, spices, vermillion, jewels— formerly had come by way of the Caspian Sea overland; and a few daring Greek sea captains, now that this route had been cut by the Huns, catching the trade winds, were sailing from Red Sea ports and loading up at Ceylon.

The sentence is passable, and is perhaps not noticeably unrhythmical. But if we read this sentence in the form in which Robert Graves actually wrote it, we shall find that it is not only clearer, it is much more rhythmical and much easier to read:

> Oriental luxury goods—jade, silk, gold, spices, vermillion, jewels—had formerly come overland by way of the Caspian Sea and now that this route had been cut by the Huns, a few daring Greek sea captains were sailing from Red Sea ports, catching the trade winds and loading up at Ceylon.

On pages 315–16 we discussed the incoherence of a passage occurring in Liebman's *Peace of Mind*. We commented in particular on the number of dead and all-but-dead metaphors. But the passage is also incoherent rhythmically. The theme is serious, the subject matter suffused with emotion, and the passage is obviously intended to appeal to our emotions, but the rhythm is broken and halting.

■ APPLICATION

The following paragraph describes the author's trip down the Yangtze River in China:

> . . . there were still the rapids, though the more dangerous rocks had now been blasted. The dreadful sucking water, with its visible, audible sucks and hisses, was still the most fearfully alive water I have seen. From what seemed most hideous depths came another skin of water, welling up and swishing itself upon the surface into a carapace design, like a turtle's back, an outline of diamond shapes, and at each angle a hole formed and sucked back into

itself, sucking back the dissolving diamond; a little farther bubbles pouted, pouting, spurting, then breaking open; and up welled and surfaced out another hexagonal animal skin. It took little time to be persuaded that one was riding the back of a prehistoric monster, whose skin wrinkled and relaxed while the monster shuffled about. A faint froth, a scarcely perceived rock just breaking the surface; and there were the whirlpools and the sudden notion that water and sky were swivelling round an almost unperceived centre of light delicate froth, which softly, softly, began its inward funnel, sucking one back into the depths from where all this came up; and this went on all the time, for two hundred kilometres of the gorges.

—Han Suyin: *The Crippled Tree.*[5]

Do you find this passage difficult to read aloud? Does it seem rhythmically disordered? Has the author tried to imitate the sounds of the rapids? Are the rhythms of the prose calculated to suggest the chaotic flow of the stream? If you think this was the writer's intention, was she, in your opinion, successful?

Is sentence 3 improved by rewriting it as follows?

Out of what seemed most hideous depths arose another skin of water, welling up, swishing around, and forming upon its surface an outline of diamond shapes, a carapace design, like the shell of a turtle. At the angle of each diamond shape, a hole opened, a funnel-shaped whirlpool, that sucked back into the depths of the stream the dissolving diamond. A little further on, bubbles pouted—pouting, spurting, then breaking open—once more turning the surface of the stream into a hexagonal-figured beast's shell or skin.

Has the rewritten sentence a smoother rhythm? Is it easier to understand? Is it better organized—grammatically and rhetorically?

Try to rewrite the rest of the passage.

Style

The reader of this text may be surprised to find that the term *style* is now appearing for the first time. He might well have expected a long discussion of style much earlier in the book. But though the term is mentioned here for the first time, actually, from the very first page of this book, we have been discussing style. The plan for conducting an argument or presenting a piece of exposition, the means for connecting paragraph with paragraph, the choice of diction, the handling of tone—all are aspects of style. Style is an overall effect: the style of a piece of prose is determined by the interplay of all sorts of elements—sentence structure, descriptive patterns, figures of speech, rhythm, and so forth. Indeed it is not always easy to pick out of a particular passage just those elements that are most important in giving the style of the writer its special quality. Such elements cannot be

[5] From *The Crippled Tree* by Han Suyin. Reprinted by permission of G. P. Putnam's Sons, publishers. Reprinted by permission of Jonathan Cape Ltd.

measured out by formula: it's quite impossible for a writer to produce a given quality of style by mechanically blending so much of this element with so much of that. A modern author puts the matter in this way: "Style is not an isolable quality of writing; it is writing itself."

So far in this chapter we have seen how difficult it is to isolate and determine the specific value of each of the factors that control tone and rhythm. And it would be much more difficult to accomplish this with respect to style in general, which is a larger concept and represents the interplay of all sorts of elements, including tone and rhythm themselves. There is no one proper shape for a sentence or length for a paragraph nor one "correct" diction. The "correctness" will depend on the occasion and the writer's purpose and the context in which the word or sentence is placed. Sometimes, as we have seen earlier, a sentence consisting of one word or a paragraph of one sentence or, with reference to diction, a slang phrase or a worn cliché may actually be the proper choice. As we have said many times in the preceding pages, it is the particular context that determines what is appropriate, and style itself is a harmonious interplay of all the elements and devices of writing.

Yet, though "style is not an isolable quality of writing," there are, nevertheless, a few *general* comments that may be worth putting on record. First, style is never to be thought of as a mere veneer, a decorative surface laid over the content. In a piece of writing, form and content interpenetrate each other and are finally inseparable.

Thus, we do not put the case accurately when we say that a writer's task is to seek a proper form—that is, a proper "container" into which to put what he wants to say. For a writer often does not know precisely what he wants to say until he has found the proper form in which to put it. (At the very beginning of this book [p. 3] we recalled the story of the old lady who, when asked to say what she meant, replied: "But how can I know what I mean till I say it?") Form and content are indeed closely related—change "how" a thing is said and you have changed, even if only so slightly, "what" is said.

Second, just because in a good style the thing said and the way of saying it are inseparable, a defective style—what we call a "bad" style—always reveals itself in some cleavage between the thing said and the saying— the content and the form. There is a disharmony between what the writer has actually put on the page and what we infer—from the existing discrepancies and disharmonies—he actually meant to say. In other words, the discordant elements call attention to themselves—they "stick out." [6]

---

[6] One must be careful to distinguish between the contradictions and confusions of a defective style and the discrepancies that one notices in an ironic statement. As we observed earlier (pp. 343–44), irony does involve a discrepancy between what is apparently said and what is actually meant. But any confusion in the reader's mind usually lasts only for a moment. He catches on that the writer is speaking ironically, and the ironic discrepancy thus proves to be a device under the writer's control—not an ineptitude. The ironic writer knows very well what he wants to say, but he is getting at his meaning *indirectly* and *obliquely*.

Originality

Finally, we ought to say something about originality. For we are constantly told that originality is the hallmark of a good style, and we are further told that the writer ought to be himself—to express his own personality—in all that he writes. One recalls Buffon's famous remark that "the style is the man." This is all very true: but the student needs to be warned against any excessive straining for originality. Instead of urging the novice writer to try to impress his unique self on his work, it is better to remind him that he will find not only what he really wants to say but also his true self through a process of exploration. Fortunately, the right kind of originality, the impress of one's unique personality, can be left to take care of itself provided that the writer manages to take care of what he can consciously control in his composition. For a style, as we have earlier remarked, is not a mere veneer; it is rather the informing principle of content. Thus a good style is bound to carry the impress of the writer's personality. Every tree in the forest has its own grain and the special quality of that tree—its unique grain pattern—will show through any honest piece of furniture made from its wood.

■ APPLICATIONS

I The following are general questions that the student should ask himself as he considers the passages quoted below.

1   What is the author's attitude toward the reader? In what way is this shown?
2   What is the author's attitude toward his material?
3   Are there any instances of sentimentality? In what way is it revealed? Are there any instances of other kinds of overstatement? Is the overstatement justified or unjustified?
4   Which of the passages, if any, makes use of understatement?
5   Do any of the passages make use of irony? Try to characterize the kind of irony in each case—sarcasm, light mocking irony, bitter irony, gay irony, and so on.
6   Are there any passages that are relatively toneless? Are there any that are confused in tone?

A   [The mate] felt all the majesty of his great position, and made the world feel it, too. When he gave even the simplest order, he discharged it like a blast of lightning, and sent a long reverberating peal of profanity thundering after it. I could not help contrasting the way in which the average landsman would give an order with the mate's way of doing it. If the landsman should wish the gang-plank moved a foot farther forward, he would probably say: "James, or William, one of you push that plank forward, please"; but put the mate in his place, and he would roar out: "Here, now, start that gang-plank for'ard! Lively, now! What're you about! Snatch it! There! There! Aft again! aft again! Don't you hear me? Dash it to dash! are you going to sleep over it! 'Vast heaving. 'Vast heaving, I tell you! Going to heave it clear astern? *Where're you going with that barrel! for'ard with it 'fore I make you swallow it, you dash-dash-dash-dashed* split between a tired mud-turtle and a crippled hearse-horse!" I wished I could talk like that.

—Samuel L. Clemens: *Life on the Mississippi.*

Characterize the tone of the mate's speech. Characterize the author's attitude toward the mate. Be as specific as you can.

B   It wasn't the bully amateur's world any more. Nobody knew that on armistice day, Theodore Roosevelt, happy amateur warrior with the grinning teeth, the shaking forefinger, naturalist, explorer, magazine writer, Sundayschool teacher, cowpuncher, moralist, politician, righteous orator with a short memory, fond of denouncing liars (the Ananias Club) and having pillowfights with his children, was taken to the Roosevelt hospital gravely ill with inflammatory rheumatism.

Things weren't bully any more;

T. R. had grit;

he bore the pain, the obscurity, the sense of being forgotten as he had borne the grilling portages when he was exploring the River of Doubt, the heat, the fetid jungle mud, the infected abscess in his leg.

and died quietly in his sleep

at Sagamore Hill,

on January 6, 1919

and left on the shoulders of his sons

the white man's burden.

—John Dos Passos: "The Happy Warrior," *1919.*[7]

C   No man could have been more bitter against opponents, or more unfair to them or more ungenerous. In this department, indeed, even so gifted a specialist in dishonorable controversy as Dr. [Woodrow] Wilson has seldom surpassed him. He never stood up to a frank and chivalrous debate. He dragged herrings across the trail. He made seductive faces to the gallery. He capitalized his enormous talents as an entertainer, his rank as a national hero, his public influence and consequence. The two great law-suits in which he was engaged were screaming burlesques upon justice. He tried them in the newspapers before ever they were called; he befogged them with irrelevant issues; his appearances in court were not the appearances of a witness standing on a level with other witnesses, but those of a comedian sure of his crowd. He was, in his dealings with concrete men as in his dealings with men in the mass, a charlatan of the very highest skill—and there was in him, it goes without saying, the persuasive charm of the charlatan as well as the daring deviousness, the humanness of naiveté as well as the humanness of chicane. He knew how to woo—and not only boobs. He was, for all his ruses and ambuscades, a jolly fellow.

—H. L. Mencken: "Roosevelt: An Autopsy," *Prejudices: Second Series.*[8]

[7] From *1919*, second volume of *U.S.A.* by John Dos Passos. Published by Houghton Mifflin Company.

[8] From "Roosevelt: An Autopsy" by H. L. Mencken. Reprinted from *Prejudices: Second Series* by H. L. Mencken, by permission of Alfred A. Knopf, Inc. Copyright 1920 by Alfred A. Knopf, Inc. Copyright 1948 by H. L. Mencken.

Both Dos Passos and Mencken exhibit definite attitudes toward Theodore Roosevelt; compare and contrast them. How does the attitude in each case color the writer's account? Cite specific instances.

II A The worst experience I ever had was being trapped in a cave. The idea of being all alone and in the dark and unable to move is enough to make most grown men afraid, and I was only fourteen. Even though the chances were I'd be found soon, I couldn't be dead sure. But I kept my head and this probably saved me from serious injury. The doctor said later that if I had tried to pull my foot loose I probably would have injured it severely. It was bad enough as it was, and the sprained ankle kept me on crutches for several weeks. My friends began kidding me about them after a while, but I think it's better to be safe than sorry. The doctor had told me to use the crutches as long as I wanted to.

B Getting trapped in a cave is no fun, but it's not the worst thing that can happen to you if you keep your head. After telling myself over and over "Keep your head, now," it struck me that it wasn't my head I was in danger of losing, it was my foot. I had to laugh, even in the fix I was in, and started telling myself, "Keep your foot, now." It sort of cheered me up and kept me from doing anything stupid.

When it was all over, people kept saying, "I'll bet you were scared to death." And my mother, after she got over her crying spell, would say, "Jimmie's not scared of anything." They were both wrong. I was scared, all right, but I kept seeing the funny side of it.

How would you characterize the tone of the first version? Of the second? Finish the account of the experience, continuing the tone of the first or the second version. Attempt to rewrite this account, giving it still another tone— say one that might be used by a much younger child, or by a philosophical old man.

III A Dear Phyllis,

Laura tells me that you are thinking of joining us on our trip through the South. I hope you can, though I wish you could have decided earlier. I will write Aunt Agnes and Mrs. Stillwell and ask them if they can find a bed for you, too. But I hope you're not expecting a deluxe suite!

I can't imagine why your mother and father should have any objections. After all, we're old enough to take care of ourselves, though our parents are a little stuffy about admitting it. I'm really looking forward to being off on our own for once.

If you do decide to come, please try to be polite to Doris. I know she gets in your hair, but after all, she's my cousin and there's no use starting trouble for me.

Love,
Evelyn

How would you characterize the writer of this letter, judging from the tone? Would the letter persuade Phyllis to go on the trip? Would it persuade her parents? Can you rewrite the letter, using a more persuasive tone?

B   Dear Phyllis,

Laura tells me that you are thinking about joining us for our trip through the South. I gather that you are all for it and it's just a question of whether your parents approve. Knowing them as I do, I'm sure they will not decide this arbitrarily. My mother, too, was a little leery at first, but after I had gone over all our plans with her, she agreed that they were perfectly sound.

The fact that we have a new car, which should eliminate any road trouble, and the fact that we'll be staying with relatives or friends every night convinced her that we'll be perfectly safe.

I remember so well the trip I made with you and your family when we were children. The old Chevrolet may have had its weak moments, but your father's ingenuity and good spirits kept us all going merrily along—to say nothing of your mother's unerring ability to spot the perfect place for stopping each night. I hope our trip turns out to be half as much fun as that one. Please give my love to everyone.

                                                                            Evelyn

Compare the tone of this letter with that in the letter above. How would you characterize the tone here? What objections is it designed to overcome? Is it designed to be shown to Phyllis's parents? If there were no parental objection to be overcome, how differently could the ideas of the letter be expressed? Try to rewrite it.

IV The two passages that follow describe scenes in the Arabian desert. The scenes are different: that by Hichens pictures a minaret and palm trees caught in a windless noon; that by Lawrence, a desert landscape, now green from recent rains. Yet the descriptions do have certain things in common, including a curiously similar way of describing the wind: "The slight winds were not at play" and "Playful packs of winds came crossing . . ." What decisively differentiates the two passages is the quality of mood, atmosphere, and tone.

Write a brief essay in which you compare and contrast the style of these two passages. Does either author make you see, vividly and clearly? Does either of them try to add a mystical element to the scene? How? Is the effort successful? Is there any straining for particular effects? Does either writer exploit suggestion? Is either passage "sentimental" and overstated? Compare the use of metaphor and rhythm in the two passages. Compare also the attitude taken toward the subject and toward the reader. In your essay be specific and give examples.

A   It was noon in the desert.

The voice of the Mueddin died away on the minaret, and the golden silence that comes out of the heart of the sun sank down more softly over everything. Nature seemed unnaturally still in the heat. The slight winds were not at play, and the palms of Beni-Mora stood motionless as palm trees in a dream. The day was like a dream, intense and passionate, yet touched with something unearthly, something almost spiritual. In the cloudless blue of the sky there seemed a magical depth, regions of color infinitely prolonged. In the vision of the distances, where desert blent with sky, earth surely curving up to meet the downward curving heaven, the dimness was like a voice whispering strange petitions. . . .   —Robert Hichens: *The Garden of Allah.*

B   . . . every hollow [was] a standing pool, and the valley beds of tall grass [were] prinked with flowers. The chalky ridges, sterile with salt, framed the water-channels delightfully. From their tallest point we could look north and south, and see how the rain, running down, had painted the valleys across the white in broad stripes of green, sharp and firm like brush-strokes. Everything was growing, and daily the picture was fuller and brighter till the desert became like a rank water-meadow. Playful packs of winds came crossing and tumbling over one another, their wide, brief gusts surging through the grass, to lay it momentarily in swathes of dark and light satin, like young corn after the roller. On the hill we sat and shivered before these sweeping shadows, expecting a heavy blast—and there would come into our faces a warm and perfumed breath, very gentle, which passed away behind us as a silver-grey light down the plain of green. Our fastidious camels grazed an hour or so, and then lay down to digest, bringing up stomach-load after stomach-load of butter-smelling green cud, and chewing weightily.

—T. E. Lawrence: *Seven Pillars of Wisdom*.[9]

[9] From *Seven Pillars of Wisdom*, by T. E. Lawrence. Copyright 1926, 1935 by Doubleday & Company, Inc. Reprinted by permission of the publisher.

PART FOUR

THE RESEARCH PAPER

CHAPTER 14

Preparation and Note-Taking

Most of the longer papers that the student will be asked to write in his college courses will be research papers.[1] That is, the student will be asked to make a study of some particular subject, to assemble materials, organize them, and incorporate them into a unified composition, with footnotes to indicate his authority for the various statements that he makes.

The research paper is a form, and a most important form, of expository discourse. We may want to investigate hydroponics or the architecture of Crusader castles or the history of a literary movement or the Battle of Hastings or the present-day do-it-yourself vogue or a thousand and one other things. But at the end of our research, after we have read our books and magazines or have gone on our field trips or carried out our experiments in the laboratory, there remains the problem of organizing the results. Our facts and opinions need to be organized so as to present their meaning as lucidly and as tellingly as possible. Even if our investigation has been extensive and thorough, it may be wasted if we present its fruits in a muddled and confusing form.

Such a muddled presentation may indeed mean that we ourselves do not know what to make of the facts we have discovered. For facts do not automatically crystallize about a meaning. We have to find what the facts mean, and this involves thinking about them, analyzing them, and working out their implications. The problems to be faced then are those that we have already studied in earlier chapters. We shall need all we have learned about exposition and argument, including definition, classification, comparison and contrast, the various kinds of analysis, the nature of evidence, and

---

[1] For a discussion of the Book Report, Summary, and Précis, see Appendix, pp. 422–25.

the principles of induction and deduction. Sometimes a piece of description may be called for; or we may need to narrate the story of a man, an event, a process, or a development. We should, therefore, by this time already know a great deal about the methods involved in working out a research paper; and by the same token, the research paper should provide us at this point with a fine opportunity to review what we have learned.

Sources

The aim of the research paper is to assemble facts and ideas from various sources, and by studying them, to draw new conclusions or to present the material in the light of a new interest. For instance, a military historian who wanted to understand why General Lee lost the Battle of Gettysburg would study the written records of orders and events, the correspondence and memoirs of witnesses, the actual terrain, and the interpretations of other historians. In the light of that evidence, he would try to frame an explanation. Or a literary critic who wanted to understand why a certain novelist often used certain themes would study the facts of the novelist's life as found in whatever sources were available (letters, memoirs, public records, biographies), the kind of education he received, the kind of ideas current in his particular place and time, and so forth. Such material would be his evidence. The researcher might discover new facts, and new facts can easily upset old theories. But he might have to depend on facts that were already available but were available only in scattered sources. Then his task would be to collect these facts and shape them into a new pattern of interpretation.

The professional historian or literary critic writing a book and the student writing a term paper use the same basic method: they collect the facts and interpret them. The term paper can be intelligent, well informed, interesting, and original. To make it so, the student must be systematic.

The first step toward making his paper systematic is to learn how to investigate his subject. There are two kinds of sources that he can use: primary and secondary. The historian going to the order book of a general or the terrain of a battlefield, the anthropologist observing the Indian tribe, or the literary scholar studying the manuscripts or letters of an author are using what are called *primary sources;* that is, firsthand information, the original documents. The college student must usually use *secondary sources;* that is, secondhand information, a report on, or analysis of, the original documents. He reads the report of the anthropologist or he studies an edition of a poet prepared by a scholar. There are also *tertiary sources*— the digest of, or commentary on, the anthropologist's report (e.g., *The Reader's Digest* and *The Book Review Digest*). The student should not use these unless he cannot get access to the secondary or primary sources. Even when he has no choice but to cite a tertiary source, he should do so with great caution. Get as close to the facts as possible. No matter how good your reasoning is, it is useless if the facts on which it works are not dependable.

Bibliography

The research paper, we have said, draws its material from many sources. It is not a digest of one book or article. But how do you get at the useful sources?

Reference books are a good starting point. Some of the more important reference books are listed below (with abbreviated entries).

GENERAL DICTIONARIES (UNABRIDGED)

Dictionary of American English. 4 vols. 1936–44.
Funk & Wagnalls New Standard Dictionary. 1964.
Oxford English Dictionary. 12 vols. and supplement. 1933.
Webster's Third New International Dictionary. 1966.

SPECIAL DICTIONARIES

Evans, Bergen and Cornelia. *A Dictionary of Contemporary American Usage.* 1957.
Follett, Wilson. *Modern American Usage, A Guide.* 1966.
Fowler, H. W. *Dictionary of Modern English Usage.* 2nd ed. rev. 1965.
Morris, William and Mary. *Dictionary of Word and Phrase Origins.* 3 vols. 1962–71.
Partridge, Eric, ed. *Dictionary of Slang and Unconventional English.* 1961.
Roget's Thesaurus of Words and Phrases. 3rd ed. 1962.

GENERAL ENCYCLOPEDIAS

Encyclopedia Americana. 30 vols.
Encyclopædia Britannica. 24 vols.

Note: Each of these encyclopedias publishes an annual supplement, which should be consulted for additional, recent information.

Americana Annual. 1923–.
Britannica Book of the Year. 1938–.
New International Year Book. 1907–.

ATLASES AND GAZETTEERS

Atlas of World History (Palmer). 1957.
Chamber's World Gazetteer. 1954.
Columbia Atlas. John Bartholomew, ed. 1954.
Columbia Lippincott Gazetteer of the World. 1952.
Encyclopædia Britannica World Atlas. 1954.
Goode's World Atlas. 12th ed. 1964.
Hammond's Ambassador World Atlas. 2nd ed. 1961.
Times (London) *Atlas of the World.* 5 vols. 1955–59.
Webster's Geographical Dictionary. Rev. ed. 1969.

YEARBOOKS—CURRENT EVENTS

American Yearbook. 1910–19, 1925–50.
Information Please Almanac. 1947–.
Statesman's Year-Book. 1864–.
Statistical Abstract of the United States. 1878–.
World Almanac. 1868–.
Yearbook of World Affairs. 1947–.

GENERAL GUIDES

Besterman, Theodore. *A World Bibliography of Bibliographies.* 4 vols.
   3rd ed. rev. 1955–56.
Books in Print, an index to the *Publishers' Trade List Annual.* 1957–.
Publishers' Trade List Annual. 1873–.
Textbooks in Print. 1956–.
United States Catalog: Books in Print. 4th ed. 1928.
   Supplement: *Cumulative Book Index.* A World List of Books in the
   English Language. 1898–.
Winchell, Constance M. *Guide to Reference Books.* 8th ed. 1967. Sup-
   plements.

GENERAL PERIODICAL INDEXES

Book Review Digest. 1905–.
Book Review Index. 1965–.
International Index to Periodicals. 1963–64.
New York Public Library Index. 1942.
New York Times Index. 1913–.
Poole's Index to Periodical Literature. 2 vols. 1802–1907.
Reader's Guide to Periodical Literature. 1900–.
Standard Periodical Directory. 1964/65–.
Ulrich's Periodicals Directory, A Classified Guide to a Selected List of
   Current Periodicals, Foreign and Domestic. 10th ed. 1963.

SPECIAL REFERENCES

Agriculture

Agricultural Index, 1916–64.
Bailey, L. H. *Cyclopedia of American Agriculture.* 4 vols. 1917.
U.S. Department of Agriculture. *Yearbook of Agriculture.* 1894–.

Art and Architecture

Art Index. 1929–.
Chamberlain, Mary Walls. *Guide to Art Reference Books.* 1959.
Fletcher, Banister. *A History of Architecture.* 17th ed. rev. 1961.
Gardner, Helen. *Art Through the Ages.* 5th ed. 1970.
Penguin Dictionary of Architecture. 1966.
Year's Art. 1880–1947. Annual.

Biography

Biography Index. 1947–.
Contemporary Authors. 1962–.
Current Biography. 1940–.
Dictionary of American Biography. 20 vols. 1928–37. Supplements.
Dictionary of National Biography (British). 22 vols. 1885–1949.
Directory of American Scholars. 5th ed. 1969.
Webster's Biographical Dictionary. 1969.
Who's Who. 1849–.
Who's Who in America. 1899–.

Business

Munn, Glenn G. *Encyclopedia of Banking and Finance.* 6th ed. 1962.
Prentice-Hall *Encyclopedic Dictionary of Business Finanace.* 1960.
Schwartz, Robert J. *The Dictionary of Business and Finance.* 1954.
U.S. Department of Commerce Publications. 1952.

Classical Literature and Mythology

Avery, C. B., ed. *New Century Classical Handbook.* 1962.
Feder, Lillian. *Crowell's Handbook of Classical Literature.* 1964.
Harvey, Sir Paul. *Oxford Companion to Classical Literature.* 1937.
Oxford Classical Dictionary. 1949.
Peck, Harry Thurston. *Harper's Dictionary of Classical Literature and Antiquities.* 1962.

Education

Ebel, Robert L. *Encyclopedia of Educational Research.* 4th ed. 1969.
Education Index. 1929–.
Monroe, P. *Cyclopedia of Education.* 5 vols. 1911–13.
Standard Education Almanac. 1968–.

History

Adams, J. T. *Dictionary of American History.* 6 vols. 1942–61.
Cambridge Ancient History. 12 vols. Rev. 1961–65.
Cambridge Medieval History. 8 vols. 1911–36.
Cole, Donald B. *Handbook of American History.* 1968.
Langer, William L. *An Encyclopedia of World History.* 4th ed. 1968.
The New Cambridge Modern History. 14 vols. 1957–70.

Literature

Bartlett's Familiar Quotations. 1955.
Brewer's Dictionary of Phrase and Fable. 1953.
Cambridge History of American Literature. 4 vols. 1917–21.
Cambridge History of English Literature. 15 vols. 1907–27.
Cassell's Encyclopedia of World Literature. 2 vols. 1953.
English Association. *Year's Work in English Studies.* 1920–.
Hart, James D. *Oxford Companion to American Literature.* 4th ed. 1965.
Harvey, Sir Paul. *Oxford Companion to English Literature.* 4th ed. 1967.

New Century Handbook of English Literature. 1956.

Oxford History of English Literature. 12 vols. 1945–63.

Reader's Encyclopedia of American Literature. 1962.

Smith, Horatio, ed. *Columbia Dictionary of Modern European Literature.* 1947.

Spiller, R. E., and others. *Literary History of the United States.* 3rd ed. rev. 2 vols. 1963.

Stevenson, B. E. *Home Book of Quotations.* 9th ed. rev. 1964.

Music

Apel, Willi. *Harvard Dictionary of Music.* 2nd ed. rev. and enlarged. 1969.

Baker, Theodore. *Biographical Dictionary of Musicians.* 5th ed. 1958.

Grove's Dictionary of Music and Musicians. 5th ed. 9 vols. 1954. Supplement, 1961.

Music Index. 1949–.

Scholes, P. A. *Oxford Companion to Music.* 9th ed. 1955.

Thompson, O. *International Cyclopedia of Music and Musicians.* 9th ed. 1964.

Ulrich, Homer, and Pisk, Paul. *A History of Music and Musical Style.* 1963.

Psychology

Drever, James. *A Dictionary of Psychology.* 1964.

Psychological Abstracts. 1927–.

Psychological Index. 42 vols. 1894–1935.

Religion

New Catholic Encyclopedia. 15 vols. 1967.

Cross, F. L. *The Oxford Dictionary of the Christian Church.* 1961.

Hastings, James. *Dictionary of the Bible.* 5 vols. 1898–1904.

Hastings, James, ed. *Encyclopedia of Religion and Ethics.* 12 vols. 1908–27.

Universal Jewish Encyclopedia. 10 vols. 1939–43.

Science and Technology

American Men of Science. 11th ed. 1968. Supplements.

Applied Sciences and Technology Index. 1913–.

Engineering Index. 1884–.

Hawkins, R. R. *Scientific, Medical, and Technical Books Published in the United States of America.* A Selected List of Titles in Print with Annotations. 1930–44. Supplements, 1950, 1953.

Henderson, I. F., and Henderson, W. D. *Dictionary of Scientific Terms in Biology, Botany, Zoology, Anatomy, Cytology, Embryology, Physiology.* 8th ed. 1963.

McGraw-Hill *Encyclopedia of Science and Technology.* 15 vols. 1960.

McGraw-Hill *Yearbook of Science and Technology.* 1969.

Van Nostrand's Scientific Encyclopedia. 4th ed. 1968.

Reference books are so numerous and sometimes so specialized that it is often helpful to consult the *Guide to Reference Books,* by Constance M. Winchell, to know where to go in the first place.

The reference book will give an introduction to a subject and certain basic facts. Best of all for the student, it will usually offer a bibliography, a list of other works on the subject—books or articles less limited in scope than the treatment in the reference book itself. With this as a starting point the student can make up his own *working bibliography* for his subject. As he reads more about his subject, he will encounter references to other works, and can gradually extend the range of his working bibliography. The subject catalogue of the library will also provide new items.

The working bibliography should be kept on convenient cards of uniform size, with only one entry to a card. This allows the student to arrange them in alphabetical or other order (by topics, for example), according to his need. The entry on the card should contain all the basic information about a book or article: the author's name with the last name first, the title of the work, the volume number, if any, the place of publication, the publisher, the date of publication. If the work appears in a periodical or collection, that fact should be indicated with the volume number, the date, and the pages occupied by the work.

This form of card entry is to be retained in making up the final bibliography to be attached to your finished paper. There the order will be alphabetical by authors. Your final bibliography may be shorter than your working bibliography, for the final bibliography should contain no entry from which you have not taken material for the actual paper, whereas certain items in your working bibliography may have been dropped as more valuable items came to light.

ENTRY FOR A BOOK

> Strachey, Lytton. <u>Elizabeth and Essex.</u> London: Chatto and Windus, 1928.

ENTRY FOR AN ARTICLE

> Barrington, Margaret. "The Censorship in Eire," <u>Commonweal,</u> XLVI (August 15, 1947), 429-32.

What items should be included in the student's working bibliography? The professional scholar may want to work through all the material on his subject, but the student preparing a term paper scarcely has the time for such a program. Many items in the bibliographies he encounters are antiquated or trivial. So to save his time and energy, he should try to select the items that will best repay his attention. There is no rule for selecting a bibliography. The student, however, can sometimes get ideas from a similarly selected bibliography in a textbook or other book on his subject. Sometimes an author will refer with special respect to certain other works on his subject. The student can also take his working bibliography to his instructor and ask for comment.

Notes

Unless you take notes on your reading you will probably not be able to remember much of the relevant material and will certainly not be able to organize it well when you write your paper. If you have taken your notes carefully, you will be able to lay out before you the whole subject and put it in order. In this way the paper will almost write itself. If the notes are to give you the most help, they must have a convenient mechanical form. Notes can be put on note cards (usually 4″ x 6″ or 5″ x 7″). Not more than one note, however brief, should be on a card. This rule should be strictly adhered to, even when the notes are on the same topic; for when you take the notes, you cannot be sure in what order you will eventually use them. Only if each note is independent can you arrange them in the order desired when you write your paper. Each note should carry at the top, at the left, or toward the center, some indication of the precise content—not the general subject of your investigation, but some subtopic. And at the top right or at the bottom, the note should carry an adequate reference to the source from which it is drawn. Presumably the full bibliographical information about that source is already in your working bibliography, and so some skeleton notation will be adequate here. (When you are taking notes not related to a working bibliography—when, for example, you are doing general reading—you should record full bibliographical information with the note.) See specimen card on the following page.

When we look at the actual note on the card we see that several other phrases might have been used to indicate the topic discussed; for instance, "American business mysticism," or "American materialism." All that is needed is a word or phrase that will remind the note-taker of the content. We notice, too, that after the direct quotation there is a parenthesis with the page number. The note-taker apparently feels that this is a telling phrase worth remembering and perhaps using. If he quotes it, he will want the exact page reference.

As for the bibliographical indication at the upper right, he might have reduced it simply to "Chesterton" if there was no Chesterton other than G. K. Chesterton in his bibliography and no other book by that author.

```
American success worship                    Chesterton, What I
                                            Saw in America,
                                            pp. 107-10.

American worship of success not materialistic.  Fact
of worship means a mystic rather than a materialist.
Frenchman who saves money to retire and enjoy his ome-
let more of a materialist.  American does not work for
the enjoyment of things, but for some ideal vision of
success.  He does not want the dollar for what it will
buy but as a symbol.  Phrase "making good" illustrates
the fact; carries a moral connotation by a "sort of
ethical echo in the word" good  (p. 108).  Not neces-
sarily an admirable morality, but a morality implied,
and idealism of a kind.
```

This, like the topic indication, is for his own convenience and need tell no more than he himself has to know to identify the source.

So much for the mechanics of note-taking. As for the process, you should make your notes relevant, accurate, and clear. To make them relevant you must keep constantly in mind the main purpose of your investigation. You are studying a particular subject with particular limits. (Remember in this connection what was said on pages 10–11 with regard to a "true subject.") You are not concerned with anything only casually associated with the subject. If, for instance, you are reading a general history to find information on the subject of the economic background of the American Revolution, you should not be distracted by the military strategy of the French and Indian War or an analysis of Puritan theology. Your job is to follow your main purpose through a body of various materials, and often what is major for you will be minor in the work you are investigating.

It is possible to take notes prematurely. Therefore, it is always best to become acquainted with a work before you take notes from it. In your first reading you may indicate material for possible notes and pass on. When you have finished the work, or those parts relevant to your interest, you can then better assess the material for possible notes. In this way you will get from any particular work only the most pertinent notes, and you will avoid duplication.

The note itself may be direct quotation or summary. If direct quotation is used, it is sometimes valuable to record the context of the quotation. What leads the author to make his statement? What point does he try to establish by it? You do not want to misinterpret your author by implication. For instance, suppose a critic should write:

> Although Herman Melville has created in Captain Ahab of *Moby Dick* a character of intense interest and monumental proportions, he has in general little sense of the shadings of personality and motive. Most of his creations are schematic, mere outlines without flesh. He lacks that basic gift of the novelist, a sense of character.

If you, assembling material for a paper on Melville as a novelist, should merely quote, "Herman Melville has created in Captain Ahab of *Moby Dick* a character of intense interest and monumental proportions," you would have a misleading note. An accurate note would run something like this:

> Even though this critic believes that Melville in general lacks a sense of character, he admits that Captain Ahab is a "character of intense interest and monumental proportions."

This principle of context holds good for both the note by summary and the note by quotation.

When you are taking notes by summary, the kind of summary to be used depends on the special case. In one case, the author's method of reasoning may be very important, and then the summary should be of a form to indicate the logical structure of the original text. In another case, where mere facts or scattered opinions are involved, the summary need record merely these facts and opinions. As for the scale of the summary, there is no guiding principle except the note-taker's need. Try to forecast what you will need when you actually come to write your paper; not merely what you will want to incorporate in the paper, but what you will need in order to understand your subject fully.

Once your notes are taken, how do you use them?[2] This again depends on the kind of subject with which you are dealing. Some subjects suggest a chronological order, others a logical order. For instance, if you are doing a paper on Keats's development as a poet, you might first arrange your notes chronologically—notes on early poems, notes on middle poems, notes on late poems. But if your subject is an analysis of the themes of Keats's poems, you might try to arrange your notes by themes, trying various classifications until you have one that seems to make sense. Or you might find, sometimes, that two levels of organization are necessary. For instance, certain themes of Keats's poems might be characteristic of certain periods. Then having established one type of classification (by theme), you might run another type (by chronology). Notes are flexible. You can use them as a device to help your thinking or to help you organize your material.

Notes record questions and issues. The different authors you have consulted have had individual approaches to the general subject, different interests, different conclusions. As you work over your cards you can locate these differences and try to see what they mean to you in your special project. Ask yourself if there is any pattern of disagreement among the authors you have consulted. List the disagreements. Are they disagreements of fact or of interpretation? Compare the evidence and reasoning offered by the authors who are in disagreement. Can you think of any new evidence or new line of reasoning on disputed points? Can you think of any significant points not discussed by your authors? What bearing would such points

---

[2] At this point it might be useful for you to look back over Chapter 3, Organizing the Composition.

have on their conclusions? Again, use your notes as a device to help your thinking.

The Outline

The outline has two uses. It can help the writer to organize his own thoughts and lay a plan for his work before he begins the actual paper. And it can help the reader to define the basic meaning and structure of what he reads. The two uses have much in common, for both mean that the maker of the outline is dealing with the structure of a discourse. In fact, once an outline is completed, an observer might not be able to tell whether it was designed by a writer or a reader.

Types of outlines

There are several common types of outlines: (1) the suggestive, or scratch, outline, (2) the topic outline, (3) the sentence outline, and (4) the paragraph outline. Variations may be worked out for special purposes.

1 **The Scratch Outline** The scratch outline is a set of notes and jottings that may be useful either for writing or for understanding and remembering what one has read. It is probably not highly organized. For instance, the student, in making a preliminary survey of his notes, may simply put down the various topics and ideas that come to him in the order in which they come. As some line of thought begins to emerge, he may indicate this, too. But his primary purpose is not to define the form and order from the beginning. It is to assemble suggestive material from his notes. He may not use some of it because, in the end, it may seem superfluous or irrelevant. The scratch outline embodies the early exploration of a subject and may be meaningless to everybody except the maker of the outline. (For an example of a scratch outline see pp. 383–84.)

2 **The Topic Outline** The topic outline does indicate the order of treatment of individual topics and does indicate in a systematic fashion, by heads and subheads, the relation among the parts in degree of importance. But as the name indicates, it proceeds, not by sentences, but by listing topics. There is, however, one exception: the outline should be introduced by a statement of the theme of the paper in the form of a fully rounded sentence. Let us set up a topic outline based on the student theme, "Why I Am for Joint Dormitories" (pp. 134–36).

> *Proposition:* Joint dormitories are desirable because they prepare for life.
> I. Aim of education to prepare for life
>   A. Acquisition of knowledge and skills
>   B. Learning to live with people
>   1. Girls as intellectual stimulus
>   2. Need for regular presence of girls

II. Objections to joint dormitories
   A. Distraction
   B. Morality
   C. College role *in loco parentis*

The student should understand that the headings in this outline do *not* correspond to paragraph divisions. One heading, for example, may correspond to only one paragraph; another heading may cover several paragraphs. That is, the outline is not by paragraphs but by topics. Not infrequently we find that a topic that looms very important in the outline will correspond to only part of a paragraph in the text. The outline indicates the relative importance of a topic and not the amount of space devoted to it.

   3 **The Sentence Outline** The sentence outline is the most complete and formal type. Here, every entry is in the form of a complete sentence. As with the topic outline, the entries in the sentence outline should correspond to the content and the order of arrangement in the text. The sentence outline differs from the topic outline in indicating more fully the content of each item and the relation among the items. To fulfill these requirements, the sentences should be very precise and to the point. Vague statements defeat the very purpose of the sentence outline and make such an outline look like merely an inflated topic outline. For the sentence outline should really take us deeper into the subject, defining the items more closely and indicating the structure more fully. By and large, the topic outline will serve for fairly simple material, the sentence outline for more complicated material. In setting up a sentence outline, main heads should be given Roman numerals; the subdivisions, scaling down in importance, should be marked *A, 1, a.* A dummy form will make the system clear:

    I. ....
      A. ....
         1. ....
           a. ....
           b. ....
         2. ....
           a. ....
           b. ....
      B. ....
         1. ....
           a. ....
           b. ....
         2. ....
   II. ....
      A. etc.

It is important to keep the indentations on the left margin consistent in each class and to be sure that a class of lower importance is more deeply indented than the class just above it. If more subdivisions are needed than are indicated here, the system can be begun over again with the key numerals and letters in parentheses. For instance, if subdivisions are needed under *a,* we can use *(I), (A), (1),* and so forth. But for ordinary purposes such an extension is rarely necessary.

Here is an example of a sentence outline made up from the student theme, "Teachers I Have Known" (pp. 75–76):

> *Statement:* Teachers can be divided into two groups—those who are interested and those who are not.
> I. Some teachers did not choose but simply drifted into the teaching profession.
> A. Certain teachers lack interest in their subject matter and these hold boring classes.
> B. Others actually hate teaching.
> II. Other teachers did choose their profession through interest in their subject or students.
> A. Some of these are intensely interested in their subject.
>   1. Some are poor communicators but their courses are worthwhile.
>   2. Others are good at putting ideas across.
> B. Other teachers are especially interested in students.
> C. A third kind of interested teacher is unfortunately an indoctrinator, having an *idée fixe* on a particular topic and the urge to insist upon it.

4 The Paragraph Outline In the paragraph outline each sentence corresponds to a paragraph in the text. In dealing with a very obviously organized piece of writing, the paragraph outline may be composed of the topic sentences, or adaptations of the topic sentences, of the paragraphs. (It is possible, of course, to make a paragraph outline of entries that are not complete sentences, but such a paragraph outline would have little utility. It would consist of little more than suggestive notes for paragraphs.) In dealing with other kinds of writing, however, it is necessary to summarize for each paragraph the content and intention. The paragraph outline has a very limited utility. On the one hand, in dealing with work composed by someone else, the paragraph outline often misses the real logical organization; for, as we have seen, paragraphs do not necessarily represent logical stages. On the other hand, in dealing in a preliminary way with material about which one intends to write oneself, not only may the outline fail to indicate the logical organization desired, but it may be arbitrary and misleading. It is very hard to predict the paragraph-by-paragraph development of any relatively extensive or complicated piece of work. To try to do so sometimes cramps and confuses the writer in the actual process of composition. The paragraph outline is chiefly valuable as a check on your own writing. In trying to make a paragraph outline of one of your own compositions, you may discover that some of your paragraphs have no proper center or function, and thus you may be led to revise.

Here is a sample of a paragraph outline taken from the student theme, "What Is a Good Coach?" (pp. 90–91).

> I. A coach is a special kind of trainer.
> II. The coach has to bring the player's body into peak condition for the particular sport he coaches.

III. The coach has to make the individual players into a team.
IV. The coach has to inspire the players' confidence in him and in themselves, a confidence that can even survive defeat.
V. Conclusion: Our Coach Hadley is a good coach.

Outlining the research paper

By working over your notes and thinking about ideas suggested in them, you will probably strike on some vague general plan for your paper. But do not commit yourself to the first plan that comes into your head. Consider various possibilities. Then when you have chosen the most promising, try to work up an outline on that basis. You will undoubtedly start with a scratch outline, the barest shadow of the paper you want to write. By checking back on your material you can begin to fill in the outline and determine the relation among the facts and ideas you wish to present. Perhaps a topic outline will serve your purpose, but at some stage a sentence outline will probably be helpful, for to make it you will have to state clearly and exactly what you mean.

Once you have an outline prepared, you can begin the actual composition. Use your outline as a guide, but do not consider yourself bound by it. As you write, new ideas will probably come to you, and if they are good ideas you should revise your outline to accommodate them. The outline is not sacred. Like your notes, it is simply a device to help you think. And remember that your paper should be a fully rounded composition, unified and coherent, emphasizing matters according to the scale of their importance. The outline is, in fact, only a start toward creating a fluent, well-proportioned discussion.

Your paper should be more than a tissue of facts and quotations from your notes. It should represent your handling of a subject and not a mere report on what other writers have said. Naturally, a large part of your material will be derived from other writers, but you should always ask yourself just what a fact or idea means in relation to your own purpose. If there is no proper place for it in your pattern, it should be excluded. A writer who has studied his subject well always has more material than he can use.

The Form of Footnotes and Bibliography

Full credit should be given for the source of every fact or idea derived from another writer. In your own text you will want to acknowledge any important item as a matter of help to your reader. It is easy to introduce a statement or a quotation by a clear explanatory phrase or sentence such as:

Charles A. Beard has proved that . . .
James Truslow Adams maintains that . . .

An excellent statement of this view is given by James Truslow Adams in his *Epic of America:* ...

As Sinclair Lewis shows in *Main Street,* the culture of the American town is ...

On the other hand, a liberal economist such as Paul Douglas holds that ...

As Thomas Wolfe observed ...

Some facts or ideas can simply be stated in your text if the fact or idea is not especially to be associated with the particular writer from whom you derived it. But in all cases, authority should be given in a footnote.

Exactly what must be footnoted? First, every direct quotation is identified in a footnote. Second, every statement of fact is referred to its source in a footnote. The student must use his discretion about documenting commonly known facts that are available in many sources. It is not necessary, for example, to cite an authority for the fact that the world is round. But it is probably necessary to document an assertion that the world is actually the shape of a grapefruit or a slightly squishy cantaloupe, the account given by present-day scientists. Third, every opinion or interpretation drawn from another writer should be referred to its source in a footnote, *even if the opinion or interpretation is one that you have independently come upon in your own thinking.* In cases where a group of facts or opinions treated together in one paragraph is drawn from the same source, one note at the end of the paragraph will serve for all the material. In cases where more than one source is involved for a single item in the text, one note will serve to acknowledge the several sources.

Footnotes

Variation in certain details is permissible in the form of footnotes—as we shall see in the discussion to follow—*but not* within the same paper. Learn one of the standard forms and use it consistently in all your work.[3] Here are a few general principles:

1   The author's name appears in direct form, not with the last name first as in the bibliography.

2   The title of a book or periodical is underlined in typescript or writing. This corresponds to italics in print. Even a relatively short piece of writing that has independent publication is considered a book. Sometimes a piece of writing, a poem for instance, first appears independently as a little book and is later included in a collection of the author's work. Practice varies in treating such items, but it is permissible to treat it as a book. Thus, we would underscore the title of T. S. Eliot's Four Quartets, but we might quote "Burnt Norton" (which is one of the four poems included) or we might underscore it.

3   The title of an item in a periodical appears in quotation marks.

---

[3] The forms for footnotes and bibliography given in this and the following chapter are based in part on those in the Style Sheet published by the Modern Language Association.

4   When an item is first mentioned in a footnote, full bibliographical information is given. Later references use a brief identifying form, to be described later.

Here are examples of various types of footnotes. Observe carefully the form of punctuation, the nature of the material included, and the order of the items presented.

FOOTNOTES FOR BOOKS

One author

¹ Gay Talese, *The Kingdom and the Power* (New York: World, 1969), p. 17.

More than one author

¹ Laurence J. Peter, and Raymond Hull, *The Peter Principle* (New York: William Morrow and Company, 1969), p. 25.

¹ Mark Schorer and others, *Harbrace College Reader:* Second Edition (New York: Harcourt, 1964), p. 542. [When a book has two authors, both names are given. When there are more than two authors, only the name listed first on the title page is given.]

Translation

¹ Alexander Solzhenitsyn, *Stories and Prose Poems,* trans. Michael Glenny (New York: Farrar, 1971), p. 125.

Work in more than one volume

¹ Morris Bishop, ed. *A Survey of French Literature* (New York: Harcourt, 1955), II, 77. [Here the abbreviation *ed.* is for editor.]

Edited work

¹ John Jay Chapman, *Selected Writings,* ed. Jacques Barzun (New York: Farrar, 1957), p. xviii.

FOOTNOTES FOR ITEMS FROM COLLECTIONS

¹ Ann Saddlemyer, "The Cult of the Celt," in *The World of W. B. Yeats,* ed. Robin Skelton and Ann Saddlemyer (Victoria, B.C.: Univ. of Victoria Press, 1965), p. 24.

FOOTNOTES FOR ITEMS FROM PERIODICALS

¹ Eric F. Goldman, "The White House and the Intellectuals," *Harper's Magazine,* 238 (Jan. 1969), 43. [Here the first number, 238, gives the volume number of the periodical. The last number, 43, is the page reference. Notice that the abbreviation *p.* is omitted for periodicals after the volume number.]

² Walter Sullivan, "Shell Collecting Tied to Spread of Starfish," *New York Times,* 30 Sept. 1969, p. 38. [When no volume number is given, the abbreviation *p.* (or *pp.*) is used.]

³ "Model VI," *The New Yorker,* 45 (Sept. 20, 1969), 35. [An unsigned article. When certain items of information are missing, as in a government document or newspaper account that has no author, put the items in the same order, simply omitting any unavailable information.]

FOOTNOTES FOR ITEMS FROM THE BIBLE

[1] Psalms 23:6-8. [Here the first number is for chapter, the others for verses, inclusive.]

[2] II Cor. 6:9. [Here the abbreviation *II Cor.* stands for Second Corinthians. Certain books of the Bible have such standard abbreviations.]

When material is not drawn directly from its original source but from some intermediary source, acknowledgment should be made to both sources. For instance, the following note indicates that the writer has used a quotation from Stephen Spender that appeared in a book by Moody E. Prior:

[1] Ralph Waldo Emerson, *Representative Men,* p. 162, quoted by Donald M. Frame, trans., *The Complete Essays of Montaigne* (Stanford: Stanford Univ. Press, 1965), p. vi.

All the forms given above indicate the first reference to a work. For subsequent references, three forms may be used. When the source in a footnote is the same as that indicated in the footnote immediately preceding, the abbreviation *ibid.* (for *ibidem:* in the same place) is used, with a new page reference if that is needed. For example:

[1] Loren Eiseley, "Science and the Unexpected Universe," *The American Scholar,* 35 (Summer 1966), 423.

[2] *Ibid.,* 424.

When the reference to be repeated does not immediately precede, either of two basic forms may be used. If only one work by a particular author is referred to in the footnotes, his last name may be used, followed by the page reference, or his last name with the abbreviation *op. cit.* (for *opere citato:* in the work cited), with the page reference. The first practice is simpler, and is becoming more common than the other. For example:

[1] Loren Eiseley, "Science and the Unexpected Universe," *The American Scholar,* 35 (Summer 1966), 423.

[2] Sir John Summerscale, ed. *The Penguin Encyclopedia* (Baltimore, 1965), p. 255.

[3] Eiseley, 424.

If the author has more than one work referred to in the footnotes, then his last name will not be enough, and an abbreviated title will be necessary.

[1] Eiseley, "Science," 464. *Or:* Talese, *Power,* p. 22. [Notice that the abbreviation *p.* is omitted in the Eiseley reference, for the reference is to a periodical, while it is used in the Talese reference, which is to a book. In other words, the short form follows the practice of the long form in this respect.]

We have already referred to the abbreviations *ibid.* and *op. cit.* But there are a number of other abbreviations found in notes and bibliographical forms. You will not find a use for all of them in your own writing, but you will sooner or later encounter them in works that you read. Some of the Latin abbreviations are now commonly replaced by English forms or may be omitted altogether (as with *op. cit.*). In using such abbreviations, the main thing is to be consistent: use either Latin or English throughout any composition.

anon.   Anonymous.

c. or ca. (circa)   About a certain date (to be used to indicate an approximate date, when the real date cannot be determined).

cf. (confer)   Compare.

ch. or chs.   Chapter(s).

col. or cols.   Column(s).

ed.   Edited by, editor, or edition.

et al. (et alii)   And others (when a book has several authors, the name of the first author followed by *et al.* may replace the full list).

f. or ff.   One or more pages following the page indicated.

ibid. (ibidem)   In the same work (referring to a work cited in a note immediately preceding).

idem   Exactly the same reference, title, and page as that given above.

infra   Below (indicating a later discussion).

l. or ll.   Line(s).

loc. cit. (loco citato)   In the place cited (when there is an earlier reference to the source).

MS., MSS.   Manuscript, manuscripts.

n.d.   No date (when publication date cannot be determined).

no.   Number (as when listing the number of the issue of a periodical or series).

n.p.   No place (when place of publication cannot be determined).

op. cit. (opere citato)   In the work cited (used with author's name to indicate source already referred to).

p. or pp.   Page(s).

passim   In various places (used when the topic referred to appears in several places in a work cited).

q.v. (quod vide)   Which see (English form: see).

rev.   Revised.

see   Used to suggest that the reader consult a certain work referred to.

seq. (sequentia)   Following (English form: f. or ff.).

supra   Above (when the topic referred to has already been discussed).

tr. or trans.   Translated by, translator, or translation.

vide   See (English form: see).

vol. or vols.   Volume(s) (but "vol." and "p." are not used if figures for both are given, as in listing a periodical reference; in such cases, use Roman numerals for volume and Arabic for page: II, 391).

Bibliography

After you have prepared a draft of your paper and established all your footnotes, you are ready to set up your final bibliography. This may differ from your working bibliography, as was pointed out above, in that it contains only items that are actually referred to in your paper, not items that have been consulted but not used.

The form for such a bibliography permits certain minor variations. For instance, the name of the publisher is sometimes omitted; and there may be differences in punctuation. For example, the following entry can be punctuated in two ways:

> Barnes, Harry Elmer. *The Genesis of the World War.* New York: Alfred A. Knopf, 1926.

or:

> Barnes, Harry Elmer, *The Genesis of the World War,* New York, Alfred A. Knopf, 1926.

But in all forms the author's name comes first (with the last name first) followed by the full title of the work, the periodical or series if any, the place of publication, the publisher (if this form is used), and the date of publication. The items may be arranged in either of two ways. First, in a straight alphabetical order, according to the last name of the author or, if there is no author, by the main word of the title. Second, alphabetically within certain groups determined by the material dealt with: "Books," "Periodicals," "Documents," and so forth. Here are some examples of entries as they might appear in the bibliography of a paper on Woodrow Wilson:

(PERIODICAL)	Baker, Ray Stannard. "Our Next President and Some Others." *American Magazine,* 74 (June 1912), 131–43.
(BOOK)	Barnes, Harry Elmer. *The Genesis of the World War.* New York: Alfred A. Knopf, 1926.
(DOCUMENT)	*Congressional Record,* 49–51. Washington: Government Printing Office, 1913–14.
(BOOK)	McAdoo, Eleanor R. W. *The Woodrow Wilsons.* New York: The Macmillan Company, 1937.
(BOOK)	Wilson, Woodrow. *The Public Papers of Woodrow Wilson.* Edited by Ray Stannard Baker and William Edward Dodd, 3 volumes. New York: Harper and Bros., 1925–27.
(PERIODICAL)	Wilson, Woodrow. "Democracy and Efficiency," *Atlantic Monthly,* 87 (March 1901), 289–99.

Notice that an overall alphabetical order is given, by author when an author is specified, and by leading word when there is no author ("Congressional"). In this short bibliography all types of sources are grouped together —books, collections, periodicals, and documents. In a long bibliography each type might be set up separately, with each group in alphabetical order.

CHAPTER **15**

The Final Version: Writing and Rewriting

Throughout this book we have been insisting that in good writing all the elements are interrelated. There is no such thing as "good" diction apart from the context in which it occurs, or "correct" tone abstracted from a specific occasion. In good writing the principles of unity, coherence, and emphasis apply at all levels—not only to the larger blocks of the composition, but to the individual phrases and even the individual words.

Though this principle of interrelation, if clearly understood by the student, can illuminate the problems of writing, it can also be inhibiting. Confronted with the demand that every item in his composition be ultimately related to everything else, the student writer may not know where to start. He may feel that in a fabric so intricately interwoven, there are no seams— no natural divisions with which to begin. It may be well, therefore, in this last chapter to do two things. The first will be to review the typical methods by which one builds up a composition. The second thing will be to point out the importance of *rewriting*. Even professional writers rarely achieve an adequate unification of elements in the first draft. In this chapter we shall want to examine very carefully—and with concrete examples—what is involved in the process of rewriting.

Writing a Term Paper

Let us assume that the student has been assigned a term paper that is to deal with some aspect of American history [1]—political, economic, cultural,

---
[1] Later in the chapter we will discuss the problems involved in writing a literary paper.

or military. He may, if he likes, write about early movies or the development of the steel industry or the exploits of John Paul Jones. He happens to be interested, however, in the American Civil War, particularly as that war revealed the adaptation to warfare of the new machines and techniques of the dawning industrial age. He first thinks about treating the use in the Civil War of balloons for military observation, but decides that this topic is rather limited. He then seriously considers discussing the development of the ironclad ship as exemplified by the *Merrimac* and the *Monitor*. Finally, it occurs to him that the role of the railroads in the Civil War might offer him not only a topic in which he has a particular interest (his uncle is an official of a railroad) but one which would allow him a good deal of scope.

On reflection, he begins to fear that the topic offers him too much scope. In an important sense the whole of the war was, he realizes, a fight for control of means of communication—railroads and navigable rivers. He is up against the problem we dealt with earlier in this book (pp. 10–11), the problem of finding a "true subject." Discussion of the total strategy of the war would be more than he wants to attempt, but he feels that in the process of research and writing he may be able to grasp his true subject. At any rate, he goes to the library and sets to work to make an exploration of the subject of the role of the railroad in the Civil War.

Bibliography

By using the card catalogue in his library and some of the general aids referred to on pages 363–66 with some help from the reference librarian, he comes up with the following list of books and articles:

BOOKS

Primary Sources

Haupt, Herman. *Reminiscences of General Herman Haupt*. Milwaukee: Wright and Joys Co., Limited Autograph Edition, July 1901.

Jacobs, M. *Notes on the Rebel Invasion of Maryland and Pennsylvania and the Battle of Gettysburg*. Gettysburg: Times Printing House, 1909.

Order Book. Civil War. Military Railroads. General Orders, Instructions and Reports. n.p., n.d. (found at the Library Bureau of Railway Economics, Association of American Railroads, Washington, D.C.). Cited as "Order Book."

The War of the Rebellion. Official Records of Union and Confederate Armies. Washington: Government Printing Office, 1902, Series 1, 53 vols.

Secondary Sources

Freeman, Douglas S. *R. E. Lee*. 4 vols. New York: Charles Scribner's Sons, 1934–36.

Turner, George Edgar. *Victory Rode the Rails*. Indianapolis: Bobbs-Merrill Company, 1953.

PERIODICALS

Weber, Thomas. Book review of *Victory Rode the Rails,* in *Mississippi Valley Historical Review,* 40, No. 4 (March 1954), 742.

MAPS

Map of United States Military Railroads, 1866 (to accompany reports of D. C. McCallum, 1861–66). Located at the Library Bureau of Railway Economics, Association of American Railroads, Washington, D.C.

(The student found many more books and articles, but these were the ones he actually sampled or read through carefully. Note that he did not use all these sources in his complete draft.)

Note-taking

Here are some sample notes taken by our student:

```
Haupt urged Burnside to cross        War of the
the Rappahannock                     Rebellion
                                     Vol. 33, 789.

1.  Supplies could be brought by water.
2.  He would have an established rail center to
    fall back on at Falmouth or
3.  to use for communication with Washington
    if he reached Richmond.
```

```
Haupt supplies Meade at       Turner, Victory Rode
Gettysburg                    the Rails, p. 280.

Haupt supplied enough materials to Meade in
four days to allow him to take the offensive.
The South was unable to do this for Lee in the
winter of 1862-1863.
```

```
┌─────────────────────────────────────────────────────────┐
│                                                           │
│   Ewell's route to        Freeman, Douglas Southall,      │
│   Gettysburg              Lee's Lieutenants, New York:    │
│                           Charles Scribner's Sons,        │
│                           1944, 3 vols., III, 36.         │
│                                                           │
│   "To Heidlersburg, on the road to Gettysburg,            │
│   'Dick' Ewell made his way before sundown on             │
│   June 30."                                               │
│                                                           │
│                                                           │
│                                                           │
│ ·                                                         │
│                                                           │
└─────────────────────────────────────────────────────────┘
```

(Note that on this third card there is full bibliographical information. The first two cards could omit it, for they refer to works already mentioned in the bibliography, where full information is given.)

■ APPLICATIONS

I Select a general topic for a research paper. The lists on pages 3, 50, and 53 will give you some ideas, or you may want to use a topic that has been assigned by an instructor in another course. Make a preliminary bibliography for your topic.

II Take notes on your subject, following the suggestions outlined in Chapter 14, pages 368–71.

III With the help of the notes you have assembled, fix upon the limited subject on which you will write.

Outline

When our student had finished his research in books and magazines, he had decided to narrow his subject to a discussion of the importance of railroads in one particular campaign, that which culminated at Gettysburg. So he jotted down the following scratch outline:

SCRATCH OUTLINE

The importance of the railroads in the Civil War can be illustrated by the Battle of Gettysburg and the events leading up to it.
Haupt's part in the Battle of Fredericksburg.
The Confederate army is forced to remain on the defensive because of the inefficiency of its railroad communications.
The next Federal offensive and the Battle of Chancellorsville.

Lee reorganizes his army and takes the offensive.
Lee's plan to cut the railroads connecting Washington with the rest of the Union.
Events that lead up to the Confederate failure at Gettysburg.
The problem of supplying Meade by railroads.
Haupt solves the problem.
Summary of Haupt's accomplishment.

First draft

Our student was aware that his scratch outline did not give him as clear an idea of the organization of the paper as might be desired. Still the scratch outline got down on paper many of the ideas that he wanted to deal with, and he still hoped that in the actual process of writing his ideas would become adequately clarified. At any rate, he decided to begin writing without going farther with his outline. Here are the first ten paragraphs of his paper.

RAILROADS IN THE CIVIL WAR

Railroads were used in the Crimean War, but the American Civil War was the first railroad war. Many historians studying the war ignore the significance of the railroads. They get bogged down in battles, by which I mean the actual fighting, or if they include them at all they include them in their passing mention of the industrial capacity of the North and South. The theme of this paper, on the other hand, is to discuss the strategic and tactical importance of the railroads in the campaigns of the Civil War by outlining their significance in the important period from the Battle of Fredericksburg to the Battle of Gettysburg. We live in an age of technology, but we did not invent it, it is well to remember.

The story of Gettysburg begins in the fall of 1862 when General Ambrose E. Burnside, who replaced General McClellan after the Battle of Antietam, moved his army to Stratford Heights and Falmouth on the north bank of the Rappahannock River overlooking Fredericksburg. In shifting position, Burnside was following the advice of his transportation chief, Herman Haupt. Even though it had to be rebuilt, Haupt favored using the Richmond, Fredericksburg, and Potomac Railroad to supply Burnside because it was a more protected road. On November 22, Haupt further advised Burnside to cross the Rappahannock, suggesting that supplies then could be carried by water, he would still have the railroad center at Falmouth to fall back on, and he would have an open means of communication with Washington if he reached Richmond.[1] It is not known to what extent this dispatch influenced Burnside, but on December 13 he attacked Lee at Fredericksburg and was defeated. The two armies spent the rest of the winter watching each other across the river.

Burnside was able to attack because Haupt had provided him with enough supplies. On the other hand, Lee was unable to take the offensive during the winter of 1862–63, even after the victory at Fredericksburg,

---

[1] *The War of the Rebellion. Official Records of Union and Confederate Armies* (Washington, D.C.: GPO, 1902), Ser. 1, XXXIII, 789.

because his men were too weak from lack of food and the animals lacked forage. Fifty miles away at Richmond there were plenty of supplies, but they could not be brought forward because of the inefficiency of the railroads.[2] Yet Lee was being supplied by the same railroad, a different section, as Burnside.

The Confederates were consequently forced to take the defensive; and in the spring of 1863 General Hooker, who had replaced Burnside, began to prepare for an offensive. Haupt, in addition to meeting the daily demands of the Army of the Potomac, landed and made ready seventy cars of supplies, material, and prefabricated bridge trusses for the "on to Richmond" movement.[3]

The ensuing Battle of Chancellorsville was a stalemate, but the Union forces suffered more physically and moralewise. The time was opportune for an offensive by the South, but again the transportation corps could not provide the necessary supplies, and forage was running out in the area of Fredericksburg. Lee concluded his best alternative was to invade Pennsylvania, for he could gather his own supplies and forage there and he might be able to isolate Washington and give encouragement to the Peace Party, which was gaining strength in the North.[4]

After the Battle of Chancellorsville and the death of Jackson, Lee reorganized his army into three corps with James Longstreet, Richard Ewell, and A. P. Hill in command of the first, second, and third corps, respectively. Lee entered his most important battle with an untested, reorganized army. The objective of the invasion of Pennsylvania was railroad centers whose destruction would cut Washington off from the north and south and this again ties into the main idea. Ewell's corps was to move up the Shenandoah from Fredericksburg with Longstreet following him and with Stuart to the right of Longstreet as a screen. Hill, by remaining at Fredericksburg, would screen the rear, but when Ewell reached the Potomac River, Hill was to follow him, and Longstreet was to move westward into the Valley and then proceed northward leaving Stuart to defend the mountain passes and screen the right.[5]

Once into Maryland, Ewell was to destroy the Baltimore and Ohio Railroad and then split up his force, part heading to Harrisburg to destroy the Cumberland Valley Railroad and part moving toward York to destroy the Northern Central. Longstreet was then to push forward to Havre de Grace and destroy the Pennsylvania Railroad main line and the great bridges over the Susquehanna River. Washington would then be isolated.[6]

Lee advanced according to schedule and on June 28, when General Meade replaced Hooker as commander of the Army of the Potomac, Ewell was only eighteen miles from Harrisburg and the Army of the Potomac was still around Frederick, Maryland. Unfortunately Stuart became separated from Lee, who then did not know where the Army of the Potomac was, and when Meade began to move after Lee, the two armies unknowingly

---

[2] Douglas S. Freeman, *R. E. Lee* (New York: Scribner's, 1934–36), II, 493–94.

[3] Haupt's dispatch to Stanton, September 8, 1863, *Order Book* (n.p., n.d.).

[4] M. Jacobs, *Notes on the Rebel Invasion of Maryland and Pennsylvania and the Battle of Gettysburg* (Gettysburg: Times Printing House, 1909), p. 1.

[5] Freeman, II, 33.

[6] George Edgar Turner, *Victory Rode the Rails* (Indianapolis: Bobbs-Merrill, 1953), p. 273.

converged on Gettysburg. Both armies were reorganized and untested; and Lee, who had given up his communications with Richmond, was living off the land. Meade did not give up his lines of communication, but he had to move so fast it became difficult to supply his army. When the two armies met July 1, 2, and 3, they were in some ways evenly matched, and a writer like Douglas Freeman seems to argue that the main difference at Gettysburg was the tactical errors made.

Perhaps the most telling fact was the reorganization of the Confederate Army and the attitude of the commanding generals. Lee was used to giving discretionary orders to Jackson, but the new commanders were used to explicit orders and lacked initiative. Several times they failed to act at crucial moments or failed to use their initiative. On July 1, Ewell and his division commanders were unwilling, after driving the enemy off Seminary Ridge, to attack Cemetery Hill, which could have been easily taken since the Union Army had not yet arrived in full force. Even more disastrous, Longstreet delayed the assault ten hours, and the next day during that time the ridge was fully fortified by forces that were just arriving. The delay was due mainly to Longstreet's disgruntled mood caused by Lee's rejection of a flanking movement he had planned. Yet Lee should have been able to shock Longstreet out of his insubordination.[7]

Another factor in the outcome was that Lee had no reconnaissance without Stuart.[8] He was like a blind man at times. Another minor factor was the poor use of Confederate artillery. The principle of converging lines of fire was ignored as were several advantageous positions and vulnerable targets.[9]

---

[7] Freeman, III, 147–50.
[8] *Ibid.*, p. 147.
[9] *Ibid.*, p. 152.

Rewriting

When the student had gotten this far, he stopped. He had become aware that his paper had lost direction. The last three paragraphs that he had written did not pertain to the thesis that he had meant to develop. A sentence like "Yet Lee should have been able to shock Longstreet out of his insubordination" touches upon a matter of interest to anyone concerned with the Battle of Gettysburg, but it really has nothing to do with the role of the railroads. At this point, therefore, the student decided to go back and rethink his paper. To this end, he resolved to make a careful outline—in this instance, a sentence outline. He hoped that the process of working out a fairly elaborate and precise outline would enable him to see how much space he should give to the Confederate difficulties of command—if any—and how to relate this matter to his general thesis.

Before working out his sentence outline, however, our student turned back to the chapter on exposition and reread the various sections, including that on expository narration, for it was apparent that a discussion of the importance of the railroads in the Civil War would make use of expository methods, and that if he discussed a particular military campaign, narrative methods would also be involved. Here follows the student's sentence outline:

SENTENCE OUTLINE

Proposition: A consideration of the Battle of Gettysburg and the events leading up to it reveals how important were the railroads in determining the strategy and the outcome of the Civil War.

I. The role of the railroads in the Civil War, a role that the historians have tended to slight, may be illustrated with the Gettysburg campaign.

II. The chief events leading up to Gettysburg were powerfully determined by problems of rail supply.

   A. Burnside and Lee fought at Fredericksburg in December, 1862, because Burnside's transportation chief, Haupt, had favored using the Richmond, Fredericksburg, and Potomac Railroad.

      1. He argued that this rail line was better protected, and that

      2. If Burnside could break through to Richmond, he would have an open means of communication with Washington.

   B. Though victorious at Fredericksburg, Lee's inefficient rail supply prevented him from going over to the offensive.

   C. When in the spring of 1863 Lee defeated Hooker at Chancellorsville, lack of supplies and forage hampered his taking the offensive.

      1. Supplies were low in the vicinity of Fredericksburg, and

      2. Inefficient rail service prevented them from being brought from more distant areas.

III. The railroads were important in shaping Lee's plan to invade Pennsylvania.

   A. He hoped, by living off the country in Pennsylvania, to ease his own problem of supply.

   B. He hoped to isolate Washington by cutting its rail connection.

      1. Ewell was first to destroy the Baltimore and Ohio Railroad, and then to destroy the Cumberland Valley Railroad and the Northern Central.

      2. Longstreet was to destroy the main line of the Pennsylvania Railroad at Havre de Grace and the bridges over the Susquehanna River.

   C. Lee followed his plan and on June 28 when Meade replaced Hooker, Lee was to the west and Meade to the east of Gettysburg, where the two forces eventually met and brought on the battle.

IV. The contribution made by Haupt's management of the railroads becomes clear when one realizes how close the Confederates came, in spite of costly mistakes, to winning at Gettysburg.

   A. Various reasons have been alleged for Lee's failure, including

      1. His lack of adequate reconnaissance because of Stuart's absence.

      2. The use of vague and discretionary orders that allowed lags and failures on the part of the corps commanders.

3. Longstreet's tardiness in carrying out Lee's orders to attack.
4. Other tactical mistakes of various kinds.
B. In spite of piecemeal rather than unified attack, the Confederate forces mounted an intense offensive that came close to winning.
C. Since none of Meade's forces had supplies to fight a three-day battle, Meade's success in holding his ground depended heavily on Haupt's ability to keep him supplied with food, ammunition, and equipment.
V. Haupt's problem in supplying Meade's army in Pennsylvania was a difficult one.
A. He first had to make the proper diagnosis of Lee's intentions.
B. The one direct rail route from Baltimore to Gettysburg had been destroyed by Ewell.
C. The closest available rail route stopped at Westminster.
1. The distance from Westminster to Gettysburg would have to be covered by wagon.
2. The rail route lacked sidings, turntables, and watering stations.
3. It could handle only four trains a day, whereas thirty were required.
VI. Haupt's success in organizing railroad supply lines was the result not only of forethought but of brilliant improvisation.
A. He had previously stockpiled materials and tools for just such an emergency.
B. On the Western Maryland he used such expedients as
1. Running the trains in convoys of five each.
2. Running the trains backwards on the return trip.
3. Replenishing water from streams by bucket brigades.
C. So successful was Haupt that by July 3, the Western Maryland's capacity had been increased tenfold.
D. Haupt also had his construction crews immediately start repairs on alternate rail lines to Gettysburg.
E. On July 5 Meade was actually being supplied beyond his daily needs.
VII. The North was indeed fortunate in having in its service a man of Haupt's special genius.

■ APPLICATION

Write a sentence outline of the paper for which you have taken notes. (See pp. 372–73.) If you have been assigned a paper in literary criticism, you may want to take into account pages 400–03 as well.

With his sentence outline before him, the student proceeded to redraft the first part of his paper and to go on to complete it. He was happy to find, as he began to write, that the sentence outline substantially justified the first four paragraphs of his first draft. He did make a number of changes, however, as you will see by comparing the first four paragraphs of the two drafts. (Most of the added matter and also of the transposed matter has been put in italics so that the reader can more easily locate the changes.) Note also the changes made in paragraphs 5 through 9. Here the student had felt the need to compress material that was not really very relevant to his thesis. He was also attempting in these paragraphs to strengthen the argument for the importance of the railroads, and to find a better transition to his account of Haupt's extraordinary feat at Gettysburg. As you read the revised paper (which follows), observe the changes.

RAILROADS IN THE CIVIL WAR

(1) *Although* railroads had been used in the Crimean War, the American Civil War was the first railroad war. *It was the first time each side utilized an extensive rail system in a total war effort.* Many historians studying the war ignore the significance of the railroads or include them in their passing mention of the industrial capacity of the North and South. The theme of this paper asserts the strategic and tactical importance of the railroads in the campaigns of the Civil War by outlining their significance in the important period from the Battle of Fredericksburg to the Battle of Gettysburg.

(2) The story of Gettysburg *really* begins in the fall of 1862 when General Ambrose E. Burnside, who *had* replaced General McClellan after the Battle of Antietam, moved his army to Stratford Heights and Falmouth on the north bank of the Rappahannock River overlooking Fredericksburg. In shifting *his* position, Burnside was following the advice of his transportation chief, Herman Haupt. *Because the Richmond, Fredericksburg, and Potomac Railroad was relatively easy to protect,* Haupt favored using it to supply Burnside *even though it had to be rebuilt.* On November 22 Haupt advised Burnside to cross the Rappahannock, suggesting that supplies then could be carried by water, *that if unsuccessful, Burnside* would still have the railroad center at Falmouth to fall back on, and *that if he did break through to Richmond,* he would have an open means of communication with Washington.[1] It is not known to what extent this dispatch influenced Burnside, *but in any case it was the duty of Burnside to judge Haupt's advice in the overall military situation. Burnside must take the responsibility for the brutal defeat he suffered when, on December 13, he attacked Lee at Fredericksburg.* The two armies spent the rest of the winter watching each other across the river.

(3) Burnside was able to attack because Haupt had provided him with enough supplies. Lee, *on the other hand,* was unable to take the offensive during the winter of 1862–63, even after the victory at Fredericksburg, because his men were too weak from lack of food and the animals lacked forage. *Only* fifty miles away at Richmond there were plenty of supplies, but they could not be brought forward because of the inefficiency of the rail *lines.*[2] Yet Lee was being supplied by the same railroad—*though* a different section *of it, of course*—as *that which served* Burnside.

(4) The Confederates were consequently forced to *remain upon* the

---

[1] *The War of the Rebellion. Official Records of Union and Confederate Armies* (Washington, D.C.: GPO, 1902), Ser. 1, XXXIII, 789.
[2] Douglas S. Freeman, *R. E. Lee* (New York: Scribner's, 1934–36), II, 493–94.

defensive; and in the spring of 1863, General Hooker, who had replaced Burnside, began to prepare *another* offensive. Haupt, in addition to meeting the daily demands of the Army of the Potomac, landed and made ready seventy cars of supplies, material, and prefabricated bridge trusses for the "on to Richmond" movement.[3] *Hooker advanced, and was badly mauled by Lee and Jackson at* the Battle of Chancellorsville. The time was *again* opportune for an offensive by the South, but again the transportation corps could not provide the necessary supplies, and forage was running out in the area of Fredericksburg. *The rich countryside of Pennsylvania looked like a promising source of supplies.*

(5)   *Lee's choice of route for the invasion was thus to a considerable extent dictated to him by the poor shape of the railroads on which he depended for much of his supplies. But railroads also figured in another way in his plans. He meant to achieve the isolation of Washington by severing the railroad lines that connected it with the north, west, and south. To cut off and seize the Northern capital would have immediate political advantage, by giving* encouragement to the Peace Party which was then gaining strength in the North.[4]

(6)   *The plan was for Lee's army, which had been reorganized after the Battle of Chancellorsville, to make the invasion in three corps:* Ewell's corps was to move up the Shenandoah Valley from Fredericksburg with Longstreet's *corps* following him, and with Stuart *and his cavalry flanking* the right of Longstreet *and acting* as a screen. Hill's *corps,* by remaining at Fredericksburg, would *protect* the rear; but when Ewell reached the Potomac River, Hill was to follow him, and Longstreet was to move westward into the *Shenandoah* Valley and then proceed northward, leaving Stuart's *cavalry* to defend the mountain passes and *to furnish* a screen *to the* right *flank.*[5]

(7)   Once into Maryland, Ewell was to destroy the Baltimore and Ohio Railroad and then split up his force, *one* part heading *for* Harrisburg to destroy the Cumberland Valley Railroad and *the other* moving toward York to destroy the Northern Central. Longstreet was then to push forward to Havre de Grace and destroy *the main line of* the Pennsylvania Railroad and the great bridges over the Susquehanna River. Washington would then be isolated.[6]

(8)   Lee advanced according to schedule, and when General Meade replaced Hooker on June 28, *Lee's forces were well up into Pennsylvania to the west and north of Gettysburg while the main Federal* army was still around Frederick, Maryland, *to the east, between Lee and his ultimate objective, Washington. Neither force had a clear notion of where the other was, and small detachments, accidentally coming into contact at Gettysburg, brought on the battle there. The battle began blind.*

(9)   *The Battle of Gettysburg has for nearly a century held the interest of military historians. Various reasons have been advanced to account for Lee's repulse in this great struggle, which probably proved to be the*

---

[3] Haupt's dispatch to Stanton, September 9, 1863, *Order Book* (n.p., n.d.).

[4] M. Jacobs, *Notes on the Rebel Invasion of Maryland and Pennsylvania and the Battle of Gettysburg* (Gettysburg: Times Printing House, 1909), p. 1.

[5] Freeman, II, 33.

[6] George Edgar Turner, *Victory Rode the Rails* (Indianapolis: Bobbs-Merrill, 1953), p. 373.

turning point of the whole war. In advancing the notion here that Haupt's ability to supply Meade was a decisive factor, I am not trying to come up with the full answer to a difficult question. I am not forgetting that Stuart's absence with the cavalry put out Lee's eyes,[7] or that Lee's army in its new organization was largely untested, or that Lee's orders were too vague or left too much to the discretion of field commanders, or that Longstreet's notorious delay in launching the attack Lee had ordered almost amounted to insubordination.[8] In fact, so much went wrong that the remarkable thing is that the Confederates were able to mount so intensive an offensive and come so close to victory. But the very narrowness of the margin between victory and defeat itself stresses the importance of Haupt's contribution. Had Meade's army been seriously weakened by a lack of supplies, it might not have managed to hold firm.

[From this point on the treatment is new.]

(10) General Haupt took charge of the railroads in Maryland and Pennsylvania on June 28, the same day that Meade replaced Hooker. The problem that confronted him was a formidable one. Meade's army had moved in four days from the Potomac to Gettysburg and some of the troops arrived on Cemetery Ridge after long hours of marching. For an unexpected, intense, three-day battle Haupt had to supply Meade's army in a position picked by accident and over rail lines the enemy had already damaged. To cap the climax, just as he was about to go to Pennsylvania, he was unexplainably delayed by the War Department.[9]

(11) When he was released from Washington, he hurried to Harrisburg but was detoured through Philadelphia because Ewell had already destroyed part of the direct route. He arrived there the evening of June 30, and Tom Scott, district manager for the Pennsylvania Railroad, reported the enemy had withdrawn from the region of Harrisburg toward Gettysburg. Scott, who had organized his own company of railroad scouts to protect his lines, thought the Army of Northern Virginia was withdrawing; but Haupt realized they were concentrating their forces to meet Meade and that there would probably be a battle at Gettysburg unless Meade altered his course. Late that night Haupt headed for Baltimore. The one rail route that went directly to Gettysburg had been destroyed by Ewell. The closest available rail route was from Baltimore to Westminster and thence by wagon to Gettysburg. The road was only twenty-eight miles long, but unfortunately there were no sidings, no turntables, no watering stations, and little wood available. Thirty trains would be needed a day; and the road could only handle four at the most, two each day.[10]

(12) On July 1, Haupt arrived in Westminster and found chaos. Supplies were trickling in, and hundreds of Meade's wagons were collecting there. Haupt had, literally, to hide from the crowd, but in several minutes he had devised a plan and before returning to Baltimore had sent several hurried telegrams. Within a few hours his construction corps began to arrive in Baltimore from Alexandria, with buckets, tools, material, and wood, supplies that Haupt had stockpiled in Alexandria for just such an

---

[7] Freeman, III, 147.

[8] *Ibid.*, pp. 147–50.

[9] Turner, p. 276.

[10] Haupt's dispatch to Stanton.

emergency. Impressed rolling stock also began to accumulate in the Baltimore yards.[11]

(13)   On July 1, trains began to roll over the Western Maryland line to Westminster, the day Meade was hurrying to reinforce the two corps who then were holding Cemetery Ridge. None of Meade's forces had supplies to fight a three-day battle. The supply trains ran in convoys of five each, at eight-hour intervals. Each convoy had time to cover the distance, unload supplies, and return with wounded before the next convoy, loaded and waiting in the Baltimore yards, pulled out. Haupt had persuaded the Quartermaster Department to supply enough men so that when the trains arrived in Westminster every car was unloaded simultaneously and then reloaded with wounded. The trains were run backwards and filled with water from streams by bucket brigades. In addition to these crews, repair crews were placed at intervals along the route to check for and repair weak places, for the road bed and track were not strong enough to handle the increased load of traffic. Haupt's men were aware of the crisis and worked like beavers; so by July 3, fifteen hundred tons were being carried daily. The capacity of the road had been increased tenfold.[12]

(14)   The great number of men involved in this operation had been supplied by Haupt, as had all the material. He even supplied the train crews. However, he did not limit his activity to the Western Maryland. He assigned a number of men from his construction corps to work on the Northern Central and York and Cumberland, which ran directly to Gettysburg. Ewell had destroyed nineteen bridges and miles of track on this route.[13] Haupt, however, realized that while the road could not be made ready for the immediate battle, it might be needed later. If the Union forces were victorious, it could easily be able to provide enough supplies for an offensive against the demoralized forces of Lee and could remove the wounded so the army could move forward quickly. In case of defeat it would facilitate retreat. Haupt's crews began work on the afternoon of July 1; and by the afternoon of July 4, the day Lee was retreating, the road was open to within fifteen miles of Gettysburg and completed just after midnight.[14] The wounded were now carried out by this route and supplies brought in through Westminster.

(15)   On July 5, Haupt was supplying Meade with supplies beyond his daily needs, and it was on this day that Haupt urged Meade to follow up his advantage. The Army of the Potomac now had an established supply line, and back in Virginia the rail lines would be badly damaged. Meade would not advance and Haupt returned to Washington and tried to get a pre-emptory order.[15] This attempt failed, and by July 14 Lee was back in the Shenandoah.

(16)   General Haupt had performed an amazing feat at Gettysburg. It is further from Baltimore to Gettysburg than from Richmond to Fredericksburg, but Haupt had done in four days of battle what the South could not

---

[11] Turner, p. 279.

[12] *Ibid.*

[13] Haupt's dispatch to Stanton.

[14] Turner, p. 280.

[15] Herman Haupt, *Reminiscences of General Herman Haupt* (Milwaukee: Wright and Joys, 1901), Limited Autograph Edition, p. 73.

do in four months of peace before Chancellorsville: he had supplied the army with enough provisions and material to take the offensive.[16]

(17)   The North was fortunate to find a man of Haupt's caliber who had the ability to utilize the potential of railroads in wartime. In one and three quarter years Haupt developed precedents for the operation of railroads in time of war, a problem never before faced by anyone, which still form the basis for the operation of railroads in war by the United States almost a hundred years later.

> Haupt was an engineering genius who helped sustain mediocre Union commanders in Virginia and who performed an outstanding feat of transportation on the Western Maryland Railroad during the Gettysburg campaign.[17]

A study of the operations of General Haupt or of the use of railroads in other campaigns and under other men would show clearly that the railroads had a decisive effect in many of the campaigns of the Civil War.

---

[16] Turner, p. 280.
[17] Thomas Weber, book review of *Victory Rode the Rails,* in *Mississippi Valley Historical Review,* XL (March 1954), 742.

At this point the student has before him a completed draft of his paper. The first section of it actually represents, as we have seen, a rewriting—a second draft. Let us stop and review that part that is a second draft, and try to follow the logic of some of the changes.

The main change has already been mentioned—the reorganization to correct the diffuse analysis of the causes of the Confederate defeat and to put the focus back on the subject of the railroads. In paragraph 9 we can see how competently the student has done this. The military aspects of the occasion are finally related to the point of the paper: "But the very narrowness of the margin between victory and defeat itself stresses the importance of Haupt's contribution"—and, of course, the importance of the railroad.

To turn to smaller concerns, we can see clear improvements in the first paragraph. The rewriting of the first sentence, with the remark about the Crimean War now put into an introductory subordinate clause introduced by the concessive *although,* sharpens the focus on the Civil War. The new second paragraph makes precise what had been vaguely implied by the phrase "railroad war" in the original first sentence. The student has also sharpened his meaning by getting rid of the sentence beginning "They [the historians] get bogged down in battles . . ." (p. 384). The metaphor of "bogging down" in battles is a poor one, both trite and inaccurate, and the fumbling explanation beginning "by which I mean . . ." doesn't help matters. In the rewriting, the student has compressed and stated more accurately his view of the historians. And he has dropped the last sentence of the paragraph, which had set up a distraction from the main idea of the paper.

If we jump ahead to paragraphs 4 and 5 (p. 389) we see some clear gains in clarity of organization. But there are gains of another sort in the revision of the clause "but the Union forces suffered more physically and moralewise" (first draft, p. 385). It is not quite clear what the student means by "suffered more physically." Does he mean that the Union army endured more casualties? Probably, but there is still a confusing margin of other possibilities of meaning.

■ APPLICATIONS

I   Reread the brief comments above on the student's revision of his paper. Can you account for the changes that have not been discussed there? Has the theme anywhere been altered for the worse? Can you suggest further changes?

1   In paragraph 9 we find the sentence: "In fact, so much went wrong that the remarkable thing is that the Confederates were able to mount so intensive an offensive and come so close to victory." In his final version the student made two changes in the sentence. Can you guess why? What changes would you make?

2   Does paragraph 14 exhibit unity? Is there material in it that should go back into the previous paragraph? If you think so, try to revise the end of paragraph 13 and the beginning of the next. Keep in mind the question of transition.

3   Go back to paragraph 1 of the second version. What is the promised subject of the paper? Now look at the last paragraph. Is it properly geared to the subject, or does it dwell too much on the personal achievement of General Haupt? Try to revise the paragraph.

II   Write the first draft of the paper for which you have made an outline.[2] (See p. 388.) Now begins the really serious work: revision. Study your paper with reference to the following considerations:

1   Have you stated the thesis or proposition of your paper? If not, is it clear by implication?

2   Does the body of the paper form a logical sequence? That is, does it present evidence and argument, if such are appropriate, in an orderly fashion? Does it give narrative, if its business is to give narrative, in such a way as to indicate cause and effect, and to give an impression of meaningful climax? And so on. Does the logical sequence, of whatever sort it happens to be, lead continuously from the first paragraph to the last? Are there any distracting digressions?

3   Are there clearly defined transitions from paragraph to paragraph?

4   Are the paragraphs organized so that they exhibit unity and coherence?

5   Check the sentence structure, the agreement of subjects and verbs, the reference of pronouns, the sequence of tenses, the position of modifiers. Check punctuation.

---

[2] If you have chosen or been assigned a literary topic, you may—unless you have already done so—want to study pages 395–98 before you embark on a first draft of that paper.

6   Have you any examples of metaphorical language? If so, are they fresh and apt? If not, try again. Do you find any points where some comparison might help?

7   To whom are you addressing your paper? What is your attitude toward your audience? What do you expect to be the attitude of the audience to your subject? What is your own attitude? In the light of these questions, do you feel that the tone of your paper is satisfactory?

8   Read your paper out loud—or better, have someone read it to you. Do you find any rhythms that are jarring or monotonous? If so, try to determine the reason. Perhaps your sentences tend to be of the same length and structure. Or perhaps they are so sprawling that the ear cannot grasp them. Try shifting the elements for variety and emphasis. Try to relate the logic of what you are saying to what your ear instinctively indicates about the rhythm.

After the first complete revision put the paper down for a day or two. Then come back to it. Try again to improve it. The writer, whether novice or veteran, must not become weary in well doing. Good writing is mostly rewriting. The sweat is worth as much as the inspiration.

Writing a Literary Paper

Let us assume that the student has been assigned a paper in literature—a paper that treats of a particular author or a literary work or a literary genre such as, say, comedy or propaganda novels. The *general* problems that are involved are the same as those already discussed and illustrated in the student paper on "Railroads in the Civil War." But papers in literature do tend to present some special problems, and it may be well to illustrate these by a concrete example, a student paper on the poetry of the great twentieth-century poet, William Butler Yeats.

This student—for ease of subsequent reference let us call her Susan—had become very much interested in Yeats's poetry. After encountering some ten or twelve of his poems in an anthology, she immediately bought a paperback selection of his poems. This further acquaintance with his poetry soon decided her to do her term paper on Yeats.

Clearly her first task was to master (as nearly as she could) Yeats's poetry; but she obviously needed also to read a life of Yeats, and she thought she ought to learn something about what the established Yeats authorities had said about the man and his work. When, however, she consulted the card catalogue in her college library, she was appalled at the number of books and articles on Yeats. In fact, she was overawed by the sheer number of plays, essays, letters, and other autobiographical documents written by Yeats himself.

Susan's difficulty here is one frequently met by a student who is planning to write on any well-known writer. Our age produces a vast number of books and articles. (Some would say that it overproduces them.) If all the books and articles that achieve print were good, one could speak of an embarrassment of riches. But the true situation is different. Though there are, to be sure, many excellent books and essays, there are also many mediocre ones, there is much duplication, and there is even some trash.

What is the student to do? He cannot read everything. How is he to know what is worth reading? Susan sensibly went first to her instructor for advice; she then made a list of works based on his suggestions and on the bibliography in her copy of the selected poems, which, her instructor said, had been edited by a sound Yeats authority. Finally, she did some vigorous sampling of each work before committing herself to reading it through.

Here is the list of books and articles that Susan drew up. Some she used in her paper and others she simply consulted casually. To see which works she actually used, check the bibliography that appears at the end of the paper (p. 419).

LIST OF WORKS CONSULTED

Berryman, Charles. *W. B. Yeats: Design of Opposites.* New York: Exposition, 1967.

Ellmann, Richard. *Yeats: The Man and the Masks.* New York: Macmillan, 1948.

Henn, T. R. *The Lonely Tower.* London: Methuen, 1950.

Jarrell, Randall. "The Development of Yeats's Sense of Reality," *The Southern Review,* 7 (1941–42), 653–66.

Jeffares, A. Norman. *W. B. Yeats: Man and Poet.* New Haven: Yale Univ. Press, 1949.

Kermode, Frank. "The Artist in Isolation," in *Yeats: A Collection of Critical Essays.* Ed. John Unterecker. Englewood Cliffs, N.J.: Prentice-Hall, 1963.

Mizener, Arthur. "The Romanticism of W. B. Yeats," *The Southern Review,* 7 (1941–42), 601–23.

Rosenthal, M. L., ed. *Selected Poems and Two Plays of William Butler Yeats.* New York: Collier Books, 1966.

Saddlemyer, Ann. "The Cult of the Celt: Pan-Celtism in the Nineties," in *The World of W. B. Yeats: Essays in Perspective.* Ed. Robin Skelton and Ann Saddlemyer. Victoria, B.C.: Univ. of Victoria Press, 1965.

Stauffer, Donald A. "W. B. Yeats and the Medium of Poetry," *ELH,* 15 (1948), 227–46.

Unterecker, John. *A Reader's Guide to William Butler Yeats.* New York: Noonday Press, 1959.

Yeats, W. B. *Autobiographies.* London: Macmillan, 1955.

———. *Collected Poems.* New York: Macmillan, 1951.

———. *Essays and Introductions.* New York: Macmillan, 1961.

———. *Explorations.* London: Macmillan, 1962.

———. *Mythologies.* New York: Macmillan, 1959.

———. *On the Boiler.* Dublin: Cuala Press, 1939.

Choosing a subject

On page 10, and earlier in this chapter, we discussed the need to discover one's true subject. With a literary topic, the problem of locating the true subject may present special difficulties. The reason is easy to see: in a literary paper the interpretative element is large, and the problems of interpretation may take subtle forms. It is much easier to evaluate the strategy in a military campaign than the literary strategy employed in a sonnet or a novel. The importance to an army of an excellent line of supply is obvious and easily stated. The importance to a poet of a certain kind of imagination is harder to make clear to a reader.

It was Susan's deep interest in Yeats's poetry that had induced her to choose it for her topic. But she wanted to do more in her paper than say over and over how much she admired Yeats's poetry. Even if she tried to tell the reader how much a particular poem—like "The Second Coming" or "A Prayer for My Daughter"—had meant to her, she feared that her merely personal response would not exert much of a claim on any reader's attention. In very skillful hands, a highly personal response might lead to a fine piece of impressionistic criticism. But Susan, in her modesty, was well aware that in her case it might simply lead to gush.

It might be worth remarking just at this point that most literary discussions may be usefully divided into three general categories: (1) Discussion that has to do with the *effects* of the literary work; for example, on the reader, as in Susan's delighted response to Yeats's poetry, or on other readers, as Yeats's influence on other modern poets or on the Irish people. (2) Discussion of the *make-up* of the work—what it means and "how" it means—its arrangement of parts, use of language, choice of metaphors, development of symbols, complications of tone, and so forth. In this category would come an analysis of a particular Yeats poem or play or of a group of his poems. (3) Discussion of the background and "causes" of the literary work. Into this category would fall essays on the various factors, historical and personal, conscious and unconscious, that had shaped Yeats's poetry. In this area of interest, the student of Yeats might write about the way in which Yeats's unhappy love affair with Maud Gonne had affected his poetry or how the climate of ideas in which he had grown up made it possible for him to write a certain kind of poetry, and so on.

Though it is true that one cannot make a rigid separation of the three areas of interest (the effects of, the make-up of, and the genesis of, a work of literature), and though the literary critics and scholars quite properly move back and forth across the boundaries between them, an awareness of these differences of interest may clarify certain problems and even help the student—as it helped Susan—to choose his true subject when he is assigned to write a literary paper.

In her search for a true subject, Susan jotted down such topics as "Yeats as an Irish Poet," "Yeats as a Modern Poet," "The Development of Yeats's Poetry," "How Yeats Became a Poet of Reality," and "What the Abbey Theatre Taught Yeats."

Susan immediately realized that the last topic, for one, was entirely too restrictive for her purposes. Yeats's practical struggles with an Irish theater and his disappointment with the way in which the Irish people responded to it may well have had a profound effect on his poetry. But Susan was not primarily interested in Yeats as a playwright, and she felt that she didn't know enough (and wouldn't have time to learn enough) about the workings of the Abbey Theatre to be able to make much of this rather special material.

As she looked again at this list of topics, she noticed that one basic idea seemed to be trying to emerge: the fact of a significant development in Yeats's poetry. At her very first reading of Yeats, she had been struck with the difference between his early, rather charmingly dreamy, lyrics and the powerfully muscled poems that came as he approached middle age. Susan soon discovered that most authorities on Yeats took some such development for granted, though they proceeded to account for it in rather different ways. At any rate, their corroboration of what she had discovered for herself gave her confidence. She would try to explore and document in her own way Yeats's development toward realism. (Perhaps *realism* wasn't the best term, but it would do until she found a better one.)

Thus, Susan's paper would fall primarily in the third area of interest described above. Yet at every point, of course, she would need to deal with the second area (the make-up of Yeats's poetry). Otherwise, she wouldn't be able to say how his early, dreamy poetry differed in quality from the tough-minded poetry of his maturity.

Susan's final sentence outline and paper follow.

From Dream to Reality:

The Poetic Development of W. B. Yeats

by

Susan Blank

Middlewestern State University

June, 1971

Sentence Outline

I. Yeats bade farewell to life in a poem celebrating life and passion.

    A. He celebrated, from Ireland's past, men of action and passion with traits like

        1. The recklessness of the country gentry.

        2. The holiness of monks, and

        3. The laughter of the drunkard.

    B. He challenged Irishmen of the future to fulfill such ideals of passionate life.

II. Yet Yeats began his career by writing a very different kind of poetry.

    A. It expressed a wish to escape the limitations of our modern world.

    B. It looked back to a simple, idyllic world.

    C. It celebrated dream, preferring it to the "Grey Truth" of science.

III. Even in Yeats's "The Song of the Happy Shepherd," however, the speaker hints that he cannot take refuge in a personal dream.

    A. By the very act of writing a poem, he shows his need to share his sorrow with someone.

    B. He expresses his belief that his sorrow can be given a permanent form and thus achieve the status of enduring truth.

IV. Though Yeats's "Wandering of Oisin" tells a story out of the heroic past about a man who tried to escape the human world, it also testifies to the fact that man cannot really escape the human condition.

   A. Oisin, even in the land of the faeries, could not put aside human sorrow, and longed to return to humankind.

   B. In the end Oisin is compelled to lose his immortality and become a mere human being once more.

V. Even in his early poetry, Yeats takes some account of the "other side" of an issue:

   A. Though "The Stolen Child" stresses the human world as a place of sorrow, it mentions some of the earth's homely joys.

   B. Other early poems reveal a similar tension between the claims of the human world and the world of the faeries.

   C. Yet, like many other poets of the 1890s, essentially Yeats was a poet in retreat from the world.

VI. Yeats hoped to recover for modern Irishmen a sense of their heroic past (including legends of the Sidhe) through ritual and literature.

   A. He planned to create a new Irish cult for which he devised a special ritual.

   B. He encouraged the writing of stories, poems, and plays based on Irish legends.

    1.   The stories and poems would draw upon the recent wave of scholarly interest in Celtic history and literature.

    2.   The plays were to be produced in the Abbey Theatre, which had been founded by Yeats and Lady Angela Gregory for this purpose.

VII. Yeats, however, was not a political activist and quarreled with Maud Gonne, who was.

    A.   Yeats had no relish for violence.

    B.   He scorned to write propaganda.

    C.   He felt that modern Ireland could achieve freedom only through a spiritual regeneration.

VIII. Yeats believed that modern Irishmen had succumbed to the ills of modernity.

    A.   They had lost contact with the heroic life of their ancestors.

    B.   They had become bourgeois in their outlook.

    C.   They were essentially divided men who needed to recover what Yeats called "Unity of Being."

IX. Yeats's increasing concern with the problems of contemporary Ireland was reflected by a change in his own poetry.

    A.   Yeats stripped his poetry of ornament and made it muscular and spare.

    B.   He cultivated in his poetry an "Image" of himself that was the opposite of all that he was in his daily life.

    C.   He employed a harsher and more realistic subject matter than in his earlier verse.

    D.   In sum, he sought to achieve the poetic effect through clarifying and intensifying the realistic, and sometimes even sordid, circumstances of the world.

X.   The change in Yeats's style had definite causes.

    A.   Maud Gonne married John MacBride.

    B.   Dublin neglected the arts.

    C.   Synge's <u>Playboy of the Western World</u> was rejected at its first performance.

XI.   Yeats transformed his disappointment at Ireland into poetic expression.

    A.   Poetry was Yeats's chief business in life, not an escape.

    B.   The poetry of his mature years reflects contemporary events.

    C.   He developed a style that could do justice to the complexities of his world.

From Dream to Reality:

The Poetic Development of W. B. Yeats

William Butler Yeats, in his valedictory poem, "Under Ben
Bulben," praises the types of men whom he had come to value during
his lifetime. He celebrates the poet, the artist, the peasant,

> Hard-riding country gentlemen,
> The holiness of monks, and after
> Porter-drinkers' randy laughter....[1]

It is a curious and interesting company: it includes no bankers,
file clerks, or real estate salesmen. Yeats urges the Irish poets
who are to succeed him to

> Sing the lords and ladies gay
> That were beaten into the clay
> Through seven heroic centuries;
> Cast your mind on other days
> That we in coming days may be
> Still the indomitable Irishry.[2]

These lines pulse with a tremendous concern for a life of action
and heroic endeavor and passion--both the monk's passion and the
drunkard's. Such a concern is typical of Yeats's later poetry.
It reflects and illuminates the experiences of his lifetime.
Indeed, poetry had become for Yeats not a prettification of life
nor an escape from life, but a clarification of the very meaning
of life.

Yet Yeats did not begin his career with this tough-minded
conception of poetry, nor could he, at the beginning of his career,

---

[1] W. B. Yeats, Collected Poems (New York: Macmillan, 1951), p. 343.
[2] Ibid., p. 343.

have written poetry of this character. As a young poet Yeats
tended to express rather directly his yearnings, dreams, and
aspirations: his earlier poems thus tend to be fantasies of
escape from the limitations of human reality rather than imaginative transformations of it. Thus, in "The Song of the Happy
Shepherd" (1889) Yeats sympathizes with the "sick children of the
world" who have to endure "all the many changing things / In dreary
dancing past us whirled."[3] In the present world of meaningless
change, it seems to him that "Words alone are certain good." The
ancient world of fauns and shepherds and pastoral poetry has passed
away. Yeats's "happy shepherd" is not really very happy. He laments
that though "Of old the world on dreaming fed, / Grey Truth is now her
painted toy." But dreaming is also truth, so the shepherd argues,
and constitutes a more rewarding truth than that offered by science.

Yet even in this poem, which celebrates the romantic past and
the poetic dreaming associated with it, the poet is not able to
divorce himself entirely from human experience. Consider, for example, some further lines from "The Song of the Happy Shepherd."

        Go gather by the humming sea
        Some twisted, echo-harbouring shell,
        And to its lips thy story tell,
        And they thy comforters will be,
        Rewording in melodious guile
        Thy fretful words a little while,
        Till they shall singing fade in ruth
        And die a pearly brotherhood;
        For words alone are certain good:
        Sing, then, for this is also sooth.[4]

---

[3] Ibid., p. 7.

[4] Ibid., p. 8.

The meaning of the passage as quoted is not altogether clear, but a number of things do emerge plainly enough: the speaker needs comfort and needs to tell his sorrows to someone or something. His fretful complaining words about life will, he asserts, if spoken into the lips of the shell, be transformed--does the shell stand for the imagination here?--into a "pearly brotherhood." (What is meant by their fading "in ruth" or how they can "die" into a "pearly brotherhood" is not made altogether clear.) But that the words of complaint become "pearls" does suggest a permanence that sets them off from the "many changing things / In dreary dancing past us whirled." Perhaps the poet is saying that poetry is the only enduring truth.

"The Wanderings of Oisin" (1887) is another poem that exhibits some of Yeats's youthful escapism. Indeed, the plot of the poem has to do with an attempt to escape from human sorrow. The hero, Oisin, abandons humankind and goes away to live a heroic life in the land of the faeries. These faeries were the gods of ancient Ireland; they are called the Tuatha de Danaan or the Sidhe. They were super-natural beings, living lives of passionate activity. With them love and youth last forever. They stand in sharp opposition to the Christianized Irishmen of a later time who impress Oisin, when he returns, as puny and unheroic, a "small and feeble populace stooping with mattock and spade, / Or weeding or ploughing...."[5] Yet it is significant that though Oisin, because of his love for the faery

---

[5] Ibid., p. 378.

Niamh, had lived for three hundred years among the Sidhe, he was never able to eradicate from his heart a sense of kinship with the mortals who live under the menace of time. The poem suggests that the youthful Yeats recognized that it was not easy and perhaps was indeed impossible to evade the penalties of the human lot. Man is mortal, and much as he may long to become a god, he cannot in fact do so.

The theme of escape to the land of the faeries is to be found in many other poems written by Yeats before 1900. For example, note the following lines from a poem entitled "The Stolen Child" (first published in December 1886).[6]

> Away with us he's going,
> The solemn-eyed:
> He'll hear no more the lowing
> Of the calves on the warm hillside
> Or the kettle on the hob
> Sing peace into his breast,
> Or see the brown mice bob
> Round and round the oatmeal-chest.
> For he comes, the human child,
> To the waters and the wild
> With a faery, hand in hand
> From a world more full of
>   weeping than he can understand.[7]

Yeats is employing here the ancient superstition that held that the faeries like to steal away to their realm children and brides on their wedding night. The source of the faeries' power to win the human being lay in the fact that mortals dread the unhappiness of the world as it is. Yet even in this poem, Yeats recognizes that

---

[6] A. Norman Jeffares, W. B. Yeats: Man and Poet (New Haven: Yale Univ. Press, 1949), p. 38.

[7] Yeats, Collected Poems, p. 19.

human life has its own pleasures, and he enumerates lovingly a
number of them--the kettle that can "Sing peace into [the child's]
breast" or the "lowing / Of the calves on the warm hillside...."
It should be noted that Yeats was willing, even in his early period,
to present the "other side" of a situation, and this honesty was a
source of strength for his poetry. In his mature work in particular,
Yeats rarely shows himself to be opinionated or cranky: he is
nearly always wonderfully fair to the complexities and even contradictions of human experience.

From the beginning, a basic theme in Yeats's poetry (see, for
example, "The Man Who Dreamed of Faeryland," "To the Rose upon the
Rood of Time," "All Things Can Tempt Me") is the tug of war between
the claims of the world of faery and the counter-claims of the
real world--between reverie and reality. If, as we have already
observed, the youthful poet too often yielded to reverie, by the
turn of century there were signs to indicate that he was becoming
aware of the weakness of vague and dreamy poetry. In a rather early
essay Yeats observes that art will probably suffer if it is divorced
from the everyday world. Thus he writes in "The Cutting of an
Agate" (1906):

> All art is sensuous, but when a man puts only his contem-
> plative nature and his more vague desires into his art, the
> sensuous images through which it speaks become broken,
> fleeting, uncertain, or are chosen for their distance
> from general experience, and all grows unsubstantial and
> fantastic. (italics supplied)[8]

---

[8] W. B. Yeats, Essays and Introductions (New York: Macmillan, 1961),
p. 293.

Circumstance and the world are the raw material of poetry, but the artist must transform them into beauty. The transformation depends for its success, however, on some resistance in the materials to be transformed: one can bend wood into a bow or forge steel into a sword, but how could one "transform" a mere cloud or a wavering band of mist into anything at all!

It is useful to compare the observation just quoted with a passage taken from a much earlier book, The Celtic Twilight (1893). Here Yeats voices a much more naive view of artistic creation and one that accords with the notion of art as an escape from the drab and humdrum world around us. Yeats writes:

> I have desired, like every artist, to create a little
> world out of the beautiful, pleasant, and significant
> things of this marred and clumsy world....[9]

In this passage, clearly the assumption is that the artist sorts out for his artistic use what is beautiful or pleasant or significant in this marred and clumsy world and discards what is ugly or un-pleasant or insignificant. Such a view of art was not of course confined to the young Yeats. It is part of the artistic credo of the 1890s. The poets of that period tended to assume that "poetry" was determined by the nature of the materials rather than by the creativity of the artist. Brought up on such a theory, the young Yeats naturally tends to run away from the streets of the city to the woodland paths of nature, from the new-fangled and "modern" to

---

[9] As quoted by Ann Saddlemyer, "The Cult of the Celt," in The World of W. B. Yeats, ed. Robin Skelton and Ann Saddlemyer (Victoria, B. C.: Univ. of Victoria Press, 1965), p. 24.

the old and familiar, from the complex to the simple. As we have observed earlier, the theme of escape comes out quite directly in a number of the earlier poems. Significantly, "The Lake Isle of Innisfree" begins "I will arise and go now, and go to Innisfree...." and "The Hosting of the Sidhe" ends with the words "Away, come away." It is not too much to say that the Yeats of the 'nineties was a poet in retreat from the world.

Yet even during the decade from 1890 to 1900, Yeats did not solely dream about escape. He wished to see Ireland unified by a cultural ideal and hoped that his own poetry might give her the spiritual strength to stand firm against England and English culture. His plan for uniting and spiritualizing Ireland had two aspects: religious and literary. As for the first, Yeats wanted to revive the ancient Druidic traditions and by combining them with his Hermetic Society for Mysticism, initiate a new Irish cult.[10] Yeats even went so far as to devise a ritual for his religious cult.

> I had an unshakeable conviction, arising how or whence
> I cannot tell, that invisible gates would open as they
> opened for Blake, as they opened for Swedenborg, as
> they opened for Boehme, and that this philosophy would
> find its manuals of devotion in all imaginative liter-
> ature, and set before Irishmen for special manual an Irish
> literature which, though made by many minds, would seem
> the work of a single mind, and turn our places of beauty
> or legendary association into holy symbols.[11]

Yeats believed that this new Irish cult could give Irishmen

---

[10] Richard Ellmann, Yeats: The Man and the Masks (New York: Macmillan, 1948), p. 115-27.

[11] W. B. Yeats, Autobiographies (London: Macmillan, 1955), p. 254.

"spiritual inspiration" and fortification.[12]

The literary aspect of Yeats's plan had to do with reviving the Irish legends and embodying them in poems, fiction, and plays. In order to provide means for producing such plays, Yeats joined with Lady Angela Gregory in founding the Abbey Theatre in Dublin in 1904. Yeats was not alone, however, in becoming interested in Irish legend. He took advantage of a general trend. Many other people were studying Irish folklore during this period.[13] The revival of the Irish stories about such heroes as Fergus and Cuchulain, Finn and Oisin, would serve to call attention to Ireland's heroic past. It was indeed a very remote past: Cuchulain was thought to have lived in the first century of the Christian era; Finn and Oisin, in the third. But Yeats sought to use the legends not to escape from the present into mythical times but to mold a new reality by changing the spiritual climate in present-day Ireland.

---

12 Ellmann, p. 122. "Maud Gonne thought that the order might work for separation of Ireland from Britain in the same way as the Masonic lodges in the north of Ireland were, she believed, working for union. It would use Masonic methods against the Masons, as another nationalistic organization, the Clan na Gael, had done. Yeats, less political in his objectives, vaguely anticipated that the order would be able to aid the movement for national independence by its magical powers.... Driven almost frantic by loving in vain 'the most beautiful woman in the world,' he thought that in collaboration with Maud Gonne in this spiritual conspiracy their minds would be so united that she would consent to become his."

13 Saddlemyer, pp. 19-21. Miss Saddlemyer lists specific publications that presented Celtic literature, beginning in the year 1856. Old Irish manuscripts were exhumed and translated by German scholars; "by the end of the century innumerable scholars, organizations and periodicals were devoted to the recovery of the Celt" (p. 20). The Pan-Celtic Society was founded in 1899; Celtic: A Pan-Celtic Magazine published its first number in 1901.

> Might I not, with health and good luck to aid me, create some
> new <u>Prometheus Unbound</u>; Patrick or Columcille, Oisin or Finn,
> in Prometheus' stead; and, instead of Caucasus, Cro-Patrick or
> Ben Bulben? Have not all races had their first unity from a
> mythology that marries them to rock and hill? We had in Ireland
> imaginative stories, which the uneducated classes knew and even
> sang, and might we not make those stories current among the
> educated classes, rediscovering for the work's sake what I
> have called "the applied arts of literature," the association of
> literature, that is, with music, speech, and dance; and at last,
> it might be, so deepen the political passion of the nation that
> all, artist and poet, craftsman and day labourer would accept a
> common design?[14]

As the foregoing comment makes plain, Yeats saw in the use of

Ireland's "imaginative stories," a way of making common cause between

the educated classes of Ireland and the uneducated classes in whose

memories and imagination these stories still lingered.

It is plain that Yeats's involvement in politics was more

mystical than militant. Indeed, he quarreled with Maud Gonne, the

woman with whom he had fallen passionately in love, because Maud

wanted to liberate Ireland by direct action--demonstrations, violent

protests, and even the use of dynamite. Yeats refers to these dis-

agreements in a number of his poems about Maud. For example, in

"No Second Troy" he writes

> Why should I blame her that she filled my days
> With misery, or that she would of late
> Have taught to ignorant men violent ways
> Or hurled the little streets upon the great....[15]

More was involved, however, in Yeats's distaste for such violence

than mere squeamishness. Yeats believed Ireland could not be freed

from foreign control unless and until she possessed her own soul.

---

[14] Yeats, <u>Autobiographies</u>, pp. 193-94.

[15] Yeats, <u>Collected Poems</u>, p. 89.

Until she had recovered her own identity and had come to terms with her own past, any freeing her from outside domination would be superficial and mechanical. Besides, Yeats scorned to write propaganda: great poetry was much more than an incitement to a particular action or political commentary on a topical event.

Yet in spite of the qualifications just made, Yeats's attempt to use poetry and drama to give Irishmen "spiritual inspiration" and to revive Irish mythology and ancient legends in order to bring about the spiritual unification of the Irish did mean involvement in the modern world. What possibly may have begun as an escape into the past and as an aesthetic indulgence in mythological glories eventually issued in a commitment to the present. Yeats had become intensely interested in the cultural life of the people around him. How intense that interest had become is revealed in some comments that he made later in his Autobiographies. He tells us that he had hoped the association of literature and music, speech and dance, would give Ireland Unity of Culture--"philosophy and a little passion."[16] What Yeats may have had in mind is suggested by a passage from "The Cutting of an Agate," published in 1906:

> My work in Ireland has continually set this thought before
> me: "How can I make my work mean something to vigorous and
> simple men whose attention is not given to art but to a
> shop, or teaching in a National School, or dispensing
> medicine?... They must go out of the theatre with the
> strength they live by strengthened from looking upon some
> passion that could, whatever its chosen way of life, strike
> down an enemy, fill a long stocking with money or move a
> girl's heart.... Their legs will tire on the road if there

---

[16] Yeats, Autobiographies, p. 195.

is nothing in their hearts but vague sentiment, and though it is charming to have an affectionate feeling about flowers, that will not pull the cart out of the ditch.[17]

Yeats hoped to give Ireland Unity of Culture by creating in all Irishmen a "Unity of Being"--a life of intellect _and_ emotion, contemplation _and_ action. For Yeats knew that Irishmen were divided beings. They had lost their hold on the high-hearted life of their ancient ancestors. They had lost the ancient aristocracy's sense of _noblesse oblige_ and the peasantry's folk imagination and folk wit. Many of them had adopted bourgeois values along with the bourgeois mode of life. This at least is the force of the taunt embodied in Yeats's poem "September 1913."

> What need you, being come to sense,
> But fumble in a greasy till
> And add the halfpence to the pence
> And prayer to shivering prayer, until
> You have dried the marrow from the bone?
> For men were born to pray and save:
> Romantic Ireland's dead and gone,
> It's with O'Leary in the grave.[18]

Modern Irishmen spent their time in "shivering prayer," hoarding their money, and in keeping their shops. Yet Yeats had hoped that the "Ireland of priest, merchant and politician," might come to "resemble 'an Ireland / The poets have imagined, terrible and gay,' might, in fact, resemble Cuchulain's Ireland, a land of reckless heroes."[19] Yeats later was to admit he had failed to attain his

---

[17] Yeats, _Essays_, pp. 265-66.

[18] Yeats, _Collected Poems_, p. 106.

[19] John Unterecker, _A Reader's Guide to William Butler Yeats_ (New York: Noonday Press, 1959), p. 19.

dream. He writes: "the dream of my early manhood, that a modern nation can return to Unity of Culture is false; though it may be we can achieve it for some small circle of men and women, and there leave it till the moon bring round its century."[20] But even if he had not succeeded in carrying out his dream, he had come to write for his own people living at his own time.

As Yeats came, more and more, to write poems about the world of contemporary Ireland and less and less indulged himself in day-dreaming about a world free from human cares, he developed a new poetic style. He stripped his own poetry of ornament and made it more spare and muscular, harder and colder and more austere. A look at such volumes as The Green Helmet (1910), Responsibilities (1914), and The Wild Swans at Coole (1919) will make this new quality fully evident. In his Autobiographies Yeats makes direct mention of his changing notion of what he had come to aim at in his own verse. He writes:

> I take pleasure alone in those verses where it seems to me
> I have found something hard and cold, some articulation of
> the Image which is the opposite of all that I am in my
> daily life, and all my country is....[21]

Yeats is correct in describing this new "image" as the opposite of all that he was in his daily life. This new, hard, cold image and the poetic form that he developed to accommodate it do represent the opposite of his real tender-hearted self. They certainly represent the opposite of all that people have taken Ireland to be. Yet one

---

[20] Yeats, Autobiographies, p. 295.

[21] Ibid., p. 274.

must be careful to see that Yeats's austere style does not represent another special means to escape from life but rather a successful way to penetrate to the inner reality of life. The proof that this is so is shown by the kinds of material that fill this new, harder, colder poetry. There are poems about thwarted love ("Adam's Curse," "No Second Troy"), about Yeats's work with the Abbey Theatre ("The Fascination of What's Difficult"),[22] and about the pettiness of some of his countrymen ("September 1913," "Paudeen").

One may sum up by saying that Yeats's more austere style is a way of putting into judged and ordered perspective the circumstances of the world that flowed around him. The poems are not, however, mere photocopies of life's circumstance, nor are they, on the other hand, ways of denying and evading it. Rather it is as if Yeats has found a special lens through which to view the world about him in all of its earthiness and ugliness and squalor, but his is a lens that gives the cluttered scene depth and clarity and aesthetic distance: what is revealed is not meaningless clutter or sordid detail but a scene heightened, clarified, intensified, and given the special radiance of great poetry.

This remarkable shift in Yeats's style probably had its relation to definite causes: Maud Gonne married John MacBride in 1903; Dublin neglected the arts and showed scant enthusiasm in raising funds to

---

[22] My curse on plays
That have to be set up in fifty ways,
On the day's war with every knave and dolt,
Theatre business, management of men....
(Collected Poems, p. 91)

provide a gallery to house the gift of Hugh Lane's pictures (1912-13); in 1907 Synge's _Playboy of the Western World_ was violently rejected at its first performance at the Abbey Theatre. Yeats was angry and disappointed with Ireland, but he had begun to find a way to deal with this disorderly world. He did not run away from it nor ignore it, but he did find a way to heighten it into poetry.

If we understand the connection between Yeats's own life and personality and the poetry of his middle and final periods, we shall be able to see the folly of charging that Yeats's poetry is an escape from life. Poetry had become Yeats's life, his world, and his business. He says in his _Autobiographies_, "I thought it was my business in life to be an artist and a poet, and that there could be no business comparable to that."[23]

Yeats's poems continued to reflect the events going on around him. In "Easter 1916" he praises the patriots--Constance Markiewicz, Patrick Pearse, Thomas MacDonough, John MacBride--who led the abortive Easter rising. Though Yeats disliked their disdain for the old aristocratic tradition and though he feared the hatred as "Peddled in the thoroughfares" by Maud Gonne,[24] among others, and though he hated John MacBride for marrying the woman with whom he was hopelessly in love--he was now able to praise the patriots, including MacBride himself. Yeats had by this time become wiser,

---

[23] P. 188.

[24] See "A Prayer for My Daughter," _Collected Poems_, p. 187.

more sensitive, more complex, and in short, more mature, and he had developed a style in which he could do justice to the real complexities of the world. In one of the great passages in his <u>Per Amica Selentia Lunae</u>, Yeats writes: "We make out of the quarrel with others, rhetoric, but of the quarrel with ourselves, poetry."[25] There is another great though brief passage in the <u>Autobiographies</u> that ought to be set beside that just quoted. There Yeats remarks: "We begin to live when we have conceived life as tragedy."[26]

---

[25] Yeats, <u>Mythologies</u> (New York: Macmillan, 1959), p. 331.

[26] Yeats, <u>Autobiographies</u>, p. 189.

Bibliography

Ellmann, Richard. <u>Yeats: The Man and Masks</u>. New York: Macmillan, 1948.

Jeffares, A. Norman. <u>W. B. Yeats: Man and Poet</u>. New Haven: Yale Univ. Press, 1949.

Saddlemyer, Ann. "The Cult of the Celt: Pan-Celtism in the Nineties," in <u>The World of W. B. Yeats: Essays in Perspective.</u> Ed. Robin Skelton and Ann Saddlemyer. Victoria, B.C.: Univ. of Victoria Press, 1965.

Unterecker, John. <u>A Reader's Guide to William Butler Yeats</u>. New York: Noonday Press, 1959.

Yeats, W. B. <u>Autobiographies</u>. London: Macmillan, 1955.

_____. <u>Collected Poems</u>. New York: Macmillan, 1951.

_____. <u>Essays and Introductions</u>. New York: Macmillan, 1961.

_____. <u>Mythologies</u>. New York: Macmillan, 1959.

THE INSTRUCTOR'S COMMENT

This is a very thoughtful paper, well organized and rather carefully written. But in paragraph 3, in which you try to show that even in "The Song of the Happy Shepherd" Yeats reveals a concern for reality, I think that your argument is a bit forced. If you are trying to say that the poet, through his very need to communicate his emotions and through his desire to find an imperishable form for them, reveals that he has a stake in the world about him, you need to make this point more specifically. I find some repetition: paragraph 8, for example, tends to repeat a point first made in paragraph 3. Yet these are minor matters. There is actually very little waste motion in your paper.

I particularly like your handling of some fairly tricky concepts—imagination as distinguished from fantasy or reverie or daydreaming. You've evidently tried to choose your terms with care and to use them responsibly.

Your choice of quotations from Yeats's writings deserves commendation. On the whole, they seem very apt and they underscore your various points quite effectively. You show a thorough knowledge of Yeats's poetry and a more than adequate knowledge of his prose writing.

I also appreciate your not leaning unduly on secondary sources but trying to establish your thesis by a direct appeal to Yeats's own work. Your thesis about Yeats is not new, but I find it to be worked out rather freshly. And you have brought your paper to a very neat conclusion.

P.S. Your metaphor of the lens in paragraph 14 is quite effective. Is it original with you?

■ APPLICATION

Do you agree with the instructor's comment? Has he been too generous with Susan? Do you find difficulties in the revised paper that he has not noted? Has he, on the other hand, failed to mention features of this paper that you think have merit?

Some general notes on literary papers

1   In writing a literary paper, it is very wise to try to determine as early as possible the primary area of interest with which one is concerned. As we noted on page 397 above, there are at least three different fields of critical and scholarly interest, and whereas the student need not try to keep strictly within the bounds of any one of them, he will find it helpful to decide at the outset the principal critical emphasis that his paper will take.

2   Even a paper stressing literary history or reader response requires that the writer possess a thorough knowledge of the character and value of

the particular literary work or works examined. This is not the place to discuss such matters, for *Modern Rhetoric* does not pretend to be an introduction to the study of literature: its purpose is to train the student to write rather than to read. Yet the two processes obviously interact, and a number of the chapters in this book—notably those on description, narration, diction, metaphor, and tone—do bear quite directly on the problem of reading and judging literature.

3   One of the special problems that comes up in writing a literary paper of any kind is the definition of terms, for literary terms are particularly difficult. Be sure that you know clearly what you mean by the terms that you are using. In rereading your paper, be on the alert for contradictory statements: they constitute good evidence that something has gone wrong.

4   Make sure that the passage you quote from an author really illustrates the point that you are making about his work. If the passage quoted does not support your statement, then keep looking until you find one that does. If, on the other hand, you cannot find a passage that really illustrates your generalization, perhaps it is your generalization that is at fault. Be prepared to revise it.

5   Try to date accurately any illustrative quotations. For example, an essay written in 1900 may not necessarily express what the writer came to feel twenty years later.

6   Be careful of what you borrow from scholars, critics, and other literary authorities. Perhaps you do not feel yourself in a position to judge which of them are really authoritative and which are not; but you can at least determine whether the statement that you are borrowing makes sense in the context in which you are using it.

7   Don't bite off more than you can chew. In saying this, we are not necessarily urging brevity, and we are certainly not urging the student to settle for an easy subject. But the effectiveness of any literary paper is seriously compromised if the writer crams in a great deal more material than is necessary to make his point, or if he presents his reader with ill-digested material which, though it may seem at a hasty reading rather learned and profound, turns out to be, when carefully inspected, pretentious nonsense.

APPENDIX:

The Book Report, Summary, and Précis

The Book Report

Your instructor may occasionally assign a book report. A book report is to be sharply distinguished from a research paper, for it deals with one book in its entirety—not with certain aspects of several books and documents as, for example, in the model research paper "Railroads in the Civil War" (pp. 389–93). The book report is also to be clearly distinguished from a book review or a critical essay, for it merely reports on a book without undertaking to compare it with other books or to pass judgment on its value.

We have said that a book report does not undertake to make comparative judgments, but it may very well include a certain amount of background material. This may have to do with the author himself, his other work, his reputation, or the circumstances under which the book was written. The presentation of such material, however, should not be allowed to become an end in itself. In scope and proportion it should be kept subordinate to the presentation of the book itself and, we may note, some book reports can dispense with it altogether.

To write a good book report you need to answer the following questions:

1 Who is the author? (What are his nationality and origins? When did he write?)
2 What other work has he done?
3 What is his reputation?
4 Are there any important or enlightening circumstances connected with the composition of this book?

5 What kind of book is this? (Is it fiction, history, literary criticism, biography, poetry, drama, or what?)
6 What is the subject of this book?
7 What material does it treat?
8 What is the theme of the book—the author's basic interpretation of the material?
9 What method of organization does he employ?
10 What are the tone and style of the book?

Note that questions 1 through 4 concern themselves with background information. If such information is needed for your book report, and is not available in the book itself or on the book jacket, consult a few standard reference works to obtain the basic facts, or look into one or two good biographies of the author or historical or critical works about him. There is no need to do a full research job (though you may find it wise to take your notes as if for a research paper so that your material will be conveniently available and easily put into proper order). Different kinds of books obviously require different handling in a book report. Here follow a few suggestions for treating three types of books:

If you are reporting on a *biography,* identify the subject of the work, summarize the subject's career as given by the biographer (including the basic pieces of evidence that the biographer employs to support his interpretation of the life he is writing), give some notion of the biographer's method of organization, and comment on his tone and style.

With regard to tone and style, you may want to ask yourself such questions as these: Is the book a scholarly treatise or a popular biography? Is the book well adapted to the audience that the biographer evidently has in mind? Does he give any interesting anecdotes and colorful touches, or does he confine himself to facts and to historical or psychological analysis?

A book report on a *novel* should define the kind of world that the author is interested in. Does he write of drawing rooms or village parlors or farms or battlefields? What kinds of characters and issues interest him? What is the outline of his plot? How do the motivations of his characters fit the plot? What is the theme of his novel? In a novel, questions of tone and style obviously are also very important.

If you are dealing with a book on *international affairs,* say, Russian influence in the Middle East, your primary concern will be to present the author's account of the situation provoking his discussion, to set forth the policy that he recommends, and to present the arguments that he uses to support that policy. You might even be led to present the philosophical or political assumptions that provide the basis for his policy. The kind of audience to whom he addresses his book will be an important consideration, and you ought to try to define it. But, in general, with books of this type, questions of tone and style—except insofar as mere clarity is involved—would be somewhat less important. In general, accommodate the shape and emphasis of your report to the kind of book on which you are reporting.

The Summary

The book report can be regarded as a kind of summary since it tells us in compact form what a particular book is about and what it says. Yet a "summary," technically considered, differs from the book report in one very important way. There is no introductory or background material on the author or the circumstances that bear on his composition of the work under consideration. *In short, there is nothing in a summary that is not actually in the work summarized.* The summary gives us in compact form the main points of the longer work; moreover, it undertakes to give *all* the main points and in their proper relation to each other.

Yet a summary is not merely a digest of a longer discourse; considered rhetorically, it is a piece of discourse in its own right. This means that it is no mere collection of words and phrases, but is composed of complete sentences, and that a person writing a summary must observe the principles of unity, coherence, emphasis, and proportion. The relation of one sentence to another must be obvious or else indicated by a suitable transition. Furthermore, if the summary extends beyond one paragraph, then the connection between the paragraphs must be made clear.

The organization of a summary is determined by the purpose that a summary is to serve. For instance, the summary may follow the order of the original text and thus give some notion of the approach used by its author. On the other hand, the summary may make use of a mode of organization quite different from that according to which the author organized the original discourse. The point is to organize your summary in the way that will best serve your purpose. At times you may want to follow the way in which the author put his article or his speech together. At other times, however, the author's way of doing this may prove quite irrelevant to your purposes.

The scale of the summary, like its organization, is determined by the purpose the summary is to serve. The real question is how much information do you need to pack into your abbreviated form? Sometimes, and for some purposes, a brief paragraph will give you an adequate digest of a whole book. On the other hand, if you are working on a finer scale, with very rich and interesting material, you may require a number of paragraphs to make a proper digest of a fairly short essay. In general, remember that a summary must summarize: unless you can squeeze down the book or article to much smaller size, then your labor has hardly been worth the trouble.

The Précis

What we call a précis (pronounced *pray-see*) is also a kind of summary, but it is more specialized than the kind that we have just been discussing. The précis retains the basic order of the original text, keeps the same proportions of part to part, and maintains the same tone. Thus, the précis has a much closer relation to the original text than do looser kinds of summary. This closer relation, however, does not mean that we should use much direct quotation or very close paraphrase. Material in the original discourse can be, and often should be, restated for economy and emphasis. Moreover, the degree of reduction, as in looser forms of summary, will be greater or smaller, depending on the purpose that the précis is to serve. But since the précis is committed to maintain the relative proportions of the original discourse, the reduction in a précis can never be so drastic as that in a "summary."

Here follows a précis of the passage from T. Harry Williams' *Lincoln and His Generals* (pp. 59–60):

> Grant was the greatest general in the Civil War, first because he was a master of global strategy. Lee is usually considered the greatest Civil War general, but he did not have the mastery of global strategy that Grant had. Grant had a modern mind; Lee, like the Confederacy, looked to the past. Whereas Grant had an expert staff that aided him with planning, Lee's staff were almost glorified clerks, which left too much detail on Lee's shoulders. Grant realized that war was becoming total and that it was necessary to destroy the enemy's economic resources; Lee, on the other hand, was old-fashioned and thought of war only as conflict between armies.

Here the original passage contains about 730 words and the précis about 112 words.

Index

exhaustive, 74–77
as a method of exposition, 68–77
schematized examples of, 68–72
systems, simple and complex, 70–71
uses of, in exposition, 72–77
see also Class, Genus, Reasoning, Species
Clay, Henry, 184 *note*
Clemens, Samuel L., *Life on the Mississippi*, 353–54
Clichés, 302–03
Cobb, Irvin, "Black and White," from *Back Home*, 324
Coffin, Patricia, "Black-White: Can We Bridge the Gap?" 22
Coherence, caution for use of controls in, 32–33
distinguished from unity, 27
logical order in, 29–30
in sentence, effect of movable modifiers on, 273 *note*
space order in, 32–34
time order in, 31
and unity in paragraph, 262
"Colors That Animals Can See, The," from *The Personality of Animals*, H. Munro Fox, 266
Columbia Forum, 16, 17
"Come on Down and Get Killed," 17–18
Common ground, in argument, 123–25
in definition, 86–87
in persuasion, 178
Communication, importance of language in, 3–4
importance of tone in, 333–34
Comparison and contrast, interest a factor in significant, 56–57
metaphorical, 325–26
as a method of exposition, 54–62
as a method of paragraph organization, 259
ways of organizing material for, 57–62
Complements, in normal sentence order, 269
Complete Book of Furniture Repair and Refinishing, Ralph Kinney, 103
Complete Fly Fisherman, The Notes and Letters of Theodore Gordon, The, John McDonald, 99
Complication, as middle of narrative, 233, 236
Composition, main intention in, 44
organizing principles in, 24–39
Conclusion, 13, 23
of a narrative, 234, 237

in reasoning, 152, 156
in syllogism, 260
two things to avoid in, 23
Concrete words, 287–88, 289–91
Conflict, in argument, 118–19
Connotation, and denotation, 286
Conrad, Joseph, "The Secret Sharer," 260–61, 263
"The Warrior's Soul," from *Tales of Hearsay*, 313
Context, importance of, in metaphor, 328–31
Contrast, *see* Comparison and contrast
Conversation, quoted, and paragraph, 256 *note*
"Cooking Syrup," student theme, 100–01
Coordination and subordination, 278–80
Corbin, John, *An American at Oxford*, 59, 259
Cowley, Malcolm, "Sociological Habit Patterns in Linguistic Transmogrification," 305–06
Craft of Fiction, The, Percy Lubbock, 257
Crippled Tree, The, Han Suyin, 351
Cross-ranking, in classification, 71

Dangling modifiers, 274
Data, 120 *note*
Da Vinci, Leonardo, excerpt, 322
Days Before, The, Katherine Anne Porter, 343–44
Death in Venice, Thomas Mann, 7
Deduction, and extended argument, 169–70
and reasoning by classes, 152–63
see also Argument, Induction Reasoning
Definition, circular, caution against, 88
classifying process in, 80–84
and the common ground, 86–87
as dictionary meaning, 77 and *note*
as an equation of convertible terms, 78–80
extended, 88–94
and generalization, 85–86
and metaphorical language, 87–88
as a method of exposition, 77–94
necessary and sufficient characteristics of, 84–85
structure of, 80–83
supportive characteristics of, 85–86
see also Identification
Defoe, Daniel, *Robinson Crusoe*, 221–22, 234–35, 247

De Kruif, Paul, *Microbe Hunters,* 130
De la Mare, Walter, *Memoirs of a Midget,* 220
Demand, the immediate practical and beyond, 4–5
Democracy, James Russell Lowell on, 12
DeMott, Benjamin, "The Age of Overkill," 298
Denotation, and connotation, 286
Denouement, as narrative end, 234, 237
Description, 196–223
  choice of words in, 211–13
  concrete and specific words in, 290–91
  dominant impression as, 205–07
  generalized, 98, 216
  impressionistic method in, 216
  intention of, 45
  and interpretation, 98
  as a kind of discourse, 45
  motivation for use of, 199
  and other kinds of discourse, 202–05
  perception in, 201
  selection of detail in, 208–09
  suggestive, 97, 197
  suggestive and the senses, 199–201
  technical (or expository) and analysis, 96–99, 196–97
  texture and pattern in, 213–19
Detroit *Free Press,* 272
Devil and Daniel Webster, The, Stephen Vincent Benét, 330–31
Dickens, Charles, *Bleak House,* 207, 210, 259
Dickinson, G. Lowes, "Red-bloods and Mollycoddles," from *Appearances,* 60–62, 267, 277
Diction, 285–310
  abstract and concrete, 287–88, 289–91
  as clichés, 302–03
  as creator of tone, 333
  dictionary explanations of, 293–96
  general and specific, 287–88, 289–91
  informal (colloquial) and formal, 296–98
  as jargon, 305–06
  as slang, 286, 297, 303–04
  as stereotypes, 303–04
  see also Language, Words
Dictionary, a record of meanings, 77 and *note,* 83, 293–96
  sample derivations in a typical, 293, 294
"Different Breed of Cats, A," student theme, 21

Differentia (ae), in refining the defining process, 81, 83, 84, 89, 90
Discourse, argument as a kind of, 45, 118–75
  description as a kind of, 45, 196–223
  as determined by intention, 44
  exposition as a kind of, 44, 48–117
  form and function of, 43
  four kinds of, 44–46
  main divisions of, 13–23
  narration as a kind of, 45, 224–52
  special problems of, 253–357
Discussion, 13, 23
  occasion of the, 132–33
Dog Fiend, The, Frederick Marryat, 221, 263
Dominant impression, 205–07
Dominant interest, paragraph organization by, 261
Donne, John, sermon, 334
Dos Passos, John, "The Happy Warrior," 354
Doubt, in argument, 118–19
Douglas, Norman, *South Wind,* 220–21
Douglas, Stephen A., debates with Abraham Lincoln, 179, 192
Dryden, John, excerpt, 283
Dublin, Louis I., *The Problem of Heart Disease,* 99
"Dutch Hustle, The," J. Wolfgang Langewiesche, 309–10
Dynasts, The, Thomas Hardy, 221

Ebb Tide, The, Robert Louis Stevenson, 218–19
Edwards, Jonathan, "Sinners in the Hands of an Angry God," 185
Either-or reasoning, 163–64
  fallacy of, 167–68
Eliot, T. S., "Burnt Norton," 186
Ellis, Havelock, 312
Elluel, Jacques, *Propaganda: The Formation of Men's Attitudes,* 193
Emotion, in persuasion, 182–84
  and reason, 120–21
Emphasis, devices for achieving, 34–36
  faulty devices of, 36
  by flat statement, 35
  as an organizing principle, 34–39
  in paragraph, 263
  by paragraph isolation, 36
  by position, 35
  by proportion, 35
  in sentence, effect of movable modifiers on, 273 *note*

Sentence, fixed word order of normal, 268–74
 length and variation in, 280–83
 loose and periodic, 280
 and the paragraph, 255–84
 parts of, 269–74
 rhetoric and grammar of the, 267–84
 rhythmic inflection of, 349
 special patterns in structure of, 274–80
 topic, 257–58
 see also Organization, Rhetoric
Sentimentality, caution against, 346, 348
Sequence, action and, in narration, 229–39
 space order in, 32–34
 time order in, 31, 260
Seven Pillars of Wisdom, T. E. Lawrence, 209, 215, 247, 259, 261, 357
Shakespeare, William, *Romeo and Juliet,* 233–34, 334
 Sonnet 154, 276
Sharp focus, in narration, 249
"Shoot the Moon," student theme, 172–74
Simile, 311 *note*
"Sinners in the Hands of an Angry God," Jonathan Edwards, 185
Slang, 286, 297
 and metaphor, 314
 and stereotypes, 303–05
Slanting, and suggestion, in persuasion, 184
Smith, J. Russell, and M. Ogden Phillips, *North America,* 197
Snow, C. P., 174 *note*
"Sociological Habit Patterns in Linguistic Transmogrification," Malcolm Cowley, 305–06
Sociological style, 306
Soldiers Three, Rudyard Kipling, 271
"Son Off to Campus Wars; Parents Sob," Art Buchwald, 335–36
Sorensen, Theodore, *Kennedy,* 247
Sources, primary, secondary, and tertiary, for research paper, 362
South Wind, Norman Douglas, 220–21
Space, arrangement of objects in, as method of paragraph organization, 260–61
 order of, in coherence, 32–34
Special problems, of discourse, 253–357
Specialized functions, paragraphs of, 267
Species, defined in relation to genus, 81, 82, 89

illustrated diagramatically, 82
Specific words, 278–88, 289–91
Standard College Dictionary, 293
Steele, Wilbur Daniel, "How Beautiful with Shoes," 212
Stein, Gertrude, *Everybody's Autobiography,* 343
Stereotypes, including slang, 303–05
Stevenson, Robert Louis, *The Ebb Tide,* 218–19
Stewart, Charles D., "The Bee's Knees," 329
Story of My Life, The, Helen Keller, 5, altered 271
Storytelling, as one type of fiction, 224 *note*
Stowe, Harriet Beecher, *Uncle Tom's Cabin,* 243
Strachey, Lytton, *Queen Victoria,* 281
Structure, and analysis and classification, 95
 of definition, 80–83
 narrative, 234–38
 of paragraph, 257–59
 of sentence, 274–80
Style, impressionistic, 216
 originality, as adjunct of, 353
 sociological, 306
 tone and other aspects of, 332–57
Subject, attitude toward, expressed by tone, 334–37
 choosing the true, 397–98
 highfalutin, 12–13
 interest as guide to finding, 10–13
 in normal sentence order, 269
 a true, defined, 11
 the true, and the proposition, 11–12
Subordination, and coordination, 278–80
"Success and Uncle Conroy," student theme, 37–38
Suggestion, and slanting, in persuasion, 184
Suggestive description, 97, 197
 and the senses, 199–201
Summary, 424
Swift, Jonathan, *Gulliver's Travels,* 286
Swinburne, Algernon, Max Beerbohm on, 273
Syllogism, 154 *note,* 156 *note*
 conditional, 164
 disjunctive, 163
 as method of paragraph organization, 260
Synonyms, 299
 definition by, 78, 88
Syntactic relationships, 269 *note*

"Teachers I Have Known," student theme, 75–76, 338, 345, 373

Technical description, 196–97
  and analysis, 96–99

Temper of Our Time, The, Eric Hoffer, 33

Tennyson, Alfred, Lord, "Flower in the Crannied Wall," 106–07

Term paper, *see* Research paper

Testimony, fact established by, 144

Texture, and pattern, in description, 213–19

Thackeray, William Makepeace, *Vanity Fair,* 249, 344

Theme, analysis of, in argument, 136–37
  development of, in argument, 170–74
  example of preparation for, 14–15
  illustrated diagramatically, 136
  relevance of, 246

Thinking, by classes, 35 *note*
  importance of straight, 115
  and language, feeling, and rhetoric, 3–8

Thoreau, Henry David, *Cape Cod,* 218
  Walden, 323

Thousand Days, A, Arthur Schlesinger, Jr., 247

Tillich, Paul, "The Lost Dimensions in Religion," from *Adventures of the Mind,* 93

Time, natural and narrative order of, 230–31
  order of, in coherence, 31
  sequence in, as method of paragraph organization, 260

Time Magazine, 17, 35, 123, 283–84

Timm, John Arrend, *General Chemistry,* 91–92

"Tinder Box, The," Hans Christian Andersen, 224

Tolstoy, Count Leo, *War and Peace,* 107, 109

Tone, effect of over- and understatement on, 345–48
  as expression of attitude toward audience, 337–38
  as expression of attitude toward subject, 334–37
  importance of, in communication, 333–34
  ironical, 343–35
  and other aspects of style, 332–57
  as qualification of meaning, 338–48

Topic sentence, 257–58

Town versus Eisner, Oliver Wendell Holmes, 286 and *note*

"Training a Dog," student theme, 51–52, 258

Transition, in paragraph linking, 264–65

Trevelyan, G. M., *History of England,* 258

True Believer, The, Eric Hoffer, 306–07

Truth, in argument, 156
  reasoning for, 188

"Two Gallants," from *Dubliners,* James Joyce, 250

Tylor, E. B., on religion, 93

Uncle Tom's Cabin, Harriet Beecher Stowe, 243

Understatement, and overstatement, effect of on tone, 345–48

Uniformity, in causal analysis, 110

Unity, and coherence, in paragraph, 262
  as an organizing principle, 24
  in sentence, effect of movable modifiers on, 273 *note*
  three tests for recognizing, 25

"Universities and the World Order, The," Quincy Wright, 330

Validity, in argument, 156

Vanity Fair, William Makepeace Thackeray, 249, 344

Variety, in extended definition, 92–93
  by sentence length, 281
  by sentence pattern, 281–82

Verbs, in description, 212
  finite, 308
  in normal sentence order, 269

Verification, acceptable, in argument, 126–27
  of fact, in evidence, 143–44

Vividness, 209, 211

Voice, 332, 348

Walden, Henry David Thoreau, 323

War and Peace, Count Leo Tolstoy, 107, 109

"Warrior's Soul, The," from *Tales of Hearsay,* Joseph Conrad, 313

Washington Post, 336 *note*

Waves, The, Virginia Woolf, 221

"We Must Learn to See What's Really New," Margaret Mead and Irene Neves, 122

Webster, Daniel, 184 *note*

Webster's New Collegiate Dictionary, 294, 295

Webster's New International Dictionary, 295

F 6
G 7
H 8
I 9
J 0

Harcourt Brace Jovanovich

0-15-562813-5